Here is a good place to start digging into today's fresh, innovative thinking in International Relations. The 16 concepts critically explored here show us why we'll all be smarter if we push the state off its lime-light-hogging center stage.

Cynthia Enloe, Clark University, USA

For at least two decades, critical imaginations have insinuated themselves into the literatures of the international relations. The essays in this volume go well beyond a mere summary of that trend. An outstanding collection of authors provides the critical thinking that students of international relations will need to imagine a global world no longer quarantined within the tradition sovereignty models and power politics paradigms that have characterized the discipline's mainstream mentality.

Michael J. Shapiro, University of Hawai'i, Mānoa, USA

This innovative book enables the reader to think differently about the closures and openings in international relations theory, for so long defined by the centrality of the state. By utilizing common and not-so-common themes the book succeeds in refreshing the theoretical imagination and thus provides an edifying experience for students and scholars alike.

Robbie Shilliam, Queen Mary University of London, UK

International relations arguably express the conditions within which political critique has been possible and certainly affirm the urgent need for a more creative political imagination. This book engages directly with concepts and principles through which critique and imagination have been re-energised in this context. Combining serious scholarship with accessible style, practical wisdom and timely provocation, it engages with many conceptual challenges facing anyone persuaded that we live in times and spaces of dramatic transformation.

R. B. J. Walker, University of Victoria, Canada

This theoretically engaging and accessibly written collection of essays enriches understandings of how state-centrism limits the intellectual and political imaginations of scholars and practitioners. It is a valuable research and teaching resource for scholars in a wide range of fields, including International Relations, Critical Legal Studies, Border Studies, Citizenship Studies and Globalization Studies.

Cynthia Weber, Sussex University, UK

CRITICAL IMAGINATIONS IN INTERNATIONAL RELATIONS

This exciting new text brings together in one volume an overview of the many reflections on how we might address the problems and limitations of a state-centred approach in the discipline of International Relations (IR).

The book is structured into chapters on key concepts, with each providing an introduction to the concept for those new to the field of critical politics – including undergraduate and postgraduate students – as well as drawing connections between concepts and thinkers that will be provocative and illuminating for more established researchers in the field. They give an overview of core ideas associated with the concept; the critical potential of the concept; and key thinkers linked to the concept, seeking to address the following questions:

- How has the concept traditionally been understood?
- How has the concept come to be understood in critical thinking?
- How is the concept used in interrogating the limits of state centrism?
- What different possibilities for engaging with international relations have been envisioned through the concept?
- Why are such possibilities for alternative thinking about international relations important?
- What are some key articles and volumes related to the concept which readers can go to for further research?

Drawing together some of the key thinkers in the field of critical International Relations and including both established and emerging academics located in Asia, Europe, Latin America and North America, this book is a key resource for students and scholars alike.

Aoileann Ní Mhurchú is Lecturer in International Politics at the University of Manchester. She conducts research on intergenerational migration, citizenship and hybridity. Her principal interest is in the changing nature of political identity and belonging in the context of increasing global migration.

Reiko Shindo is Teaching Fellow at the Department of Politics and International Studies at the University of Warwick. She conducts research on migrant activism and diaspora politics. Her principal interest is in examining various forms of resistance and investigating how they are transforming the boundary of the political community.

INTERVENTIONS

Edited by:
Jenny Edkins, Aberystwyth University and Nick Vaughan-Williams, University of Warwick

The series provides a forum for innovative and interdisciplinary work that engages with alternative critical, post-structural, feminist, postcolonial, psychoanalytic and cultural approaches to international relations and global politics. In our first 5 years we have published 60 volumes.

We aim to advance understanding of the key areas in which scholars working within broad critical post-structural traditions have chosen to make their interventions, and to present innovative analyses of important topics. Titles in the series engage with critical thinkers in philosophy, sociology, politics and other disciplines and provide situated historical, empirical and textual studies in international politics.

We are very happy to discuss your ideas at any stage of the project: just contact us for advice or proposal guidelines. Proposals should be submitted directly to the Series Editors:

Jenny Edkins (jennyedkins@hotmail.com) and
Nick Vaughan-Williams (N.Vaughan-Williams@Warwick.ac.uk)

'As Michel Foucault has famously stated, 'knowledge is not made for understanding; it is made for cutting'. In this spirit the Edkins–Vaughan-Williams Interventions series solicits cutting edge, critical works that challenge mainstream understandings in international relations. It is the best place to contribute post-disciplinary works that think rather than merely recognize and affirm the world recycled in IR's traditional geopolitical imaginary.'

Michael J. Shapiro, *University of Hawai'i at Mānoa, USA*

Critical Theorists and International Relations
Edited by Jenny Edkins and Nick Vaughan-Williams

Ethics as Foreign Policy
Britain, the EU and the other
Dan Bulley

Universality, Ethics and International Relations
A grammatical reading
Véronique Pin-Fat

The Time of the City
Politics, philosophy, and genre
Michael J. Shapiro

Governing Sustainable Development
Partnership, protest and power at the world summit
Carl Death

Insuring Security
Biopolitics, security and risk
Luis Lobo-Guerrero

Foucault and International Relations
New critical engagements
Edited by Nicholas J. Kiersey and Doug Stokes

International Relations and Non-Western Thought
Imperialism, colonialism and investigations of global modernity
Edited by Robbie Shilliam

Autobiographical International Relations
I, IR
Edited by Naeem Inayatullah

War and Rape
Law, memory and justice
Nicola Henry

Madness in International Relations
Psychology, security and the global governance of mental health
Alison Howell

Spatiality, Sovereignty and Carl Schmitt
Geographies of the nomos
Edited by Stephen Legg

Politics of Urbanism
Seeing like a city
Warren Magnusson

Beyond Biopolitics
Theory, violence and horror in world politics
François Debrix and Alexander D. Barder

The Politics of Speed
Capitalism, the state and war in an accelerating world
Simon Glezos

Politics and the Art of Commemoration
Memorials to struggle in Latin America and Spain
Katherine Hite

Indian Foreign Policy
The politics of postcolonial identity
Priya Chacko

Politics of the Event
Time, movement, becoming
Tom Lundborg

Theorising Post-Conflict Reconciliation
Agonism, restitution and repair
Edited by Alexander Keller Hirsch

Europe's Encounter with Islam
The secular and the postsecular
Luca Mavelli

Re-thinking International Relations Theory via Deconstruction
Badredine Arfi

The New Violent Cartography
Geo-analysis after the aesthetic turn
Edited by Sam Okoth Opondo and Michael J. Shapiro

Insuring War
Sovereignty, security and risk
Luis Lobo-Guerrero

International Relations, Meaning and Mimesis
Necati Polat

The Postcolonial Subject
Claiming politics/governing others in late modernity
Vivienne Jabri

Foucault and the Politics of Hearing
Lauri Siisiäinen

Volunteer Tourism in the Global South
Giving back in neoliberal times
Wanda Vrasti

Cosmopolitan Government in Europe
Citizens and entrepreneurs in postnational politics
Owen Parker

Studies in the Trans-disciplinary Method
After the aesthetic turn
Michael J. Shapiro

Alternative Accountabilities in Global Politics
The scars of violence
Brent J. Steele

Celebrity Humanitarianism
The ideology of global charity
Ilan Kapoor

Deconstructing International Politics
Michael Dillon

The Politics of Exile
Elizabeth Dauphinee

Democratic Futures
Revisioning democracy promotion
Milja Kurki

Postcolonial Theory
A critical introduction
Edited by Sanjay Seth

More than Just War
Narratives of the just war and military life
Charles A. Jones

Deleuze & Fascism
Security: war: aesthetics
Edited by Brad Evans and Julian Reid

Feminist International Relations
'Exquisite corpse'
Marysia Zalewski

The Persistence of Nationalism
From imagined communities to urban encounters
Angharad Closs Stephens

Interpretive Approaches to Global Climate Governance
Reconstructing the greenhouse
Edited by Chris Methmann, Delf Rothe and Benjamin Stephan

Postcolonial Encounters in International Relations
The politics of transgression in the Maghreb
Alina Sajed

Post-tsunami Reconstruction in Indonesia
Negotiating normativity through gender mainstreaming initiatives in Aceh
Marjaana Jauhola

Leo Strauss and the Invasion of Iraq
Encountering the abyss
Aggie Hirst

Production of Postcolonial India and Pakistan
Meanings of partition
Ted Svensson

War, Identity and the Liberal State
Everyday experiences of the geopolitical in the armed forces
Victoria M. Basham

Writing Global Trade Governance
Discourse and the WTO
Michael Strange

Politics of Violence
Militancy, international politics, killing in the name
Charlotte Heath-Kelly

Ontology and World Politics
Void universalism I
Sergei Prozorov

Theory of the Political Subject
Void universalism II
Sergei Prozorov

Visual Politics and North Korea
Seeing is believing
David Shim

Globalization, Difference and Human Security
Edited by Mustapha Kamal Pasha

International Politics and Performance
Critical aesthetics and creative practice
Edited by Jenny Edkins and Adrian Kear

Memory and Trauma in International Relations
Theories, cases, and debates
Edited by Erica Resende and Dovile Budryte

Critical Environmental Politics
Edited by Carl Death

Democracy Promotion
A critical introduction
Jeff Bridoux and Milja Kurki

International Intervention in a Secular Age
Re-enchanting humanity?
Audra Mitchell

The Politics of Haunting and Memory in International Relations
Jessica Auchter

**European-East Asian Borders
in Translation**
*Edited by Joyce C.H. Liu and
Nick Vaughan-Williams*

**Genre and the
(Post)Communist Woman**
Analyzing transformations of the
Central and Eastern European
female ideal
*Edited by Florentina C. Andreescu and
Michael Shapiro*

**Studying the Agency of
Being Governed**
*Edited by Stina Hansson, Sofie Hellberg
and Maria Stern*

Politics of Emotion
The song of Telangana
Himadeep Muppidi

Ruling the Margins
Colonial power and administrative rule
in the past and present
Prem Kumar Rajaram

**Race and Racism in
International Relations**
Confronting the global colour line
*Alexander Anievas, Nivi Manchanda and
Robbie Shilliam*

**The Grammar of Politics
and Performance**
*Edited by Shirin M. Rai and
Janelle Reinelt*

**War, Police and Assemblages
of Intervention**
*Edited by Jan Bachman, Colleen Bell and
Caroline Holmqvist*

**Re-imagining North Korea in
International Politics**
Problems and alternatives
Shine Choi

On Schmitt and Space
Claudio Minca and Rory Rowan

Face Politics
Jenny Edkins

Empire Within
International hierarchy and its imperial
laboratories of governance
Alexander D. Barder

**Sexual Politics and
International Relations**
How LGBTQ claims shape
International Relations
*Edited by Manuela Lavinas Picq and
Markus Thiel*

Emotions, Politics and War
Edited by Linda Åhäll and Thomas Gregory

**Jacques Lacan: Between
Psychoanalysis and Politics**
Edited by Samo Tomšič and Andreja Zevnik

The Value of Resilience
Securing life in the 21st century
Chris Zebrowski

Political Aesthetics
Culture, critique and the everyday
Arundhati Virmani

Walzer, Just War and Iraq
Ethics as response
Ronan O'Callaghan

Politics and Suicide
The philosophy of
political self-destruction
Nicholas Michelsen

Late Modern Palestine
The subject and representation of the
second intifada
Junka-Aikio

Negotiating Corruption
NGOs, governance and hybridity in
West Africa
Laura Routley

The Biopolitics of Lifestyle
Foucault, ethics and healthy choices
Christopher Mayes

**Critical Imaginations in
International Relations**
Aoileann Ní Mhurchú and Reiko Shindo

**Time, Temporality and Violence
in International Relations**
(De)fatalizing the present, forging
radical alternatives
*Edited by Anna M. Agathangelou and
Kyle Killian*

Lacan, Deleuze and World Politics
Rethinking the ontology of the
political subject
Andreja Zevnik

The Politics of Evasion
A post-globalization dialogue
Robert Latham

CRITICAL IMAGINATIONS IN INTERNATIONAL RELATIONS

Edited by Aoileann Ní Mhurchú and Reiko Shindo

Routledge
Taylor & Francis Group

LONDON AND NEW YORK

First published 2016
by Routledge
2 Park Square, Milton Park, Abingdon, Oxon OX14 4RN

and by Routledge
711 Third Avenue, New York, NY 10017

Routledge is an imprint of the Taylor & Francis Group, an informa business

British Library Cataloguing in Publication Data
A catalogue record for this book is available from the British Library

Library of Congress Cataloging in Publication Data
A catalog record for this book has been requested

ISBN: 978-1-138-82319-8 (hbk)
ISBN: 978-1-138-82320-4 (pbk)
ISBN: 978-1-315-74216-8 (ebk)

Typeset in Bembo
by Taylor & Francis Books

Printed and bound in Great Britain by
Ashford Colour Press Ltd, Gosport, Hampshire

MIX
Paper from
responsible sources
FSC
www.fsc.org FSC® C011748

CONTENTS

List of contributors   *xv*
Acknowledgements   *xx*

 1 Introduction: being critical and imaginative in
    International Relations   1
    Aoileann Ní Mhurchú and Reiko Shindo

 2 Borders   11
    Nick Vaughan-Williams

 3 Citizenship   28
    Peter Nyers and Zeina Sleiman

 4 Community   41
    Laura Brace

 5 Creativity   56
    Christine Sylvester

 6 Difference   70
    David L. Blaney and Naeem Inayatullah

 7 Globalisation   87
    V. Spike Peterson

 8 Knowledge Practice   102
    Aoileann Ní Mhurchú

 9 Law   120
    Andreja Zevnik

10 Narrative   136
    Carolina Moulin

11 Power   153
    Rita Abrahamsen

12 Resistance   166
    Reiko Shindo

13 Sovereignty   182
    Jens Bartelson

14 Space   195
    John Agnew

15 Subjectivity   212
    Shiera S. el-Malik

16 Technology   228
    Benjamin J. Muller

17 Theory   245
    Ching-Chang Chen and Young Chul Cho

18 Time   262
    Tom Lundborg

Index   277

LIST OF CONTRIBUTORS

Rita Abrahamsen is Professor in the Graduate School of Public and International Affairs at the University of Ottawa. She is the author (with M.C. Williams) of *Security Beyond the State: Private Security in International Politics* (Cambridge University Press, 2011) and *Disciplining Democracy: Development Discourse and the Good Governance Agenda in Africa* (Zed Books, 2000). Her articles have appeared in leading journals including *African Affairs, Alternatives, International Political Sociology, Journal of Modern African Studies, Political Studies, Third World Quarterly* and *Review of African Political Economy*. She was joint-editor of *African Affairs*, the highest ranked journal in African studies, from 2009 to 2014.

John Agnew is Distinguished Professor of Geography and Professor of Italian at the University of California, Los Angeles (UCLA), USA. From 2011 to 2014 he was Visiting Professor of Political Geography at Queen's University, Belfast. In 2008–9 he was President of the American Association of Geographers. He is the author, among other books, of *Hegemony: The New Shape of Global Power* (Temple University Press, 2005) and *Globalization and Sovereignty* (Rowman & Littlefield, 2009). He is on the editorial boards of *International Political Sociology, Review of International Political Economy* and the *European Journal of International Relations*. He is the Editor-in-Chief of the Regional Studies Association journal *Territory, Politics, Governance*.

Jens Bartelson is Professor of Political Science, at Lund University. His fields of interest include international political theory, the history of political thought, political philosophy and social theory. Jens Bartelson has written mainly about the concept of the sovereign state and the philosophy of world community. He is the author of *Visions of World Community* (Cambridge University Press, 2009), *The Critique of the State* (Cambridge University Press, 2001) and *A Genealogy of Sovereignty* (Cambridge University Press, 1995).

David L. Blaney is James Wallace Professor of Political Science, Macalester College, USA, and writes on the political and social theory of international relations and global political economy. His two books (co-authored with Naeem Inayatullah), *International Relations and the Problem of Difference* (Routledge, 2004) and *Savage Economics: Wealth, Poverty, and the Temporal Walls of Capitalism* (Routledge, 2010), explore international relations/political economy as a cultural project constructing a modern Western identity that makes it complicit with colonialism. With Arlene Tickner, he has edited *Thinking International Relations Differently* (Routledge, 2012), which shows how IR knowledge is actually produced around the world. A second edited volume with Tickner, *Claiming the International* (Routledge, 2013), explores the possibilities and paradoxes of alternative modes of worlding. He is beginning work on a book, *Justifying Suffering*, exploring the political economy tradition from Smith to neoclassical economy, and contemporary rationalist IPE.

Laura Brace is Senior Lecturer in Political Theory at the University of Leicester. She is author of the book *The Politics of Property* (Edinburgh University Press, 2004), and is currently working on a companion volume, *The Politics of Slavery* and, with Julia O'Connell Davidson, on an edited collection of essays on *Slaveries Old and New* for the British Academy. Her work on community and migration appears in a journal article for *Citizenship Studies* (2013) and in a chapter in *Citizenship and its Others* edited by Bridget Anderson and Vanessa Hughes (Palgrave, 2015).

Ching-Chang Chen is Associate Professor in the Department of Global Studies and a research fellow in the Afrasian Research Centre at Ryukoku University, Japan. His research interests cover international relations theory, critical security studies and East Asian politics. He has published on the relationship between threat perceptions and national identity construction in journals such as *Issues & Studies* and *Journal of Chinese Political Science*, as well as on the theory and practice of non-Western international relations in *International Relations of the Asia Pacific, Asian Perspective* and *Perceptions*. He is a co-editor of *The North Korea Crisis and Regional Responses* (East-West Center, 2015). He is a graduate of National Taiwan University and received his Ph.D. in International Politics from Aberystwyth University, Wales.

Young Chul Cho (co-first author) is Assistant Professor in the Faculty of International Studies at Chonbuk National University, South Korea. His research and teaching interests are international relations theory, critical/popular geopolitics, social research methods, Northeast Asia and South Asia. His articles have been published in *Cambridge Review of International Affairs, International Relations of the Asia-Pacific, Japanese Journal of Political Science, Pacific Focus*, and so on. He completed his Ph.D. in International Relations at the University of Manchester, UK. Before joining the current institution, he was Korea Foundation Visiting Professor at Leiden University in Holland and Associate Professor at O.P. Jindal Global University in India. He can be reached at youngchul.cho@gmail.com.

Shiera S. el-Malik is Associate Professor at DePaul University in Chicago where she teaches and writes in the area of colonialism and political thought and international political theory. She has published in the *Review of International Studies*, *African Identities*, *Journal of Contemporary African Thought*, *Politics, Groups and Identities*, *Irish Studies in International Affairs* and in edited volumes.

Naeem Inayatullah is Professor of Politics at Ithaca College. His work locates the Third World in international relations and global political economy. With David Blaney, he is the co-author of *Savage Economics: Wealth, Poverty, and the Temporal Walls of Capitalism* (Routledge, 2010) and *International Relations and the Problem of Difference* (Routledge, 2004). He is the editor of *Autobiographical International Relations* (Routledge, 2011), and co-editor of *Interrogating Imperialism* (Palgrave Macmillan, 2006) and *The Global Economy as Political Space* (Lynne Reiner, 1994). Recent journal articles include 'Gigging on the World Stage: *Bossa Nova* and *Afrobeat* after De-Reification', forthcoming in *Contexto Internacional*; 'Pulling Threads: Intimate Systematicity in *The Politics of Exile*', *Security Dialogue*, special issue 44(4), 2013: 331–345; 'Liberal Fundamentals', *Journal of International Relations and Development* (2012) and 'The Dark Heart of Kindness', *International Studies Perspectives* (2012). He serves as the Associate Editor for the first few issues of the *Journal of Narrative Politics*.

Tom Lundborg is Research Fellow at the Swedish Institute of International Affairs, where he is the principal investigator of a project on Time and Discourses of Global Politics, funded by the Swedish Research Council, 2014–2017. He is also Senior Lecturer in Political Science at the Swedish Defence College. His research centres on theories of security and international relations, with a special focus on the role of time for studying and analysing global and international politics. His publications include *Politics of the Event: Time, Movement, Becoming* (Routledge, 2012), as well as articles published in *European Journal of International Relations*, *Review of International Studies*, *Alternatives: Global, Local, Political*, *International Political Sociology* and *Theory & Event*.

Carolina Moulin is Assistant Professor at the Institute of International Relations, Pontifical Catholic University of Rio de Janeiro, Brazil. She is Chief Editor of *Contexto Internacional: Journal of Global Connections*. She holds a Ph.D. in Political Science from McMaster University, Canada. Her research interests revolve around the international politics of refugee and migrant protection, with a focus on processes of resistance and mobilisation in contexts of territorial and social exclusion in urban and rural settings.

Benjamin Muller is Associate Professor in Political Science at King's University College at the University of Western Ontario in London, Canada. In addition to teaching in the fields of Critical Security Studies and Borderland Studies, Dr. Muller also served as President of the Canadian section of the International Studies

Association (2015–2016). Dr. Muller has published widely on borders, surveillance and identification technology, security, sovereignty, and IR theory, including two monographs: *Security, Risk, and the Biometric State: Governing Borders and Bodies* (Routledge, 2010); and, with Samer Abboud, *Rethinking Hizballah: Legitimacy, Authority, Violence* (Ashgate, 2012). Dr. Muller has provided invited expertise to NATO, Canadian Parliamentary Committees and various stakeholder groups, as well as being an invited guest of a number of universities in North America and Europe. To advance his research on the Sonoran Borderlands, in 2014–2015 Dr. Muller held the Inaugural Visiting Scholar position at *Confluencenter for Creative Inquiry* at the University of Arizona.

Aoileann Ní Mhurchú is Lecturer in International Politics at the University of Manchester. Her research explores the changing nature of political identity and belonging in the context of increasing global migration, looking specifically at questions of time and space, intergenerational migration, hybrid subjectivity and sovereignty. She is author of *Ambiguous Citizenship in an Age of Global Migration* (Edinburgh University Press, 2014) and has published articles with *International Political Sociology*, *Alternatives: Local, Global, Political* and *Citizenship Studies*.

Peter Nyers is Associate Professor of the Politics of Citizenship and Intercultural Relations in the Department of Political Science, McMaster University, Canada. He is the author of *Rethinking Refugees: Beyond States of Emergency* (Routledge, 2006) and the editor or co-editor of several books on the politics of citizenship, migration and security, most recently the *Routledge Handbook of Global Citizenship Studies* (Routledge, 2014, co-edited with Engin F. Isin). He is currently completing a book manuscript on the politics of deportation and anti-deportation called 'Irregular Citizenship'. Nyers is one of the Chief Editors of the journal *Citizenship Studies*.

V. Spike Peterson is Professor of International Relations in the School of Government and Public Policy at the University of Arizona, with courtesy appointments in the Department of Gender and Women's Studies, Institute for LGBT Studies, International Studies and Center for Latin American Studies. Her current research focuses on informalisation, global householding, queering IR theory/practice and the politics of insecurities in the context of critically analysing global political economy.

Reiko Shindo is Teaching Fellow in the Department of Politics and International Studies at the University of Warwick. Her research areas include citizenship, borders, and language and translation. Her articles have appeared in *Citizenship Studies, International Political Sociology* and *Third World Quarterly*. In 2011, she worked as a programme adviser at the Secretariat of the International Peace Cooperation Headquarters, Cabinet Office, Japan.

Zeina Sleiman is a Ph.D. candidate in political science at McMaster University. Her research interests focus on transnational forms of citizenship, security, statelessness and sanctuary practices across the US and Canada.

Christine Sylvester is Professor of Political Science and Women's Studies, University of Connecticut, and Professorial Affiliate of the School of Global Studies, Gothenburg University. She is interested in the arts and IR (*Art/Museums: International Relations Where We Least Expect It* [Routledge, 2009] and 'Power, Security and Antiquities' in Edkins and Kear [2013]) and is editor of the Routledge series *War, Politics, Experience*, where she recently contributed *Masquerades of War* (ed., Routledge, 2015), *War As Experience: Contributions From International Relations and Feminist Analysis* (Routledge, 2013) and *Experiencing War* (ed., Routledge, 2011). She has received three awards from the International Studies Association (ISA), was Hesselgren Professor for Sweden, and was presented with an honorary doctorate in the social sciences by Lund University.

Nick Vaughan-Williams is Professor of International Security and Head of the Department of Politics and International Studies at the University of Warwick, UK. His research, supported by the British Academy and ESRC, focuses on the relationship between sovereignty, subjectivity and the spatial dimensions of security – particularly the changing nature and location of borders in global politics. He is author of *Europe's Border Crisis: Biopolitical Security and Beyond* (Oxford University Press, 2015) and *Border Politics: The Limits of Sovereign Power* (Edinburgh University Press, 2009, 2012, Gold Winner of the Association for Borderlands Studies Book Award), co-author of *Critical Security Studies: An Introduction* (Routledge 2010, 2015, with Columba Peoples), and co-editor of five volumes including *European-East Asian Borders in Translation* (Routledge, 2014, with Joyce C. H. Liu) and *Critical Theorists and International Relations* (Routledge, 2009, with Jenny Edkins). He is founding co-editor of the Routledge 'Interventions' book series (with Jenny Edkins).

Andreja Zevnik is Lecturer in International Politics at the University of Manchester. She is convener of the Critical Global Politics research cluster at the University of Manchester. She is author of *Laclan, Deleuze and World Politics: Rethinking the Ontology of the Political Subject* (Routledge, 2016), and co-editor of *Jacques Lacan: Between Psychoanalysis and Politics* (Routledge, 2015, with Samo Tomšič.

ACKNOWLEDGEMENTS

The idea behind this book arose from a conversation we had outside, one bright sunny day in Aberystwyth several years ago and is based in an important friendship. Both editors thank each other for a hugely enjoyable personal as well as working relationship over the past few years. We are very grateful to Jenny Edkins and Nick Vaughan-Williams for their support in the idea behind this book from its inception. It has also been a great privilege for us as editors to work with the authors who contributed to this book. Their belief in the idea of the book, their generosity in producing brilliant chapters, their participation in the mutual peer-review process and their patience sustained this project throughout.

This book is dedicated to the people – our family and friends as well as teachers, supervisors and colleagues – who have been instrumental in our 'education'. They encouraged us to imagine a world freely and fearlessly in ways that have been instrumental in how we engage in international politics as an exciting, dynamic and creative space.

Aoileann (Manchester) and Reiko (Tokyo)
June 2015

1

INTRODUCTION

Being critical and imaginative in International Relations

Aoileann Ní Mhurchú and Reiko Shindo

Critical and imaginations

The discipline of International Relations (IR) is driven by a desire to be critical and imaginative. Its so-called disciplinary history, if there is one, is fraught with debates between schools of thoughts, some of which have been identified as 'Great Debates'. Once introduced, concepts and theories are constantly under scrutiny. They are relentlessly re-invented to address the inadequacy of the old ones, to replace them and, eventually perhaps, to be replaced by others. In this regard, despite many strands of theories and 'isms' gracing their work, one of the underlying aspirations shared by IR scholars is arguably to possess and exercise a 'critical imagination'. As Jim George said, to be critical is to engage in 'the search for thinking space' where scholars share an enthusiasm for 'alternative explanations of how we got to the present and why we think the way we do about the contemporary world' (1989: 273). To be fair, phrases such as 'critical' and 'imaginations', used by George but not limited to him, are often attached to particular approaches in IR that are identified as 'alternatives to rationalist theories of international relations' (Smith 2001: 224). However, given the continuous attempts to explore different ways of thinking and talking about the world, it can also be said that IR scholars share, in a broad sense, a desire to think and act imaginatively and critically. As IR scholars we are encouraged to challenge what appears to be true, what is believed to be unquestionable and what seems to be taken for granted.

In this book we specifically use the phrase critical imagination to explore possibilities of world politics that do not reproduce state-centred politics. The IR discipline witnessed a surge of interest in challenging state-centric thinking in the late 1980s and early 1990s, through the notable development of postmodernist/poststructuralist, feminist, and postcolonial approaches in IR (for example, Campbell 1992; Der Derian and Shapiro 1989; Edkins 1999; McClintock et al. 1997).

These approaches attempt to critically examine the state-centred understanding of politics to explore different possibilities of the international, the political and the relational beyond a necessary focus on the state. They challenge an understanding of the world which is made up of bounded subjects within bounded political communities. The state-centred approach to world politics requires binaries, such as identity/difference, inside/outside, national/international, past/present, and development/underdevelopment as a necessary starting point for thinking about international politics. These binaries are relentlessly questioned and fiercely resisted by poststructuralist, feminist and postcolonial approaches. Such approaches instead focus on key concepts discussed within IR and show how these concepts work *through and beyond* binaries. This critical exploration of the world beyond various statist boundaries continues to this day (see, for example, Abrahamsen 2000; Inayatullah and Blaney 2004; Lundborg 2013; Nyers 2006; Peterson 2003; Sylvester 2009; Vaughan-Williams 2012).

This book situates itself in this ongoing attempt to critically interrogate state centrism. It does so by selecting various key concepts that have been discussed separately across existing studies and bringing them together in a single volume. In doing so, it encourages readers to understand IR as more than a discipline. It is a site where relations between various groups such as nations, states and political communities, have been imagined and reimagined. These relations are questioned and contested through key concepts in this edited book. This book unpacks these concepts and explores what possibilities they suggest in forming relations and ways of being in world politics that do not reproduce state centrism.

To critically examine the state's ontological and epistemological status in IR does not mean to dispense with it. Rather it is to consider how the state itself is constituted by a set of practices, ideas and imaginaries that articulate particular relations in world politics.[1] In other words, this book offers neither an outline of how we 'move away' from the state nor an image of how the world looks once we move away from the state. What lies beyond nation-state-led politics is not the answer that this book intends to offer. Instead, it offers an overview of how various key concepts have been used to imagine and reimagine the conditions of nation-state-led politics. Put simply, it looks at concepts which have been used as toolkits to rethink the possibilities of international relations. Thus, this book is not designed as the endpoint of a journey, but as a companion which inspires us in ongoing attempts to challenge (reimagine) the possibilities of state-based international relations.

This book focuses on sixteen key concepts to think about how state centricity limits our imaginations of political life and how this can be or has been challenged. For this book we chose concepts based on two criteria. First, we selected concepts which have prompted the emergence of new fields of study in thinking about non-state-centric worlds in IR. Second, we selected concepts which address underlying themes shared among critical scholarship in its attempt to think beyond a state-sovereign-oriented world. The former includes concepts such as borders (critical border studies), citizenship (critical citizenship studies, critical migration studies), globalisation (critical global studies), narrative (autobiographical and fictional studies), technology (science and technology studies) and law (critical legal studies). The latter group of concepts include community, sovereignty, subjectivity, creativity, knowledge practice, difference, power, resistance, space, theory and time.

The concepts discussed in the book are not necessarily absent in state-centred approaches to IR. Instead they are made invisible, or 'silenced' in Agnew's term (see Agnew in this book), in different ways. This book investigates the ways in which these concepts are rendered invisible and how a specific kind of world view has become more legitimate than others as a result. It also explores how different worlds might look through a renewed engagement with these concepts. If imagination helps us to 'construct a creative space that is not filled by existing ideas and information' (Park-Kang 2015: 370), it is through these concepts that this book endeavours to find such a 'creative space' in IR.

By focusing on concepts, we put ideas to the forefront of analysis rather than starting with a set of theories or specific theoretical frameworks. Chapters in this book are designed to allow readers to explore and think about what 'critical' IR can be in its various conceptual manifestations. Each chapter provides a discussion about how the concept can play a key role for reflecting on state centrism in IR and for envisioning the world through and beyond the state. Furthermore, the chapters draw connections between concepts to address common concerns and challenges in imagining IR. By doing so, the book allows readers to refer to one concept at a time while also linking together different concepts. The chapters not only illuminate key debates around these concepts but also provide thought-provoking insight into the concepts themselves for the study of international relations, especially when discussing their critical potential, which will be of interest to both students new to IR and anyone interested in original and critical perspectives on state-centric IR.

The chapters are written by a wide range of authors, both established and emerging academics located in Asia, Europe, Latin America and North America because we wanted to generate as broad a discussion as possible. Each chapter in the book is written by someone whose own research draws upon the respective concept, and illustrations are given in that context. Although there is no uniform structure to the chapters as such, each chapter addresses the following five points:

(A) A reflection on why the concept is important and how it acts as a tool for re-thinking international relations.
(B) An overview of the core principles, ideas and/or contentions associated with the concept; in particular the way in which the concept has come to be understood in critical thinking such that it challenges a statist starting point.
(C) A discussion of the critical potential of the concept to interrogate the limits of state centrism.
(D) Connections with key thinkers and other ideas.
(E) A list of suggestions for further reading, briefly annotated.

By addressing these points, each chapter aims to reappraise conceptual grounds on which IR theories are based instead of offering another set of facts and data to counter the existing ones. They initiate readers to '*think* rather than reproduce accepted knowledge frames' and thereby to 'create the conditions of possibility for imagining alternative worlds (and thus to be able to recognize the political commitments sequestered in every political imaginary)' (Shapiro 2013: xiv, emphasis original).

Critical versus traditional approaches?

By adding the term 'critical' before imaginations, we are aware of the danger of creating two camps within IR arbitrarily, if not unnecessarily. Indeed, this is the concern explicitly addressed by several contributors. For instance, in her chapter on power, Rita Abrahamsen warns that the traditional/critical dichotomy will prevent us from being self-reflective of our own approaches because we assume the other – in this case, any approach identified as conventional – to be 'by its very nature unable to be critical' (Abrahamsen: 162). She goes on to say: '[l]ittle is gained by such dichotomies and there is a need to be alert to the dangers of caricaturing other approaches as somehow stuck in outmoded understandings'. She suggests that 'in discussing so-called critical approaches, we need to be sufficiently reflexive and attuned to the forms of productive power at work in designating some approaches as "critical" and others as "traditional" or "conventional"' (ibid.: 163). Abrahamsen's challenge for nuanced reflection on the traditional/critical dichotomy is taken up throughout this book. Indeed, some chapters link contemporary debates and issues to older ones to address the question of continuity. For example, the chapter on knowledge practice by Aoileann Ní Mhurchú considers a neo-Kantian influence in critical engagement with understandings of 'knowledge as practice'. In their chapter on difference, David Blaney and Naeem Inayatullah also discuss the influence of thinkers such as Hedley Bull, Karl Polanyi and Ashis Nandy on their critically engaged understanding of difference: thus mixing so-called traditional and critical writers together to look for imaginative insights. By doing so, these chapters question the idea that critical thinking involves a radical new break with the so-called traditional. They emphasise the ways in which classical and non-classical thinking have become intertwined rather than the idea that the latter simply surpasses the former.

Other chapters interrogate the field of 'critical IR' to question any neat understanding that can be contrasted with 'traditional IR'. For example, in the chapter on creativity, Christine Sylvester expresses her frustration that many of the approaches called 'critical' remain largely concerned about theory and meta-theory at the expense of the everyday. Jens Bartelson, Andreja Zevnik, Reiko Shindo and Shiera el-Malik also express frustration in their chapters about the literature that is supposedly offering a 'critical' analysis within postmodern, poststructuralist, postcolonial or feminist traditions. In his chapter on sovereignty, Bartelson interrogates the critical understanding of sovereignty as contingent and considers the implications and limitations of such an understanding. In Zevnik's chapter on law, she argues that critical IR scholarship is largely reticent about law other than looking at it as a limitation or a practice of governance which she contrasts with seeing law as a productive force with emancipatory potential. She refers to this as the 'curious absence' of law, and points out that a mechanism of repression is in operation in supposedly 'critical' works as a result. In her chapter on resistance, Shindo argues that, despite the traditional/critical division, studies on resistance tend to collectively focus on visible forms of resistance that are driven by the will to change the status quo. She argues that to gain a fuller picture of resistance we must also consider unintentional and hidden protests conducted without the will to undermine state centricity. el-Malik's chapter on subjectivity also notably shows how critical IR scholarship often reifies gendered and ethnic forms of subjectivity by not paying enough attention to macro power relations embedded in subjectivities.

What this draws attention to is how a critically focused interrogation of state-centred politics does not produce a single 'critical' alternative approach to world politics which can be clearly demarcated from an approach that is 'non-critical'. Rather critical interrogation of state-centred politics produces many different, and often competing, ideas about what world politics *can* be across past and present, the traditional and the critical, the national and international, the everyday and meta-theory, and so on. In doing so, what each chapter highlights is the power of 'critique' itself in *producing* IR; that is, the way in which critique can help us to develop different ways of talking about, evaluating, doing and interrogating the changing nature of politics, relations and experiences of the international in a globalising world.

The rest of this chapter looks at four key areas of interrogation associated with this commitment to ongoing critique which can be seen throughout the book. These areas are first, interrogation of the disciplinary boundary of IR; second, of the division between engaging narrators and objective observers; third, of territorial space; and finally of a necessary ideal of progressive politics.

Interrogating the disciplinary boundary of IR

The chapters in this book point repeatedly to the need to rethink the disciplinary boundary of IR when examining the tradition/critical distinction. Contributors do this by explicitly addressing the limits of the IR discipline as a sole source of imaginations and call for more inclusive and innovative approaches in thinking about international relations. This is most directly addressed in the chapter by Blaney and Inayatullah. They argue that 'IR reduces others' differences to threat, without considering that encounters with others also present possibilities for attraction, exchange and learning' (Inayatullah and Blaney: 71). From this standpoint, Blaney and Inayatullah suggest the need to focus on difference beyond the language of threat and control which has become the norm in IR. In thinking about creativity as 'a form of making' (Sylvester: 57), Sylvester similarly suggests the need to go beyond the IR discipline in searching for vocabularies that enable us to be creative.

She argues that '[c]reativity in our field would seem to require that the IR thinker journey for inspiration beyond the customs, sources, and regulatory mechanisms that constitute the core of the field' (ibid.).

Indeed, rethinking the state-centric view of the world in IR through key concepts in this book, we are invited to question the disciplinary boundary set out as 'IR'. For example, drawing on science and technology as well as popular film, Benjamin Muller notes in his chapter on technology that '[t]raditional notions of space, inside and outside, us and them, (dis)order, security, threat, and so on, are radically reimagined in contemporary global politics, and IR is increasingly challenged, disrupted, motivated, and open to a variety of interdisciplinary influences under these conditions' (Muller: 288). In selecting the key concepts for this edited book, we, as editors, too, have realised how difficult it is to contain the scope of this book solely within the IR discipline. As noted above, many of the concepts chosen for the book play a central role in developing new fields of study, each of which encompasses different disciplines beyond IR, including geography, sociology, science, philosophy, history, anthropology and economics, which the chapters in this book draw constant attention to.

Challenging the idea of IR scholars as objective observers

The challenge to a traditional/critical distinction also leads contributors in this book to question the assumed sacred line that protects 'academics' as detached and aloof observers of the world. This point comes out strongly in Carolina Moulin's chapter on narrative. Moulin demonstrates various ways in which IR scholars engage with their own subject materials. By looking at several exemplary works, she problematises the objective/subjective distinction assumed in some approaches in IR. She introduces a way of reading IR as a series of narratives which 'necessarily blur fact and value, authorship and readership, characters and audiences' and 'escape claims about mere truth, and about reality, for theirs is the realm of performativity' (Moulin: 145). In similar vein Shindo's chapter on resistance starts from the recognition that it is difficult and even dangerous to identify particular social movements and incidents as 'resistance'. She considers how our understanding of 'resistance' is not a matter of observation but is embedded in particular political and ethical views upheld by IR scholars. From this standpoint, she raises a series of questions that put the researchers' embeddedness in their research topics at the forefront of studies on resistance and IR scholarship more generally.

In his chapter on time, Tom Lundborg addresses the involvement of theorists in their analysis of time. By showing how particular assumptions of time and progress inform specific views of history, Lundborg explores the idea of 'a pluralism of time' (Lundborg: 272). Drawing, for example, on the work of Kimberly Hutchings, he notes that this idea 'offers a useful way of questioning the role of the theorist as someone who occupies a privileged position in a unified present, on the basis of which he or she can act as both "prophet and time-traveller"' (ibid.). The call for 'a pluralism of time' is shared by Ching-Chang Chen and Young Chul Cho in their chapter on theory. They argue that IR theories are reflective of the cultural contexts in which IR theorists are living. The state-centric view 'does not come from a cultural vacuum. Rather, it reflects a particular understanding about territory, statehood and authority derived from Western/European history, philosophy and culture' (Chen and Cho: 251).

In other words, these contributors question the seemingly innocuous belief in imagination assumed by IR scholars. Considering that any academic theorising is a political act, it is crucial to ask what sorts of politics IR scholars are involved in when they explore alternative possibilities of politics and call for the need to 'imagine' the world differently. This is what the chapters in this book draw attention to. The search for alternatives to state centricity requires IR scholarship to question the limit of the imaginable and hence broaden the scope of 'imagination'. To do so, as Ní Mhurchú argues, is to reflect upon 'knowledge' as that which needs to be interrogated in and of itself. She notes that this involves refusing to start with key concepts on the presumption that these can be simply used to explain the world. What must be unpacked and investigated is not the question of what these concepts do but how we practice them and the way we come to rely upon particular understandings of key concepts *in* international politics.

Although imagination is said to be a key intellectual activity in scholarship, the practice of imagination hardly receives any attention on its own, with a few important exceptions (Mills 1959). Somehow the meaning of imagination is assumed to be evident, apolitical and uncontroversial. By directly identifying IR scholars as providers of specific ways of imagining worlds, the chapters in this book show that challenging the traditional/critical distinction entails politicisation of *both* IR scholars themselves and their 'imagination'. To borrow Milja Kurki's phrase, they show how we need to investigate the 'epistemological and ontological decisions IR theorists make' (2011: 133) to envision worlds differently.

Disorienting space

Many contributors specifically highlight the spatial implications of rethinking the traditional/critical division. They argue that thinking critically about international relations necessarily requires re-engagement with a previously held spatial understanding of the world. In his chapter on space, for example, John Agnew points out that world politics is constituted in and circulated across networks and flows, and place-making around the world. He notes how a geopolitics of knowledge 'can help us understand more adequately the paths of contemporary world politics' (Agnew: 209). The development of such 'paths' is further complicated by Nick Vaughan-Williams' chapter on borders. His chapter highlights the fluidity of borders and how these are no longer to be found only at traditional entry/exit points, nor are they always 'territorial' in a straightforward sense. It is in light of an understanding of fluidity as part of geopolitics that Muller discusses the concept of technology. In his chapter he challenges the idea that technology is only used by the powerful in the international arena, and explores instead how IR can be seen as a technology of power itself which sets the limits of possibility for how we conceive of and interpret global politics.

In her chapter on globalisation, Spike Peterson shows further the spatial complexity of the contemporary world by linking globalisation to everyday activities, political and economic controversies, and international affairs. According to Peterson, globalisation both unfolds democratic deficits, anglo-centric tendencies, and ideological manipulation and presents opportunities for challenging these state-oriented structures. She notes that to understand globalisation is to understand the difficulty of ever pinning it down because 'the contexts in which globalisation has currency are especially diverse in disciplinary, epistemological and ideological/political investments' (Peterson: 88). In their chapter on citizenship, Peter Nyers and Zeina Sleiman similarly question any straightforward attempts to link citizenship to a simple idea of globalising Western liberal norms. Instead, they argue that the idea of citizenship is shaped by simultaneous processes of both globalisation *and* localisation.

Interrogation of progressive politics

What underlines the chapters in this book is not least a question of how we have come to understand progressive politics. In thinking about the critical potential for different concepts, contributors refuse to provide clear visions as to how they should be thought about. This destabilises the ground on which IR scholars have come to stand. This is a dislocation of the *terra firma* upon which IR scholars have come to expect their explorations may start, and end up as well. For example, in her chapter on community, Laura Brace disrupts the normal association between community and commonality (inclusion), exploring instead the exclusionary basis of community as common membership (without ever reducing community simply to exclusion). She argues that 'we cannot assume … communities are unified systems of social cooperation without steadfastly ignoring the ways in which they are structured by property and power, to exclude outsiders who do not belong' (Brace: 51). Yet she notes that there are no easy alternatives and refuses to simply dismiss liberal notions of community and in particular its relationship to property and ownership that in large part produces the aforementioned exclusions and insecurities. Along with all of the chapters in this book, Brace's chapter emphasises the need to unsettle and disturb – rather than simply abandon – how we have come to know and deploy a certain concept in order to imagine politics otherwise. Her chapter suggests that we cannot settle on any one path as a necessarily 'better' way of doing politics.

Despite these four ways in which the chapters engage with the critical/traditional relationship, we interpret their engagement as embodying a unified message: to engage in critical imagination is to understand world politics in fluid and indefinite terms. It develops myriad ways of talking about, evaluating and interrogating the changing nature of world politics. In short, to engage in critical imagination is not to give answers but to keep asking. As such, what unites the chapters in this book is a commitment to critique itself, the activity vital to the process of imagining International Relations.

In conclusion we hope that people will return to this volume for many years to come in order to reflect upon ongoing debates about various key concepts within the field of IR. Our intention is that this book will act as a source of inspiration for how these debates are developing, their many twists and turns, and the ways in which they open up many possible lines of inquiry into international relations. In other words, this book is not driven by the need to set boundaries around the 'critical' so that we can teach, understand or write about the world around us coherently. It is worried even less about encapsulating the social reality of critical imagination in IR. Rather, the book is driven by a desire to explore the fluidity of critical imaginations in IR, so as to embrace and give voice to that fluidity, the tensions it comprises and the imaginative potentials it opens up.

Note

1 Our focus here on the state as something which is insufficient yet still hugely important can be linked to Chakrabarty's argument about Europe/European thought which he identifies as being 'both inadequate and indispensable' (2007: 16). We would like to thank Carolina Moulin for pointing this out.

Bibliography

Abrahamsen, R. (2000) *Disciplining Democracy: Development, Discourse and Good Governance*, London: Zed Books.

Campbell, D. (1992) *Writing Security: United States Foreign Policy and the Politics of Identity*, 2nd edition, Minneapolis: University of Minnesota Press.

Chakrabarty, D. (2007) *Provincializing Europe? Postcolonial Thought and Historical Difference*, Princeton, NJ and Oxford: Princeton University Press.

Der Derian, J. and Shapiro, M. (eds) (1989) *International/Intertextual Relations: Postmodern Readings of World Politics*, Lexington, MA: Lexington.

Edkins, J. (1999) *Poststructuralism and International Relations: Bringing the Political Back In*, Boulder, CO: Lynne Rienner.

George, J. (1989) 'International Relations and the Search for Thinking Space: Another View of the Third Debate', *International Studies Quarterly* 33(3): 269–279.

Inayatullah, N. and Blaney, D. (2004) *International Relations and the Problem of Difference*, Abingdon: Routledge.

Kurki, M. (2011) 'The Limitations of Critical Edge: Reflections on Critical and Philosophical IR Scholarship Today', *Millennium: Journal of International Studies* 40(1): 129–146.

Lundborg, T. (2013) *Politics of the Event: Time, Movement, Becoming*, Abingdon: Routledge.

McClintock, A., Mufti, A. and Shohat, E. (eds) (1997) *Dangerous Liaisons: Gender, Nation and Postcolonial Perspectives*, Minneapolis and London: Minnesota University Press.

Mills, C.W. (1959) *The Sociological Imagination*, New York: Oxford University Press.

Nyers, P. (2006) *Rethinking Refugees: Beyond States of Emergency*, New York and London: Routledge.

Park-Kang, S. (2015) 'Fictional IR and Imagination: Advancing Narrative Approaches', *Review of International Studies* 41(2): 361–381.

Peterson, S. (2003) *A Critical Rewriting of Global Political Economy: Integrating Reproductive, Productive and Virtual Economies*, Abingdon: Routledge.

Shapiro, M. (2013) *Studies in Trans-Disciplinary Method*, Routledge: London.

Smith, S. (2001) 'Reflectivist and Constructivist Approaches to International Theory', in John Baylis and Steve Smith (eds), *The Globalization of World Politics*, 2nd edition, Oxford: Oxford University Press, pp. 224–252.

Sylvester, C. (2009) *Art/Museums: International Relations Where We Least Expect It*, Boulder, CO: Paradigm Publishers.

Vaughan-Williams, N. (2012) *Border Politics: The Limits of Sovereign Power*, Edinburgh: Edinburgh University Press.

2

BORDERS

Nick Vaughan-Williams

Introduction

The concept of the border of the state has acted – and indeed continues to act – as a lodestar in the practice and theory of international relations. It structures the modern geopolitical imagination and dominant ways of dealing with questions relating to, *inter alia*, identity, security and belonging. A simplifying device for understanding the location of political authority, the concept of the border of the state organises the otherwise messy, overlapping and interconnecting nature of global politics into two supposedly distinct realms: the 'inside' of the state characterised by normality, friendship, security and progress; and the 'outside' of the international, associated with enmity, insecurity and anarchy.

Yet despite the considerable work that the concept of the border of the state does in shaping the modern geopolitical imagination, traditional discourses have tended to take this concept somewhat for granted. In the discipline of International Relations (IR) 'borders' have for the most part been treated as a static, ahistorical, territorial given: a mythical line in the sand assumed to be located at the outer-edge of the modern sovereign state. In the context of debates about globalisation, transnational flows of people, capital and goods were often said to be eroding borders between states. Following 9/11 the pendulum swung the other way and imperatives of national security led many analysts to pronounce the reassertion of the border. What these debates arguably missed, however, was the possibility that the concept of the border may itself be undergoing a series of transformations in contemporary political life. As well as problematising the work that this concept does in shaping the modern geopolitical imagination, a raft of critical scholarship has recently sought to diagnose the ways in which the nature and location of borders are not what or where they are supposed to be according to the modern geopolitical imagination. While there is no doubt that many stubborn borderzones persist and often with violent effects on local and migrant populations – as illustrated by the paradigmatic US–Mexico case – borders are not only to be found at traditional entry/exit points, and neither are they always 'territorial' in a straightforward sense.

If the analytical focus is shifted away from 'the border' as a given to the more active notion of 'bordering practices' – understood broadly as *attempts* to identify and control the mobility not only of people, but also of services and goods – then the picture becomes far more complex. Bordering practices are increasingly *offshored* beyond that which they aim to secure; *outsourced* to third states, private security companies and citizens as part of the risk management cycle; *preemptive* so that movements deemed to be 'irregular' and 'risky' are targeted *before* a person or object begins to move in the first place; and geared not simply towards the prevention of movement, but also to the *enhancement* of certain types of mobility deemed to be 'regular'. For these reasons, traditional understandings of the concept of the border of the state – and accompanying metaphors of 'lines', 'walls', and 'limits' – have been presented with a number of challenges, and various authors have called for the development of alternative border imaginaries in IR.

This chapter explores how IR has been imagined and reimagined in relation to the concept of the border of the state. The discussion begins with an overview of how that concept has operated within contemporary IR theory: as an assumed ground in traditional approaches and as a site of inquiry and repoliticisation in more critical work. From here the imaginative potential of focusing on the changing nature and location of 'the border' is explored. By highlighting the contingency of borders – and their intrinsic relationship with violence – it is argued that we can denaturalise present structures and sites of political authority. Finally, in reflecting on connections between critical approaches to borders in IR and key thinkers in social and political theory, the chapter concludes by reading poststructural thought as an effort to unsettle and disturb – rather than simply abandon – bordering practices in order to imagine politics otherwise.

Core ideas

According to what John Agnew (2003) refers to as the 'modern geopolitical imagination', borders between states are typically understood to be territorial markers of the limits of sovereign juridical–political authority. Central to this imagination is an historical account of the transition from overlapping jurisdictions in Medieval Europe to the modern sovereign territorial state (Walker 1993; see also Anderson 1996, Elden 2013). In this narrative, which typically begins with the end of the Thirty Years War and the Treaties of Westphalia in 1648, non-territorial dynastic rule gave way to a system of states defined precisely by strict territorial delimitations (Jackson 2000: 318). Irrespective of conceptual or historical 'accuracy', this account has had – and continues to have – a powerful grip on the practice and theory of politics and international relations (Agnew 2005; Walker 1993; see also Agnew in this book). While orthodox approaches to IR have typically taken borders for granted, a number of perspectives have sought to recognise and in more radical guises problematise the work that borders do in (re)producing this particular (and political) imagination.

Taking borders for granted

At base, the concept of the border of the state conditions the very possibility of both 'domestic' and 'international' political structures. Domestically, it is integral to conventional notions that the limits of political authority are coterminous with territorial limits. This is illustrated in Max Weber's influential definition of the state as: 'a human community that (successfully) claims the monopoly of the legitimate use of force *within a given territory*' (Weber 1948: 78, emphasis added). In the context of the international, the concept of the border of the state enables the core principle of territorial integrity enshrined in Article 2 Paragraph 4 of the United Nations (UN) Charter: 'All Members shall refrain in their international relations from the threat or use of force against the territorial integrity or political independence of any state.' Since the end of World War II, this principle has acted as the cornerstone for regulative ideals such as: the legal existence and equality of all states before international law; protection against the promotion of secessionism by some states in other states' territory; and territorial independence and preservation (Elden 2006). Without the concept of the border, the notion of independent states with contiguous – as opposed to overlapping – territories would be unimaginable.

As Anthony Jarvis and Albert Paolini (1995: 1–4) have pointed out, the concept of the border of the state also allows for an intellectual division of labour between the academic disciplines of politics on the one hand and IR on the other. In this view, the former takes as its focus matters considered proper to the internal functioning of the sovereign territorial state (for example, justice, rights and democracy) while the latter engages with issues arising from relations among states (for example, the balance of power, conflict and war). Yet, despite its privileged epistemological and ontological position, the concept of the border of the state has traditionally been somewhat taken for granted in both disciplinary contexts: Politics and IR, respectively, operate either side of the border without taking its constitution and reproduction as an object of substantive analysis. Thus, according to Chris Brown (2001: 117) 'neither modern political theory nor IR theory has an impressive record when it comes to theorising the problems posed by borders'. Similarly, Robert Jackson (2000: 316) has argued that 'it is remarkable that state borders are usually taken for granted by international relations scholars. They are a point of departure but they are not a subject of inquiry.'

This lacuna is symptomatic of the statist paradigm within which orthodox approaches have typically imagined IR. As John Gerard Ruggie (1983) noted in his review of Kenneth Waltz's *Theory of International Politics* [1979], structural realism assumes an idealised form of the Westphalian system without acknowledging it as a historically contingent set of spatial–temporal relations. Equally, although Hedley Bull's *The Anarchical Society* [1977] offers a tantalising glimpse of the possibility for new forms of political organisation, he concedes that his argument is ultimately 'an implicit defence of the state system' (Bull 2002: 247). In *Social Theory of International Politics* [1999] Alexander Wendt notes that borders are historically contingent phenomena that vary in breadth, depth and degree of completion, but beyond this recognition, the concept of the border of the state is once again left rather hostage to fortune in his analysis: 'an enquiry *among* states must take territory as in some sense given' (Wendt 1999: 211).

Problematising borders

The main problem with conceptualising the spatiality of power in terms of pre-existing blocs and fixed identities, as Agnew puts it, is that such a view takes 'the coercive power of territorial states for granted as a fixed feature of the modern world rather than seeing it as the outcome of a number of historical contingencies' (Agnew 2003: 69). An account of this nature not only de-historicises the evolution of the state and states-system, but it also implies a notion of power as the mono-poly of control exercised equally over anywhere within a given territory. In turn, this glosses over the fragility of the very power upon which the legitimacy of the state rests. An unproblematised understanding of the modern geopolitical imagi-nation thus has something of the 'we came, we knew, we conquered' mentality: one that traditional IR has serviced in a purportedly 'objective' manner for the sake of upholding modern statecraft (Agnew 2003: 60).

In contrast to the approaches above, a diverse range of scholarship in IR has sought to recognise and problematise the work that the concept of the border of the state does in both enabling and constraining the modern geopolitical imagina-tion. That imagination, according to Mathias Albert, David Jacobson and Yosef Lapid (2001: 8), has translated into a particular 'territorialist epistemology' in IR. Various normative IR theorists have moved beyond the limitations of earlier approaches by considering how borders play an active role in shaping ethical limits and practices in contemporary political life. For example, Jackson (2000) has pointed to the way in which state borders not only delimit spheres of national interests and security, but also define sovereign rights and duties such as those relating to intervention. A related argument is pursued by Williams who, drawing on Bull and Hannah Arendt, argues borders between states perform an ethical role by ensuring 'state independence, *limits* on violence, sanctity of agreement or the stability of possession' (Williams 2002: 739–40).

However, complicating the view that borders between states are harmless 'fences between neighbours' that serve to *delimit* violence, William E. Connolly (1995: 163) points to their rather more Janus-faced character when he argues that 'boundaries form indispensable protections against violation and violence; but the divisions they sustain also carry cruelty and violence'. In support of this argument, Connolly refers to the etymology of the concept of territory as deriving from the Latin root *terrere* meaning to frighten or terrorise (ibid.: xxii). Indeed, Connolly suggests that territory can be thought of as precisely 'land occupied and bounded by violence' (ibid.: xxii). In this view, to territorialise is 'to establish boundaries around [territory] by warning other people off' (ibid.). Echoing the connection between violence and territory made by Connolly, the work of R.B.J. Walker has argued that borders between states should not be read as sites of 'airbrushed achievement', but re-appraised and repoliticised as a 'site of struggle' (Walker 2002: 22).

Repoliticising borders

Of all scholars in IR, R.B.J. Walker arguably offers the most sustained critique of the concept of the border of the state and the work that it does in shaping the modern geopolitical imagination: 'One has to ask how have we so easily forgotten the concrete struggles that have left their traces in the clean lines of political cartography and the codifications of international law' (Walker 1990: 159). Unlike orthodox approaches that treat space as an unexamined background against which international relations play out, Walker's work seeks to diagnose what is at stake in the constitution and performative reproduction of the modern geopolitical imagination. Rather than a natural or neutral starting point, Walker shows how such an imagination is based on the historically constructed principles of the homogeneity, infinitude and invariability of space associated with Euclidean geometry. He argues that these ideas gave rise to the principles of state sovereignty, sharply delimited space and territorial integrity in post-Renaissance Europe, which were then exported around the globe via colonialism (see also Brace in this book).

For Walker, the principle of state sovereignty crystallised in early modern Europe amid growing cultural crises, and the medieval world of hierarchies and continuities gave way to a modern one of autonomies and separations. An alternative was required to the so-called 'Great Chain of Being' (the Western medieval conception of the order of the universe characterised by strict hierarchical links to God). Walker argues that the principle of state sovereignty 'offers both a spatial and a temporal resolution to questions about what political community can be, given the priority of citizenship and particularity over universalist claims to a common human identity' (Walker 1993: 62). The principle provides a double resolution to the problem of universality and particularity: on the one hand, the existence of an international sovereign states-system permits cultural particularity ('citizenship') within a broader framework of universal norms of interaction ('common human identity'); on the other hand, the generalisation of the sovereign state as a particular form cuts across all cultures. The resolution 'one world, many states' both enables and depends upon a spatial demarcation between inside and outside, which, in the context of the Westphalian system, is manifested as the concept of the border of the state.

Spatially, the principle of state sovereignty 'fixes a clear demarcation between life inside and outside a centred political community' (ibid.: 62). This allows for reason, justice and democracy to be aspired to *inside* the sovereign state against the backdrop of perpetual warfare and barbarism *outside* in the sphere of the international. It also permits notions of 'here' and 'there', 'us' and 'them', and affirms the presence of a political community. Temporally, these demarcations also provide the condition of possibility for notions of 'progress' and 'development' inside states as defined against what happens outside them: 'between states […] the lack of community can be taken to imply the impossibility of history as progressive teleology, and thus the possibility of merely repetition and recurrence' (ibid.: 63). As such, Walker argues that it is precisely this spatial–temporal resolution provided by the logic of 'inside/outside' that makes orthodox theories of IR distinctive. Walker's diagnosis of the relationship between sovereignty and the inside/outside problématique adds an important dimension to any attempt to examine the concept of the border of the state. Following his argument, the many paradoxes and contradictions glossed over by the principle of state sovereignty can be 'read as points, lines, and planes, as monopolies of power and authority, borders and territories' (Walker 2002: 10). These coordinates are often taken for granted, but Walker insists that 'as historical constructs, conceptions of space and time cannot be treated as some uniform background noise, as abstract ontological conditions to be acknowledged and then ignored' (Walker 1993: 131). The recognition that modern notions of inside and outside are merely historical constructs which 'have allowed us to situate and naturalise a comfortable home for power and authority' highlights not only the contingency of borders, but also the politics of global space more generally (ibid.: 178).

However, while Walker's diagnosis helps to understand modernity as a structure of insides and outsides that both enable and reproduce the state/states-system, it is possible to identify something of an unresolved tension in his book *Inside/Outside*. On the one hand, the logic of inside/outside is treated as a sort of 'iron cage' within which the modern geopolitical imagination and IR is trapped. On the other hand, there are also moments in Walker's work when he suggests that this logic is no longer apposite to contemporary conditions. For example, in the opening paragraphs of *Inside/Outside* it is claimed that 'ours is an age of speed and temporal accelerations' and at various points throughout the text it is implied that the concept of the border of the state is undergoing a series of transformations (ibid.: 20, 159, 161). Yet, while Walker (ibid.: 159) acknowledges that 'better explanations […] are no doubt called for', such explanations are ultimately not offered in *Inside/Outside*. Further still, Walker argues that alternatives 'are unlikely to emerge without a more sustained reconsideration of fundamental theoretical and philosophical assumptions than can be found in most of the literature on international relations theory' (ibid.). *Inside/Outside* thus poses and yet leaves in abeyance the tantalising question of whether it is possible – and/or indeed politically desirable – to think 'outside' the modern geopolitical imagination of insides and outsides.

Walker is not alone in expressing the idea that the traditional inside/outside logic associated with the modern geopolitical imagination is increasingly at odds with the complexities of contemporary political life. A growing number of scholars across the humanities and social sciences have also pointed to the increasingly paradoxical nature and location of borders, which are not always what or where they are supposed to be according to that imagination. Chief among these commentators is Étienne Balibar (1998: 217–8) who has famously argued: '*Borders* are vacillating […] they *are no longer at the border*, an institutionalised site that could be materialised on the ground and inscribed on the map, where one sovereignty ends and another begins.' Similarly, Achille Mbembe (2005: 31–32) writes: 'In [the] heteronymous organisation of territorial rights and claims, it makes little sense to insist on distinctions between "internal" and "external" political realms, separated by clearly demarcated boundaries.' Eyal Weizman (2007: 13) articulates a common complaint when he writes: 'New and suggestive cartographic representations of today's world [are required] […] a departure from the traditional view of a world that consists of a series of more or less homogeneous nation states separated by clear borders in a continuous spatial flow.' It is precisely to this quest for alternative border imaginaries in a range of critical scholarship that the discussion now turns.

Critical potential

Since the end of the Cold War, the fall of the Berlin Wall and the emergence of the discourse of globalisation, it is possible to identify two prominent and competing discourses related to the concept of the border of the state: the first is the claim that borders between states are withering away; the second is the notion that borders not only remain, but are becoming increasingly significant. According to the former, the transformation of global production is said to have ushered in new patterns of governance, in which the role of the modern, sovereign, territorially bordered state has diminished. Thus, it is often argued that the erosion of state borders over recent decades has come to threaten the very idea of the Westphalian territorially defined international state-system (Scholte 2000: 135–6). By contrast, the latter discourse maintains that national economies have been left intact if not actually strengthened by globalisation and the modern state continues to remain the primary political entity in world politics. Moreover, especially since the attacks on the Twin Towers of the World Trade Centre and the Pentagon on 11 September 2001, there have been a number of challenges to the concept of globalisation and discourses relating to borderlessness in the face of renewed national security imperatives. In the face of US military aggression and various (albeit sometimes contradictory) reassertions of territorial sovereignty, some writers argue that state borders are more important than ever before (Starr 2006). Evidence can be mounted in defence of either position, but both ultimately work within and further entrench the modern geopolitical imagination. What this debate excludes, moreover, is the possibility that the concept of the border of the state is undergoing a series of transformations in contemporary political life. While the idealised image of the concept of the border of the state may also be challenged historically (Anderson 1996) and/or by looking beyond Western geocultural contexts (Liu and Vaughan-Williams 2014), a wider range of critical scholarship has typically sought to emphasise the increasing complexity of transnational bordering practices (see Peterson in this book).

What and where is the border?

The technological sophistication with which attempted controls on movement are performed, the diversity of geographical locations where these performances take place, and the speed at which decisions about whom and/or what is considered 'regular' and/or 'irregular' are all factors commonly cited in support of the view that borders are changing and that alternative border imaginaries are required beyond the dominant inside/outside frame (Johnson et al. 2011; Kumar Rajaram and Grundy-Warr 2007; Parker and Vaughan-Williams 2009, 2012; Rumford 2008).[1] For example, borders have been reformulated in terms of mobile sites of preemptive risk assessment and identity management that facilitate the faster mobility of the trusted few at the expense of an array of suspicious Others (Amoore 2006; Bigo 2007); as a spatiotemporal continuum of controls on movement stretching between domestic/foreign domains and from now into the future (Bialasiewicz 2011; Vaughan-Williams 2009); and as a set of sovereign rituals through which the fiction of the modern subject, state and state-system is continually (re)produced, performed into being, and whose contingency is ultimately concealed and forgotten (Salter 2012; Walker 2010).

The changing nature and location of 'EUrope's' borders provide a striking illustrative case in point.[2] In 1985 the Schengen Agreement pledged to apply the principle of the free movement of people, services and goods by abolishing border controls between France, Germany, Belgium, the Netherlands and Luxembourg. With several rounds of enlargement and the accession of new Member States to what is now the European Union (EU), the Schengen zone has grown considerably since its inception. However, as William Walters (2002: 573), among others has shown, the condition of possibility of this 'area of freedom, security, and justice' is a series of compensatory measures that have turned the border into a 'diffuse, networked, control apparatus'. With the advent of identity cards, hotel registers, health certificates and a range of surveillance technologies, Didier Bigo (2001) has likewise argued that 'internal' and 'external' categories no longer make sense: borders in the traditional sense have given way to a 'field of (in)security' involving methods of 'unease management' such as risk profiling, the detention of 'irregular' populations (for example, undocumented migrants) and the enhanced mobility of 'regular' citizen-subjects (for example, tourists).

Further illustrating these points, another strand of critical scholarship has examined the 'off-shoring' and 'out-sourcing' of EUropean border controls. Attempts at policing 'irregular' migration, for example, now commonly take place in neighbouring third states, typically in Turkey and across North Africa (Bialasiewicz 2011). These extra-territorial projections of the border characterise aspects of the work of FRONTEX – the European Agency for the Management of Operational Cooperation at the External Borders of the Member States of the EU. Established in 2004, FRONTEX is an Agency of the EU Commission and has sought to characterise itself as a technocratic risk manager and mere coordinator of EU Member States' border controls. However, with access to a pool of nearly 2,500 personnel, 196 coastal patrol vessels and 53 helicopters, FRONTEX is akin to a military-style force and has embarked on a range of operations designed to stem 'irregular' migration thousands of miles away from Member States' territories in West Africa. Such projections have also given rise to the out-sourcing of bordering practices not only from EU Member States to third states, but also from the authorities of third states to local militias. As is well documented, research produced by NGOs demonstrates that the off-shoring and out-sourcing of Europe's borders has led to the deferral of responsibility for asylum and international production, which routinely leads to the dehumanisation and even death of some 'irregular' migrants (Vaughan-Williams 2015; see also websites of Migreurop and Statewatch below under 'further readings and useful websites'). The bordering practices of FRONTEX and its proxies in third states demonstrate that the territorial limits of the EU on the one hand are increasingly incongruent with the attempted reach of EU border control on the other hand: there has been a series of spatial–temporal displacements of the border, which bears little resemblance to that concept as it has been traditionally understood in the context of the modern geopolitical imagination.

Critical border studies

By now a considerable body of scholarship has responded to the need for alternative border imaginaries, and a more theoretically reflective and self-consciously 'critical' approach to the study of borders has emerged in IR and related disciplines (see *inter alia* Johnson et al. 2011; Kumar Rajaram and Grundy-Warr 2007; Parker and Vaughan-Williams 2009, 2012; Rumford 2008; Squire 2011). Seeking to move beyond the impasse reached in zero-sum debates about the continued 'presence' or increasing 'absence' of borders, the interdisciplinary field of Critical Border Studies (CBS) – broadly conceived – has challenged traditional statist notions of what and where borders are supposed to be according to the modern geopolitical imagination and shown how borders are increasingly fractured and multiple while often no less violent in their effects. Much of this literature has sought to 'decentre' the border so that it is not taken as a straightforward foundation for political analysis, but treated precisely as a site of interrogation in its own right. Central to this decentring has been a move towards a more sociological treatment of borders as a set of contingent *practices* throughout societies with performative effects. The move from 'border' to 'bordering practice' gives added weight to routine and everyday attempts to control mobility alongside more spectacular and exceptional sites and events. In turn, this enables greater attention to the role that non-state actors play in performing what Chris Rumford (2008) has referred to as 'borderwork': not only private security companies, for example, but also increasingly citizens, as part of the risk management cycle.

According to a multi-authored 'Agenda' for CBS, one of the tasks facing scholars is to 'extrapolate new border concepts, logics, and imaginaries that capture the changing perspective on what borders are supposed to be and where they may be supposed to lie' (Parker and Vaughan-Williams et al. 2009: 2). A recent development in the critical study of borders, especially against the backdrop of the 'War on Terror', has been the shift from a *geopolitical* line of inquiry to a *biopolitical* horizon of analysis. Whereas the former centres on the study of territory and power, the latter has urged, following the work of Michel Foucault (1978), closer attention to the relationship between techniques of government and the management of populations. This move has prompted a number of new border concepts, logics and imaginaries that seek to complicate the inside/outside logic associated with the modern geopolitical imagination. For example, in her analysis of US homeland security initiatives, Louise Amoore draws on Foucault to diagnose what she refers to as the 'biometric border': a 'mobile regulatory site through which people's everyday lives can be made amenable to intervention and management' (Amoore 2006: 337). So-called 'smart' technologies designed to risk-assess prior to travel are less associated with the 'geopolitical policing' of borders than with biopolitical modes of governing populations (ibid.).

Didier Bigo (2007) has developed the concept of the 'ban-opticon', which can be understood as another biopolitical border imaginary – drawing partly on the work of Giorgio Agamben (1998). This concept, a play on Jeremy Bentham's figure of the panopticon as featured in the work of Foucault, characterises logics of surveillance and profiling that create a transnational field of unease and (in)security management. The use of the term 'ban' refers to the device used by Agamben to understand the 'potentiality […] of the law […] to apply in no longer applying' (Agamben 1998: 28). Agamben uses the figure of *homo sacer* from Roman law to characterise the way in which sovereign power operates by banning certain lives from juridical–political structures: the former are subject to the latter, but do not benefit from any of the rights of the citizen. With the border concept of the ban-opticon, Bigo seeks to grasp the way in which populations such as 'irregular' migrants are often subjected to practices of surveillance that may lead to their abandonment and exposure to death.

For my own part, I have advanced the concept of the 'generalised biopolitical border' in order to characterise the reformulation of the border throughout Agamben's work as a performative decision about the worthiness of different lives (Vaughan-Williams 2009). Such a 'decision' is not necessarily taken by a singular source and neither is it inevitably 'successful' in its effects or met without resistance or contestation from those whom it targets. Rather it constitutes an *attempt* by diverse 'petty sovereigns' to use Judith Butler's (2004: 61–2) phrase – for example FRONTEX border personnel engaged in push-back activities on land and at sea – to performatively produce and secure the borders of political community. Such borders are inscribed via a cut between the politically qualified life of the citizen (whose identity, rights and security are assured) and that of contemporary *homines sacri* (whose subject position is unstable, denied access to 'normal' juridical–political structures and placed in insecure zones of habitual jeopardy). Beyond the more well-known aspects of his thought, Agamben also offers a series of devices – not only the ban, but also zone of indistinction, logic of the field, and *nomos* – to rethink the relationship between sovereignty and political space without relying upon a straightforward inside/outside topology (Minca 2006; Vaughan-Williams 2009).

But while there has been a spirited uptake of Agamben in some quarters of CBS, a number of scholars have also expressed caution when focusing on sovereign power, the politics of exceptionalism and (a particular reading of) Agamben's *homo sacer* thesis. Vicki Squire claims that, contrary to some Agambenian readings, contemporary borderzones are not exceptional spaces and should more accurately be conceptualised as sites of political struggle, rather than of biopolitical control (Squire 2011: 15). This is because, in Squire's view, 'borderzones may be marked by struggles around abjectification, but do not necessarily produce abject subjects' (ibid.: 14). To focus on such abjection, which Squire claims that the Agambenian account does, is to ignore what she refers to as the political agency of 'irregular' migrants – 'the different ways in which irregularity is contested, resisted, appropriated and/or re-appropriated – often by those who are constituted or categorised as such' (ibid.: 8). In a similar vein, Anne McNevin rejects Agambenian approaches in the light of her fieldwork with irregular migrant communities in Berlin, which revealed them not to be akin to the figure of *homo sacer*, but rather as 'politically active people' (McNevin 2013: 184). What is common to these critiques, as Heather Johnson puts it, is the argument that Agambenian analyses fail 'to begin from the position of the migrant', which means that there is a tendency to treat every borderzone and all irregular migrants as the same, rather than appreciating how the contested politics of mobility and struggles around border control play out differently across multiple sites with varying effects and implications (Johnson 2013: 84).

Agamben's work is unapologetically philosophical and his paradigmatic analysis seeks to make intelligible various structures of violence and exclusion on which contemporary political life is predicated. For this reason, Agamben can be read as a political polemicist who brings into association a broad range of hitherto unconnected phenomena in order to construct a series of deliberately provocative diagnoses and interventions. Read in these terms, his approach is not so much to offer more 'empirically accurate' understandings of contemporary phenomena, but to challenge existing frameworks of interpretation by revealing their limits and putting forward alternative problematisations. Yet despite this counter-argument, a number of critics have suggested that Agamben's diagnoses are perhaps least insightful from the perspective of populations targeted by biopolitical techniques of government.[3] In the context of CBS, this demands greater attention to the site of mutual encounter between bordering practices and 'irregular' migrants, which reveals not only the violence of attempts to police mobility, but also how apparatuses of control are often resisted, appropriated and/or escaped (Mezzadra and Neilson 2013; Stierl 2012; see also Shindo in this book).

Connections with key thinkers and other ideas

Underpinning the CBS research agenda are a number of philosophical backstops whose work has provided key concepts, logics and methodologies for diverse problematisations of the border. As we have already seen, Michel Foucault's (1978) paradigmatic account of biopolitics has set the stage for many recent interventions in the attempt to reconceptualise borders beyond the limits of the modern geo-political imagination. Foucault traced from the eighteenth century the emergence of new forms of knowledge that brought biological life into the heart of political calculations and mechanisms. Changes wrought by industrialisation and demographic growth meant that modern politics were increasingly driven by the optimisation of the life of man-as-species. Biopolitical modes of governance operate not by enclosing and disciplining individual bodies, but via the management and intervention in the population as a whole. This paradigm has implications for rethinking the border because 'security' refers not only to the fixing and demarcation of territory, but also to the enhancement of mobility and circulation of populations in order to sift and cancel out perceived threats within populations.

Despite these insights, however, Foucault's account of biopolitics has been taken in different directions in the contemporary philosophical literature and this has influenced various strands of thought within CBS. Agamben's (1998) reintroduction of sovereign power within the biopolitical paradigm is associated with a 'negative' or thanatopolitical impulse (in Greek mythology *thanatos* was the personification of death), which prioritises the often lethal ways in which some lives are killed in order to optimise those of others. By contrast, another strand in contemporary biopolitical theory – one often linked to the work of Antonio Negri – emphasises the more 'positive' or vitalist dimensions of biopolitics, which prioritises the power *of* life rather than power *over* life. In broad terms, these poles have translated into works that tend either to emphasise border control on the one hand or migrant mobility on the other hand (McNevin 2013). However, a number of research agendas in CBS have sought to move beyond this dichotomy by focusing, for example, on the concepts of irregularity (Squire 2011), ambivalence (McNevin 2013) and (auto)immunity (Vaughan-Williams 2015).

More generally, it is not by coincidence that CBS has drawn largely upon a range of thinkers associated with poststructural thought. Though heterogeneous and often rejected by those very thinkers, poststructuralism nevertheless shares a broad interest in critically questioning the logic and practice of borders understood in a general sense. Thus, in addition to Foucault, Agamben and Negri, the works of Baudrillard, Deleuze, Derrida and Nancy – to name only a few – refuse to take entities (the state, the subject, the community, and so on) as separate phenomena to begin with (Edkins and Vaughan-Williams 2009). Rather than taking such entities as somehow distinct from the outset in order that the relations between them might then be analysed, these thinkers all work with a more radically *relational* ontology. That is to say, their interest is precisely in tracing and ultimately problematising the work that different types of borders and bordering practices do in producing these phenomena *as* distinct. Furthermore, a hallmark of this work is a sustained interest in identifying and interrogating the often violent methods and outcomes of drawing (and obscuring) these kinds of distinctions. Once the constitution of elements of the social order is foregrounded as a site of analysis then the radical contingency of the constituted order is revealed *as such*. Attention is drawn to radical openness and interconnectedness on which society is founded and also to the violence with which that is often otherwise concealed. Via a recovery of this openness – or 'undecidability' in Derridean terms – it then becomes possible to 'bring the political back in' (Edkins 1999) and recall the potential for imagining alternatives to the present in all its dominant forms. Ultimately, poststructural thought does not simply embrace 'open borders' as a normative position, but rather challenges us to repoliticise all distinctions, borders and bordering practices – including the concept of the border of the state – as foundations for political thought, judgement and action.

Conclusion

As we have seen, the concept of the border of the state has enabled a dominant conception of juridical–political order that is central to the modern geopolitical imagination: an idealised view of that order as being divided between domestic and international realms and largely settled and stable. Yet, as Agnew, Walker, and others have pointed out, the work that this concept does is not a natural or neutral practice, but one that serves to benefit those whose interests are bound up in maintaining the status quo. Consequently, accounts of IR that rely upon an unre-flective usage of the concept of the border of the state are complicit in practices of forgetting the contingency of the juridical–political order and the reification of it. More recently, a range of critical scholarship associated with CBS has not only sought to problematise the concept of the border of the state, but also to trace the multiple ways in which borders are undergoing a series of spatial and temporal displacements and deferrals. Rather than a static thin line at the outer-edge of the state, CBS reorientates the analysis of the border so that it effectively becomes a verb: a series of practices that attempt to control the mobility of people, services and goods at diverse sites. Once borders are reconceptualised as bordering practices we are better able to identify and interrogate the work that they do – and the violence that they perform and (re)produce – in the name of securing political communities. This method of repoliticisation opens up questions such as: How do efforts to secure mobility affect different populations in different ways? What is at stake in the cultivation of unease and suspicion for the purpose of attempting to control movement in public spaces? Should citizens be border guards and what kind of society does this give rise to?

Rethinking borders biopolitically means that traditional geopolitical notions of 'inside' and 'outside' are complicated rather than abandoned: conventional coordinates of the subject, state and states-system are unsettled and demand renewed investigation. The decentring of the border in this way has potentially radical implications for the way in which IR has imagined itself and core themes including sovereignty and the very notion of the 'international': to decentre the border is to highlight the con-tingency of the modern system of insides and outsides and to repoliticise questions of identity, security and belonging (on the latter see Nyers and Sleiman in this book).

Despite the advances of CBS, however, more work is needed in order to extend the range of concepts, vocabularies and imaginations apposite to the contemporary transformation of the border. Equally, there remains considerable scope for scholars working with CBS approaches to engage in deeper international political socio-logical analyses of the manifold effects of bordering practices from the perspective of populations interpellated in diverse ways by those practices. For these reasons, one of Walker's (2010: 6) predictions – that the future of IR will need to 'think much more carefully about how complex practices of drawing lines have come to be treated as such a simple matter' – would appear to be a rather safe bet.

Acknowledgements

I would like to thank the editors of this volume and one anonymous reviewer for their detailed and constructive engagement with earlier drafts of the chapter. All remaining errors or limitations are entirely my own.

Notes

1 'Irregularity' is used here in inverted commas in order to denaturalise the category as one that is performatively produced by apparatuses of border security (see Squire 2011).
2 The term 'EUrope' has gathered increasing popularity in the critical literature in order to acknowledge that while related, the spatial and legal limits of the 'EU' are not coterminous with that of 'Europe' (see Bialasiewicz 2011).
3 For an alternative reading of Agamben and the possibility of political contestation see Edkins and Pin-Fat (2005).

Further reading and useful weblinks

FRONTEX – the official website of the EU external border management agency: http://frontex.europa.eu, accessed 13 February 2015.

Migreurop – an observatory on borders in Europe: www.migreurop.org/?lang=en, accessed 13 February 2015.

Parker, N. and Vaughan-Williams, N. (eds) (2012) *Critical Border Studies: Broadening and Deepening the 'Lines in the Sand' Agenda*, London and New York: Routledge. A collection of essays that seeks to formalise the CBS research agenda.

Statewatch – A non-governmental organisation that monitors states and civil liberties in Europe: www.statewatch.org, accessed 6 June 2015.

Watch The Med – a platform monitoring migrant deaths and human rights abuses at Europe's maritime borders: http://watchthemed.net, accessed 13 February 2015.

Walker, R.B.J. (1993) *Inside/Outside: International Relations as Political Theory*, Cambridge: Cambridge University Press. A seminal interrogation of the concept of the border in the modern geopolitical imagination.

Weber, L. (ed.) (2015) *Rethinking Border Control for a Globalizing World: A Preferred Future*, London and New York: Routledge. Offers a series of attempts to think through the possibility for alternative border logics in global politics.

Wilson, T. and Donnan, H. (eds) (2012) *A Companion to Border Studies*, Oxford and New York: Wiley-Blackwell. Provides a comprehensive overview of the main developments in the interdisciplinary field of border studies.

Bibliography

Agamben, G. (1998) *Homo Sacer: Sovereign Power and Bare Life*, trans. D. Heller-Roazen, Stanford, CA: Stanford University Press.

Agnew, J. (2003) *Geopolitics: Re-Visioning World Politics*, London and New York: Routledge.

Agnew, J. (2005) 'Sovereignty Regimes: Territoriality and the State Authority in Contemporary World Politics', *Annals of the Association of American Geographers* 95(2): 437–461.

Albert, M., Jacobson, D. and Lapid, Y. (eds) (2001) *Identities, Borders, Orders: Re-Thinking International Relations Theory*, London and Minneapolis: University of Minnesota Press.

Amoore, L. (2006) 'Biometric Borders: Governing Mobilities in the War on Terror', *Political Geography* 25: 336–351.

Anderson, M. (1996) *Frontiers: Territory and State Formation in the Modern World*, Cambridge: Polity Press.

Balibar, É. (1998) 'The Borders of Europe', in P. Cheah and B. Robbins (eds), *Cosmopolitics: Thinking and Feeling Beyond the Nation*, trans. J. Swenson, London and Minneapolis, MN: University of Minnesota Press, pp. 216–229.

Bialasiewicz, L. (ed.) (2011) *Europe and the World: EU Geopolitics and the Transformation of European Space*, Farnham and Berlington, VA: Ashgate.

Bigo, D. (2001) 'The Möbius Ribbon of Internal and External Security(ies)', in M. Albert, D. Jacobson and Y. Lapid (eds), *Identities, Borders, Orders: Re-Thinking International Relations Theory*, London and Minneapolis, MN: University of Minnesota Press, pp. 57–101.

Bigo, D. (2007) 'Detention of Foreigners, States of Exception, and the Social Practices of Control of the Banopticon', in P. Kumar Rajaram and C. Grundy-Warr (eds), *Borderscapes: Hidden Geographies and Politics at Territory's Edge*, London and Minneapolis: University of Minnesota Press, pp. 91–106.

Brown, C. (2001) 'Borders and Identity in International Political Theory', in M. Albert, D. Jacobson and Y. Lapid (eds), *Identities, Borders, Orders: Re-thinking International Relations Theory*, London and Minneapolis: University of Minnesota Press, pp. 117–136.

Bull, H. (2002) *The Anarchical Society: A Study of Order in World Politics*, 3rd edition, Basingstoke and New York: Palgrave Macmillan.

Butler, J. (2004) *Precarious Life: The Powers of Mourning and Violence*, London and New York: Verso.

Connolly, W.E. (1995) *The Ethos of Pluralization*, London and Minneapolis: University of Minnesota Press.

Edkins, J. (1999) *Poststructuralism and International Relations: Bringing the Political Back In*, Boulder, CO: Lynne Rienner.

Edkins, J. and Pin-Fat, V. (2005) 'Through the Wire: Relations of Power and Relations of Violence', *Millennium: Journal of International Studies* 34(1): 1–23.

Edkins, J. and Vaughan-Williams, N. (2009) 'Introduction', in J. Edkins and N. Vaughan-Williams (eds), *Critical Theorists and International Relations*, London and New York: Routledge, pp. 1–6.

Elden, S. (2006) 'Contingent Sovereignty, Territorial Integrity and the Sanctity of Borders', *The SAIS Review of International Affairs* 26(1): 11–24.

Elden, S. (2013) *The Birth of Territory*, Chicago, IL and London: University of Chicago Press.

Foucault, M. (1978) *The Will To Knowledge: The History of Sexuality: Volume 1*, London: Penguin.

Jackson, R. (2000) *The Global Covenant: Human Conduct in a World of States*, Oxford and New York: Oxford University Press.

Jarvis, A. and Paolini, A. (1995) 'Locating the State', in J. Camilleri, A. Jarvis and A. Paolini (eds), *The State in Transition: Reimagining Political Space*, Boulder, CO: Lynne Rienner, pp. 3–19.

Johnson, C., Jones, R., Paasi, A., Amoore, L., Mountz, A., Salter, M. and Rumford, C. (2011) 'Intervention: Rethinking the Border in Border Studies', *Political Geography* 30(1): 61–69.

Johnson, H. (2013) 'The Other Side of the Fence: Reconceptualizing the "Camp" and Migration Zones at the Borders of Spain', *International Political Sociology* 7: 75–91.

Kumar Rajaram, P. and Grundy-Warr, C. (eds) (2007) *Borderscapes: Hidden Geographies and Politics at Territory's Edge*, London and Minneapolis: University of Minnesota Press.

Liu, J.C.H. and Vaughan-Williams, N. (eds) (2014) *European-East Asian Borders in Translation*, London and New York: Routledge.

Mbembe, A. (2005) 'Necropolitics', trans. L. Meintjes, *Public Culture* 15(1): 11–40.

McNevin, A. (2013) 'Ambivalence and Citizenship: Theorising the Political Claims of Irregular Migrants', *Millennium: Journal of International Studies* 41(2): 182–200.

Mezzadra, S. and Neilson, B. (2013) *Border as Method, or, the Multiplication of Labor*, Durham, NC and London: Duke University Press.

Minca, C. (2006) 'Giorgio Agamben and the New Biopolitical Nomos', *Geografiska Annaler* 88B(4): 387–403.

Parker, N. and Vaughan-Williams, N. et al. (2009) 'Lines in the Sand? Towards an Agenda for Critical Border Studies', *Geopolitics* 14(3): 582–587.

Parker, N. and Vaughan-Williams, N. (eds) (2012) *Critical Border Studies: Broadening and Deepening the 'Lines in the Sand' Agenda*, London and New York: Routledge.

Ruggie, J. G. (1983) 'Review: Continuity and Transformation in the World Polity: Toward a Neorealist Synthesis', *World Politics* 35: 261–285.

Rumford, C. (ed.) (2008) *Citizens and Borderwork in Contemporary Europe*, London and New York: Routledge.

Salter, M. (2012) 'Theory of the /: The Suture and Critical Border Studies', *Geopolitics* 17: 734–755.

Scholte, J. A. (2000) *Globalization: A Critical Introduction*, Basingstoke and New York: Palgrave Macmillan.

Squire, V. (ed.) (2011) *The Contested Politics of Mobility: Borderzones and Irregularity*, London and New York: Routledge.

Starr, H. (2006) 'International Borders: What They Are, What They Mean, and Why We Should Care', *The SAIS Review of International Affairs* 26: 3–10.

Stierl, M. (2012) '"No one is illegal!" Resistance and the Politics of Discomfort', *Globalizations* 9(3): 425–438.

Vaughan-Williams, N. (2009) *Border Politics: The Limits of Sovereign Power*, Edinburgh: Edinburgh University Press.

Vaughan-Williams, N. (2015) *Europe's Border Crisis: Biopolitical Security and Beyond*, Oxford and New York: Oxford University Press.

Walker, R.B.J. (1990) 'Sovereignty, Identity, Community: Reflections on the Horizons of Contemporary Political Practice', in R.B.J. Walker and S. Mendlowitz (eds), *Contending Sovereignties: Redefining Political Community*, Boulder, CO: Lynne Rienner, pp. 159–185.

Walker, R.B.J. (1993) *Inside/Outside: International Relations as Political Theory*, Cambridge: Cambridge University Press.

Walker, R.B.J. (2002) 'After the Future: Enclosures, Connections, Politics', in R. Falk, L. Ruiz and R.B.J. Walker (eds), *Reframing the International: Law, Culture, Politics*, London and New York: Routledge, pp. 427–449.

Walker, R.B.J. (2010) *After the Globe, Before the World*, London and New York: Routledge.

Walters, W. (2002) 'Mapping Schengenland: Denaturalising the Border', *Environment and Planning D: Society and Space* 20(5): 564–580.

Weber, M. (1948) 'Politics as a Vocation', in H. Gerth and C. Wright Mills (eds), *From Max Weber: Essays in Sociology*, London: Kegan Paul, pp. 77–128.

Weizman, E. (2007) 'On Extraterritoriality', in G. Agamben et al. (eds), *Arxipèlag D'Excepcions*, Barcelona: Centre de Cultura Contemporania.

Wendt, A. (1999) *Social Theory of International Politics*, Cambridge: Cambridge University Press.

Williams, J. (2002) 'Territorial Borders, Toleration and the English School', *Review of International Studies* 28(4): 737–758.

3

CITIZENSHIP

Peter Nyers and Zeina Sleiman

Introduction

The study of citizenship has undergone a number of important developments over the past few decades. Not least among these innovations has been a willingness to theorise and analyse citizenship in ways that challenge the state-centricity of the concept. Modern political thought has conferred near monopoly rights to the state over the governance of citizenship. Today, however, citizenship is being increasingly investigated as occurring in unusual and uncommon sites and enacted by unexpected and unanticipated subjects. The emergence of cosmopolitan citizenships, diasporic citizenships, indigenous citizenships, and non-citizen citizenships, to name but a few, have deeply complicated and contested the idea that citizens are legally bound to the territorial sovereign state. These shifts in how the concept of citizenship is being studied are reflective of a number of important transformations, such as the rise of global forms of connectivity, migratory trends, and border politics. These changes have provoked new ways to think about political belonging, the governance of political subjects, and the enactment of political subjectivities.

Transformations in citizenship have profound implications for many of the key concepts in International Relations (IR), including sovereignty, territoriality, and authority. The territorial sovereignty principle, with its account of citizenship as a bounded and legal identity, is increasingly in competition with the de-territorialised global connectivity principle, where political belonging is not necessarily synonymous with the sovereign territorial state (Isin 2012). Central to thinking about citizenship in non-statist ways is to approach citizenship as a performative concept that is defined as much by its contextual enactments as by its formal and legal dimensions. And yet, discussions about citizenship have mostly occurred in the fields of sociology, anthropology, and geography. Despite the important interventions made by Andrew Linklater (1990), Jan Jindy Pettman (1999), and R.B.J. Walker

(1999), IR scholars – both mainstream and critical – have been reluctant to investigate citizenship as an intervening force in international politics. When citizen action is included in these analyses, it is more commonly done through subsuming citizenship into larger categories such as 'global civil society'. Citizenship, it would seem, is largely outside the analytical focus of most investigations of international relations.

This chapter seeks to critically examine the potential of citizenship within the study of international relations. We argue that the inclusion of citizenship within IR scholarship has the potential to break through the field's state-centrism and allow for thinking critically about global political struggles. The chapter will, therefore, explore the ambiguities and political paradoxes of this challenge posed by citizenship in a range of scholarship. Citizenship poses a challenge because it introduces a 'domestic' category to investigations of the 'international'. Including citizenship in the conceptual armoury of IR scholarship, therefore, has the potential to break down the inside/outside walls of conventional IR frameworks and consider how non-state actors act as an intervening force in international politics.

We will outline these complex and paradoxical developments in this chapter by, first, discussing the ambiguities and tensions of citizenship as a form of control versus its potential for critical transformation. While this is often characterised as a division between the legal and performative, we argue that citizenship is most productive as an analytic when it includes both the formal and performative dimensions. The critical potential of citizenship to break through the confines of state-centric IR can be found in the tensions between the formal and performative. Specifically, the formal–performative tension creates an opening for investigating citizenship in non-statist terms in at least two ways. First, it provokes us to question what kind of political community is being constituted by these performances and practices. Second, it allows us to see how citizenship can be performed as much by non-citizens as by formal citizens. This has the effect of provoking some fundamental questioning of the nature of political subjectivity, agency, and power in international politics. Taken together, both the space and subject of citizenship are revealed as ambiguous, up for grabs, and open to retaking and reshaping along non-statist lines (Ní Mhurchú 2014). The next section of the chapter illustrates some of the contemporary enactments of this kind of citizenship by analysing the re-emergence and spread of sanctuary cities. Sanctuary cities constitute themselves in an act of refusal to abide by the citizen/migrant distinction and, instead, view all residents, regardless of their legal status, as possessing rights to the city. These cities represent an ideal site from which to assess how new spaces (the urban), actors (cities), and subjectivities (undocumented citizens) can enact international politics in ways unaccounted for by traditional state-centric approaches in IR. Finally, we conclude the chapter by reflecting on the possibilities, but also the limits, that critical approaches to citizenship have for understanding world politics.

Citizenship between the formal and performative

Given its centrality to modern political thought, why does citizenship occupy such a marginal position within IR? Linklater (1990) famously characterised the development of the modern practice of international relations as the result of the early modern trade-off between 'men' and 'citizens'. Faced with a conflict between ethical universalism and ethical particularism, figures like Hobbes prioritised claims to the obligations we have to fellow citizens in the particular political association of the state. This move has resulted in a paradoxical positioning of citizenship in modern political thought. On the one hand, the figure of the citizen is central to the domestic realm of civil society and democratic governance. On the other, it is relatively absent in thinking about the external politics of the international. The familiar story of international relations is that it is a set of practices meant to secure, protect, and maximise the interests of this polity in relation to the dangerous, volatile, and anarchical realm of the international. The citizen is that subject who is protected, secured, and kept safe from the dangers of the external realm. In this way, the violent and unsavoury practices of international relations find legitimacy. This is because states claim that they are taking the necessary measures to protect their citizens. In doing so, they establish an important condition of possibility for the fulfilment of citizenship's potential. Protected from external violence and domination, citizens become free to participate in the determination of the 'good life' within the polity (Walker 1993).

While this constitutive narrative about IR has been disrupted and problematised by other narratives (e.g. globalisation), many of the central debates in the field nonetheless proceed with the assumption that the inside/outside narrative still has contemporary purchase. The endurance of this narrative is perhaps best illustrated in the resilience of the communitarian–cosmopolitanism debate. As with Linklater's (1990) 'man/citizen' tension, what animates this debate is a disagreement over where to draw borders on political community and ethical responsibilities. What are the limits of political community? Where do we draw the line for ethical responsibilities? In this debate, cosmopolitans adopt an ethos of universality and champion the obligations owed to the global human community (Archibugi 2008). Communitarians, by contrast, emphasise the individual's attachment to the national community. The universal moral vocabulary of cosmopolitanism – mobilised to achieve the aims of universal justice – is often portrayed as being at odds with the cultural diversity provided for by local community (Brown 1995; Miller 1995). At stake in this debate are complicated and at times seemingly intractable positions on the nature and scope of moral and political principles, norms, and values, such as human rights or justice. Despite the divergence of views, the binary spatial order of inside/outside continues to define the debate, constraining rather than liberating the options for political subjectivity and community (see Brace in this book).

The inside/outside narrative also prevails within citizenship studies, as it remains a field of study that is primarily centred on the individual's relationship to the state to which they belong. Studies on citizenship usually start with a number of assumptions, the most common one being that citizenship is a legal category that defines one's membership to a particular sovereign state. This assumption has generated a vast scholarship on the various national laws, rules, and regulations that govern citizenship. Citizenship studies scholars have investigated, often in quite critical terms, the combination of rights and duties that defines a citizen's relationship to the state. Following the work of British sociologist T.H. Marshall (1950), these rights have traditionally been described as civil (right to liberty and equality before the law), political (right to vote and participate in the political process), and social (right to participate fully within the social order). The responsibilities and duties of citizenship vary historically and geographically, but the three most commonly cited examples are conscription (military or national service), taxation, and participation (voting, jury duty). While other rights and duties, such as sexual, cultural, and environmental, have expanded the scope and depth of citizenship, the legal definition of citizenship orients scholarship on these rights and duties in relation to the authorities and institutions of the sovereign state.

This tradition of taking a legal perspective on the formal institution of citizenship has been criticised for how it can downplay the social struggles, past and present, which shape and reshape the formal parameters of citizenship. As a result, a growing body of scholarship investigates citizenship as a performative concept (McNevin 2011). These studies are interested in how citizenship is done, enacted, and put into play in various contextualised social, cultural, economic, and political milieus. In the area of security studies, for example, citizenship has been analysed in terms of the expectations placed upon it to contribute to the reproduction and legitimation of the national security efforts of the state. The governmentalities that provoke feelings of anxiety and unease within the polity also provoke the desire for security among the citizenry (Nyers 2009; Fournier 2014).

To appreciate how citizenship can interrupt the dominant inside/outside narrative of IR, the formal and performative dimensions of the concept should be employed simultaneously. This is because, by itself, the legal or formal perspective on citizenship does not tell us much about how citizenship is experienced. Similarly, an exclusive focus on the performative element of citizenship can miss some of the important structural and contextual limitations and possibilities for action. Consequently, both the legal and performative dimensions of citizenship are important: the legal aspect of citizenship both enables and provokes the performative element of citizenship.

How do the tensions found in the formal–performative approach allow citizenship to be mobilised as an analytic that can challenge the state-centricity of IR scholarship? This challenge can be addressed in two ways. The first proceeds by investigating other forms of political sites and communities – that is, other than the state – where the formal elements of citizenship are performatively enacted and negotiated. It is clear that citizenship is no longer an identity that is the exclusive domain of sovereign states. If citizenship can be broadly defined as an institution that mediates the relationship that political subjects have with the polity to which they belong (Isin and Nyers 2014b: 1), it is by no means a foregone conclusion that this polity must always be the state. Other forms of political community have existed historically and persist as coeval forms of belonging today. The fact that citizenship is no longer considered to be an exclusively domestic identity – citizenship has been globalised along with many other political categories – only strengthens and deepens the challenge it poses to IR. The rise of dual, multiple, and diasporic citizenship regimes over the past several decades has challenged the long-held requirement by states that citizens be loyal to one and only one sovereign authority. There has also been a significant expansion of supranational institutions and covenants, as well as a growth in the scope of local, city, regional, and trans-national-based authorities. These spaces and sites do not fit easily within the inside/outside logic of state sovereignty. All this places the citizen in a network of rights and responsibilities that are performatively negotiated in increasingly complex ways that, paradoxically, both exceed and reinforce the state-centrism of the concept.

The formal–performative tension allows for a second critical stance toward state-centrism. It allows for an appreciation of the political struggles that are immanent to the concept of citizenship. Rights are rarely conferred magnanimously by state authorities or out of their own altruism. Rather, rights have historically emerged through social struggles against established norms, authorities, dominations, and power relations. Citizenship, therefore, is not only about the 'right to have rights', as Arendt (1951: 294–95) famously described the concept. Better, in our view, is Engin Isin's (2012: 109) formulation: the 'right to claim rights'. By replacing 'have' with 'claim', the active and dynamic elements of citizenship are placed at the forefront. This phrase, Isin (2012: 109) explains, 'highlights the idea that before there are any rights, there is the right to be political and that the right to be political can only exist by exercising it'. This may sound like a tautological formulation, but only if one starts with the assumption that being political comes after citizenship. Isin's argument is that individuals enact themselves as political subjects prior to being the bearer of rights. Political subjectivity, in other words, precedes citizenship. The struggle for rights itself presupposes a subject who can make a claim for these rights. These claims often involve social mobilisations that draw upon existing (or newly invented) social, cultural, religious, and economic resources.

An important implication of this dynamic definition of citizenship is that it allows for non-citizens to be included in the frame of analysis. To say that citizenship is about the 'right to claim rights' is to leave the status of the subject who is making these claims ambiguous. Those who do not have the status of citizenship nonetheless make claims to citizenship and negotiate many rights and duties. The citizenship of non-citizens opens up a broad range of critical questions about some of the basic categories of politics, both international and domestic. If our category to describe 'insiders' (citizenship) is to include the acts of 'outsiders' (non-citizenship), then it becomes possible to start a critical questioning of the analytical and political purchase of the inside/outside distinction of modern politics. In the section below, we explore the implications of these critical challenges posed by citizenship in the context of sanctuary cities that open themselves up as spaces where state citizenship is not a requirement for membership, belonging, and rights.

Citizenship's critical potential: sanctuary practices

Citizenship, we have seen, has the critical potential of opening up new sites of investigating global political processes and struggles. It also has the critical potential to expand the range of actors involved in these processes and struggles. These advances are not only numerical (more sites, more actors), but also transformative: a different kind of politics is being enacted, performed, and negotiated in these sites. The struggles of citizenship are, therefore, not only about rights and recognition, but also about the contested constitution of subjectivity and polities themselves. If citizenship involves the 'right to claim rights', one can begin to identify not only the substance of these rights claims, but also the state and non-state entities to which these claims are directed. For example, when non-status Sudanese refugees occupied a public square in Cairo for three months, their claims were not directed at the Egyptian state. With the slogan 'We live in the country of UNHCR', the refugee protesters directed their claims about protection, living conditions, and international mobility rights to the UN refugee agency (Moulin and Nyers 2007). There are many other examples of rights claims being directed by citizens and non-citizens to state and non-state entities. In this section, we illustrate how sanctuary cities are creating a space for contesting citizenship, and forming a foundation for citizenship that is enacted within cities and regions. We do this by, first, outlining the emerging power of cities and sanctuary movements. Next, we elaborate on the potential of these sites and movements for conceiving a form of citizenship that is not centred on or over-determined by the logic of the sovereign state.

The movement to provide protection and security to non-citizens through sanctuary practices is a centuries-old practice, and one that has seen a significant revival in cities and towns across the globe (Lippert and Rehaag 2013). An important part of this movement has been to extend the space of sanctuary beyond that of churches and other sacred spaces to secular sites such as universities, schools, community centres, and so on. In various and diverse ways the space of the city has emerged as a key site of sanctuary. These sanctuary practices have been enacted at a municipal level, and take a variety of forms. For example, Cities of Refuge provide sanctuary to individual authors who are facing persecution from their home governments for their written or spoken words (Nyers 2008). The City of Sanctuary movement, to cite another example, has spread to over thirty-five cities, towns, and villages in the UK. This movement is primarily aimed at locally welcoming and providing hospitality to asylum seekers waiting for their applications to be processed (Squire and Darling 2013). By contrast, sanctuary cities in the United States and Canada – including major metropolitan areas such as Los Angeles, Chicago, New York, and Toronto – take a more active public policy agenda with city governments making municipal services available to all residents of the city, regardless of their formal status. The services made available in these cases touch on important issues of social citizenship, border policy, and immigration policy and, in doing so, challenge the state's claim to monopolise these areas of governance – areas that are extremely sensitive for how sovereign states legitimate their authority.

Sanctuary practices exemplify the way in which citizenship can be conceived not only as a technology of rule and order, but also as a political dynamic that generates ruptures in existing rules and orders. Cities, including municipal government and localised actors, are able to take some control of immigration policy, and thereby challenge the state's claim to monopolise this area. This provides a space for thinking critically of sanctuary cities and how they provide residents – irrespective of their legal status – with the rights and services normally accorded to citizens only by the state. While cities can only provide rights and services that are mandated by the municipality (and, therefore, cannot issue passports), sanctuary cities nonetheless challenge the state-centric conception of citizenship. This is because sanctuary cities challenge the state's claim to monopolise matters of immigration by providing a welcoming space and rights to people that the state has denied entry or formally refused status. In return, residents of the city are required to fulfil basic citizenship duties, such as abiding by the law, and thereby creating a basis for citizenship in regions within the state.

Sanctuary cities and migrant citizenship involve some significant challenges – conceptual, political, and ethical – to the state-centricity of IR. In the first place, sanctuary cities represent a conceptual challenge in thinking about agents and actors in global politics. Researchers have long shown how cities can be important sites of contestation that challenge state power. Cities are not only the sites where social movements arise, but some movements actually 'impose the city as the basic cell of a new socio-political organization' (Castells 1983: 14), thereby opening up a perspective on this city as a powerful political entity that challenges 'existing spatial and social forms, the exploration of new social meanings and, finally, the demand for an alternative social order' (Portaliou 2007: 167).

In this way, cities are expressive of all sorts of hopes, aspirations, and possibilities for inventing new forms of political community, authority, and subjectivity (on the importance of such spaces see Brace in this book). Cities are not only subservient to state power, but can function as their own powerful entity alongside states – particularly in relation to social movements. This challenges the current understanding of world order since cities are actually a central force in which human life is negotiated. As Magnusson (1994: 629) argues, 'Viewed from an urbanist's perspective, city life is where the principles of state sovereignty – and the complementary principles of individual sovereignty – fall apart in the face of the complexity of human existence'. Thinking of the city in this light allows us to think 'simultaneously of the local and the global, the universal and the particular' (ibid.: 630) in ways that does not reproduce the hierarchies of state sovereignty. Instead, cities, states, and other forms of political communities can be seen as being coeval, coexisting albeit in a highly contested way (see Peterson this volume).

An analysis of sanctuary practices allows us to look at alternative forms of transnational powers that may have the potential to establish universal human rights among people regardless of citizenship, race, religion, or nationality – a task that has been traditionally the responsibility of the state as the 'rights giver'. In this case, such a study can help us document the emerging ways in which state powers can and are exercised by actors other than the state or international organisations. It also highlights the ways in which power within international politics is being negotiated and shifted by transnational entities (see Abrahamsen in this book). Sanctuary practices, and particularly sanctuary cities, derive some power by providing an avenue in which refugees, stateless people, and undocumented residents are making claims to rights outside the avenue of the state.

Sanctuary cities and sanctuary practices, particularly those enacted by municipal governments, provide an avenue in which acts of citizenship can be performed. Isin uses the term 'acts of citizenship' (Isin 2009; cf. Isin and Nielsen 2008) to describe how rights and duties are claimed and enacted by people who may or may not be officially authorised to claim and perform these rights and duties. These acts of citizenship happen when people – either citizens or non-citizens – disrupt what he calls the dominant 'script' that is provided by the state. An act, therefore, is a political intervention that disrupts the received narratives about the nature, scope, and subjects of 'politics'. Citizenship is not only a matter of laws, status, and governing practices, but is also a site of creativity, inventiveness, and experimentation with new forms of being political. With acts, it is the transversal transformations that are of central importance, not the re-inscription of dominant identities and practices. At the same time, an act goes beyond disruption, and also provides something 'new' to the usual script. This is a realm of 'insurgent' citizenship where people make claims to entities other than that of the state, such as through activist networks and through sanctuary movements (Darling 2014; Ridgley 2008).

In a similar way, sanctuary cities do not worry about asking 'who is a citizen?' but instead constitute a site through which subjects can produce themselves as citizens by making claims to rights that they would otherwise not be authorised to. Sanctuary cities redefine who should be included in the political community and are providing a space in which the official 'script' of citizenship can be rewritten. We can witness a disruption of state authority, even though such ruptures take place in a city space that is nonetheless internal or immanent to the state. In many ways, acts of citizenship are facilitated through these city policies by providing a 'safe haven' for contesting the state's judgement on who it lets in and out. This challenges the state's authority on regulating borders, but it also means that cities are acting alongside states at a global level.

Providing a space for residents to enact citizenship, when they have been denied by state authority, forms the potential of creating citizenship that is not based within the state or a transnational form of citizenship. These have also changed the way in which borders are conceived, and as a result are changing the nature of the state as a 'rights giver' since (some) rights can be given and taken within regions of a state. Isin's analysis of the enactment of new forms of citizenship lies within a criticism of the shifting dynamics of the state within global politics. Consequently this places into question the relationship between the state and the nation (and therefore the citizen) by critically assessing the relationship between the nation and the state as 'natural' associations. By doing this, he demonstrates that 'the idea here is that the existence of rights presupposes political subjectivity and rights are effective only in practice' (Isin 2012: 90). Therefore the idea of a nation or a political community with rights and privileges can potentially exist outside the state, or in this case within a city. In other words, this can occur, when cities and localised communities begin enacting the power that states hold in welcoming 'outsiders', by providing them a safe space to live and access to local services. This can essentially form the foundation for a community that, in some regards, has been rejected by state authority, yet welcomed at a more local level.

The emerging power of sanctuary cities is an example that can help us understand how the borders that shape who belong and who does not are changing (see Vaughan-Williams in this book). Cities that enforce sanctuary policies include 'symbolic declarations of city space as sanctuary, restrictions on the use of local resources for enforcing federal [immigration] law, and policies to ensure all city residents have equal access to rights and entitlements' (Ridgley 2013: 19) regardless of their official membership status to the state. The power of the city can transcend that of the state, which functions to create a form of political community that provides rights to people living within its borders. In this case, forming a type of membership that is confined to the borders of the city.

Sanctuary practices and sanctuary cities challenge the mainstream understanding of 'relevant' actors in international relations as they challenge state power and authority in a number of ways. This particularly relates to the ways in which they directly challenge the state's decision-making when it comes to border control and governing the rights of social citizenship. Viewed from the perspective of the formal dimensions of citizenship, sanctuary cities provide more expansive formal or legal rights to irregular migrants. From the perspective of the performative dimension of citizenship, sanctuary cities develop out of the struggle for irregular migrants to acquire rights, and who do so by enacting the 'right to claim rights'. They claim those rights through municipal authorities and local organisations instead of state authorities. In these cities, it is residents, not citizens, who claim rights and perform duties, thereby demonstrating the ways in which citizenship can be considered autonomous from the state, in, admittedly partial, yet still significant ways.

Conclusions and further questions

This chapter has sought to demonstrate that the concept of citizenship can be productively mobilised to reveal new insights about non-statist forms of world politics. It did so in a number of ways. First, while citizenship is famously a state-centric concept, it is also constantly unbinding itself from the embrace of the state. In this way, citizenship is both a site of sovereign control and an enactment of creative transformation. It is the site of statism and represents the potential to move beyond, side-step, or otherwise evade statism and invent something new. Second, in order to appreciate this duality, we argue that the formal and performative dimensions of citizenship be investigated simultaneously. The formal–performative perspective on citizenship allows for critical questions to be posed about both the site and subject of political community. In other words, the concept of citizenship allows us to identify movements that challenge and contest the state-centric vision of political community and identity. We explored this with the example of sanctuary cities. These cities are not just another 'level' of analysis to 'add on' to an otherwise state-centric model of world politics. Rather, they represent a site where some of the fundamental categories of politics – citizen, non-citizen, political agency, and community – are being reinvented anew. Third, the concept of citizenship is not doomed to be an exclusionary concept, central to the self/other bordering practices of the state. As illustrated through the example of sanctuary cities, the borders between citizen and non-citizen, documented and undocumented, member and non-member are rendered marginal in this kind of local/global politics.

We conclude the chapter with a few questions about citizenship in critical IR scholarship. Our hope is that these questions will lead to many more about how the contested enactment of political subjectivity can act as a critical force in world politics.

1. Introducing citizenship to the study of international relations involves taking a critical stance toward IR, but also to citizenship studies itself. What does it mean to speak of 'critical citizenship studies'? What does it mean to be 'critical' in this context? Guillaume (2013: 29) argues that criticality involves taking a 'self-conscious posture' that would allow one to 'avoid thinking about the state and the international as the state would like to be thought'. We can add 'citizenship' to this formulation as well. Much of the scholarship in citizenship studies is already acutely aware of the inequalities and arbitrariness of citizenship regimes. But despite this awareness, all too often this recognition is pro forma only, with studies bracketing off the outsider and focusing on the figure of the citizen alone. However, it is doubtful that citizenship can be conceived, proceed, or exist without its constitutive outsiders. Therefore, what is critical about this scholarship is its refusal to accept these analytical borders. Instead, it explores the complex interconnections that citizens, semi-citizens, and non-citizens engage in, both routinely and exceptionally, expectedly and unexpectedly, locally and globally.

2. Is it possible to 'take apart' citizenship – that is, remove it from its statist foundations – without abandoning the concept entirely? When making the claim that citizenship can potentially exist 'outside' the governmental regime of the state, one is also forced to confront the difficult task of liberating the concept from the state's classification regime that seeks to capture and claim the idea of 'citizenship' as its own. How then can we assess when citizenship is creative and transformative, and when it is co-opted by the state? Indeed, to create or reclaim a mode of thinking that can dissociate the citizenship from the state is no small task. However, a dynamic group of scholars is looking at citizenship in this way. Their substantive concerns are diverse and inter-disciplinary. Many are outside the disciplinary confines of IR and yet write on themes that are nonetheless central to the field, such as war, security, borders,

and the global political economy (Cowen and Gilbert 2008; Guillaume and Huysmans 2013).

3. Is there a danger of enacting a kind of conceptual colonialism by classifying all political struggles under 'citizenship'? How should we analyse the struggles of marginalised people who are themselves ambivalent about category of citizenship (Chatterjee 2004)? These questions raise important challenges to how we perceive the origins of citizenship. To be sure, citizenship has a history of being deployed in order to draw a hierarchical distinction between the 'Europe' or the 'West' and the rest of the world. There are deep power relations involved in this formulation. We can see the contemporary manifestation of this discourse in arguments for the global spread of 'liberal democracy' as the supposedly only legitimate model of governance. But the idea that citizenship is somehow a uniquely Western institution that stands in contrast to the despotic regimes of the 'East' is full of historical hubris. When citizenship is investigated more broadly as the mediating institution between political subjects and their polities (not necessarily or only the state) to which they belong, the game of benchmarking with 'liberal democracy' is disrupted. What emerges instead is a focus on the ways in which the cornerstone of any political order – the political subject – is brought into being. There is an increasing interest in this kind of 'global' citizenship studies. Rather than globalizing Western liberal norms about political subjectivity, these studies focus on the simultaneous processes of globalisation and localisation of citizenship (Isin and Nyers 2014a).

Further reading and useful weblinks

Balibar, E. (2004) *We, the People of Europe? Reflections on Transnational Citizenship*, Princeton, NJ: Princeton University Press.

City of Sanctuary (UK): http://cityofsanctuary.org, accessed 1 May 2015.

Dreamers USA: www.thedream.us, accessed 1 May 2015.

Goldring, L. and Landolt, P (eds) (2013) *Producing and Negotiating Non-Citizenship: Precarious Legal Status in Canada*, Toronto: University of Toronto Press.

Health Care for All: www.healthcareforall.org, accessed 1 May 2015.

Holston, J. (2009) *Insurgent Citizenship: Disjunctions of Democracy and Modernity in Brazil*, Princeton, NJ: Princeton University Press.

NoBorder Network: www.noborder.org, accessed 1 May 2015.

No One Is Illegal – Vancouver: https://noii-van.resist.ca, accessed 1 May 2015.

Rygiel, K. (2010) *Globalizing Citizenship*, Vancouver: University of British Columbia Press.

Shachar, A. (2009) *The Birthright Lottery: Citizenship and Global Inequality*, Cambridge, MA: Harvard University Press.

Solidarity City Network: http://solidaritycity.net, accessed 1 May 2015.

Stevens, J. (2010) *States without Nations: Citizenship for Mortals*, New York: Columbia University Press.

Tyler, I. and Marciniak, K. (eds) (2014) *Protesting Citizenship: Migrant Activisms*, London: Routledge.

Bibliography

Archibugi, D. (2008) *The Global Commonwealth of Citizens: Toward Cosmopolitan Democracy*, Princeton, NJ: Princeton University Press.

Arendt, H. (1951) *The Origins of Totalitarianism*, New York: Harcourt, Brace & Co.

Brown, C. (1995) 'The Idea of a World Community', in K. Booth and S. Smith (eds), *International Relations Theory Today*, University Park: Pennsylvania State University Press, pp. 90–109.

Castells, M. (1983) *The City and the Grassroots: A Cross-Cultural Theory of Urban Social Movements*, London: E. Arnold.

Chatterjee, P. (2004) *The Politics of the Governed: Reflections on Popular Politics in Most of the World*, New York: Columbia University Press.

Cowen, D. and Gilbert, E. (eds) (2008) *War, Citizenship, Territory*, London: Routledge.

Darling, J. (2014) 'Asylum and the Post-Political: Domopolitics, Depoliticisation and Acts of Citizenship', *Antipode* 46(1): 72–91.

Fournier, P. (2014) 'The Neoliberal/Neurotic Citizen and Security as Discourse', *Critical Studies on Security* 2(3): 309–322.

Guillaume, X. (2013) 'Criticality', in M.B. Salter and C.E. Mutlu (eds), *Research Methods in Critical Security Studies*, London: Routledge, pp. 29–32.

Guillaume, X. and J. Huysmans (eds) (2013) *Security and Citizenship: the Constitution of Political Being*, London: Routledge.

Isin, E.F. (2009) 'Citizenship in Flux: the Figure of the Activist Citizen', *Subjectivity* 29(1): 367–388.

Isin, E.F. (2012) *Citizens without Frontiers*, London: Bloomsbury.

Isin, E.F. and Nielsen, G. M. (eds) (2008) *Acts of Citizenship*, London: Palgrave Macmillan.

Isin, E.F. and Nyers, P. (eds) (2014a) *Routledge Handbook of Global Citizenship Studies*, London: Routledge.

Isin, E.F. and Nyers, P. (2014b) 'Globalizing Citizenship Studies', in E.F. Isin and P. Nyers, (eds), *Routledge Handbook of Global Citizenship Studies*, London: Routledge, pp. 1–11.

Linklater, A. (1990) *Men and Citizens in the Theory of International Relations*, 2nd edition, London: MacMillan.

Lippert, R.K. and Rehaag, S. (eds) (2013) *Sanctuary Practices in International Perspectives: Migration, Citizenship and Social Movements*, New York: Routledge.

Magnusson, W. (1994) 'Social Movements and the Global City', *Millennium: Journal of International Studies* 23(3): 621–645.

Marshall, T.H. (1950) *Citizenship and Social Class and Other Essays*, Cambridge: Cambridge University Press.

McNevin, A. (2011) *Contesting Citizenship: Irregular Migrants and New Frontiers of the Political*, New York: Columbia University Press.

Miller, D. (1995) *On Nationality*, Oxford: Oxford University Press.

Moulin, C. and P. Nyers (2007) '"We live in the country of UNHCR": Refugee Protests and Global Political Society', *International Political Sociology* 1(4): 356–372.

Ní Mhurchú, A. (2014) *Ambiguous Citizenship in an Age of Global Migration*, Edinburgh: Edinburgh University Press.

Nyers, P. (2008) 'Community without Status: Non-Status Migrants and Cities of Refuge', in D. Brydon and W. Coleman (eds), *Renegotiating Community: Interdisciplinary Perspectives, Global Contexts*, Vancouver: University of British Columbia Press, pp. 123–138.

Nyers, P. (ed.) (2009) *Securitizations of Citizenship*, London: Routledge.

Pettman, J.J. (1999) 'Globalisation and the Gendered Politics of Citizenship', in N. Yuval-Davis and P. Werner (eds), *Women, Citizenship and Difference*, London: Zed Books.

Portaliou, E. (2007) 'Anti-Global Movements Reclaim the City', *City* 11(2): 165–175.

Ridgley, J. (2008) 'Cities of Refuge: Immigration Enforcement, Police, and the Insurgent Genealogies of Citizenship in U.S. Sanctuary Cities', *Urban Geography* 29(1): 53–77.

Ridgley, J. (2013) 'The City as Sanctuary in the United States', in R.K. Lippert and S. Rehaag (eds), *Sanctuary Practices in International Perspectives: Migration, Citizenship and Social Movements*, New York: Routledge, pp. 219–231.

Squire, V. and J. Darling (2013) 'The "Minor" Politics of Rightful Presence: Justice and Relationality in the City of Sanctuary', *International Political Sociology* 7(1): 59–74.

Walker, R.B.J. (1993) *Inside/Outside: International Relations as Political Theory*, Cambridge: Cambridge University Press.

Walker, R.B.J. (1999) 'Citizenship and the Modern Subject', in Kimberly Hutchings and Roland Dannreuther (eds), *Cosmopolitan Citizenship*, London: Macmillan, pp. 171–200.

4

COMMUNITY

Laura Brace

Introduction

This chapter on community explores some of the different meanings of community as belonging. It follows Gerard Delanty's argument (2009) that community has an inescapable normative dimension, that belonging is never finite and the longing for community can never be fulfilled. As Delanty argues, the search for belonging takes place in an insecure world, structured by the boundaries of community and by exclusion, so that belonging itself is insecure. What does it mean not to belong, not only on a local, regional or national level, but also to the international? People argue not only about the authenticity of the community, but about the status and the value of its members, and there is a broad range of critical literature on the idea of 'community' that relates to questions of identity and difference, and to the social relations of power embedded in structures of class, race, gender and nation. Drawing on my own research in addition to that of others, I will focus on a particular, liberal notion of community and in particular its relationship to property and ownership. I will then go on to consider how these constructions of community play out in international politics, in particular at the borders of the nation state and in the social and political relations of colonialism. This focus draws out the normative dimensions of community and its connection to the value of power relations, expressed through notions of honour and dishonour, distinction and degradation.

These liberal meanings of community are inseparable from what it means to be independent and autonomous, and what it takes to secure the individual to the community. In Locke's seventeenth-century theory of the social contract, for example, belonging to the community is intimately connected to a set of rights and credentials that determine personhood. Lockean individuals, in order to count as individuals, are expected to lead their own lives, without being dependent on anyone else, taking responsibility for themselves, their conscience, their labour and their reason. Property theory often rests on the assumption of rational, independent agents who are able to perceive their own self-interest and respect the equally rational and justifiable claims of others. From there, they are understood to be capable of building their own communities based on reasonableness and consent. This raises the question of who counts as a member of this community, defined by their enterprise and self-ownership, according to Macpherson (1962: 157). These solid individuals with secure roots in their own property-holding form a 'virtual community of people linked by their citizenship in Europe at home and abroad ... and constituted in opposition to their indigenous subjects' (Mills 1997: 29). The answer to the question of who belongs, in other words, comes out of a tangle of norms, assumptions, power relations and inequalities that are attached to race, class and gender, and to ideas about labour and freedom as well as belonging. Property relations are forged at the intersection of the natural and the social, where the boundary between self and other is expected to be fixed in nature, but where what counts as natural and real is constantly shifting. This is the contested moral and political space of community. Property functions as a set of legal relations, making it contingent and constantly in flux. At the same time, the volatility of property is offset by its 'strong connection with the essential, the authentic, the permanent, the territorial and the individual' (Davies 1999: 342). This tension between the fragility and the permanence of property is reflected in conceptions of community as vulnerable and constantly threatened by loss, and at the same time as natural and permanent.

The first section of this chapter explores how community is imagined out of self-ownership, and the particular view of freedom that emerges from liberal thinking based on possessive individualism, where being free and autonomous means having the capacity to exclude others from an impregnable internal fortress. In this particular world view, individuals are by nature equal, rational, self-interested and competitive. In pursuing their individual appetites and aversions, they can expect to find themselves in conflict with one another, and one person's absolute autonomy will come to rely on extinguishing the autonomy of another individual. The only way to prevent these conflicts from escalating out of control is for each individual to recognise every other individual as equally rational and self-interested, and as ultimately separate from them. Property in this discourse acts as a means of separation between individuals, and the basis for cooperation and a minimalist version of community. It is linked to a vision of separate, radically abstracted selves able to relate to each other through competition and exchange, with fixed boundaries around the individual who can then choose his or her degree of belonging to any given community.

This chapter explores the construction of what Bridget Anderson has called 'the community of value', made up of citizens who are understood fully to own themselves and to be ethically incorporated into a particular moral, economic and social space that is then imagined as a community. The chapter looks at some of the dimensions of outsiderness that are generated by the search for belonging to this community of value in an insecure world. Establishing the criteria of social belonging tells us who is included and who is excluded from 'the circle of those entitled to a just distribution and reciprocal recognition' (Fraser 2009: 17); in other words, who is entitled to be a member of the community of value. Using this core idea, the chapter looks at how liberal ideas of community are inflected by property thinking, and at how that affects our notions of the public good, our connections to one another and how we deal with people beyond our borders. The critical potential of this chapter lies in interrogating what it means to use the idea of community to draw barriers around ourselves to protect us from potentially harmful intrusions. In considering the 'cosiness' of certain forms of community, the challenges of not taking personhood for granted and the role of labour in under-standing membership, this chapter connects with the ideas of Rawls, Hegel, Hobbes and Locke as well as with critics of liberal property thinking such as Waldron, Penner and Mills.

Territories of the self

A territorial understanding of the self encourages an identity based on a fixed and unbreachable boundary between self and other. It creates particular relations of honour and status between individuals. People tend to see all others as external to their identity, and as possible threats to their own integrity. This approach to thinking about the self as contained and enclosed, and protected by private prop-erty, rather than as constituted by the common and forged in relation to others, links it to a particular way of imagining community (Brace 1997, 2004). The atmosphere of mutual fear, distrust and diffidence creates a sense of a self constantly on its guard, alert to the possibility of danger and invasion, inevitably taking up the stance of distrust and self-defence. This is a vision of non-community closely associated with Hobbes' conception of the state of nature, that also finds its echoes in Kant's 'unsocial sociability of men', where man has an inclination to associate with others, but also a strong propensity to isolate himself from others. Any rela-tionships between people are bound to be based on suspicion, as Kant says each seeks to 'achieve a rank among his fellows whom he cannot tolerate but from whom he cannot withdraw' (Kant 1963). People meet to trade with one another, for example, and 'a certain Market-friendship is begotten' which is based more on jealousy than on true love (Warrender 1983: 42). They meet for pleasure and recreation in order to satisfy their own vainglory by making comparisons with the defects and infirmities of others. They 'wound the absent' by condemning and jud-ging them (ibid.). At the same time, as both Hobbes and Rousseau recognised, they are afflicted by the unremitting rage to distinguish themselves from others and to pursue glory through self-aggrandisement and the potential to exercise power over others. Property relations that arise from this territorial understanding of the self, coupled with the rage to distinguish the self from others, are centrally concerned with the capacity to exclude. In this discourse, it is the capacity to exclude others, to refuse to acknowledge them as members of the community, that according to

Macpherson 'makes a man human' (1962: 142). The individual subject is under-stood to be defined by independent labour, appropriation and acts on the outside material world (Coleman 2005). Such individuals are able to define their own terms of possession, and to treat others as external threats to their own identity and integrity. They are understood to have the capacity to enclose and husband themselves. This particular conception of property in the person grounds a claim for integration into a normative order of rights and duties, into the welfare of the collective, and so membership of the community. Charles Mills points out that this concept of personhood has to include the concept of a 'subperson' – not an inan-imate object, and not entirely outside the imagined moral community, but not fully a person. Subpersons are defined in contrast to those who own themselves, and it is generally understood that they 'can be encroached upon with impunity' (Mills 1997: 7).

James Penner argues that the 'hold of property on our imaginations' (Penner 2009: 195) means that we apply the concept of property beyond the realm of genuine property rights to other very different sorts of social relations. For him, the concept of distributive justice only makes sense where individuals view the law as 'an alien body of norms which confine and restrain them by threats of sanction' (ibid.: 198), and where members of the community, such as hedge fund managers who resist regulation, treat their relations with others as a series of extractions. While more modern liberalism has dissipated the strength of suspicion and distrust, the residue of exclusion, drawing the boundaries around the self, encroaching on others with impunity and 'wounding the absent' remains. As Nick Blomley argues, a distributive model of justice and social interaction presupposes what he calls a 'propertied' view of social life where subjects are constituted as individualised bearers of resources engaged in market-like transactions (1997: 211–12). In this account, Rawls' basic liberties – liberty of conscience, freedom of association, freedom of speech and liberty, the right to vote, hold public office, and so on – are essentially freedoms from the interference of others; and the difference principle, which ensures that any social and economic inequalities are to be to the greatest benefit of the least-advantaged members of society, is a 'defensive stance' (Penner 2009: 199) designed to draw barriers to protect us from the potentially harmful intrusions of others.

Such a defensive, distributive approach to community means that justifications of private property start from the perspective of the rights and interest of the potential proprietor, and only then take into account the perspective of society as a whole (Waldron 2009). This model of property and community tends to set it up so that the hard cases for private property are phrased in social terms around issues of pollution, for example, and patterns of inequality and poverty. Waldron argues that this takes us to an aggregative approach of the general good, to a vision of the communal within which 'the particularity of individual predicaments disappears from view' (Waldron 2009: 171). In this airbrushing out of particularity, it comes to look as though only the interests of individual owners are at stake in justifica-tions of private property. Those without property are rendered absent. We need, as

Waldron argues, to think about those who have no property at all, who bear all the restraints but enjoy none of the benefits of private property. It is their interests 'to whom, *above all*, a justification of property is owed' (ibid.: 172). For Waldron, there are grave dangers for the poor in having their poverty categorised as a social problem to be fixed. In the process, they will be treated like an oil slick or a component of a decaying infrastructure, as 'broken' (Cameron 2011).[1] Each poor man, woman and child, Waldron argues, has a 'human status as an individual, an agent, a proper subject of freedom, and a potential bearer of obligations' (2009: 172–3). This is almost exactly what is denied to those identified by Mills as sub-persons, who can be encroached upon with impunity. It is one of the functions of 'community' to police who is afforded this human status. Traditional property theory takes personhood for granted 'and thus excludes the differential experience of those who have ceaselessly had to fight to have their personhood recognised in the first place' (Mills 1998: 9).

Homelessness, community and gentrification

Those who qualify as subjects of freedom and bearers of obligation are often those who are allowed to count as citizens, to participate in the social contract, and it is from them that our states and institutions claim allegiance (see Nyers and Sleiman in this book). Waldron's argument is that justifications of private property con-centrate on this group of people, defined as potential property owners, and any regulatory scheme considers the advantages that might accrue to them, as its likely beneficiaries. He uses the example of the regulation of public spaces, and cam-paigns to clean up urban parks so that they are not filled with litter, human waste, needles, bed rolls and condoms, and people can use them without feeling harassed or intimidated by other users. Such campaigns set rules so that people feel welcome in public spaces, but the rules are made in a society where there are large numbers of homeless people who have no private space and so no alternative but to live all their lives in public. The background conditions of homelessness make the pro-posals to regulate the parks unfair because of the disparities the beneficiaries and the homeless people will experience in bringing their behaviour into line with the rules (Waldron 2009: 178). There is a real, palpable difference between the impact of the regulation on a person who has a home in contrast to someone who is homeless, and this affects their 'human status' within the community.

Prohibiting people from sleeping is stopping them from doing something that they need to do. Being prevented from sleeping is not only uncomfortable and degrading, but painful, dangerous and impossible, almost literally unbearable, as Waldron points out. For Waldron, this example poses fundamental questions about who counts as a member of the community. In a situation where those without a private place to live are stopped from sleeping and urinating, they are being treated like an alien group, and not as the proper subjects of freedom or the potential bearers of obligations. Instead, they are coded as intruders into public space 'in a way that makes public places uncomfortable for members of the community'

(Waldron 2009: 185). They are 'space invaders' (Puwar 2004), and strangers. This fits with Zygmunt Bauman's (2000) analysis of the boundaries of new communities that are constructed to exclude strangers. The homeless people in Waldron's account (2009: 186) both enforce and problematise social and cultural boundaries, and the boundary between self and other. They are especially troubling strangers because they share 'common citizenship' and a common place of residence with the other members of the community. Their membership is not about civic or national belonging, but about the moral boundaries of property and the performance of self-ownership. Homeless people are marked as mobile, rootless, anti-social and threatening, and treated as needing to be removed from sight. They are the social other of the residents, cast as both flawed consumers and vagabonds (Marotta 2002: 44), rather than strongly associated with permanence and authenticity. They represent the contingency and volatility of specific ways of understanding private property as the basis of community, and show how this constellation distributes subpersonhood and insecurity. Their treatment is conflated with measures to deal with anti-social behaviour. In the controversy over the use of 'homeless spikes' in London, Tesco defended their use as deterrents to anti-social behaviour such as smoking and drinking, which they interpreted as intimidating for their customers (before removing the spikes in response to protests). Campaigners against the spikes outside luxury apartments in central London declared that: 'We don't want to live in a society where public space is covered in spikes. Homeless people are not pigeons' (Halliday 2014).

The online protests on change.org and on twitter against the use of the spikes to deter people from sleeping in doorways can be read as using the new technologies of communication to create a communicative space 'where a kind of proximity is to be found' (Delanty 2009: 157), a flexible community within which belonging is generated through participation in communication. This expresses the idea that communities can be untethered from the insecurities of the world and exist without being grounded in a collective identity. These virtual spaces are often idealised as universally accessible public domains, outside the institutions of the state, and offering the possibility of a public sphere that permits a 'rational, well-informed conversation between equals capable of resolving their differences by non-coercive means' (Schlesinger and Kevin 2000: 207). Questions remain however about what kind of proximity and conversation these spaces offer, when some of the protestors were arguing that flowerpots would have been a better and more aesthetically pleasing solution than the unsightly spikes. As Waldron argues, responses to the diverse demands on public spaces are often about keeping poverty out of sight, and relieving the distress of the rich by sheltering them from the disturbing spectacle of the 'strangers' who live among them (Waldron 2009: 187).

Nick Blomley's description of the 'geographies of property' at the 'gentrification frontier' in Vancouver in the late 1990s (Blomley 1997: 194) reflects some of the same cosmetics of community, covering over the wound of absence. The Downtown Eastside in Vancouver was a densely populated inner city neighbourhood of several thousand people, but was described as 'empty' by developers. The people who lived there were a mobile, socially marginal and criminalised population who were easily characterised as outsiders with little stake in the neighbourhood. They were regarded as unstable, contingent and in flux, divorced from the authentic, the permanent and the territorial. Once they had been characterised as outsiders and strangers, they were understood to have no real identification with the place. Improvement and revitalisation of the neighbourhood was only possible if property owners moved in and 'the marginal and dangerous move out' (ibid.: 196). Those who resisted gentrification responded by emphasising the stability of the displaced population, characterising the neighbourhood as a settled community of residents and stressing the loyalty of many elderly men to it as their home. They insisted on the entitlement of long-term working-class residents to the neighbourhood by invoking the dignity of masculine labour, and the 'implicit Lockean landscape that the resource worker created in his prime' (ibid.: 209). Blomley quotes the words of one of the residents campaigning against the developers: 'They think that every-body down here is just a transient. But this is a community. It is a neighbourhood. There are actual people living down here' (ibid.: 201 n.41). The developers and the realtors co-opted the narrative of community and property to 'configure the neighbourhood as an empty, speculative site, rather than a viable community space' (ibid.: 203). In response, the protestors imbued the neighbourhood with local meanings, presenting it as a place of 'shared sentiment and symbols' (ibid.: 205), collective memories and the creation of an imagined community. The symbolic effect of the different readings of property at work here was to 'map a border – both real and metaphorical – between an inside and an outside' (ibid.: 206). In the process, oppositional property narratives emerged between the 'good property' of the poor and marginalised and the 'bad property' of prevailing capitalist relations (ibid.: 205).

Blomley's analysis of gentrification echoes the colonial discourse of property relations where the Lockean landscape of ordered and disciplined improvement and productivity was created against a backdrop of the myth of vast tracts of vacant land, awaiting development and improvement. Under colonialism, the formation of identities and communities was played out in 'the definition of entitlement to welfare and to property rights, both within the metropole and on the periphery' (Daunton and Halpern 1999: 6). Endowment, anchorage and membership were all mediated through property rights in land, persons and labour. The volatility and flux of property meant that these rights were constantly renegotiated and contested. As Delanty (2009) argues about belonging, it is never established as final: there is always contestation over claims to community. The English colonists used their own ideas about proper land use and ownership to displace the indigenous people of America, marking them as wandering, transient and potentially troublesome. Their mobility was coded as resistance to the 'English colonial agenda of fixity and social place' (O'Brien 1999: 206), and their capacity to define the terms for possessing the land was crowded out by enclosures and the conception of private property in land, structured by the right to exclude. Their version of ownership was stigmatised as non-improving, wasteful and linked only to subsistence rather than fully integrated into the market relations that underpinned the currents of world trade and the meanings of citizenship and belonging. They had failed to fulfil God's injunction to subdue the earth. As a result, they were regarded as fugitives and exiles in their own land, unable to define their own terms of possession and community.

The theme of loss

These oppositional narratives of 'good' and 'bad' property fluctuate and change their meanings in response to the volatility and flux of property, and to the social relations of power involved in defining its meaning. The 'good', improving property of enclosure was contrasted to the 'bad' stewardship of the indigenous peoples, but also to the 'bad' corporate greed of the developers. This is related to the ways in which 'community' is positioned as the defining other of capitalist modernity, contrasting direct, local relationships with more abstract relations. Community is understood to emerge from face-to-face encounters and to be sustained by naturalised boundaries that exist 'through reference to place or race or culture or identity' (Joseph 2007: 58). Miranda Joseph identifies a romantic narrative of community that places it prior to 'society', and then sees it as destroyed by capitalism and modernity as economic values became predominant. The modern discourse of community 'has been dominated by a theme of loss' (Delanty 2009: 7). This has the effect of cutting community off from capital by sealing it in the past. This sealing-off neatens the edges of community and allows us not to think about the social relations of power involved, and to ignore the question of who belongs and on what terms. In her critique of Robert Putnam and his analysis of social capital, Joseph argues that he gives to 'community' the values of trust, norms and networks that can sustain economic cooperation, and divorces them from the background conditions of exploitation and subordination (Joseph 2002: 12). This romantic narrative of community, Joseph argues, is then complicit with capital and deployed to maintain or elaborate domination and exploitation (ibid.: 19–21).

Waldron uses the homelessness example to express his doubts about 'community' as an adequate response to being 'poor, deprived and displaced' (2009: 189) when the problem is one of exclusion or expulsion from the community. His article is a critique of 'cozy forms of community' where those who are privileged as members enjoy one another's company, take responsibility for their neighbourhood and celebrate their loyalty, shared values and communal solidarity (ibid.: 190). As part of the construction and maintenance of such cosy communities, their members recoil from the homeless people who live amongst them, and try to ensure that they 'come nowhere near their gates, nowhere near the public places where they walk their prams or hold their barbecues' (ibid.). They demonstrate and act upon an impulse to protect their given form of community, but also to prevent the formation of an alternative form of community by the disadvantaged. This is part of the same process that crowded out indigenous meanings of property and alternative forms of ownership under colonialism. Those who count as the proper subjects of freedom and the potential bearers of obligation are also in control of the narratives of possession and community and able to define the terms of membership. As Waldron argues, the small-scale example that he uses applies on a much wider scale to people who band together to defend their jobs and industries, their own property in skill and membership, 'no matter what the cost to poor people beyond their borders' (ibid.: 191), who are figured as outsiders, refugees and migrants and treated with suspicion.

This exclusion of poor people beyond borders is inextricably linked to the insecurity of the world and of belonging, and to the role of labour in determining membership and the meaning of community. The prosperous market economy of Waldron's account is a moral and political as well as an economic space, and the borders are drawn around individuals as well as around states. The territorial self claims a monopoly, a right to exclude competitors and contestants as potential invaders, and at the same time has to legitimate itself in relation to others through notions of honour and degradation which consist in comparison. The liberal subject defined by Hobbes as a fortress, by Locke as an enterprising owner and by Rawls as the self-authenticating source of valid claims, owns his or her labour, and not only finds his or her work developing and liberating, righteous, industrious and creative, but constitutive of his or her membership of a civil society and of his or her citizenship. It can ground their collective responsibility, their sense of identity and honour, and their assurance of economic security. In the process, they are defined in relation to what others lack (Hall 2000: 230). Some people's labour is stigmatised as inefficient, as unskilled and unimproving, as drudgery that bears no relation to the welfare of the collective. As I have argued elsewhere, this is particularly the case for poor women who work in the economy of makeshifts, outside the protection of the guilds and other mechanisms of ethical incorporation into civil society (Brace 2002, 2013). Those who labour without honour and recognition become freelance hustlers with nothing to sell except themselves, and find themselves on the outside of the 'community of value' (Anderson 2013), marked by race and by gender, and denied the 'human status' that can ground their belonging.

In Mills' account of the racial contract, white people are defined as white on the basis that they have the capacity to exclude others and to exercise despotic dominion over themselves. This helps us to understand whiteness as a probationary and as a moral category, where whiteness is a status and a property in membership. It becomes inextricably linked to a set of expectations, privileges and benefits that are affirmed and legitimated by law and by the norms of belonging. Being white involves being able to protect yourself from subpersonhood and from strangerhood. Race in this account is a 'marker of entitlement or dispossession, civilisation or barbarism, normative inclusion or normative exclusion, full or diminished personhood' (Mills 1997: 127). It is also deeply connected to labour, and the powerful myth that African slaves, in need of direction and compulsion, were only fitted for certain kinds of labour and needed to be disciplined (Brace 2004: 174). This was a myth that fixed slaves in their place, and broke the connection between labour and honour, rationality and autonomy. This dishonouring of labour was an important dimension of racialised dispossession and exclusion. At the same time, the link between industry and righteousness is also broken by mobility, and those whose labour is stigmatised as inefficient are also constructed as vagrant, marginal, wandering and transient. Their mobility is a sign that they are not keeping their place, and the problem of migration is perceived as being that people are seeking to work in the wrong place, undermining the livelihoods of settled members of the community, and refusing to accept their position (Anderson 2013: 27).

Migration and the human project

The sense of stability that underpins both communal and individual identity is thrown into disorder by the processes of migration. Endowment and entitlement are understood to require anchorage, so that membership rests on property rights in land, persons and labour that are supposed to be fixed, 'assuming, apparently, that people usually stay where they are supposed to be' (Pettman 1998: 394). Those who do not stay where they are supposed to be, like the original peoples of America or homeless people living in parks or sheltering in doorways, are marked as potentially troublesome, and then as lacking in self-control and the inclination to labour. Poor people who move and migrate have somehow not rooted themselves in improvement and ownership of a property in the person, or in their own communities; they are understood not to be masters of themselves, to lack the 'durable solidity' that forms the core of the liberal subject's identity (Brace 2010).

This durable solidity is inflected by gender. Women are supposed to find it in the family, in their domestic duties and responsibilities and their fixed loyalties to their culture and community. In the traditional migration story, it is assumed that they are left behind or attached to male migrants as dependants. Women from poorer South and Southeast Asian states who migrate to work in richer South and Southeast Asian and Gulf states in domestic labour and sex work inhabit 'a strange in-between space, between the public and the private, the domestic and the market' (Pettman 1998: 398). It is a space that is somehow outside community, and the women are understood to be suspended there, in a world of 'fraught commitments and fragmented loyalties' (Gardiner Barber 2006: 73).

Standing, as Judith Shklar and Charles Mills argue, was defined by citizens distinguishing themselves from non-citizens, and members of communities distinguishing themselves from strangers, through a dialogue between the liberal subject and its others within which 'people who are not granted [the] marks of civic dignity feel dishonored, not just powerless and poor' (Shklar 2001: 2). Somewhere in this complicated dialogue about social standing, inclusion and community, there is a story about migration and the processes that construct belonging. The figure of the 'high-value' migrant will be an entrepreneur, an investor, a doctor, a research scientist, a software engineer or 'the privileged employee of a multinational company' (Agnew 2008: 184; UKBA 2010). They are able to rely on their own capacities, their grounding in self-ownership and improvement, to claim 'citizen-like entitlements' (Ong 2006: 501) on the basis of their respectable standing (Shklar 2001: 17). The link between their labour and righteousness, their enterprise, is unbroken by their mobility and they are able to continue to define their own terms of possession. In their negotiation of national and international spaces, their 'frequent flying' and 'net surfing' (Pettman 1998: 389), they are not constructed as vagrants. The terms of belonging are related to the 'somatic norm' of being white and male, but some others, including women, 'can pass as the universal human' if they are protected by their skills or their aspirations, or by the 'privilege of being racially unmarked' (Puwar 2004: 10–11). The 'property of membership' (Somers 1996: 67) is required to support the rights and duties that underpin human status and the community of enterprisers, and is embodied in notions of skilled and fair labour which are withheld from the poor (and in particular from poor women) who migrate for work.

As Waldron argues about the rules preventing homeless people from using the parks, in part this exclusion is a question about negative liberty, about asking 'why do we think we are justified in stopping them from acting in these ways?' (Waldron 2009: 180). When we think about community, citizenship and migration, in a context where migration is considered in terms of rates and targets, the abuse of free movement and the idea of 'pull factors' to particular countries (BBC 27 February 2014), the particularity of the individual predicaments of migrants disappears from view. It is not only the interests of 'the brightest and the best' migrants or of 'working families who work hard and do the right thing' (Meredith 2014) that need to be considered in justifying borders. Individual property rights require a collective context for their exercise and realisation. Private property 'is held by virtue of communal relations' (Davies 1999: 341). Property, as Penner points out, is a normative achievement, a site where individuals are able to act communally. Property, he argues, serves as an indicator of the inadequacies of community – there is something wrong when significant numbers of people cannot make property rights their own (Penner 2009: 211). Collective concerns cannot be separated from issues of relative power, the realm of social relations and membership of the imagined community. By assuming that each individual is sovereign over him or herself and free to exclude others, we neglect 'the value people may place on the kind of power relations in which they stand to others' (Cohen 1995: 80). In other words, we cannot assume, with Rawls, that communities are unified systems of social cooperation without steadfastly ignoring the ways in which they are structured by property and power, to exclude outsiders who do not belong.

Penner (2009) quotes from Rawls to make his point. 'Now obviously', Rawls says, 'no one can obtain everything he wants; the mere existence of other persons prevents this'. In this territorial world view, others work to prevent my getting what I want, unless I can arrange it so that they serve my interests. Penner concludes that in Rawls' scheme, the only conceivable appreciation of others is 'as either impediments to or tools for the realization of my goals' (Penner 2009: 201). Against this, Penner draws on Hegel to stress the central importance of recognition by other rational wills, and the possibility of forming associations in which we act together rather than in conflict with each other. This raises the possibility of acting jointly, of treating everybody as subjects of freedom and potential bearers of obligation. It opens up the scope of community membership, and of human status: 'To be human is necessarily to value, and care about, not just our own lives but the way the whole human project is going' (Penner 2009: 204). This vision of community is about self-respect linked to participating with others in the human project, and for Penner this is only possible to imagine when property rights are kept in their place. As Davina Cooper's (2007: 236) research on Summerhill School shows, in imagining community, we should be 'thinking about property as a set of networked relations in which the subject is embedded'. Mastery and dominion can be decentred by placing limits on what she terms 'propertization', dispersing rights and limiting power (Cooper 2007: 636). She argues for a broader conception of property and community 'organized around relations of belonging rather than control, where rights are fragmented and institutional authority dispersed' (ibid.: 627). Rather than structuring communities around self-interest, the problem of fairness and the fetishisation of property in self-ownership, we need to think differently about the existence of other people. Our understanding of what it is to flourish and what it is for our lives to have meaning is 'ineluctably a matter of situating ourselves within the history of the human species' (Penner 2009: 216).

Conclusion

This chapter has explored some of the core ideas linked to community, and in particular to the idea of the community of value, structured by the state and the labour market, as well as by social relations of gender, race, nation and class. The critical potential of community as a concept is dependent on finding a way of detaching it from the distributive assumptions of property fetishism and of the territorial self. This involves thinking about international politics in a way that moves beyond 'border thinking' that takes it for granted that national citizenship is the ground on which rights and belonging ought to be organised. As other thinkers have argued about the social contract and about migration, we need to think about community through 'ordinary human relations' (Zerilli 2005: 77). We need an international politics that can understand how the nation state is implicated in reproducing the territorial understanding of the self and recognise that what happens at the borders of communities is about the production of power through relations of dependency, belonging and insecurity (Anderson et al. 2010: 8).

Acknowledgements

Particular thanks are due to Patrick Joseph Cockburn and the other members of the Politics of Property specialist group. Many of the ideas in this chapter come out of papers and discussions at our 2014 meeting.

Note

1 In the wake of the riots in London and other English cities in 2011, David Cameron declared that the 'slow motion moral collapse' that had led to a 'broken society' was back

at the top of his political agenda. He pledged to tackle children without fathers, schools without discipline and communities without control (Cameron 2011).

Further reading and useful weblinks

Bauman, Z. (1988–1989) 'Strangers: The Social Construction of Universality and Particularity', *Telos* 78: 7–42.

Benhabib, S. (1992) 'Autonomy, Modernity and Community: Communitarianism and Critical Theory in Dialogue', in A. Honneth et al. (eds), *Cultural-Political Interventions in the Unfinished Project of Enlightenment*, Cambridge, MA: MIT Press.

DeFilippis, J., Fisher, R. and Shragge, E. (2009) 'What's Left in the Community? Oppositional Politics in Contemporary Practice', *Community Development Journal* 44(1): 38–52.

Young, I. M. (1986) 'The Ideal of Community and the Politics of Difference', *Social Theory and Practice* 12(1): 1–26.

Walker, R.B.J. (1993) *Inside/Outside: International Relations as Political Theory*, Cambridge: Cambridge University Press.

For discussion of an alternative community, see: www.transitionheathrow.com/grow-hea throw and www.farmgarden.org.uk

On campaigns for migrant rights, see: http://precariousworkersbrigade.tumblr.com/antiraids campaign

Bibliography

Agnew, J. (2008) 'Borders on the Mind: Re-framing Border Thinking', *Ethics and Global Politics* 1(4): 175–191.

Anderson, B. (2013) *Us and Them? The Dangerous Politics of Immigration Control*, Oxford: Oxford University Press.

Anderson, B., Sharma, N. and Wright, C. (2010) 'Editorial: Why No Borders?' *Refuge* 26(2): 5–18.

Bauman, Z. (2000) *Community: Seeking Safety in an Insecure World*, Cambridge: Polity.

BBC News (2014) 'Big Increase in Net Migration in Europe', 27 February, www.bbc.co.uk/news/uk-politics-26367391, accessed 18 August 2014.

Blomley, N. (1997) 'Property, Pluralism and the Gentrification Frontier', *Canadian Journal of Law and Society* 12(2): 187–218.

Brace, L. (1997) 'Imagining the Boundaries of a Sovereign Self', in L. Brace and J. Hoffman (eds) *Reclaiming Sovereignty*, London: Cassell, pp. 137–154.

Brace, L. (2002) 'The Tragedy of the Freelance Hustler: Hegel, Gender and Civil Society', *Contemporary Political Theory* 1(3): 329–348.

Brace, L. (2004) *The Politics of Property*, Edinburgh: Edinburgh University Press.

Brace, L. (2010) 'Improving the Inside: Gender, Property and the Eighteenth-Century Self', *British Journal of Politics and International Relations* 12(1): 111–125.

Brace, L. (2013) 'Borders of Emptiness: Gender, Migration and Belonging', *Citizenship Studies* 17(6–7): 873–885.

Cameron, D. (2011) 'England Riots: Broken Society is Top Priority', *BBC News*, 15 August 2011, www.bbc.co.uk/news/uk-politics-14524834, accessed 8 June 2015.

Cohen, G.E. (1995) *Self-Ownership, Freedom and Equality*, Cambridge: Cambridge University Press.

Coleman, J. (2005) 'Pre-modern Property and Self-ownership Before and After Locke: or, When did Common Decency become a Private Rather Than a Public Virtue?', *European Journal of Political Theory* 4(2): 125–145.

Cooper, D. (2007) 'Opening up Ownership: Belonging, Belongings and the Productive Life of Property', *Law and Social Inquiry* 32(3): 625–664.

Daunton, M. and Halpern, R. (eds) (1999) *Empire and Others: British Encounters with Indigenous Peoples 1600–1850*, London: UCL Press.

Davies, M. (1999) 'Queer Property, Queer Persons: Self-Ownership and Beyond', *Social and Legal Studies* 8(3): 327–352.

Delanty, G. (2009) *Community*, 2nd edition, London: Routledge.

Fraser, N. (2009) *Scales of Justice*, New York: University of Columbia Press.

Gardiner Barber, P. (2006) 'Locating Gendered Subjects in Vocabularies of Citizenship', in E. Tastsoglou and A. Dobrowolsky (eds), *Women, Migration and Citizenship*, London: Ashgate, pp. 61–84.

Hall, S. (2000) 'Conclusion: the Multi-cultural Question', in B. Hesse (ed.), *Un/settled Multiculturalisms: Diasporas, Entanglements, Transruptions*, London: Zed Books, pp. 209–241.

Halliday, J. (2014) 'Tesco to Remove Anti-Homeless Spikes from Regent Street Store After Protests', *The Guardian*, www.theguardian.com/society/2014/jun/12/tesco-spikes-remove-regent-street-homeless-protests, accessed 18 August 2014.

Joseph, M. (2002) *Against the Romance of Community*, Minneapolis: University of Minnesota Press.

Joseph, M. (2007) 'Community', in B. Burgett and G. Hendler (eds), *Keywords for American Cultural Studies*, New York: New York University Press, pp. 57–60.

Kant, I. (1963) *Idea for a Universal History from a Cosmopolitan Point of View*, translated by L.W. Beck, Indianapolis, IN: Bobbs-Merrill Co., www.marxists.org/reference/subject/ethics/kant/universal-history.htm, accessed 18 August 2014.

Macpherson, C.B. (1962) *The Political Theory of Possessive Individualism*, Oxford: Oxford University Press.

Marotta, V. (2002) 'Zygmunt Bauman: Order, Strangerhood and Freedom', *Thesis Eleven* 70(1): 36–54.

Meredith, C. (2014) 'David Cameron: "We Need to Help Hard-working Families with their Household Bills"', *Express*, 26 April, www.express.co.uk/news/uk/394950/David-Cameron-We-need-to-help-hard-working-families-with-their-household-bills, accessed 22 August 2014.

Mills, C.W. (1997) *The Racial Contract*, Ithaca, NY and London: Cornell University Press.

Mills, C.W. (1998) *Blackness Visible: Essays on Philosophy and Race*, Ithaca, NY: Cornell University Press.

O'Brien, J. (1999) '"They are so Frequently Shifting their Place of Residence": Land and the Construction of Social Place of Indians on Colonial Massachusetts', in M. Daunton and R. Halpern (eds), *Empire and Others: British Encounters with Indigenous Peoples, 1600–1850*, London: UCL Press, pp. 204–217.

Ong, A. (2006) 'Mutations in Citizenship', *Theory, Culture and Society* 23(2–3): 499–505.

Penner, J.E. (2009) 'Property, Community, and the Problem of Distributive Justice', *Theoretical Inquiries in Law* 10(1): 193–216

Pettman, J.J. (1998) 'Women on the Move: Globalisation and Labour Migration from South and Southeast Asian states', *Global Society* 12(3), 389–403.

Puwar, N. (2004) *Space Invaders: Race, Gender and Bodies out of Place*, London: Berg.

Sargisson L. and Tower Sargent, L. (2004) *Living in Utopia: New Zealand's Intentional Communities*, London: Ashgate.

Schlesinger, P. and Kevin, D. (2000) 'Can the European Union become a Sphere of Publics?', in E.O. Eriksen and J.E. Fossum (eds), *Democracy in the European Union: Integration Through Deliberation?* London: Routledge, pp. 206–229.

Shklar, J. (2001) [1991] *American Citizenship: The Quest for Inclusion*, Cambridge, MA: Harvard University Press.

Somers, M. R. (1996) 'The "Misteries" of Property: Relationality, Rural-Industrialization, and Community in Chartist Narratives of Political Rights', in J. Brewer and S. Staves (eds), *Early Modern Conceptions of Property*, London and New York: Routledge, pp. 62–94.

UK Border Agency (2010) www.ukba.homeoffice.gov.uk/sitecontent/newsarticles/2010/nov/14-theresa-may-speech, accessed 21 July 2014.

Waldron, J. (2009) 'Community and Property – For Those who Have Neither', *Theoretical Inquiries in Law* 10(1): 161–192.

Warrender, H. (1983) *The Clarendon Edition of the Philosophical Works of Thomas Hobbes*, Volume III: 'De Cive', English Version, Oxford: Clarendon Press.

Zerilli, L. (2005) *Feminism and the Abyss of Freedom*, Chicago, IL: University of Chicago Press.

5

CREATIVITY

Christine Sylvester

Is IR creative? The broad outlines of the field vary from place to place; yet wherever I have gone to work in IR – in the USA, Zimbabwe, Australia, the Netherlands, Britain, Scandinavia – I have sensed unease about IR's bounty of knowledge at a time of global tensions around the 'new' wars and new antagonisms in our time. It is not that IR lacks imagination. The field has traditionally imagined an international filled with – take your pick – states, non-states, decision makers, systems, norms, firms, regimes, terrorists, IGOs and NGOs, and developing countries. A number of dynamics attach to the various imaginaries – anarchy, conflict, threat, cooperation, exchange, rationality, balances, globalisation, patriarchy, underdevelopment, transgression, and so on. Yet IR's worlds have mostly been imagined through the linking of concepts or data points, which leaves the field with a certain social hollowness at the core of the canon, an emptiness where people, who are going about their lives experiencing and influencing international relations, should be. Some among these invisibles can get into the IR picture if they display monumental, can't-miss-it agency in international relations. Their techniques and even some of their proper names flash up in the various Springs and Winters of recent Middle East politics, or in connection with spectacular terrorist tragedies of 2001 in New York and 2015 at the offices of 'Charlie Hebdo' magazine in Paris. Utterly faceless subalterns of IR work in the bowels of international political economy as garment workers in South Asia, join militias, or become targets of them; occasionally they pop up in texts of IR when writers want to bolster arguments about the consequences of higher, more central dynamics of international politics (e.g. Mearsheimer and Walt 2007; Sylvester 2013a).

I want to argue that much of IR lacks the creativity necessary to place itself in the world of people and their politics rather than above it. Creativity is not the same as imagination. Cognitive psychologists Etienne Pelaprat and Michael Cole (2011: 399) posit that 'imagination is the process of resolving and connecting the fragmented, poorly coordinated experience of the world so as to bring about a stable image of the world. Thereby a feeling of oneself in relation to the world emerges.' Creativity is 'a form of making, the making of "the whole world of culture" based on the products of imagination' (ibid.). In that understanding, creativity is measured by the making of something out of imagination, which society allows and then decides is creative. Others who study imagination and creativity argue that creativity is difficult to speak about in a general way, without taking into account the various levels and criteria that exist for creativity in organisations, commercial products, scholarship, and artworks (e.g. Surkova 2012).

The literature on imagination and creativity is large and nonconsensual, but we might find a starting point by thinking about IR as a field that connects fragments and brings about stable images of the world, but 'feels' itself removed from the world it imagines and has trouble thinking of, let alone making, those 'whole worlds of culture' that Pelaprat and Cole (2011: 399) posit. When people rise up and topple regimes in wars of international significance, the creative void in IR is very evident. It cannot easily use abstract theories and models to address the social power of contemporary international relations (see Sylvester 2013c). Creativity in our field would seem to require that the IR thinker journey for inspiration beyond the customs, sources, and regulatory mechanisms that constitute the core of the field. Such journeys are underway in corners of IR, where epistemic camps have formed around ideas borrowed heavily from scholarship outside usual IR purviews (Sylvester 2007). The camps of international political sociology, feminist IR, and the global south, all part of a burgeoning critical IR, have made their disagreements with the inherited field known and have moved on in the many new journals that steal thunder from the conventional field of realisms and liberalisms. Yet even these critical camps have inherited a tendency from IR past to stay up in the heavens of theory and philosophy rather than muck about down with the people of international relations. It is still assumed, if I may put it colloquially, that the higher you can climb the ladder of abstraction, the better, the more profound, and the more real your analysis of international relations.

I do not question the profundity, the smartness, and the importance of the new critical traditions in IR; I, for one, am grateful that the new camps now exist. What I question is whether even they are creative enough to *be in the world as it is and speak to and with it, not just to one another about it.* This is a concern Milja Kurki (2011; see also Murphy 2007) raises about critical IR interventions: what have they achieved for the world? Adding on to that, what have they achieved for many people at the front lines of today's international relations? Could it be that some critical IR responses to a field tied to the state system and its dynamics lost some creativity along the way, as aficionados eased into new camps and found them commodious? Possibly, but this condition has not afflicted all in critical IR. Some continue to turn their imaginations into creative works, and with room to mention only a few, let me start with Jenny Edkins and Adrian Kear (2013). They have created a new academic entity at Aberystwyth University at the cusp of IR and performance studies. That entity brings very different fields into conversations with one another and creates spaces to address *both* theoretical *and* practical issues of international politics that range from humanitarian interventions that worsen matters on the ground (Opondo 2013) to the classroom lecture on international relations that seems inadequate to the difficult issues IR faces, even to the IR professor delivering it (e.g. Inayatullah 2013). Michael Shapiro has made numerous forays into IR from a background in literary analysis. Some of his contributions soar to the land of abstract 'juxtapositions that disrupt and/or render historically contingent accepted knowledge positions' (2013: xv). Others can descend into the local to telescope one American mother's political response to the senseless death of her son in the Iraq war (Shapiro 2011).

Swati Parashar (2014) has made many personal journeys to the edge of IR – to talk to Maoist insurgents in India and militant women in Kashmir, and to Sri Lankan war zones to interview Tamil Tiger women combatants during the last months of their ultimately unsuccessful war. Parashar makes fieldwork locations her home in IR, her go-to places of knowledge, where she listens and sometimes worries about the war stories she hears and the circumstances she faces (Parashar 2011). Then there is Stephen Chan, a poet, diplomat, and martial arts master as well as prolific writer in IR. He creates spaces in-between all of his arenas and always lets the light of ordinary people shine through. They are the wise expert observers of international relations in his *Out of Evil: New International Politics and Old Doctrines of War* (2005) and *Grasping Africa* (2007).

Very earthshaking indeed are the new forays into 'fictional' IR made by Elizabeth Dauphinee in her groundbreaking *The Politics of Exile* (2013), Richard Jackson's fiction about conversing with a terrorist (2014), and Sungju Park-Kang's (2014) fictional scenarios that fill gaps in the Korean record of Cold War international relations. Each author defies the usual separation maintained between social science and humanities and uncovers knowledge and insight residing in shadows – of their own lives or among real or imagined people, IR might never register as possible agents of international relations. Hit by the last form of analysis many expected within IR boundaries, it is still unclear how the field is accommodating fiction writing as a methodological tool, albeit, some critical IR journals have taken up the challenge with enthusiasm (e.g. *Security Dialogue* 2013).

In the following pages I highlight the work of two additional IR scholars who impress me with their creativity. Cami Rowe (2013) journeys to anti-war movements in the USA with insights from performance studies that are augmented by personal participation in and observation of activist events. Elina Penttinen (2013) moves boldly across psychology, physics, philosophy, literature, film and her own interviews to talk about a seemingly verboten topic in IR – joy – and how it manifests even in war zones. Before turning to their contributions, I return to the notion of creativity and consider the characteristics of creative people presented by some in the arts and by a researcher who has been examining the issue of individual creativity for years.

Individual creativity

It can be surprising to learn that artists, who are most often associated with the so-called creative arts, are not the ones who usually want to talk about creativity. They do not like the term; nor do some art analysts, who maintain that there is too much bad or kitschy work masquerading as art and killing the creativity of real art (Baudrillard 2005; Greenberg 1985), or those who claim that the art market determines creativity as that which sells big (e.g. Wu 2002). Some art students at the California Institute of the Arts (Cal Arts), one of America's top programmes, report that creativity is 'a lovely-dovey cliché used by people who are not professionally involved with art' (Thornton 2008: 63). Artists do not label themselves creative any more than prominent authors refer to their craft as creative writing, the common name given to writing courses in many universities. Nonetheless, the president of Cal Arts reports that the creative students he has observed have 'inherent originality, eccentricity or even cussedness, on edge with their world' (ibid.). He implies that students arrive with those traits rather than learning creativity there.

Nancy Andreasen (2014: 70), a leading psychiatrist and neuroscientist, has studied creativity and the brain extensively and finds that creative people exhibit a number of traits that correspond with the Cal Arts impressions. Creative individuals are 'better at recognizing relationships, making associations and connections, and seeing things in an original way – seeing things that others cannot see'. Not necessarily IQ geniuses or major leaders in their areas, they are 'polymaths, people with broad interests in many fields' (ibid.: 72). This suggests to her that the tradition of separating the sciences from humanities, and insisting that a person slots better into one or the other, can be a creativity killer. Creative people, she finds, are 'adventuresome and exploratory. They take risks' (ibid.: 74). They do not follow the crowd, the canon, the accepted formulas; and when others praise them for doing very creative work, such individuals are often surprised, for their ideas seem so obvious. Andreasen tells us that creative people tend to find that 'standard ways of learning and teaching are not always helpful and may even be distracting … they prefer to learn on their own' (ibid.: 75). And that means taking off in directions that some would find eccentric, if not outright unacceptable. Finally, Andreasen (2014) claims that creative people persevere with their own ideas even in the face of criticism and rejection. They can see what those tied to convention do not, and they can create what they see and imagine beyond it. They do not crave social approval, nor do they find established social institutions especially useful in developing their ideas.

Cami Rowe and Elina Penttinen are in IR but not party to its problems with creativity or its unease. The criteria I use to make that determination draw on Andreasen's research, suggesting that to be creative in IR as elsewhere one must be a polymath, come up with new relationships, take risks in choice of puzzle, persevere in a different way of thinking, and be fiercely independent in efforts to learn what is needed to know outside standard courses and methods of a field. In addition, the works produced should be in those extra- and post-disciplinary modes that show that the researcher is in the world rather than above it.

The IR of performance and joy: Rowe and Penttinen

Rowe wrote her Ph.D. in the UK under my supervision, and I was the external examiner for Penttinen's Ph.D. in Finland. Right from the start, I could see that both oozed creativity and showed little anxiety about how their intended work would or would not be received in IR. They displayed a risk-taking world awareness that set them apart from other students, and were eager to enter into the spaces they studied. Ph.D.s easily won, both gained academic positions and both have books out in the Routledge series on *War, Politics, Experience* (Penttinen 2013; Rowe 2013).[1]

Cami Rowe: *The Politics of Protest and US Foreign Policy*

The Politics of Protest and US Foreign Policy carves out, stakes out, and hangs out at a fulcrum of performance theory and anti-war activism around the latest Iraq War. Rowe is interested in how recent protest groups have endeavoured to get people to think outside the box of patriotic American war discourse, by devising strategies that resonate with aspects of performance thinking. Activist groups historically have turned around dominant images, meanings, and identities of despised foreign policies and have created alternative positions that citizens should hold. Often this has been achieved by magnifying one unifying characteristic of group members. The Greenham Common anti-war movement, for example, was comprised of women, many of them mothers, who used their gender identities to feminise the aura of cruise missile bases in the UK. Rather than leave their women's tools at home, they attached prosaic items to the barbed wire fences of the bases and set up daily routines near these. The point was to minimise boundaries between the military warriors and the everyday social encounters of civilian life. Occasionally, they would clip the fences, rush onto the bases, and climb up onto cruise missiles as though these were fair rides, thereby challenging the audacity of security and numbering themselves among the 'specialists' who could breach it. To Rowe, the strategies of such peace groups 'may have operated under banners of motherhood and soldier-hood … [but] their actions did not succeed in complicating public notions of those categories; soldiers were still widely seen as the enemies of those who opposed the Vietnam War, and were mistreated accordingly. Women were likewise margin-alised by mainstream anti-war communities, being granted positions of inferiority within the organisational structures of those bodies' (2013: 4).

Drawing on two recent anti-Iraq war groups, Code Pink and Iraq Veterans Against the War (IVAW), Rowe points to a key shift in protest strategy and tactics. These groups aimed to reveal the mistake made by high-level decision makers in starting the Iraq war, while simultaneously destabilising their own public identities as tame, motherly women or America's heroic vets. Code Pink sought to catch the attention of those responsible for the war and not target the soldiers made to conduct the war, as had been the case in the Vietnam era. An initial step they took was to supercharge the colour pink, a commonplace code for girls and women, by dressing in feminine pinks while engaging in activities that severely critiqued the interventionist mistake of America in Iraq. Dressed like 'nice women', and with smiles on their faces, some Code Pink members publicly presented Condoleeza Rice and Hillary Clinton, both supporters of the war, with pink slips (lingerie) as symbols of the common understanding that getting a pink slip means 'you're fired'. IVAW targeted the military, Washington officials, and average citizens through public narrations and street performances that relayed the ugly realities they had encountered and been forced to oversee in Iraq.

To performance theorists, all performance is 'action that is conducted with the intention of being to some degree witnessed by another' (Rowe 2013: 8). But the point of performance thinking is that it helps the researcher or spectator spot and evaluate all the components of a performance, instead of dwelling on the storyline or message theatrically presented, which is where political performances directed by polls and consultants want the public to linger. Rowe notes that social science uses of the term performance or performativity rarely reference the literature of performance studies, which can mean that they miss fine but important points about performance and audience reception. There is, of course, a long tradition of associating the arts with knowledge that is irrelevant to IR's social science, historical, philosophical, normative and natural science traditions.[2] That belief remains a stubborn artefact of disciplinary organisation in the academy, a split that Patrick Jackson (2011: 195) endorses in his recent dismissal of the arts as a mode of inquiry for IR, on the grounds that it is not-science.[3]

Rowe happily breached the social science/arts gap and also became personally involved in the protests she was researching. She joined pink-clad women pushing a bed into a busy D.C. intersection and then shouting that Washington should wake up. Her costume was a pink nightgown, slippers, and curlers for the morning rush-hour event, timed to impact a large audience that would presumably be impatient to get to work unless quickly engaged. Presenting as sweet innocents costumed in lovable pink got everyone watching what seemed at first to be a non-threatening joke, until it became the set for a vigorous anti-war performance. The actors for such performances were always women, plus the odd male police officer they flirtingly persuaded to stand down from his insistence that they move on. As to the genre, another key concept in performance studies, Code Pink performances were at the cusp of comedy and tragedy.

Rowe learned that IVAW also recognised the importance of self-presentation and always wore imitation military uniforms for their protest activities. Thus clothed, they enacted counterinsurgency dramas on the streets of Times Square, New York and in Union Station, D.C., suddenly putting ordinary people inside war activities that vets had experienced and perpetrated in Iraq towns. Just as powerful in a different way were the individual testimonies about their experiences in Iraq, relayed during a four-day Winter Soldier hearing/gathering in 2008.

Rowe, who observed both types of IVAW events, describes Winter Soldier as a 'prolonged performance' (Rowe 2013: 43) relative to the short shocks of the counterinsurgency acts. Both made demands on the vets and on those caught up in instant street wars or in listening to one after another lengthy, difficult, and, at times, horrifying recitation of war experience. As an audience member at Winter Soldier, Rowe reports that she experienced mental exhaustion, physical disturbance, and an 'immediacy of awareness that had previously been subsumed under layers of academic distancing and comforting prior experience with the topic' (ibid.: 44). Interviews with other observers/spectators confirmed her own experience and indicated that the layers of normality that normally shielded people living outside war zones from the actions inside them were peeled away by the painstaking performance of testimony. By becoming the audience for IVAW instead of an actor, as she was with Code Pink, Rowe placed herself in a space of war, protest, and performance new to IR and to performance studies.

I would like to see greater empirical development of Rowe's conviction or 'strong sense that all of the anti-war organizing in the United States did coalesce in a way that exerted pressure on politicians' (ibid.: 134–135). I can readily see that the new movements did give 'a visible voice to political positions that were otherwise largely suppressed or invisible' (ibid.: 135). But whether they had an impact on the foreign policies and conduct of the war, or on the withdrawal from it, requires further analysis. I applaud, however, Rowe's steadfast belief that aspects of the arts can send light into dark corners of IR if we are willing to be mavericks, outlaws, or iconoclasts, and embrace the challenges of creative ways of knowing without flinching.

Rowe's approach to researching these war protests fits Andreasen's (2014) characterisation of the creative person. Rowe displayed the tendency of the polymath to pull in knowledge from seemingly unconnected realms – in her case, combining IR with performance studies and actual performances. Her methodology, of being in and of some of the performances and an audience for others, enabled her to make associations and connections at the fulcrum of performance and daily life within IR that others had not yet noted. Rowe took risks in choosing her puzzle and methodology, persevered in a different way of thinking, and did so independently and with determination. She created a new framework for appreciating citizen activist modes of presentation and their careful play of space, genre, costuming, and interchange with audiences, and used methodologies that matched the creativity of the protest movements she was studying. It should also be noted that Rowe's push beyond the usual texts, personages, and genres of mainstream and critical IR did not leave her professionally stranded. Ph.D. in Politics and International Relations in hand, she is a faculty member in the Department of Performance Studies at the University of London's Goldsmith's College.

Elina Penttinen: *Joy and International Relations: A New Methodology*

Why does IR focus on negative processes and outcomes of international politics and neglect to study situations in which people flourish, even in the midst of upheaval? That question compels the rather obvious fact that the field focuses on identifying problems rather than identifying solutions. And when solutions do appear, say, in the public policies of post-genocide Rwanda, the human positives in that situation can get buried in critiques and put-downs of President Kagame, one of the more forward-thinking leaders on gender equality. In Penttinen's exploration of the reasons why IR is so excited by negative events, she singles out critical IR, including feminist IR, for particular finger-wagging. Although their intentions are noble, she argues, critical IR has an orientation to the world that prevents it from smelling the roses; and the built-in negativity of the IR traditions pulls it closer to conventional IR than one might realise. Central to Penttinen's thesis is the claim that all of IR overemphasises struggle, conflict, oppression, loss and vulnerability as the realities of international relations. In doing so, everyone overlooks the radiance and joy of life that can make it possible for disagreements to be resolved, the horrors of war to be handled by ordinary people through resilience and self-healing, and individual joy to emanate despite violent international relations. To put this in her words, Penttinen sees critical IR in particular as:

> a circulating practice in which first there is research on what is wrong in the world and how to analyze it, and next research on what is wrong with the research or analysis of others. In turn this circular motion of criticism operates as a self-serving function which creates and maintains the identities and subjectivity of academics in IR, who proclaim an objective or clearer view of the reality of international relations than those lay persons in the midst of it.
>
> *(Penttinen 2013: 14)*

'What if the world [i]s not a problem to be fixed?' (ibid.: 12). Penttinen embarks on a quest to fashion a way out of this circular negativity by introducing a variety of scholarly traditions that incorporate more positive assumptions about human life. These include posthumanist new materialism, literary analysis, positive psychology, aspects of quantum physics, a bit of Buddhism, and film studies. Not one of these traditions features in most IR tool kits, because each puts some emphasis on locations and instances of liveliness, positive emotion, and belief that humans actively and mindfully create positive possibilities, even in the midst of war and conflict. Penttinen does not dispute the seriousness of ongoing crises in the Middle East, nor would she minimise Ukrainian struggles with Russia, and the wars and accompanying gender-based violence in several African countries. What she disputes is the breezy conviction in the social sciences that solutions come from 'a person [or institution or state] named "someone else" who will fix it … and that focusing on … what is wrong in the world and discussing it within academia, will somehow bring the solution' (ibid.: 14).

Here is a polymath fascinated by ways of knowing, that address exactly the same kinds of issues and challenges IR does, but in remarkably different ways. Convinced not just of the superiority of these approaches but the importance of learning from them, Penttinen presents several pathways to better IR around a series of examples of cooperative, life-affirming, and joy-inducing situations. Each exemplifies the ability of ordinary people to absorb the demands of their contexts, work with those demands, and come out stronger. One case focuses on Finnish women police officers working in international crisis management contexts as humanitarian agents of the UN in Kosovo; Penttinen interviewed women returning from such demanding missions. Other cases feature her analysis of two novels that depict women in extreme situations of conflict in Rwanda and Serbia working through their fears and anger to reach understandings of violence that are personally empowering and quietly joyous. Three more cases focus on the positive personal testimonies of women's experiences in World War II in Finland, as well as the films *Stormheart* and *The Men Who Stare at Goats*, with their posthumanist antics of imagining agency in war. She presents quite a range of exemplars, geospaces, and time periods of international relations – more than many IR analysts would attempt to address in one book. Penttinen dives in, however, with each chapter stronger than the one preceding it.

The case of the Finnish police women shows determined individuals taking the measure of painful situations and operating within them effectively and kindly, using what Penttinen calls ethical action competence tinged with an 'open-hearted, nonjudgmental, positive attitude to everyday life' (ibid.: 61). Instead of being put off by the challenges in a post-war area that is swarmed by a multicultural, multinational team of specialists, each with his or her notions of what should be done, the Finnish police women impress her with their ability to 'surrender to the present moment' (ibid.: 54). To the women, '[t]he operation and the field were seen to be filled with possibilities instead of being infested with unsolvable problems' (ibid.: 55). Difference all around them seems to be creatively embraced rather than controlled. The women police officers on assignment in Kosovo creatively manage their assignments and themselves, instead of trying to manage the locals and the internationals. This seems to make them happy as well as effective.

Penttinen then moves to the theme of self-healing in post-conflict zones, a process of individual reconciliation that features minimal help from outsiders. Her entry point here is not a set of interviews but rather literary analysis of a number of narratives. One is a novel, *The Cello of Sarajevo* (Galloway 2008), whose main character becomes an anti-sniper seeking to protect a cellist playing in memory of people who were mowed down while they waited in a queue for food. The other is a memoir, *Left to Tell* (Ilibagaza 2006), from a psychological journey a woman finds herself taking to survive and emerge mentally healthy from the Rwandan genocide raging around her. Two aspects of these tales strike Penttinen as experiences IR overlooks to its detriment. One is the healing power of communicating a survival tale your own way and in your own voice. Rowe observed this factor at the Winter Soldier hearings, where telling one's story and hearing many other stories of war had a powerful effect on the tellers and those who listened through the four days. There is a simple lesson in this that Penttinen encourages IR to take up: people are experts on their lives; so talk to them. Too often, those who experience war are not afforded opportunities by grief counsellors or academics 'to name and define …' (Penttinen 2013: 75). The experts do that for them, producing an arc of failed imagination that keeps rehearsing the old saw that 'war is a source of human suffering' (ibid.: 76). To Penttinen, war can be the source of suffering and also of creativity, a point Jean Bethke Elshtain also made in her path-breaking book *Women and War* (1987).

The final parts of Penttinen's book consider a collection of memoirs and pictures of women taken during World War II Finland. It is intriguing that much of this material focuses not on war as a problem but rather on 'how the women make it through everyday life under such conditions … how one meets the challenges that war creates' (Penttinen 2013: 79). Most of them find their return to the gendered status quo ante far more traumatising than the war itself. Indeed, some recall the minimal war they experienced in the north of Finland as more socially engaging than anything that comes with peace; many especially comment on the mutual friendliness of Finns and Germans stationed in the region. Penttinen takes away from this the sense that women should not be presented in set war categories – as victims, Rosie Riveters, or soldiers. They participate in the heightened sociality of war and, like many soldiers, can remember it fondly. Animals also participate, and Penttinen winds up considering war through the eyes of a dog adopted by a Finnish family in Berlin as the Wall comes down in 1963, and a film that satirises the ideal masculine soldier and replaces him with a new-age, slow food, meditating, and mostly unarmed group of 'soldiers'. These sources amplify Penttinen's claims that people show resilience, fortitude, and positive emotions in situations of considerable danger.

Eager to challenge IR and create new sources of salient knowledge and new ways of gathering it, the book probably introduces far more streams of thought and concepts than the author can fully integrate. As well, it is one thing to 'imagine for a moment that the world is not broken' (ibid.: 106), and another to look at moments or episodes of world time with Penttinen's confidence that they are, in fact, not broken entirely; that life continues on with an uncertain and changing dynamic that need not be reduced to something to fix. Surely, she exclaims, there are numerous tendencies across the world that make it wise to be modest in claims about any of them. Feminist IR locates the international and its relations in people, locations, and modest activities; but Penttinen is right when she accuses even feminist IR of dwelling on problems in the world. I remember my mother lamenting that academics 'spoil things for people by always looking for trouble'. She hated it whenever I picked holes in a film she liked or refused to appreciate the televised excitement when the candidate I had not supported was giving his victory address. What if we did start at another position? Could we do it and would we last as creative students of joy and international relations, students of animal points of view on war, of praxis sensitive to local concerns and not higher power concerns? That is Penttinen's creative provocation, and I find it unique among the creative IR texts mentioned earlier.

And so, back to creativity and IR

Creativity is not every scholar's strong point. Andreasen (2014) insists that creativity has a lot to do with temperament, attitude, and capacity to withstand withering comments by colleagues who follow the research rules and want to make sure that others, especially new scholars, do so too. The field of IR has made room for so many new topic areas in recent decades that there should be lots of creative air to imbibe. In fact, creativity is not exactly bursting out all over IR. Nearly every conference I attend leaves me wondering where creativity is hiding out.[4] Recall Andreasen's definition of creative people as those who are 'better at recognizing relationships, making associations and connections, and seeing things in an original way – seeing things that others cannot see' (2014: 70). That last phrase tells it all. If one sees things others cannot see, then one is something of an anomaly, apart from the others – even others who are also creative in their own ways.

Nonetheless, the classroom environment has taught me that people can have latent or undiscovered bits of creativity that they require the permission of an authority figure to pull out. Like talent, creativity can be encouraged and practised if – and these are big ifs – the environment is initially safe enough to enable a potential creator to think outside, not just 'the' box but as many boxes as possible. To do so in IR requires two additional conditions: willingness to take risks and to play like children with the material of IR; and efforts to bring in even more situations, locations, and sources of knowledge that are not-IR.[5] As one example, knowing through one's senses can be as important as reaching knowledge through rationality. What does war taste like? What aspects of war touch our bodies even when we are outside war zones? How does joy feel – and do we even know how it should feel? How about visual and aural acuities in war? How many Winter Soldier tales of horror can we hear without walking away or looking at our phones? How long does it take before a Dutch still-life painting – lush with peeled fruits, flowers on the edge of wilting, and toppled wine glasses – begins to connect our thoughts, say, on war, or trafficking, or refugee life, or Ebola, or whatever relationships our minds go to? And then there is determination and practice, which should hone a scholar's ability to discern a strong from a weakly creative point and pull back when something clearly does not work. One art sociologist insists that 'art requires not merely a creator but also an audience who will receive the work, and who will thereby allow it *to work*' (Garlick 2004: 123, emphasis original). Who is the audience for the (art)work of a creative scholar – other creative scholars, students, the imaginative but uneasy enterprise of IR? That remains to be seen.

One mutual strength of the two scholars highlighted here is their scholarly immersion in the worlds of their research. Like the other creative scholars sketched earlier, their creativity takes the esoteric field of IR to places where people live, work, read, write, struggle, shape, and adjust to international relations around them; in that regard, their work echoes aspects of Parashar's remarkable relationship with fieldwork in South Asia. Such are the locations of scholarship that need to be nurtured by IR: the places of ordinary folks, who, as Code Pink, IVAW, and police women from Finland in Kosovo show, can be creative in facing international relations. Penttinen says that IR is always looking for trouble, trouble, trouble, defying the resources of the human spirit in doing so. My view is that IR is looking for the politics of the international in obvious and overworked places full of foreign policy elites, major named institutions, firms, statistics, and field-recognisable power moves. Historically, IR reaches above people and lets anthropology and social work nestle down with them. At a time when people and their political arts are forcing major changes in the world, sidelining them or the scholars who research them would be uncreative, devoid of sense, and do nothing to ease the unease of a discipline aloft and aloof.

Notes

1 Routledge (London) seems the publisher of choice for IR scholars pursuing creative research – although I am impressed that Princeton University took on Daniel Drezner's wonderful *Theories of International Politics and Zombies* (2011) and has sent it into a second 'revived' edition.
2 Yet one finds in IR writings mention of the art of war, the art of politics, and the art of diplomacy. I see this as a tacit acknowledgement that social science explanations and understandings of war, politics, and diplomacy miss something important that can only be evoked as 'art' (Sylvester, 2006).
3 See response by Sylvester (2013b).
4 One exception that comes to mind is the BISA Critical Terrorism Studies Annual Conference I keynoted in 2012. It was absolutely brimming with creativity.
5 My harbour of inspiration is the art museum – any art museum will do.

Further reading

Ackerly, B., Stern, M. and True, J. (2006) *Feminist Methodologies for International Relations*, Cambridge: Cambridge University Press.

Acuto, M (2014) 'Everyday International Relations: Garbage, Grand Designs, and Mundane Matters', *International Political Sociology* 8(3): 345–362.

Kaufman, C. (2009) *Creativity 101*, New York: Springer Publishing.

Kopper, A. (2012) 'The Imaginary of Borders: From a Coloring Book to Cezanne Paintings', *International Political Sociology* 6(3): 277–293.

Leavy, P. (2015) *Method Meets Art: Arts-Based Research Practice*, 2nd edition, New York: The Guildford Press.

Shilliam, R. (2012) *International Relations and Non-Western Thought: Colonialism and Investigations of Global Modernity*, Abingdon: Routledge.

Soreanu, R. (2010) 'Feminist Creativities and the Disciplinary Imaginary of International Relations', *International Political Sociology* 4(4): 380–400.

Sylvester, C. (2009) *Art/Museums: International Relations Where We Least Expect It*, Boulder, CO: Paradigm Publishers.

Sylvester, C. (2015) (ed.) *Masquerades of War*, New York: Routledge.

Bibliography

Andreasen, N. (2014) 'Secrets of the Creative Brain', *The Atlantic* 314(1) (July/August): 62–75.

Baudrillard, J. (2005) *The Conspiracy of Art*, ed. S. Lotringer, trans. A. Hodges, New York: Semiotrext(e).

Chan, S. (2005) *Out of Evil: New International Politics and Old Doctrines of War*, London: I.B. Tauris.

Chan, S. (2007) *Grasping Africa: A Tale of Tragedy and Achievement*, London: Tauris.

Dauphinee, E. (2013) *The Politics of Exile*, London: Routledge.

Drezner, D.W. (2011) *Theories of International Politics and Zombies*, Princeton, NJ: University of Princeton.

Edkins, J. and Kear, A. (eds) (2013) *International Politics and Performance: Critical Aesthetics and Creative Practice*, London: Routledge.

Elshtain, J.B. (1987) *Women and War*, New York: Basic Books.

Galloway, S. (2008) *The Cellist of Sarajevo*, London: Atlantic Books.

Garlick, S. (2004) 'Distinctly Feminine: On the Relationship Between Men and Art', *Berkeley Journal of Sociology* 48: 108–125.

Greenberg, C. (1985) 'Avant-Garde and Kitsch', in F. Frascina (ed.), *Pollock and After: The Critical Debate*, London: Chapman, pp. 21–23.

Ilibagiza, I. (2006) *Left to Tell: Discovering God Amidst the Rwandan Holocaust*, Carlsbad: Hay House.

Inayatullah, N. (2013) 'Impossibilities: Generative Misperformance and the Movements of the Teaching Body', in J. Edkins and A. Kear (eds), *International Politics and Performance: Critical Aesthetics and Creative Practice*, London: Routledge, pp. 150–158.

Jackson, P.T. (2011) *The Conduct of Inquiry in International Relations*, New York: Routledge.

Jackson, R. (2014) *Confessions of a Terrorist: A Novel*, London: Zed Books.

Kurki, M. (2011) 'The Limitations of the Critical Edge: Reflections on Critical and Philosophical IR Scholarship Today', *Millennium: Journal of International Studies* 40(1): 129–146.

Mearsheimer, J. and Walt, S. (2007) *The Israel Lobby and American Foreign Policy*, New York: Farrar, Straus, and Giroux.

Murphy, C. (2007), 'The Promise of Critical IR, Partially Kept', *Review of International Studies* 33(Supplement 1): 117–133.

Opondo, S. (2013) 'Stagecraft/Statecraft/Mancraft: Embodied Envoys, "Objects" and the Spectres of Estrangement in Africa', in J. Edkins and A. Kear (eds), *International Politics and Performance: Critical Aesthetics and Creative Practice*, London: Routledge, pp. 130–149.

Parashar, S. (2011) 'Embodied "Otherness" and Negotiations of Difference', *International Studies Review*, part of Forum: Emotion and the Feminist IR Researcher, 13(4): 696–699.

Parashar, S. (2014) *Women and Militant Wars: The Politics of Injury*, London: Routledge.

Park-Kang, S. (2014) *Fictional International Relations: Gender, Pain and Truth*, London: Routledge.

Pelaprat, E. and M. Cole (2011) '"Minding the Gap": Imagination, Creativity, and Human Cognition', *Integrative Psychological and Behavioral Science* 45(4): 397–418.

Penttinen, E. (2013) *Joy and International Relations: A New Methodology*, London: Routledge.

Rowe, C. (2013) *The Politics of Protest and US Foreign Policy*, London: Routledge.

Security Dialogue (2013) Special Issue on Elizabeth Dauphinee's *The Politics of Exile* 44(4): 281–297.

Shapiro, M. (2011) 'The Presence of War: Here and Elsewhere', *International Political Sociology* 5(2): 109–125.

Shapiro, M. (2013) *Studies in the Trans-Disciplinary Method: After the Aesthetic Turn*, London: Routledge.

Surkova, I. (2012) 'Towards a Creativity Framework', *Society and Economy* 34(1): 115–138.

Sylvester, C. (2006) 'Bringing Art/Museums to Feminist International Relations', in Brooke Ackerly, Maria Stern, and Jacqui True (eds), *Feminist Methodologies for International Relations*, Cambridge: Cambridge University Press, pp. 201–220.

Sylvester, C. (2007) 'Whither the International at the End of IR?' *Millennium Journal of International Studies* 35(3): 551–573.

Sylvester, C. (2013a) *War as Experience: Contributions from International Relations and Feminist Analysis*, London: Routledge.

Sylvester, C. (2013b) 'The Elusive Arts of Reflexivity in the "Sciences" of IR', *Millennium: Journal of International Studies* 41(2): 309–325.

Sylvester, C. (2013c) 'Experiencing the End and Afterlives of International Relations/ Theory', *European Journal of International Relations* 19(3): 609–626.

Thornton, S. (2008) *Seven Days in the Art World*, London: Granta.

Wu, C. (2002) *Privatising Culture: Corporate Art Intervention Since the 1980s*, London: Verso

6

DIFFERENCE

David L. Blaney and Naeem Inayatullah

Introduction

The discipline of international relations (IR) constructs its object as a unitary world of actors, relations, and structures. At its most ambitious, IR seeks to 'discover' the laws of international and global society. Yet John Hobson (2012: 344) ends his recent book with the charge that IR 'fails to deliver'. Rather than providing a 'positivist, value-free analysis and universalist theories of world politics', IR produces a Eurocentric vision where the West is the sole agent of modernity and the source of progress (see also Chen and Cho in this book). What happens beyond the European core is treated as secondary or rendered as barbaric. By excluding the story of imperialism from the centre of inquiry, IR appears as a form of colonial knowledge. Yet, inquiry into colonial relations explodes these Eurocentric 'myths'; it treats the world as a co-construction of West and non-West and challenges the mapping of self and other onto civilisation and barbarism (ibid.: 14–21).

We earlier traced IR's denial of its own colonial character to the problem of difference (Inayatullah and Blaney 2004). We spoke of difference in the language of 'culture'. Culture, we wrote, points us to a human commonality: the capacities to create, perform, and transform meaningful forms of life. But culture(s) reminds us that human endeavours in meaning-making and world-making are multiple and diverse – and thereby partial. Despite the tendency to put 'global' in front of so many processes – global flows, global development, global consumption, etc. – culture still points us always to a terrain of 'partiality and diversity' (Inayatullah and Blaney 2004: 16–17). And IR, in our account, fears full exploration of partiality and diversity, instead translating difference as otherness. Like Hobson, we locate the sources of these denials and deferrals in a historical account of how modern social and political thought structures IR as colonial knowledge and practice.

In this chapter, we begin by sketching how the problem of difference emerged in the early modern era. Difference appeared from the confluence of inside and outside: from violent religious schism and from the simultaneous 'discovery' of new continents and peoples. These events threatened to crack European cosmology by undermining its creation myths. In response, theorists of this period struggled to restore a single church and the unity of creation – to construct, as James Tully (1995) has it, an 'empire of uniformity'. Such an empire understands difference as a threat to be contained, denied, or deferred. This empire's efforts extend to space and time; it homogenises varying peoples and places into bounded states located along a ladder of developmental stages – a response that continues to structure the limits and possibilities of much of IR's engagement with difference, even Hedley Bull's promising efforts. In the second section, we highlight Karl Polanyi's contribution to our engagement with difference, noting how the writings of Tzvetan Todorov and Ashis Nandy shape our reading of Polanyi. Polanyi, in our terms, allows an ethnological critique of modern capitalism that draws on ethical/political resources from multiple times and places. To conclude this section, we draw attention to other work on difference in IR, noting the multiple sources employed by scholars and the growing number of authors students might consult. Third, we demonstrate the critical potential of IR as a site for the exploration of difference. We point to scholars who resist Eurocentric readings with histories that document the co-construction of the world by self and other. We illustrate the critical power of locating the other *within* as a source of critical self-reflection in our work on Adam Smith and the work of those who recover as coeval the voices of protest of the colonised against Western dominance. Nor need we seal ourselves within a particular location within developmental time; alternative times/places abound and we can find in them vast creativity for thinking alternative political possibilities. We conclude with thoughts on politics/ethics and knowledge production in IR.

Core ideas: difference, threat, and deferral

IR is an encounter with difference. Though IR can best be understood as heterology, i.e. the study of the many modalities of difference (de Certau 1986), much of IR reduces others' differences to threat, without considering that encounters with others also present possibilities for attraction, exchange, and learning. The continuum of possibilities is 'split' into two, such that threat and violence are attributed to the outside while the inside receives the affirmative qualities (Benjamin 1988: 218–220). A stable polity and prospects for social and economic development are claimed to depend on this homogenisation of internal space and identities. Difference is displaced to the outside as danger and threat, at best contained by borders and the balance of power.

We have traced this equation of difference with danger to early modern social thinkers' efforts to contain the eruption of difference evident in the wars of religion and the 'discovery' of the Americas (Inayatullah and Blaney 2004: Chapters 1 and 2). The Reformation fractured the pretensions of a universal church. Catholics and

Protestants each declared the other idolaters, killing believers, sacking churches, and de-legitimating rulers. Rulers set upon their dissident populations with fire and sword, practising a form of internal crusade. General warfare broke out, halted as the sides became exhausted, only to break out again in the Thirty Years' War – perhaps the bloodiest period in European history until the twentieth century. Traumatised leaders and populations eventually exhausted their religious zeal and reluctantly moved towards regarding religious difference as a stain with which they would have to live. An uneasy peace resulted, defended by a balance of power and the begrudging acceptance that princes could define the religion of their realm.

But what seemed lost in all this was a justification for political authority. In this context, as Stephen Toulmin (1990) notes, thinkers tried to reestablish political stability and moral consensus on a new rational and certain basis. Thomas Hobbes, Hugo Grotius, and John Locke sought a common basis for rule that was consistent with emergent understandings of nature as 'homogenous, uniform, symmetrical' (Funkenstein 1986: 29). These thinkers deduced the necessary motivations, institutions, and laws necessary to establish political authority and maintain political stability. They did so by placing humans in the 'state of nature' – a natural state prior to society from which authority naturally and certainly arises. If Europe's internal violence was due to uncertainties about legitimate rule rooted in differences in religion and culture, then stable polities required an end to uncertainty and the imposition of cultural and legal uniformity noted by Tully (1995). We read these understandings of political authority as a deferral of the problem of difference, as a refusal to face the ubiquity of difference, as a denial of a potentially rich relationship with difference, and, most important, as the naturalisation of an active hostility towards diversity. This heritage continues to haunt us.

The discovery of a new world similarly challenged Europe's grasp of the social world as emerging from a single creation and guided by God's plan toward redemption and unification (Hodgen 1964; Pagden 1982). The commitment was to universal teleology and a single Edenic origin that constructed difference not as intrinsic human richness, but as a fall from grace and degeneration from God's initially perfect creation. The previously unknown peoples of the Americas were difficult to fit into such an interpretive grid. Their obscure origins prompted imagining them as the result of God's multiple creations or as lost Christian tribes. Many saw their strange ways as satanic or animalistic, not worthy of the designation 'human', and were therefore subject to enslavement or eradication. For others, the isolation of these peoples from the Word of God was a scandal, but one that could be remedied with missions to Christianise and civilise this new world. Here, difference would be washed away along with sin. In either case, difference generated doubt and anxiety, producing efforts that would contain or vanquish threats to Europe's originary myths and cosmology. Mostly missed in this response was the opportunity to see difference as a resource – something that might be explored in order to expose and oppose the stifling constraints of uniformity.

Although eventually accepted as human, the Amerindian other was nevertheless located at the temporally opposite pole from Christian Europe. Amerindian religious and cultural abominations were the result of their drifting away from the Christian heartland – a travel that explained their degeneration from God's original perfection. In this way, spatial distance between Europeans and others was converted into temporal difference (Hodgen 1964), and European thinkers established the temporal backwardness of Amerindians via meticulous (if often fanciful) comparisons with the ancient Greeks (White 1972). Europeans and Amerindians emerged from the same single source, the same family. The Europeans, however, retained Christian origins and their advanced civilisation. Meanwhile, Amerindians had lost the way and were arrested in a degenerate or savage past. Europeans imagined the Amerindian as a temporally prior self, who might rejoin Christian civilisation via education; European conquest developed thereby an explicitly pedagogical purpose.

Inside and outside were interconnected: if we can think simultaneously of Europe's internal religious wars and its imperial justifications in the Americas, we can see how Hobbes', Grotius', and Locke's search for an unchallengeable basis for rule merges with their enunciation of societies' natural laws of progress and development (Inayatullah and Blaney 2004: Chapters 2 and 3). Specifically, spatial/cultural difference is imagined as temporal/developmental difference, with non-European societies seen as backward, no longer coeval with Europe (Fabian 1983). Here, difference is seen always as degeneration, not as opportunity. This is the foundation of Enlightenment notions of progress, nineteenth-century evolutionary theories, twentieth-century understandings of development, and twenty-first-century humanitarian interventions. The good life made possible within the boundaries settled by international society may not be secured immediately, but appears as an inevitable and inexorable outcome of the spread of modern ideas, practices, and assistance for those who find themselves stuck on a lower rung of development.

Admittedly, this inside/outside structure central to much of IR (Walker 1993) grants to outside others a measure of difference in terms of sovereignty and self-determination, but the distinctive good life of the political community depends on homogenising political and social structures across time and space. Differences may persist but they are located 'securely' outside, certainly beyond the West and sequestered within the boundaries of other states, always something to be excluded, and deterred, if eventually assimilated.

Hedley Bull, unlike most of the key figures in IR, takes up this issue, self-consciously grappling with the problem of difference when he draws the distinction between international system and international society. Bull counterposes interactions among self-regarding states, answering only to themselves, with interactions informed by common values (Bull 1977: Chapter 1). This distinction plays a central role in Bull's influential historical account of how interacting polities and peoples come to be joined in a *society* of states. The world becomes a society not simply by conquest, though conquest was a necessary condition of bringing far-flung peoples and polities into the European international society. The world becomes an international society through the gradual acceptance, even embrace, of a set of European rules and norms. Of particular importance, international society favours the independence of states, the right to sovereignty – a right extended finally to the peripheries of Europe and non-European states in the twentieth century after decades of struggle (see Bull and Watson 1984).

Far from sanguine, Bull recognises the limits of this international society. Preserving the independence of states depends on an imbalance of power and a hierarchical legal order, where the interests and independence of small powers may be sacrificed, and where war often retains value as a tool for maintaining this order. Despite these limits, states, including the weakest powers, value international society because its norms and operations provide some check on the imperial ambitions of great powers and create the basis for demands for greater equality (Bull 1977: Part 2; Bull 1983; Inayatullah and Blaney 1995).

In our reading, Bull provides a double response to difference. On the one hand, his defence of the independence of states supports difference contra the homogenisation produced by empire, forms of global government, or a decline into a system of unchecked competition (Bull 1984; Bull 1977: Chapter 14). On the other hand, Bull remains ambivalent about difference. The minimal respect available for the self-determination of states depends on substantial commonality: a common form of polity, international rules and norms, and growing economic and social interconnections. He reminds us that this commonality grows from European subjugation of much of the rest of the world. Indeed, the very possibility of any protection of difference seems to require continuing subordination of much of the world to elements of commonality established with and imposed by (European) international society: predominately European understandings of rule/authority, nation-statehood and liberal norms of governance, and social and economic development in modern capitalist terms. Bull endorses greater equality among states, but he remains wary, since he identifies Third World demands for equality, particularly cultural recognition, as a grave danger to the minimal respect for sovereignty achieved in international society. These demands threaten to undercut the dominance of Western values that provides the commonality on which respect for difference within sovereign states depends (Bull 1983).

If Bull values difference, as we have seen, it also lurks as a threat – something beyond European norms of order. Only European values can be extended to re-imagine international society or some other global order. Bull excludes the possible value of other world orders whose difference is not something from which we might learn. For Bull, other civilisations can contribute little to global or regional conversations about the meaning of order or justice.

Nevertheless, the importance of Bull's suspicions of notions of world government or global society should not be underestimated. Other scholars within the English School tradition (who Bull might label 'solidarists') show less restraint, actively embracing notions of global society and governance (see Dunne 2013). Andrew Linklater (1998), for example, takes the limits of international society as identified by Bull to indicate that the project of establishing global community remains unfinished. A greater universality, a world where violence is restrained, individual rights respected, and liberal governance performed, is immanent within international society. Similarly, work more narrowly focused on human rights (see Dunne and Wheeler 1999) suggests a more expansive and pervasive role for European norms in civilising a global society. Though imagined as diffusion from the West to the rest of the world, these normative principles spread to the non-West most effectively when leveraged by alliances of transnational activists and Western governments (Keck and Sikkink 1998). Likewise, development, in the form of capital investment, knowledge transfers, and the intensification of market relations, promises the end of poverty and the flourishing of international peace and domestic civility (Sachs 2005). For all these scholars, the world's disorders and backwardness cannot be allowed to hide behind the principle of the sovereignty of states in an international society. Bull's defence of sovereignty may appear quaint or out of joint with the times where the empire of uniformity moves to root out and eradicate difference via aid programmes for development and military intervention for nation- and state-building.

It is not simply that a Eurocentric IR fails in its universal explanatory project, that it ignores difference and misunderstands the universe that we occupy, as Hobson stresses. Rather, difference serves as the other against which much of IR constructs itself as a universal project: its singular modern world of like units, moving in circuits of trade and financial flows, subject to global norms. International society extends European values in the name of the universal, constructing a world of states where difference is contained and erased. Hedley Bull remains noteworthy because he departs from this script at key points. He recognises the role of conquest in the creation of an international order and his defence of that order, whatever its warts, turns on the preservation of a space for difference. Though Bull fears movements that challenge European international society in the name of equality and difference, he still rejects the homogenising aspirations of projects for global governance.

Key thinkers: Polanyi, Todorov, and Nandy

Karl Polanyi's *The Great Transformation* (1957) is a classic of international political economy. Polanyi's critique of free-market orthodoxy as disembedding the economy from society and thereby exposing human labour, livelihood, and habitation to degradation remains timely. We have highlighted Polanyi's account of this degradation as principally 'cultural' – a 'debasement' or 'lethal injury' to entire forms of life, where 'self-respect and standards' are damaged (1957: 157–158; Inayatullah and Blaney 2004: Chapter 5). More precisely, we read Polanyi as a champion of difference, whose response to capitalism turns on a dialogic or perspectival political economy.

Our reading of Polanyi draws inspiration from the work of Bulgarian-French literary therorist, Tzvetan Todorov (1984) and Indian psychologist, social theorist, and gadfly, Ashis Nandy (1983, 1987) on the colonial relations of self and other: Todorov on the conquest of the Americas and Nandy on British colonialism in India. For both English and Spanish colonisers, native peoples became legitimate objects of domination because they fell below the threshold of full humanity: either as wickedness subject to annihilation; or as children in need of tutors, women in need of subjugation, and heathens in need of conversion. Both Todorov and Nandy emphasise that colonial violence and oppression depend on tropes that separate and oppose self and other and refuse an overlap or continuity that might place self and other in the same moment.

Conversely, as Todorov (1984: 249) emphasises, to the extent that the other is seen as like the self, the other is assimilated to the self; any recognition of equality involves the denial of genuine difference. In colonial encounters, then, the other appears as separate and inferior and subject to violence, exploitation, and physical eradication. Or the other is granted equality but only at the price of erasing difference via colonial missions and postcolonial economic and political development. The material impact of colonial domination is certainly vast and continues to weigh on the present, but both authors stress that these material conditions shouldn't obscure the pervasive and persistent 'psychology of colonialism' (Nandy 1983: ix–xii) or the *contemporary* terrain of self and other shaped by conquest (Todorov 1984: 1).

Todorov and Nandy respond to this colonial legacy in strikingly similar ways. Both directly challenge the separation and distancing of self and other that makes domination possible. For Todorov (1984: 1), the self is never complete, always standing in a relation of alterity to itself. This alterity, Todorov (1984: 185–193, 225, 240–241) observes, opens a space for engagement with the other that moves beyond either domination of an inferior other or a denial of difference. The encounters in the Americas reveal not only cruelty and insensitivity, but also learning and growth and the emergence of responses that begin to move against the temptation to demonise or assimilate the other.

We do find in Todorov the possibility of adopting a kind of 'perspectivism' in which the cultural practices of the other are placed beside one's own, both differences and commonality and strengths and weaknesses noted, and a certain overlap of views revealed and constructed. Todorov calls this an 'ethnological stance' where the fears and doubts associated with the other are turned into a resource for a self-examination that might substantially alter not only how the self sees the other, but also how the self views itself. Where difference becomes a resource it is possible to join a conversation that 'contributes to the reciprocal illumination of one culture by another' (Todorov 1984: 240).

Likewise for Nandy (1987: 2, 4, 17, 54–55), the polarisation of self and other wrought by colonialism hides that cultures and traditions intersect and overlap; they are layered, comprised of 'different levels or parts', or perhaps dominant and recessive moments. And no matter how different, the subjects of colonial encounters can find connections and overlaps between their own values and visions and the other's various cultural practices and traditions. These connections and overlaps suggest that interactions are not fixed and the possibility of re-negotiating colonial polarities into a dialogue where self and other meet on the basis of equality. Dialogue does not uncover an 'integration of visions', some universal that might be imposed on the world, but draws connections between various understandings of and responses to a world of inequalities and oppressions. The other may serve as a source of critical self-reflection as long as we recognise that the other is also within us and that our common experience of suffering may establish connections between self and other.

Karl Polanyi is rarely associated with these authors. He is best known for his critical history of the political institutionalisation of 'free' markets and the movements of societal self-protection that necessarily arise in response. Yet we find at the heart of this history a perspectivism not unlike that embraced by Todorov and an ethical practice that engages in the cultural dialogue that Nandy endorses.

On the one side, Polanyi (1977) refuses what he calls 'the economistic fallacy' that assimilates all human efforts at want-satisfaction, if not all human interactions, into a market imaginary. The maximising of ends with finite means (or economising) becomes the paradigm for human action and markets become the model for all practices and institutions. Market logic, instead of a particular historical form, is taken as a universal. Any appearance to the contrary, where human behaviour seems governed by an alternative moral or social logic, is either immediately and inexorably rendered intelligible in market terms, or is attributed to some form of backwardness/underdevelopment. Polanyi recognises that this fallacy justifies market economics theoretically and institutes the marketisation of social space practically. Difference appears as a threat to our understanding of natural laws that must be erased with proper economic pedagogy, structural adjustments, and development projects.

On the other side, Polanyi's perspectivism makes him attentive to the multiplicity of economic forms across cultures and human history (Polanyi 1968, 1977). He acknowledges the universal human necessity to satisfy material needs and wants, but highlights the variability and plurality of these practices: organised at different scales, with multiple forms of reciprocity, embedded in differing social visions, both hierarchical and egalitarian, and serving varying societal and human values. With this move, Polanyi shifts our understanding of self and other in ways that open us to critical self-reflection. It becomes clear that what he calls a 'market mentality' fails to illuminate the human condition and redress our current maladies. The effort to impose markets damages human cultures, impairs the security of livelihood, and fouls the earth, as Polanyi stresses in *The Great Transformation* (1957). It also excludes the possibility of learning from the multiplicity of human experience if we see others as earlier stages of the self that are beyond the pale of civilisation and contemporary political relevance. Rather than distancing himself temporally or spatially from the other, Polanyi brings others close, providing an encounter with our contemporary values and visions. The possibilities for critical self-reflection expand when, as Nandy might suggest, we draw not only on values and visions internal to a market mentality but can also use the recessive others within and values and visions beyond as a mirror for the self.

Following Todorov, we would describe Polanyi's strategy as ethnological and propose rethinking international political economy (IPE) as an ethnological practice. Contemporary IPE has largely become disconnected from the idea that institutions or practices have ethical content beyond economising (see Ashley 1983; Cohen 2008). Resisting this economistic fallacy alters the boundaries of IPE and deepens the archives on which it might draw. Looking beyond the variations offered by multiple forms of capitalism, we might investigate the multiplicity of non-market practices and hybrid forms for human possibilities now proscribed by a market imaginary. Many of the alternative visions and forms of life that might serve as interlocutors in the dialogue among traditions that Nandy embraces remain inaccessible to political economy. They speak in voices unfamiliar to social scientists and in texts placed in obscure sections of libraries or not archived at all. Often, they respond to questions that we fail to ponder or do not know how to ask. Accessing these visions requires opening oneself to the other both within and beyond the self.

Finally, we want to stress that other scholars also draw on Tordorov, Nandy, and Polanyi to think through the problem of difference in ways that complement and inform our work. Polanyi figures in many accounts that point us beyond the imaginary of development and modernisation (e.g. Blaser 2010; Escobar 1995; various authors in Sachs 1992) or towards alternative economies (Gibson-Graham 2006). In and around IR, Todorov finds a place in Connolly (1991) and Neumann (1999) in exploring the function of the other in constructing boundaries. Nandy appears in Shilliam (2011) as he attempts to think beyond the West in IR and Krishna (1999) in his analysis of postcolonial security. IR scholars who reflect on difference draw on a panoply of additional authors who explore colonial knowledge production, modern conceptions of history, and/or the ethics of self–other relations. A short list includes Bahktin (Guillaume 2011); Derrida and Levinas (Campbell 1998; Edkins 1999); Fanon (Shilliam 2013); Said (Krishna 1999; Neumann 1999); Spivak and Chakrabarty (Hutchings 2008); and the feminist standpoint theory of Sandra Harding (J. A. Tickner 2011; A. B. Tickner 2013).

Also, many feminists in IR foreground how the gendered norms and practices constitute a binary by which the self is masculinised and the other is feminised (J. A. Tickner 1992 and the essays in Peterson 1992 and Grant and Newland 1991 are foundational). In our work, Jessica Benjamin's arguments in *The Bonds of Love* (1988) have figured powerfully. Specifically, we (Inayatullah and Blaney 2004: 11, 44, 53, 73, 158) rely on her account of how the (culturally constructed) spectrum of masculine and feminine characteristics is first separated or 'split' and then apportioned to male and female bodies (1988: 25–32, 62–63). If we have not been sagacious enough to foreground her influence on our thinking, this is so for three reasons. First, Benjamin's social theory works primarily in the psychoanalytic tradition; while she makes powerful claims about the 'macro', she ventures into IR only tangentially. Second, we hesitate to endorse feminisms of various types without first having done our own work on what parts of that vast corpus remain under the influence of the imperial/colonial and what parts overlap with our more postcolonial aspirations (see Mohanty 1997). Benjamin herself worries that she projects almost exclusively from middle-class, heterosexual, two-parent families (Benjamin 1988: footnote page 75, footnote page 104–105). Third, our favoured category is not gender, or class, or race. Rather, we propose that processes of 'Indianising' of others best fit the international/global disorder (Inayatullah and Blaney 2004: ix–x). 'Indianising' highlights the splitting of self and other where others are simultaneously but not identically named as feminine, proletariat, and black/brown. The term 'Indian' travels from continent to continent as a catalysing misnomer – South Asians, the indigenous of the Americas, and the aboriginals of all continents. But it correctly names those it describes as colonised – where 'colonisation' is not just a metaphor (Tuck and Yang 2012).

We might conclude then that the resources for exploring difference within IR are now rich and themselves diverse. Yet, as we saw earlier, IR tends to reproduce the early modern resistance to engaging the other as a resource, instead drawing boundaries that secure the self from the doubts and fears associated with difference. In this way, much of IR preserves its aspiration to construct a singular world politics but at the price of not knowing the world – not knowing itself, the other, and possibilities for remaking the world.

Critical potentials: connected histories, recessive selves, and dialogical criticism

If we follow Nandy, Todorov, and Polanyi, we might unlearn disciplinary habits that immediately separate and oppose self and other and eschew the rewards that reproduce Eurocentric IR. Doing so requires cultivating different disciplinary habits. While Eurocentric accounts in political economy, for example, assume ontologically separable units, we might begin instead by assuming connections and overlaps of self and other and then learn to treat these connections and overlaps as opportunities for learning and resources for political and ethical exploration.

Though too often ignored, we can find IR scholars who reject the Eurocentredness of the discipline by emphasising, as Barkawi and Laffey (2006: 348–352) put it, the 'mutually constitutive character of world politics' – a world of 'relations' more than 'separate objects'. Here, following Todorov, Nandy, and Polanyi, self and other are placed on a footing of equality without assimilating one to the other. This move resists assumptions of a state of original poverty from which some, through exceptional capabilities and efforts, blaze their paths to development, while others lack these capacities, lagging behind and requiring assistance. In this spirit, L.S. Stavrianos (1981) produced a history of the Third World written against the grain of the idea of separate national development. He documents the creation not of separate countries but peripheral and central zones all interconnected and moving via processes of global capital accumulation. These processes don't simply polarise Western Europe (and later North America and Japan) as the centre while simultaneously producing Third World forms as the periphery; both centre and periphery contain elements of the other. With these tools, Stavrianos explains the contemporary rifts and connections between rich and poor within and across regions. And, as emphasised also by Janet Abu-Lughod (1989), the world prior to European exploration, conquest, and hegemony was already interactive and interconnected, though European zones were peripheral to the powerful centres and major commercial empires of the Middle East and East, South, and Southeast Asia. Abu-Lughod (1989) argues that these earlier world systems contributed to later European advance, so that contemporary European dominance cannot be separated from its earlier and continuing connections.

More recently, John Hobson (2004) has intensified the onslaught against Eurocentric IR. He notes that, for the exceptional role of European states to be sustained, IR (and other disciplines) must erase the dynamic activity of regions beyond the West. While paying homage to the earlier work of Abu-Lughod (1989: 305–306), Hobson suggests a more expansive accounting of the 'origins' of the modern West: the nineteenth-century emergence of the West depends on innovations in science and mathematics that it inherits from Arabs; agrarian and industrial advancements borrow from a Chinese ability predating the boom in commercial agriculture and the industrial revolution in Europe; European military, navigational, and commercial technologies are inherited from various parts of the world and then transmitted via networks of trade and conquest dominated by others; and resource transfers, more than institutional innovation, explain spurts in European growth. None of this, Hobson assures us, is meant to deny European contributions in science, industrial technologies, ideas, and social practices, but he refuses the picture of an already stagnant East that the West eclipses based on some internal genius and energy. Rather, Hobson characterises the West as a late-developer. Development or progress is not a Western invention but emerges from a co-construction of West and East, a co-constitution of self and other.

Postcolonial and feminist scholars also try to undo the colonial exclusions of IR, by working to recover the responses of subaltern others (Hutchings 2011; J. A. Tickner 2011). Nandy (1983: 47–63) usefully reminds us, however, that excluded voices might be found as recessive themes within the dominant self, as Gandhi did when he invoked softer, feminine aspects of the British self to resist British colonialism. More generally, Nandy (2002: 4) calls our attention to 'disowned cultures and states of consciousness about which the presently dominant global middle-class culture of knowledge knows nothing'. As we shall see, reimagining the canon of IR involves incorporating dominant and recessive elements of both self and other (see el-Malik in this book).

Our work on Adam Smith applies Nandy's insight in recovering recessive elements to rethink IPE (Blaney and Inayatullah 2010: Chapter 2). Mentioning Smith usually evokes the invisible hand, harmonious markets, and progress towards civilisation, where modern society supersedes all prior stages of human history. It is the savage societies of hunters and gatherers that provide the most common baseline for Smith's comparisons; their limited productive capacities are accompanied by low living standards, brutality, undeveloped institutions, and unrefined moral sentiments. Only with the extension of the division of labour and the spread of commerce does humanity grasp the possibilities of advance beyond this savage stage. How then could we not favour the conditions and perspectives of the most advanced?

Nevertheless, unlike most contemporary acolytes of free markets, Smith also identifies how a modern civilised society fails. In his major and minor works, Smith catalogues (see Blaney and Inayatullah 2010: 46–57) the low living standards of common people, the resulting inequalities that provoke resentment, the moral and physical degradation of workers in factories who are subject to the influence of dangerous demagogues, and the temptation towards empire that favours a narrow elite and damages peoples in other parts of the world. Most strikingly, Smith explores his doubts by employing savage societies as a perspective from which to mark contemporary weaknesses. Factory work appears crippling in its drudgery and narrowness *in comparison with* the savage's more holistic knowledge and greater civic spirit. Similarly, Smith notes the free time for singing and dancing possessed by savages while pointing to long hours worked by common people in modern society to meet their needs. Smith thereby brings forward the social forms of backward peoples that he otherwise relegates to a superseded life. Savages now appear as allies in critical self-reflection and their values appear as a recoverable if recessive part of the self. Readers might rightly be confused at this point as we uncover, not the canonical Smith, but another Smith, the savage Smith.

This savage Smith, who enlists critical standards beyond the modern, seems far from contemporary IPE, but it might remind us of Polanyi's ethnological strategy of drawing connections between resistance to capitalism and other social forms. We should not be surprised that contemporary anthropology similarly utilises findings about hunter-gatherers to speak directly to political economic issues. Most prominent is Marshall Sahlins (1972), who draws on the ethnographic record to demonstrate that many hunting and gathering groups can be seen as affluent, meeting their limited needs with ease. Scarcity appears, then, not as an affliction of pre-modern societies but as a distinctly modern condition resulting from the increasing time and energy required in meeting expanding needs. Smith also understood that the material requirements for social respectability expanded along with the accumulation of wealth. Other ethnographers refine Sahlins' claims, exploring the way certain hunters and gatherers see the environment as abundant, supporting this generalised security of livelihood with social practices that enforce sharing, limit consumption, and proscribe accumulation (see for example, Bird-David 1990; Wiessner 1982). The result of all this is that we might learn from those who have structured their lives around limiting their needs; that neither human happiness nor human freedom is strictly tied to expanding material abundance (Gowdy 1999). We can thereby resist the unacknowledged blackmail of today's capitalists and modernisers who threaten a return to an assumed original poverty if we balk at their recommendations. We can turn our attention instead to issues of inequality and shift social life away from market-driven competitive acquisitiveness towards developing the institutions that support greater sharing.

These examples suggest that temporally or spatially displaced others might be key to dialogical criticism (see Brace this volume). We can explore this idea more fully using explicitly anti-Eurocentric work from within IR. As we have seen, Bull falters precisely where such dialogues might begin: he recognises others' differences but regards them as temporally superseded, not coeval; he cannot therefore allow them a role in reconfiguring international society. Contra Bull, we might locate counter-imperial currents within colonised spaces as *coeval* with the West's modernity, not simply as a late or inferior derivative, and therefore a crucial part of a conversation about the possible futures. Inspired by C.L.R. James' *The Black Jacobins* (1989), IR scholars have recovered voices of the colonised that rework and extend modern ideas of equality and freedom. As examples, IR scholars have turned to thinkers from Francophone Africa, that pit a vision of more egalitarian, non-racist world orders against French colonial ideologies that preserved empire in the name of freedom (Grovogui 2006); or to liberation movement leaders in Portuguese colonies who challenged notions of culture as racialised that justified colonialism in the name of difference (Jones 2011); or perhaps to Caribbean intellectuals' use of the notion of the creole to break down polarisations of self and other that underwrote non-Western inferiority (Munro and Shilliam 2011). As this growing literature suggests, the West holds no monopoly on the meaning of the modern; the spatial other might be central to critical ethical/political reflection on the present and the possibilities for the future.

However, this characterisation of the other in terms of alternative modernities might unnecessarily restrict the scope of critical dialogue. The modern, however variable and layered, does not exhaust the diversity of selves available to us. IR might draw into dialogue others that appear only recessive in relation to modern selves. Shilliam (2013) argues that Caribbean slaves imagined redeeming themselves (and slave owners) via religious practices, quite contrary to conventional histories where abolition comes via the extension of legal rights. For Blaser (2010), indigenous peoples in Paraguay often defy the idea that they have a special place in sustainable development by imagining their role as creatively enacting the eternal relations of human and natural that subvert the notion of development itself. And Kichwa women's formulations of demands for self-rule invoke notions of multiple and overlapping spaces quite foreign to modern notions of sovereignty (Picq 2013). These voices may be harder to hear, since they run counter to modern sensibilities, but, if Nandy is correct that we can locate others as recessive moments of the self, then these voices are not exotic. They may resonate with a persisting sense that modern notions of rights do not exhaust what emancipation might mean; that development seems to turn our relation to nature destructive; that the borders we use to demarcate the possibilities of rule violate other notions of belonging and accountability; that modern international society might draw on the values and visions it claims to have suppressed as key to reimagining its future.

Conclusions

The resources available for a dialogical criticism suggest the promise of a discipline that engages the political and ethical possibilities of difference. Though brief, our account indicates that engaging difference will draw us to critical reflection on key aspects of international society, like sovereignty, and bring old and new voices to key debates about time and space, borders and globalisation. What's more, the problem of difference challenges us to rethink what it means to know international relations.

Further reading and useful weblinks

We feel the students should read Todorov, Nandy, Benjamin, and Polanyi for themselves, since our presentations are all too brief and our reading of Polanyi might be thought contentious. We also encourage reading other key texts that have inspired postcolonial IR and the creative exploration of difference. As much as we value the work of Shilliam, Guillaume and Neumann, we see value in returning directly to Fanon, Said, and James.

Karl Polanyi Institute of Political Economy (www.concordia.ca/research/ polanyi.html) at Concordia University, Montréal, Canada, is dedicated to preserving Polanyi's legacy.

Community Economies Research Network (CERN) and the Community Economies Collective (CEC) (www.communityeconomies.org) work on new visions of economy.

The Disorder of Things (http://thedisorderofthings.com) solicits comments on and around IR.

Bibliography

Abu-Lughod, J.L. (1989) *Before European Hegemony: The World System A.D. 1250–1350*, Oxford: Oxford University.

Ashley, R. (1983) 'Three Modes of Economism', *International Studies Quarterly* 27(4): 463–496.

Barkawi, T. and Laffey, M. (2006) 'The Postcolonial Moment in Security Studies', *Review of International Studies* 32: 329–352.

Benjamin, J. (1988) *The Bonds of Love: Psychoanalysis, Feminism, and the Problem of Domination*, New York: Pantheon.

Bird-David, N. (1990) 'The Giving Environment: Another Perspective on the Economic Systems of Gatherer-Hunters', *Current Anthropology* 31(2): 189–196.

Blaney, D.L. and Inayatullah, N. (2010) *Savage Economics: Wealth, Poverty and the Temporal Walls of Capitalism*, London: Routledge.

Blaser, M. (2010) *Storytelling Globalization from the Chaco and Beyond*, Durham, NC: Duke University.

Bull, H. (1977) *The Anarchical Society: A Study of Order in World Politics*, New York: Columbia University.

Bull, H. (1983) *Justice in International Relations*, Waterloo: University of Waterloo.

Bull, H. (1984) 'Introduction' in H. Bull (ed.), *Intervention in World Politics*, Oxford: Oxford University, pp. 1–4.

Bull, H. and Watson, A. (eds) (1984) *The Expansion of International Society*, Oxford: Oxford University.

Campbell, D. (1998) *National Deconstruction: Violence, Identity, and Justice in Bosnia*, Minneapolis: University of Minnesota.

Cohen, B.J. (2008) *International Political Economy: An Intellectual History*, Princeton, NJ: Princeton University.

Connolly, W.E. (1991) *Identity/Difference: Democratic Negotiations of Political Paradox*, Ithaca, NY: Cornell University.

de Certau, M. (1986) *Heterologies: Discourse on the Other*, Minneapolis: University of Minnesota.

Dunne, T. (2013) 'The English School' in T. Dunne, M. Kurki, and S. Smith (eds), *International Relations Theories: Discipline and Diversity*, Oxford: Oxford University, pp. 132–152.

Dunne, T. and Wheeler, N.J. (eds) (1999) *Human Rights in Global Politics*, Cambridge: Cambridge University.

Edkins, J. (1999) *Poststructuralism and International Relations: Bringing the Political Back In*, Boulder, CO: Lynne Rienner.

Escobar, A. (1995) *Encountering Development: The Making and Unmaking of the Third World*, Princeton, NJ: Princeton University.

Fabian, J. (1983) *Time and the Other: How Anthropology Makes its Object*, New York: Columbia University.

Funkenstein, A. (1986) *Theology and the Scientific Imagination*, Princeton, NJ: Princeton University Press.

Gibson-Graham, J.K. (2006) *Postcapitalist Politics*, Minneapolis: University of Minnesota.

Gowdy, J. (1999) 'Hunter-Gatherers and the Mythology of the Market' in R.B. Lee and R. Daly (eds), *The Cambridge Encyclopedia of Hunters and Gatherers*, Cambridge: Cambridge University, pp. 391–399.

Grant, R. and Newland, K. (eds) (1991) *Gender and International Relations*, Bloomington: Indiana University.

Grovogui, S. (2006) *Beyond Eurocentrism and Anarchy*, New York: Palgrave.

Guillaume, X. (2011) *International Relations and Identity: A Dialogic Approach*, London: Routledge

Hobson, J.M. (2004) *The Eastern Origins of Western Civilization*, Cambridge: Cambridge University.

Hobson, J.M. (2012) *The Eurocentric Conception of World Politics: Western International Theory, 1760–2010*, Cambridge: Cambridge University.

Hodgen, M.T. (1964) *Early Anthropology in the Sixteenth and Seventeenth Centuries*, Philadelphia: University of Pennsylvania.

Hutchings, K. (2008) *Time and World Politics: Thinking the Present*, Manchester: Manchester University Press.

Hutchings, K. (2011) 'Dialogue between Whom? The Role of the West/Non-West Distinction in Promoting Global Dialogue in IR', *Millennium* 39(3): 639–647.

Inayatullah, N. and Blaney, D.L. (1995) 'Realizing Sovereignty', *Review of International Studies* 21(1): 3–20.

Inayatullah, N. and Blaney, D.L. (2004) *International Relations and the Problem of Difference*, New York: Routledge.

James, C.L.R. (1989) *The Black Jacobins: Toussaint L'Ouverture and the San Domingo Revolution*, 2nd edition, New York: Vintage.

Jones, B.G. (2011) 'Anti-Racism and Emancipation in the Thought and Practice of Neto, Cabral, Mondlane and Machel' in R. Shilliam (Ed.), *International Relations and the Non-West*, London: Routledge, pp. 47–63.

Keck, M. and Sikkink, K. (1998) *Activists Across Borders: Activist Networks in International Politics*, Ithaca, NY: Cornell University.

Krishna, S. (1999) *Postcolonial Insecurities: India, Sri Lanka, and the Question of Nationhood*, Minneapolis: University of Minnesota.

Linklater, A. (1998) *The Transformation of Political Community: Ethical Foundations of the Post-Westphalian Era*, Columbia: University of South Carolina.

Mohanty, C.T. (1997) 'Under Western Eyes: Feminist Scholarship and Colonial Discourses' in A. McClintock, A. Mufti, and E. Shohat (Eds), *Dangerous Liasons: Gender, Nation, and Postcolonial Perspectives*, Minneapolis: University of Minnesota, pp. 255–277.

Munro, M. and Shilliam, R. (2011) 'Alternative Sources of Cosmopolitanism: Nationalism, Universalism and Créolité in Francophone Caribbean Thought' in R. Shilliam (ed.), *International Relations and the Non-West*, London: Routledge, pp. 159–177.

Nandy, A. (1983) *The Intimate Enemy: Loss and Recovery Under Colonialism*, New Delhi: Oxford.

Nandy, A. (1987) *Traditions, Tyranny, and Utopias: Essays in the Politics of Awareness*, New Delhi: Oxford.

Nandy, A. (2002) *Time Warps: Silent and Evasive Pasts in Indian Politics and Religion*, New Brunswick, NJ: Rutgers University.

Neumann, I.B. (1999) *Uses of the Other: 'The East' in European Identity Formation*, Minneapolis: University of Minnesota.

Pagden, A. (1982) *The Fall of Natural Man: The American Indian and the Origins of Comparative Ethnology*, Cambridge: Cambridge University.

Peterson, V.S. (ed.) (1992) *Gendered States: Feminist (Re)Visions of International Relations Theory*, Boulder, CO: Lynne Rienner.

Picq, M.L. (2013) 'Indigenous Worlding: Kichwa Women Pluralizing Sovereignty' in A.B. Tickner and D.L. Blaney (eds), *Claiming the International*, London: Routledge, pp. 121–140.

Polanyi, K. (1957 [1944]) *The Great Transformation*, Boston, MA: Beacon.

Polanyi, K. (1968) 'The Economy as an Instituted Process' in G. Dalton (ed.), *Primitive, Archaic, and Modern Economies*, Garden City, NY: Anchor.

Polanyi, K. (1977) *The Livelihood of Man*, New York: Academic.

Sachs, J.D. (2005) *The End of Poverty: Economic Possibilities for Our Time*, New York: Penguin.

Sachs, W. (ed.) (1992) *The Development Dictionary: A Guide to Knowledge as Power*, London: Zed.

Sahlins, M. (1972) *Stone Age Economics*, Chicago, IL: Aldine.

Shilliam, R. (2011) 'The Perilous but Unavoidable Terrain of the Non-West', in R. Shilliam (ed.), *International Relations and the Non-West*, London: Routledge, pp. 12–26.

Shilliam, R. (2013) 'Black Redemption, Not (White) Abolition' in A.B. Tickner and D.L. Blaney (eds), *Claiming the International*, London: Routledge, pp. 141–158.

Stavrianos, L.S. (1981) *Global Rift: The Third World Comes of Age*, New York: William Morrow.

Tickner, A.B. (2013) 'By Way of Conclusion: Forget IR?' in A.B. Tickner and D.L. Blaney (eds), *Claiming the International*, London: Routledge, pp. 214–232.

Tickner, J.A. (1992) *Gender and International Relations: Feminist Perspectives on Achieving Global Security*, New York: Columbia University.

Tickner, J.A. (2011) 'Dealing with Difference: Problems and Possibilities for Dialogue in International Relations', *Millennium: Journal of International Studies* 39(3): 607–618.

Todorov, T. (1984) *The Conquest of America: The Question of the Other*, New York: Harper and Row.

Toulmin, S. (1990) *Cosmopolis: The Hidden Agenda of Modernity*, Chicago, IL: University of Chicago.

Tuck, E. and Yang, K.W. (2012) 'Decolonization is Not a Metaphor', *Decolonization: Indigeneity, Education, & Society* 1(1): 1–40.

Tully, J. (1995) *Strange Multiplicity: Constitutionalism in an Age of Diversity*, Cambridge: Cambridge University.

Walker, R.B.J. (1993) *Inside/Outside: International Relations as Political Theory*, Cambridge: Cambridge University.

White, H. (1972) 'The Forms of Wildness: The Archaeology of an Idea' in E. Dudley and M. Novak (eds), *The Wildman Within: An Image in Western Thought from the Renaissance to Romanticism*, Pittsburgh, PA: University of Pittsburgh, pp. 3–38.

Wiessner, P. (1982) 'Risk, Reciprocity and Social Influence on !Kung San Economics' in E. Leacock and R. Lee (eds), *Politics and History in Band Societies*, Cambridge: Cambridge University, pp. 61–84.

7

GLOBALISATION

V. Spike Peterson

Introduction

The concept of 'globalisation' took hold in academic discourse during the second half of the twentieth century. It referenced a number of interacting socio-cultural, economic, political and technological developments that appeared to erode and/or transcend state/nation boundaries, with perplexing implications for the theory and practice of IR. Defining globalisation was, and remains, controversial: sceptics questioned to what extent and with what effects territorial, national boundaries and state-centric power were actually being superseded (e.g. Hirst and Thompson 2007). Yet adoption of the term has been rapid, and in the twenty-first century references to globalisation are ubiquitous. Youngs and Kofman (2008: xi) suggest that this embrace of the concept is due to 'its relevance as much to individuals as to major institutions, to the ways in which they think about the actions and justifications of their governments, the functioning (or not) of their economies, their work destinies and consumption habits, their concerns about the environment, new and changing migration patterns, and so on'.

In short, talking about globalisation has become commonplace because changes associated with it affect virtually all of us, from intimate relations and everyday activities to political and economic controversies and international affairs. Yet in spite of its pervasive deployment, disagreement continues over the meaning of globalisation and interpretation of its effects. On one hand, making basic sense of globalisation is difficult because the scale and extent of changes associated with it are quantitatively large and challenge our ability to generate comprehensive yet coherent studies. On the other hand, many of the changes are qualitatively 'different': they unsettle ideas and practices that seemed familiar – and often comfortable – and thus challenge us to rethink conventional categories and explanatory frameworks (see Ní Mhurchú in this book). Moreover, all meanings depend on context, and the contexts in which globalisation has currency are especially diverse in disciplinary, epistemological and ideological/political investments. In the social sciences, where positivist and modernist orientations predominate, economic, political and institutional practices tend to be foregrounded, and operations of power are highlighted. In the humanities, where interpretive, historical and post-structuralist orientations predominate, culture, discourse and representational practices are more likely to feature, and globalisation is more often interpreted in terms of media and cultural trends.

Ideologically, it is no surprise that those who appear to benefit, or whose interests appear to benefit from globalisation, tend to regard it positively: for example, as promoting shared norms, enabling economic growth or advancing particular political interests. Others are less sanguine, noting that for all its 'cosmopolitan' and 'unifying' potential, globalisation in the twenty-first century, and as a projection into the future, poses numerous problems: for example, its starkly uneven effects, 'democratic deficits', Anglo-centric tendencies and ideological manipulation.

What seems most obvious and unequivocal is that globalisation since the latter half of the twentieth century constitutes an unprecedented scale of inter-connectedness (due primarily to new technologies), that its implications for people's lives are extensive (few remain untouched by globalising processes) and at the same time, its effects on people's well-being are not homogeneous (inequalities of sex/gender, class, race and national location are pervasive). More obvious still is that globalisation as a concept and practice is singularly key to critically re-imagining the state-centricity of International Relations (IR). In particular, globalisation exposes how the meaning, constitution and effects of borders – conceptual, terri-torial and, especially, statist – are being radically transformed and in ways that require radical rethinking.

The development of information and communication technologies (ICTs) is widely acknowledged as key to the speed and scale of these transformations. I have argued elsewhere (Peterson 2003) that these technologies not only enable the 'global' in globalisation, but transform the world as we 'know' it. The point here is that globalisation involves not only empirically observable changes in scale and scope, but also analytical challenges posed by information technologies and their unprecedented fusion of culture and economy – of virtual and material dimensions. Key to IR and global political economy (GPE), these technologies also enable linked transformations in production processes (how and what work is valued and who does it) and financial markets (how money moves and is valued, and who has it). By intensively and extensively structuring work and wealth, these transforma-tions deeply affect everyday life worldwide. Given the circuits of power and deepening inequalities involved, exploring the critical potential of globalisation is a timely, even urgent, project.

To explore these issues, in this chapter I review definitional debates involving the temporality and spatiality of globalisation processes, and identify various approaches to analysing these complex developments. I introduce a *critical intersec-tional* approach as more adequate for addressing the uneven effects of globalisation manifested especially in inequalities of sex/gender, ethnicity/race, culture, class and national 'difference'. I argue that the critical potential of globalisation is how it compels us to rethink not only territorial (empirical) boundaries, but also and inextricably, conceptual (analytical) boundaries. I explore this rethinking by briefly discussing issues of governance, legitimacy, inequalities, informal work, migration politics and a queering of states/nations, before concluding with suggested directions and future concerns.

Core ideas

Time matters

Lack of agreement on defining globalisation complicates assigning dates to the emergence or *temporal* span of these complex social processes. Mittelman (2000: 18–19) identifies three possible 'starting points' of globalisation. The first dates to the origins of civilisation (early state-making, approximately 5,000 years ago) when diverse peoples came into contact through long-distance trade and conquest. The second dates to the development of capitalism in Western Europe approximately 400–500 years ago. The third dates from the 1970s, when capitalism itself underwent fundamental change in respect to recessionary dynamics, debt dependency, deregulation of capital markets and deterritorialisation.

A 'long view' of globalisation acknowledges that exchange activities, markets and long-distance trade have existed from ancient times, with significant effects on social orders, trans-regional circulation of goods and, perhaps more importantly, ideas. This view aligns with 'world system' advocates (for example, Denemark et al. 2000; Frank 1998; Frank and Gills 1996) who posit a 5,000-year history of capital accumulation and centre–periphery exchange, understood as globalising processes. The critique of Eurocentrism foregrounded by taking a longer and more external-relations-oriented view of capitalism and world history is an important, and under-acknowledged, perspective. Yet even world system accounts ignore heteropatriarchal (merged heteronormative and patriarchal) premises and related structural hierarchies that are key to centralisation and accumulation dynamics that the long view illuminates (Lerner 1986; Peterson 2010c, 2014a).

At odds with the long view are important distinctions made by 'world system' advocates (for example, Amin 1996; Wallerstein 1974). The latter view the 'long sixteenth century' (1450–1640) as a qualitative transformation in which capitalism both commodifies labour power and institutionalises 'ceaseless accumulation', with the effect of subordinating social relations more generally to the economic imperative of pursuing profit. In both of these perspectives the temporality of globalisation has a long yet varying history, and its extent and effects are shaped by exchange relations and political dynamics.

The majority of IR and GPE scholars today, however, focus on globalisation since approximately the 1970s, both as a continuation of capitalist dynamics *and* new trends due to neoliberal policies. This period of globalisation is foregrounded in the present discussion as well, primarily to bring critical attention to twenty-first-century realities and pervasive inequalities. But I also note the decisive importance of ICTs in this, arguably just the most recent, phase of globalisation.

Space matters

Globalisation has also been characterised as *spatial* expansion of transnational practices and cross-cultural interaction. Viewed positively and/or negatively, this spatial expansion is especially legible in the modern era of technological innovations and processes of industrialisation, capitalism and colonisation. Since at least the seventeenth century, economic processes and geopolitical developments established 'globalising' patterns of exploitation and inequalities that variously continue into the twenty-first century. Contemporary geographers remind us that the organisation of space is not simply a feature of but constitutes social relations: in important senses, who we are and how we act is both determined by and determines the 'ordering' of space. Whoever controls the ordering of space – through architecture, city planning, transportation infrastructures and territorial borders – has power over people's lives. In this important sense, 'space' as a concept and practice is itself political.

Since the 1970s, spatial dynamics have been reconstituted by the development of information and communication technologies and their global application. Important here is what the critical scholar David Harvey (1989) characterised as 'time-space compression', which for some analysts marks a qualitatively new era of globalisation, captured by the now familiar metaphor of a 'shrinking world'. At issue is the extent, intensity and accelerating pace of interconnectedness as electronic and wireless transmissions are dematerialised (digitally coded symbols/signals) and deterritorialised (transmitted through frictionless space), with the effect of 'collapsing' temporal and spatial 'distances'. Traditional boundaries and borders that deeply structured social relations no longer have the same meaning or power, as near and far, local and global interact and operationally 'merge' in real time (instantaneous broadcasts, a global audience). This is not to claim the political significance of geography/space is eliminated but that it is reconfigured, as power is concentrated in old and new nodes of networking circuits (Castells 2000).[1] These processes of time-space compression are radically accelerated by the miniaturisation, symbolisation and dematerialisation enabled by ICTs and also encouraged by competitive practices and technocratic commitments promoted by neoliberal capitalism.

In these senses, globalisation shapes and is shaped by the interaction of technological *and* socio-cultural/political/economic developments (see Muller in this book). In the twenty-first century, globalisation clearly disrupts territorial presumptions previously dominant in Economics and IR, and challenges us to rethink how power operates within, across and beyond state borders. In particular, IR's conventional conceptualisations of sovereignty, nationalism, inside–outside and levels of analysis are problematised by transnational/global developments.

Difference matters

Controversies regarding the meaning and effects of globalisation also complicate easy distinctions between dominant and critical understandings of the concept. To suggest some differentiations, I paraphrase six 'approaches' to globalisation identified by Bayliss et al. (2011: 7–8) in the Introduction to their popular IR textbook. *Realists* acknowledge increasing interconnectedness between economies and societies, but deny system-transforming erosion of territoriality or the power politics of competitive nation-states, and maintain the importance of threatened or actual use of force. *Liberals* see globalisation as a long-running transformation in state-centric agency that undermines realist accounts, recognise the system-transforming effects of ICT-generated interconnectedness and favour a metaphor of web-like relations. For *Marxists*, globalisation is neither new nor a transformation of world politics, but simply a Western-led, latest stage of global capitalism that deepens economic inequalities, especially between the core, semi-periphery and periphery. *Constructivists* criticise representations of globalisation as an external force that reduces state agency (permitting elites to deny accountability/responsibility), and they favour using technologies to mould globalisation processes, especially via transnational social movements. For *poststructuralists*, globalisation is less an external 'reality' than a discourse that is itself shaped by a nexus of power/knowledge relations, and to uncover how power is operating requires detailed historical analyses. *Postcolonial* scholars share Marxist claims regarding continuity of exploitative, colonial practices and deepening inequalities, including a silencing of subaltern voices and perpetuation of class and geopolitical domination.

To these, and overlapping some of them, we can identify a *critical intersectional* approach.[2] Even as ICTs enable integration and may enhance cultural homogenisation, the uneven effects of globalisation are manifested in continuing and new structural inequalities of sex/gender, ethnicity/race, culture, class and national 'differences'. Advocates of globalisation avoid theorising the nature and role of oppression in relation to neoliberal policies, and critics typically focus on one or another of these hierarchies. The point here is that theoretical attention to inequalities as a *structural* feature of globalisation, and especially their complex and often unexpected *intersections*, remains underdeveloped. A more adequate approach would entail critical attention to inequalities and would have to address affect and emotion, not least as they shape investments in particular 'differences' and thus shape continuing and new global hierarchies.

Critical potential

Conceptually, the critical potential of globalisation is arguably most significant in calls for *fundamental rethinking* that it engenders. In Mies' words 'questions of conceptualization are questions of power' (Mies 1986: 36). Given the extent, scale and intensity of visible (material) changes in everyday life and larger patterns of human interaction, as well as the less visible disruption of familiar categories and bounded/

boundary concepts that globalisation involves, at stake are not only territorial borders but analytical categories and premises.

Many contemporary social theorists critique the binary logic that prevails in positivist and 'rationalist' epistemologies still favoured in orthodox IR. The point of such critiques is to problematise *essentialised* (ahistorical and reductive) assumptions exemplified in conventional and too-often-taken-for-granted binaries: fact–value, reason–emotion, order–anarchy, peace–war, public–private, political–economic, self–Other, masculine–feminine. Power operates when assuming these binaries because the terms are not equally valorised – the first term is favoured or privileged over its 'opposite', for example, by valuing reason over emotion. Whatever the philosophical debates, actual practices of globalisation reveal the ambiguity, fragility and indeterminacy of categorical distinctions (boundaries) presumed in these binaries. In particular, globalisation indisputably reveals the interplay of politics and economics, the permeability of borders/boundaries and the instability of state-centric power. More effectively perhaps than philosophical arguments, globalisation forces us to realise how untenable and limiting the presumption of static, ahistorical, decontextualised categories is, and how crucial it is to fundamentally rethink IR's conventional starting points.

Governance and legitimacy

First and most familiar are issues of governance, as globalisation undermines categorical claims – and disciplinary premises! – regarding state sovereignty and autonomy. In actuality, states have always competed for and 'shared' power among diverse sources, but globalisation – especially the neoliberal promotion of market forces – has increased the number and power of actors that national governments confront. These multiple and diverse sources of power complicate how we understand and practice state-centric accountability, legitimate authority and political organisation. States now 'share' governing processes with increasing numbers of private, non-governmental actors, variously defined social movements, transnational associations and multilateral agencies. International governmental organisations (IGOs) like the International Monetary Fund and World Trade Organization generate policies that affect the lives of people worldwide, without any institutionalised accountability to those people. Geopolitically powerful states are more likely to influence IGO decision-making, yet even they must negotiate in a field of shifting norms, priorities, institutional practices and power-wielding players. Governance is also troubled when establishing 'ultimate' legislative and jurisdictional authority is no longer 'obvious'. The presumed authority of laws and courts within state boundaries is increasingly complicated by the growth of transnational and international legislative bodies regarding rights, justice, trade and monetary arrangements. Today, the multiplicity of legal and judicial sites worldwide poses difficult questions of 'whose rules rule?'

Governance is inextricable from issues of whose force, or threat of it, is backing up claims to legitimate authority. The complexity of these issues is intensified by information, communication, surveillance and military technologies associated with globalisation and widely deployed by multiple state *and* non-state actors. In many contexts, insecurities proliferate as it is increasingly difficult to determine who 'has' legitimate authority, how they got it, how they use it and to whom they are accountable. Examples include the rights and privacy issues of data mining and internet surveillance, and the more directly violent threats posed by drone warfare and ever more 'secretive', less detectable modalities of destruction. Threats and insecurities take many forms. Consider how ICTs not only 'collapse' time and space, but also facilitate cross-border flows – of unregulated financial assets, 'radical ideas', illicit goods, diseases, pests and pollutants. The effects may entail rewards for some and tremendous risks to others. Risks and insecurities are arguably most visible in the ways neoliberal globalisation deepens inequalities that constitute lives of poverty for too many, differentiate more and less environmentally vulnerable populations and fuel resentments that may materialise in violent conflicts.

This wide-ranging and no doubt expanding array of governance quandaries presents daunting but unavoidable challenges. Some imagine that awareness of heightened interdependence and progressive use of ICTs can promote global civil society or cosmopolitan democracy (Held 1995). Yet realising these objectives is hampered by the stark reality of deepening inequalities and the effects of envy and resentment that attend them.

Inequalities and informal work

The argument underpinning these claims is that *neoliberal* globalisation has systemically 'restructured' GPE and exacerbated inequalities. Critics argue that decades of neoliberal policies (liberalisation, deregulation, privatisation) have reduced most states' capacity for and/or commitment to public welfare provisioning, while these same policies have 'flexibilised' production processes (downsizing, subcontracting), eroded the power of labour, variously exacerbated un- and under-employment, and deepened inequalities within and between nations. Flexibilisation[3] is key and both *feminises* employment (more women working for income and a deterioration of labour conditions [Peterson 2003]) and shifts production away from formal (secure, reliable, regulated) employment opportunities. Deteriorating economic conditions increase the vulnerability of the global majority; facing limited options, most take whatever work they can find. The erosion of labour power exacerbates a decline in household income that 'pushes' more people into informal (precarious, unregulated) work,[4] while flexibilisation reduces tax revenues, which reduces resources for welfare provisioning, and spurs informal work to compensate in part for this loss. Flexibilisation thus fuels informalisation, and both involve feminisation. These developments – as well as recent crises – have dramatically increased both inequalities (APSA 2008; Cornia 2004) and the scale and significance of informal activities (Barta 2009; Chant and Pedwell 2008). Concluding a recent and exceptionally comprehensive survey of the literature, Godfrey (2011: 270) states that 'informal economic arrangements represent a dominant form of exchange for many of the world's peoples and, depending on how one defines informality, may be the dominant model of economic organization'.

Dominant studies of global political economy (e.g. Cohn 2012; Oatley 2012), focus on formal (official, recorded, taxed, regulated) activities that generate forms of monetary and presumably market-based compensation. But this focus excludes far too much. First, it excludes the socially necessary but unpaid domestic labour that ensures both family/household survival and the intergenerational reproduction of appropriately socialised individuals (citizens, workers), upon which state-centric continuity depends. Second, it conventionally excludes illicit economic activities, which are increasingly significant both because of their global scale and value, and their clandestine nature, with its potential for funding or fueling illegal, even war-making, activities. Third, a narrow focus on formal, market-based production marginalises myriad forms of 'work' (subsistence, street vending, peasant farming) that constitute the primary source of income in the global South, shape the resource-pooling strategies of households worldwide and are an increasingly significant aspect of economic life in the global North.

Informal work is thus much more important – socio-culturally, economically and politically – than is generally acknowledged. It reveals not only how economic and political arrangements are inextricable, but also how these arrangements are shaped by and affect the economic life of households, which directly and indirectly shapes the lives of *all* workers and indeed non-workers worldwide. Most visible through even conventional lenses is the dramatic expansion of informal work already noted. While informal work may appeal to and be rewarding for some individuals, the vast majority of informal labour is precarious and poorly paid. In effect it constitutes devalorised (feminised) work, and structural hierarchies of gender, ethnicity/race, class and nation shape which devalorised (feminised) workers are most likely to be doing it: poor people, ethnic minorities, women, youth, migrants, the urban 'underclass', the global South. The point here is that theorising informal work invites, indeed requires, analyses that can address how 'differences' are crosscutting, that is, intersecting, and such analyses are essential for critically re-imagining states, IR and globalisation (see Blaney and Inayatullah in this book).

Informalisation that is less visible but growing in significance reveals disturbing linkages between precarious – uncertain, unreliable, risky – forms of work and widely experienced conditions of *insecurity*. The latter include, but are not limited to, conditions of direct and indirect (structural) violence that are conventionally understood in political, military and geopolitical terms. For example, economic informalisation is structurally linked to *political* informalisation, which is a feature of states weakened by economic restructuring but is especially problematic in the context of increasingly numerous 'civil wars', or what Mary Kaldor characterises as 'new wars' (Kaldor 2001). In conflict zones there are powerful incentives for seeking, and multiple opportunities for securing, resources and profits through both licit and illicit informal activities and unregulated financial transfers. States weakened by neoliberal policies and/or protracted conflict are less able – and sometimes insufficiently motivated – to impose and maintain law and order, even when peace is proclaimed. Without effective public control and authority, post-conflict reconstruction may be continually undermined by established and effective networks of private – and often illicit – resource provision. These points suggest the importance of analysing politics and economics as inextricable, and addressing the *systemic* aspect of informality which links household reproduction, economic processes, state politics, 'governance gaps' and global insecurities (Peterson 2010b).

Informal work has additional significance for feminist and other critical approaches to the study of political economy. First, the *systemic* aspect of informalisation reveals how political economy is gendered: informality cuts across and links the conditions and activities of unpaid domestic-caring labour (assigned primarily to women and neglected in most economic theory) with the conditions and monetised valorisation of formal market activities (focused on in economic theory and increasingly feminised). Second, how symbolic devalorisation of feminised work and workers is 'translated' into material devalorisation is especially visible through a lens on informalisation. Power operates in informalisation through intersections of feminised, racialised 'work', histories of exploitative colonisation, geopolitical hierarchies and global migration flows (ibid.). Inequalities feature here by virtue of historical, structural hierarchies shaping whose vulnerability renders them subject to economic migration, what education and training they have received, what forms of relatively devalorised labour they can access and to what extent 'old' hierarchies and identity politics are reproduced in new contexts. In effect, informalisation and its inequalities both 'produce' economic migrations, and informal work is a 'product' of migrations insofar as it constitutes a primary mode of income generation, especially for recent migrants.

Inequalities and migration politics

The global 'care economy' reveals intersecting gender, ethnicity/race and class dynamics in several global trends, especially the feminisation of employment and labour migration. Women now constitute one-half of those migrating internationally, and increasingly do so as the primary income earner (Piper 2006). Women in the global South typically leave deteriorating economic conditions to seek more lucrative work in the global North where a 'care deficit' exists (Ehrenreich and Hochschild 2002). The latter reflects increasing needs for (privatised) care-giving and health services (as ageing populations entail more medical attention and long-term care), at the same time as neoliberalised states reduce public spending in support of social services. In effect, when women of relative privilege gain formal employment in the 'productive' economy, this generates informalised, reproductive labour for 'Other' women who are positioned less favourably in terms of ethnicity/race and class, and in the global domestic and care economy, less favourably in terms of national location.

Moreover, the global care economy is only part of larger migration politics that are shaped by and challenge state-centricity. Between-nation inequalities, and global awareness of them, are powerful migration motivators, and since the 1980s income gaps between rich and poor countries have become both much more extreme and more predictive of one's life chances (Milanovic 2012). While inequalities induce migration pressures, migration itself is marked by new patterns of experience and identification that have implications for state-centrism (Portes and DeWind 2007). First, ICTs are significant for altering virtually every aspect of im/migration processes – not least for making new and sustaining old networks, and facilitating remittance flows that shift responsibility for economic development onto those who migrate, rather than those who benefit most from globally uneven development. Second, globalisation is significant for reconfiguring family/household formations – not least for expanding the presence of 'transnational (global) households' that 'remodel' traditional arrangements and arguably involve as much as one-sixth of the world's population[5] (Peterson 2010a, 2014b). In short, the who and how of migration are changing, and also the experience of migrants in relation to states.

In particular, studies of migration document meaningful shifts in subjective experience. For example, migrants report more ease transitioning to, living in and culturally identifying with more than one nation. Those comfortable with new or even multiple identities are more likely to experience a corollary sense of agency, which in turn may be expressed in political activism at, or affecting, multiple sites (see Shindo in this book). These fluid social spaces, cultural hybridities and plural allegiances variously trouble nationally bounded identity and citizenship claims. They also suggest an unprecedented increase in the number of *non*-migrants variously affected or 'touched' by migration processes, especially when we include vast numbers involved in transnational householding. Moreover, even as inequalities increase migration pressures, the contentious arena of immigration policies presents formidable challenges for state-centric policy making, as well as governance issues of 'securing borders'.

Queering states

I turn finally to the critical potential of feminist and queer studies for rethinking state-centricity. Feminists have long and variously both criticised the state as a resiliently patriarchal institution and considered how the power of the (liberal) state might be deployed in support of women's equality. Queer studies have focused on the state's legislative, medical and policing power, exercised for the most part at the expense of LGBT recognition, rights and protection from homophobic violence. Here my focus is the heteropatriarchal principles of states, specifically, how they constitute family forms and shape transmission of property and membership claims in ways that warrant much more critical attention.

The central claim is that familiar sex and gender binaries and patriarchal relations are not naturally 'given' (without history, prepolitical) but constituted and normalised in contingent, historical processes of early state formation (AKA the 'rise of civilisation').[6] Once normalised, gender ideologies and patriarchal principles persisted – often enhanced by the spread of monotheistic religions – and were taken as 'given' in the context of modern European state-making, where they underpinned the constitution of 'family/household' units as essential socio-economic building blocks for consolidating and sustaining sovereign states. Whereas liberal theorists of the time rejected the principle of inherited *monarchical* rule, they retained the principle of *patriarchal* rule in both public and private domains. What matters here is that heteropatriarchal principles determine not only the transmission of property claims (shaping, and generally reproducing, inequalities of gender, sexuality and class), but also the transmission of membership/citizenship claims (shaping access to rights within states and inequalities between states). In addition, birthright citizenship – increasingly the norm worldwide – is inextricable from the production of ethnic and racial categorisations and the hierarchical relations they enable (Stevens 1999, 2010).

The implication of this argument is that heteropatriarchal norms – codified in marriage, family and other laws ordering inheritance of property and citizenship claims – are key to the production and continuity of intersecting structural inequalities. In other words, these norms not only produce inequalities of gender and sexuality, but also of class, race and national location. Consider, for example, that citizenship rules simultaneously establish the in/exclusions of membership and, in effect, operationalise the in/exclusions of state *boundaries*. The troubling issue here is that the state's use of (birthright, inherited) citizenship claims to control cross-border mobility of individuals structurally *precludes* the reduction of inequalities that labour migration would actualise; hence exacerbating between-nation inequalities, while increasing immigration pressure (Milanovic 2012).

These norms are historically constructed, and in important ways are currently deconstructed by globalising dynamics. On one hand, feminist and queer theory/ practice criticises and resists the politics of gender hierarchy and heteronormativity, not least the exclusions of conventional marriage and family law. On the other hand, the globalising effects of neoliberal capitalism – including demographic and socio-cultural trends – are transforming family/household formations and their hetero-patriarchal norms, not least in transnational households that affect vast numbers of people, with multiplying implications for sending and receiving countries. In sum, globalisation is visibly changing people's lives 'from the bottom up' as well as 'from the global downward' – better stated, there are no discrete levels or unidirectional causes. Globalisation exposes the constructedness, hence, fluidity, instability and indeterminacy of sex as well as states. This presents numerous quandaries for IR and social theory/practice more generally.

Connections and conclusions

Given the extent and array of changes and challenges to state-centricity posed by globalisation, the range of scholars engaging the concept is extensive. Points raised above draw from multiple disciplines and particularly the work of critical, feminist and postcolonial scholars ('feminist IR' sources are now far too numerous to specify!): for example, Isabella Bakker and Nancy Folbre on feminist economics; Lourdes Beneria and Shirin Rai on social reproduction; Geeta Chowdhry, Chandra Talpade Mohanty, Aihwa Ong and Gayatri Spivak on postcolonial studies; Nira Yuval-Davis and Jacqueline Stevens on citizenship and nationalism; and David Harvey, Naomi Klein, Mark Rupert, Saskia Sassen, Jan Aarte Scholte and Immanuel Wallerstein on critical approaches to neoliberal globalisation.

Given the centrality of globalisation processes to changes in how we think about, imagine and practice state-centricity, the points raised above engage most of the concepts addressed in this book. This is most obvious regarding chapters featuring borders, citizenship, difference, power, sovereignty, space, technology and theory. Relationships among these concepts are especially visible when we examine linkages among households ('personal', family relations), markets (economic relations) and states (political, legal and militarised relations), and how these are being shaped by, and in turn shaping, globalising processes. A second confluence of related topics involves intersections of sex/gender, race, class and national location, and theoretical developments indicating that 'taking critiques of sex/gender seriously' (Peterson 2010c) is key to more adequate analyses, and potential amelioration, of the many intersecting inequalities that already harm arguably the majority of the planet, and ultimately pose perilous futures for all of us.

Notes

1 First, the resources – material infrastructure, intellectual capital, education and training required for advanced technologies – are unevenly distributed, managed and controlled, which shapes who the key players are and whose rules dominate in the 'virtual economy' (Peterson 2003). Second, what and whose information, images and ideologies circulate is shaped by power differentials among, and the selective priorities of, media and marketing decision makers.

2 Intersectionality signifies 'the complex, irreducible, varied, and variable effects which ensue when multiple axis of differentiation – economic, political, cultural, psychic, subjective and experiential – intersect in historically specific contexts' (Brah and Phoenix 2004: 76).

3 Flexibilisation refers to shifts in production processes away from large, integrated factory work sites, unionised workers, and mass production of standardised consumer goods to spatially dispersed (global) production networks, increasingly casualised (temporary and part-time) and informalised workers, and small batch, 'just-in-time' procurement and production.

4 Informal activities, informality and informalisation share a reference to *work* that falls outside formal (regulated, taxed) economic arrangements. Activities range from domestic care work, subsistence, street vending, seasonal harvesting and home-based production, to micro-enterprises, tax evasion and trafficking in drugs and arms; they occur in urban and rural locales, in industrialised, transitional and developing countries, and in household, corporate and government domains. And their effects are felt at all levels, as shifts in divisions of labour alter roles, subjectivities and power relations.

5 Households are the foundations of socio-economic systems and crucial sites for analysing continuity *and* change in social orders. They are primary sites of the processes of (intergenerational) social reproduction involving multiple life-cycle 'stages' – pursuing marriage/partnership, earning income, securing childcare, eldercare, healthcare and education, acquiring domestic 'help,' relocating for retirement – and increasingly occur across

national boundaries. Douglass (2010) multiplies the total number of migrants (214 million in 2013) by four or five non-migrating household members to estimate numbers of people (approximating 1 billion in 2013) engaged in global households.

6 For argumentation developed at length and extensive references in support of claims in this final section, see Peterson (2010c, 2013, 2014a, 2014b).

Further reading and useful projects

Readings

Appelbaum, R.P. and Robinson, W.I. (eds) (2005) *Critical Globalisation Studies*, New York: Routledge.

Barker, D.K. and Feiner, S.F. (2004) *Liberating Economics: Feminist Perspectives on Families, Work, and Globalisation*, Ann Arbor: University of Michigan Press.

Cornia, G.A. (ed.) (2004) *Inequality, Growth, and Poverty in an Era of Liberalization and Globalisation*, Oxford: Oxford University Press.

Krishna, S. (2008) *Globalisation and Postcolonialism: Hegemony and Resistance in the Twenty-first Century*, Lanham, MD: Rowman and Littlefield.

Marchand, M.H. and Runyan, A.S. (eds) (2011) *Gender and Global Restructuring: Sightings, Sites and Resistances*, 2nd edition, London: Routledge.

Runyan, A.S. and Peterson, V.S. (2014) *Global Gender Issues in the New Millennium*, 4th edition, Boulder, CO: Westview.

Rupert, M. and Solomon, M.S. (2006) *Globalisation and International Political Economy: The Politics of Alternative Futures*, Lanham, MD: Rowman and Littlefield.

Scholte, J.A. (2005) *Globalisation: A Critical Introduction*, 2nd Edition, Hampshire: Palgrave Macmillan.

Shields, S., Bruff, I. and Macartney, H. (eds) (2011) *Critical International Political Economy: Dialogue, Debate and Dissensus*, London: Palgrave.

Tabak, F. and Crichlow, M.A. (eds) (2000) *Informalization: Process and Structure*, Baltimore, MD and London: The Johns Hopkins University Press.

Zein-Elabdin, E.O. and Charusheela, S. (eds) (2004) *Postcolonialism Meets Economics*, London and New York: Routledge.

Projects

The University of California Atlas of Inequality combines GIS (Geographic Information System) and database technology with internet multi-media components to provide online resources that enable users to examine global change. Available at http://ucatlas.ucsc.edu/index.php.

The International Labour Organization (ILO) is the UN agency that brings together governments, employers and workers of its member states in common action to promote better labour conditions throughout the world. For their projects and research specific to informal work, see their website www.ilo.org.

Operating over a decade, the Sarai programme at the Center for the Study of Developing Societies (CSDS) provides a platform for interpreting and researching contemporary transformations, especially with regard to the interface between information technology, society and culture. See the Cybermohalla Project at http://sarai.net/projects.

Feminists working in IR have probed endless variations of what it might mean to 'take gender seriously' in the central areas of inquiry associated with the discipline – states, security, global political economy – and invariably extending well beyond it. Feminists have documented and theorised linkages between intimate and international (in)security, especially through critiques of masculinist privilege operating throughout the world (dis)order. See the website at www.genderandsecurity.org to appreciate the range of issues emerging from the 'gender and security' inquiries.

Bibliography

Amin, S. (1996) 'The Ancient World-System Versus the Modern Capitalist World-System', in A.G. Frank and B.K. Gills (eds), *The World System: Five Hundred Years or Five Thousand?* London: Routledge, pp. 247–277.

APSA (American Political Science Association) (2008) *The Persistent Problem: Inequality, Difference, and the Challenge of Development. Report of the Task Force on Difference, Inequality, and Developing Societies.* July. Available at: www.apsanet.org/Portals/54/files/Publications/TF_Persistent_Problem_Inequality_2008.pdf, accessed 18 March 2010.

Barta, P. (2009) 'The Rise of the Underground', *Wall Street Journal* March 14: Global Economics Section, W1.

Bayliss, J., Smith, S. and Owens, P. (eds) (2011) *The Globalization of World Politics: An Introduction to International Relations*, 5th edition, Oxford: Oxford University Press.

Brah, A. and Phoenix, A. (2004) 'Ain't I A Woman? Revisiting Intersectionality', *Journal of International Women's Studies* 5(3) (May): 75–86.

Castells, M. (2000) *The Information Age*, Vol. 1, *The Rise of the Network Society*, 2nd edition, Oxford: Blackwell.

Chant, S. and Pedwell, C. (2008) *Women, Gender and the Informal Economy: An Assessment of ILO Research and Suggested Ways Forward*, Geneva: ILO.

Cohn, T.H. (2012) *Global Political Economy*, 6th edition, Boston, MA: Longman.

Cornia, G.A. (ed.) (2004) *Inequality, Growth, and Poverty in an Era of Liberalization and Globalization*, Oxford: Oxford University Press.

Denemark, R.A., Friedman, J., Gills, B.K., and Modelski, G. (eds) (2000) *World System History: The Social Science of Long-Term Change*, London: Routledge.

Douglass, M. (2010) 'Globalizing the Household in East Asia', *Whitehead Journal of Diplomacy and International Relations* 11(1) (Winter/Spring): 63–77.

Ehrenreich, B. and Hochschild, A.R. (eds) (2002) *Global Woman*, New York: Metropolitan Books.

Frank, A.G. (1998) *Reorient: Global Economy in the Asian Age*, Berkeley: University of California Press.

Frank, A.G. and Gills, B.K. (1996) 'The 5,000-Year Old System', in A.G. Frank and B.K. Gills (eds), *The World System: Five Hundred Years or Five Thousand?* London: Routledge, pp. 3–55.

Godfrey, P.C. (2011) 'Toward a Theory of the Informal Economy', *The Academy of Management Annals* 5(1): 231–277.

Harvey, D. (1989) *The Condition of Postmodernity*, Oxford: Basil Blackwell.

Held, David. (1995) *Democracy and the Global Order: From the Modern State to Cosmopolitan Governance*, Cambridge: Polity Press.

Hirst, P. and Thompson, G. (2007) *Globalization in Question*, 3rd edition, Cambridge: Polity Press.

Kaldor, M. (2001) *New and Old Wars: Organized Violence in a Global Era*, Stanford, CA: Stanford University Press.

Lerner, G. (1986) *The Creation of Patriarchy*, New York: Oxford University Press.

Mies, M. (1986) *Patriarchy and Accumulation on a World Scale: Women and the International Division of Labor*, London: Zed Books.

Milanovic, B. (2012) 'Evolution of Global Inequality', *Global Policy* 3(2) (May): 125–134.

Mittelman, J.H. (2000) *The Globalization Syndrome: Transformation and Resistance*, Princeton, NJ: Princeton University Press.

Oatley, T. (2012) *International Political Economy*, 5th edition, Boston, MA: Longman.

Peterson, V.S. (2003) *A Critical Rewriting of Global Political Economy: Integrating Reproductive, Productive, and Virtual Economies*, London: Routledge.

Peterson, V.S. (2010a) 'Global Householding Amid Global Crises', *Politics and Gender* 6(2): 271–281.

Peterson, V.S. (2010b) 'Informalization, Inequalities and Global Insecurities', *International Studies Review* 12(2): 244–270.

Peterson, V.S. (2010c) 'A Long View of Globalization and Crisis', *Globalizations* 7(1) (March): 187–202.

Peterson, V.S. (2013) 'The Intended and Unintended Queering of States/Nations', *Studies in Ethnicity and Nationalism* 13(1) (April): 57–68.

Peterson, V.S. (2014a) 'Sex Matters: A Queer History of Hierarchies', *International Feminist Journal of Politics* 16(3): 389–409.

Peterson, V.S. (2014b) 'Family Matters: How Queering the Intimate Queers the International', *International Studies Review* 16(4): 604–608.

Piper, N. (2006) 'Gendering the Politics of Migration', *IMR* 40(1) (Spring): 133–164.

Portes, A. and DeWind, J. (eds) (2007) *Rethinking Migration*, New York: Berghahn Books.

Stevens, J. (1999) *Reproducing the State*, Princeton, NJ: Princeton University Press.

Stevens, J. (2010) *States Without Nations*, New York: Columbia University Press.

Wallerstein, I. (1974) *The Modern World-System* I, New York: Academic Press.

Youngs, G. and Kofman, E. (2008) 'Preface', in E. Kofman and G. Youngs (eds), *Globalization: Theory and Practice*, 3rd edition, London and New York: Continuum, pp. xi–xii.

8

KNOWLEDGE PRACTICE

Aoileann Ní Mhurchú

> To think (rather than to seek to explain) ... is to invent and apply conceptual frames and create juxtapositions that disrupt and/or render historically contingent accepted knowledge ... to unbind what is ordinarily presumed to belong together and thereby challenge institutionalized ways of reproducing and understanding phenomena.
>
> *(Shapiro 2013: xiv)*

> What is questioned is the way in which knowledge circulates and functions, its relations to power. In short, the *régime du savoir*.
>
> *(Foucault 1982: 212)*

Introduction

One key way of understanding knowledge practice (the relationship between knowledge and practice) within International Relations has been to emphasise the idea of accumulating knowledge – about ourselves and about the world – through increasingly nuanced forms of practice – from measurement to observation and reflection. Here the world and our place in the world are understood as knowable (if somewhat incompletely) through key concepts such as statehood, nationality, citizenship, individuality, humanity and sovereignty. What is explored and focused upon is how 'we' – as individuals and groups of individuals – can live more harmoniously, more peacefully, more democratically in 'the world', which is made up of sub-national, national and supra-national communities.

However the idea of knowledge practice has also been linked to the way in which knowledge (of ourselves and the world) is a result of different practices of knowing the world and of being subjects *in* the world. In contrast to the former understanding, here the emphasis is no longer on how we – as pre-existing individuals, citizens, humans or states – act in the world and come to know the world. Instead knowledge practice from this latter perspective is understood as a process of acting politically: of developing different interpretations of the social order (the world) and our role (as subjects) in this *through* ideas such as 'individuality', 'citizenship', 'statehood', 'humanity', 'sovereignty', 'Western', and so on. This approach is subversive of state centricity because it eschews the idea that we must start from a centralised source of power in key concepts in order to inquire into politics but instead links 'politics' to debate, discussion and rethinking itself (Edkins 1999). Such an approach emphasises the importance of recognising the value in disrupting what we 'know', as Shapiro and Foucault note above, and thus where we presume 'politics' lies. This approach is hugely influenced in IR by broader feminist, postmodern and postcolonial studies, which have developed around interrogating dominant practices of 'knowledge'. It is reinvigorated by the changing nature of the world as we 'know' it, due to processes of globalisation and shifting practices of technology, governance, mobility, community and control (see Agnew, Brace, Muller, Peterson and Vaughan-Williams in this book).

This chapter will explore what is involved in this latter understanding of knowledge practice. It will first discuss the nature of this understanding – which is based on refusing to start with key political concepts to explain the world and which instead seeks to unpack and investigate key political concepts themselves. The chapter then moves on to focus on three core approaches within this critical knowledge practice: problematisation, disorientation, and questioning of a necessary way forward. As indicated by Foucault in the quote above, this critical approach involves a shift away from asking 'how do we know that what we know is true?' (the epistemological question of truth) and thus away from focusing on general ideas of truth. Instead it asks 'how is our understanding of ourselves and of the world *implicated* in what is taken to be knowledge?'

Grammars of inquiry

One of the key ways in which knowledge is practised within International Relations as a discipline, and more generally within the social sciences, is by focusing on particular concepts such as democracy, global justice, humanitarian intervention, citizenship, or gender and asking questions about these. For example, to ask questions such as, 'do current citizenship regimes help reduce or merely exacerbate global justice?'; 'how democratic are international institutions such as the UN or the EU?'; 'what responsibility do we have to strangers?'; 'what is the relationship between the role of women in international institutions and gendered inequality?'. The emphasis here is on using key political concepts as starting points in order to build upon existing knowledge of the world: to explain, analyse and understand better existing ideas of how the world is made up of individuals – understood as men and women, citizens and strangers, us and them – and groups of individuals – including nation-states, ethnic and national groups, non-governmental organisations and trans-national as well as trans-regional groups.

Despite the nuance with which these key political terms are engaged, the emphasis remains on generating and testing explanations about the world within already acknowledged and taken-for-granted frameworks – what Shapiro calls 'grammars of inquiry' (2013: 3–8). Examples of such grammars of inquiry include dualisms such as particularism versus universalism; national relations versus international relations; citizenship (nationalism) versus non-citizenship (common humanity). We can take the example of the book *Saving Strangers: Humanitarianism in International Society* by Nicholas Wheeler (2002). This book explores how humanitiarian intervention can be justified even in the face of absolute state sovereignty as a norm of the international system. In doing so, this book assumes that political possibility is always a trade-off between the duties which states have to citizens within their borders (inside) *or* to strangers beyond their borders (outside). It does so by taking as its starting point the idea that state intervention is normally reserved by states for its own citizen members: those already living within a nation-state. Based on this understanding, it explores then how interventions beyond the borders of a state are being considered when a high threshold of unspeakable violence to non-citizens ('strangers') elsewhere takes place despite the accepted norm of non-intervention within the international system.

What is important to note is that 'citizenship' is taken here as that which explains something rather than something that needs explaining. It explains the responsibility which states have to those within their borders; what is discussed then is the idea that this is changing because states are also recognising responsibility to those outside of borders who are non-citizens. The emphasis, as such, remains on developing further our existing general understandings (knowledge) about the world by exploring how this operates in terms of a (an evolving) relationship between citizenship inside the state versus non-citizenship outside the state. This type of work can be contrasted, however, with that of authors who refuse to start with key concepts under the presumption that these explain the world, but instead who make these key concepts their focus.

In his work, for example, Engin Isin (2002) does not take the concept of citizenship as his starting point nor does he presume the link between being a citizen and being a national; instead citizenship *is* the focus of his study. Isin does not discuss how citizenship can be used to explain and thereby further analyse and understand existing knowledge about the world. Instead he considers how citizenship has come to be understood in a particular way, linked to nationality, which has been (and is) part of generating knowledge about the world. Put simply, Isin refuses to take for granted any common sense understanding about citizenship such as the association of citizenship with a necessary accumulative (social, political and economic) inclusion over time and the juxtaposition between citizenship (belonging) and non-citizenship (strangerhood). Rather, he posits 'citizenship' *as* a site of struggle over broader meanings of political identity and belonging. He explores, for example, how citizenship has been produced as a process of inclusions and exclusions linked to struggles by slaves, Jews, craftsmen, tradesmen, women, prostitutes, vagabonds, working classes, plebeians and aborigines to produce different types of belonging. Focusing on these moments of instability which underlie how this concept has been drawn and re-drawn, Isin explores an alternative understanding of citizenship which is produced *through* strangerhood, otherness and outsiderness rather than against it.

Doing so, Isin makes 'citizenship' the outcome of his investigation rather than its starting point. He questions the way in which citizenship has been 'coded' (Shapiro 2013: xii) through comparisons between particularism and universalism, nationhood and strangerhood, the national and the international, inclusion and exclusion, community and non-belonging. He explores how citizenship is made sense of through these binaries. In other words, his work highlights the link between the idea of citizenship and what is produced by this idea. That is, citizenship produces a particular image of identity and belonging which has an effect on how we understand the world (as made up of national and international spaces, forms of belonging and non-belonging, etc.) and our role (as strangers or as nationals, as included people or excluded people, as citizens or as migrants) in the world. Doing so, it helps to begin to link 'citizenship' to 'a thoroughly heterogeneous ensemble consisting of discourses, institutions, architectural forms, regulatory decisions, laws, administrative measures, scientific statements, philosophical, moral and philanthropic propositions – in short, the said as much as the unsaid' (Foucault 1980: 196). Isin's work highlights the way in which citizenship is being contested, rethought and experienced in many different ways through gaps, silences and fissures within various parts of an ensemble (for other examples, see Bosniak 2006; McNevin 2011; Ní Mhurchú 2014; Nyers and Rygiel 2012).

We can say that in the type of approach that Isin's work represents, in contrast to that of the type of approach that Wheeler's work represents, attention is drawn to the question of *how* we have come to know what we know – in terms of distinctions between nationalism and internationalism, citizenship and strangerhood, universalism and particularism. It investigates the limitations of this way of thinking – in particular how and where it is contested, challenged, rethought or fails to manifest; it does this rather than merely amending, providing nuance and developing more sophisticated understandings about how we have come to know the world *in* these terms. (See also, for example, Balibar [2012] on 'community'; Closs Stephens [2013] on 'nationalism'; Squire [2011] on 'mobility'.)

This critical approach to knowledge practice can be linked to a neo-Kantian philosophy (Shapiro 2013). The Enlightenment saw a shift towards objective reality, prioritising appearance, passive perception and observation instead of perception, religion and spirituality. It was Kantian philosophy which allowed for a return to experience with an emphasis on the conditions of possibility for something to appear. It re-emphasised a productive mode of consciousness: intuition, senses and (un)consciousness. It did so however by privileging the question of common sense: a sense which is common to all based on the reasoning human mind. As Shapiro (2013) points out, unlike Kantian philosophy, neo-Kantian philosophy,

exemplified in the work of people like Michel Foucault (or Deleuze and Rancière), emphasises dissensus and discord: an attitude of permanent critique.[1] The
point is that Kantian-inspired (phenomenological) understanding of knowledge
practice seeks to explore the subjective nature of the world – senses, perception,
emotion and unconsciousness – in the same way as we might study the objective
nature of the world, that is, through a concern with existing objects of knowledge
such as the individual, democracy, nation-states, etc. Whereas, a neo-Kantian
approach emphasises *social relations*: that is, the historical context of problems as a
starting point for knowledge practice. Rather than a concern with relationships
among existing objects of knowledge, '[i]t encourages inquiry into the forces
that have brought such objects and their interrelations to one's attention' (Shapiro
2013: 6).

The emphasis here is not on developing knowledge about ourselves and about
the world as already made up of states, citizens, foreigners, the national and the
international through increasingly nuanced forms of practice – observation, reflection
and/or measurement – but on exploring the way in which knowledge (of ourselves and the world) in terms of concepts such as 'state', 'citizen', 'foreigner' and
'humanity' is a result of different ways of positioning these terms – for example, of
seeing citizenship as synonymous with statehood and of understanding humanity as that
which transcends statehood. The way we study the world, in other words, is linked in
such an approach to how we *understand* the world. This understanding is recognised to
have implications for how we see the types of subjects and events which the world
can be made up of (see Moulin in this book). As discussed by Aradau and Huysmans (2014), this is to link questions about knowledge and politics to method –
understood as devices that enact worlds and acts that disrupt particular worlds – as
well as to ontology, epistemology and theory. What is refused from such a perspective which emphasises the productive nature of knowledge is 'the notion that
method is a set of pre-given, neutral techniques that can be applied to diverse
objects without fundamentally altering the ways in which they are constructed and
understood' (Mezzadra and Neilson 2012: 66). Instead, it involves for example
negotiating/recognising the different kinds of knowledges that are produced *around*
ideas of foreignness, citizenship, border, mobility, limits, etc. and asking what types
of subjectivities and ways of acting in the world come into being through such
ideas, and in what ways these conflict as well as complement each other.

What we have then is an approach based upon what Foucault (2000) called 'a
critical attitude' derived from reading Kant's work; this is one which encourages
self-reflection rather than acquiescence to already institutionalised spaces of identity
within prevailing power relations. Below I explore three core (although not
exhaustive) approaches which help us to understand better what a critical attitude
to knowledge practice involves: these are problematisation; disorientation; and
rethinking. These approaches to knowledge practice enable us to constantly question and self-reflect upon key concepts (ibid.: 49) and the distinctions which these
concepts impose. In doing so, the aforementioned three approaches provide an
alternative attitude to that attitude which has traditionally started with key concepts

(existing objects of knowledge) and moved on to observe, reflect, and/or measure the relationships between them.

Problematisation

A focus on problematisation involves exploring how 'different solutions to a problem have been constructed and made possible by the way the problem is posed in the first place' rather than by virtue of a subjectively shared world (Campbell 1998: x). Instead of an understanding of the world in terms of an independent realm of 'problems' and 'solutions' which we (as citizens, or strangers, nationals or non-nationals, free or unfree subjects) encounter, it is to explore how our understanding of ourselves as these types of subjects is *implicated* in the process through which we have defined the problems we encounter as problems of freedom, citizenship, nationality, gender relations, mobility, etc. Doing so is to shift away from the centrality of individual subjects – the idea of persons as having a unified personality – and from an emphasis on the inner lives of individuals as reflecting an inner truth about the world. The emphasis moves instead towards the question of how a particular problematisation shapes and reshapes the enduring reality of the world (Shapiro 2013: 12).

Coined by Michel Foucault, a problematising approach explores how subjects emerge *in* the way problems are formulated rather than by coming to problems as pre-existing citizens, nationals, strangers or humans. Through the concept of problematisation we are able to move from the emphasis which is traditionally placed on 'experiences' to explore that of *practices* as the games of truth through which people are 'led to focus their attention on themselves' (Foucault 1986: 5).

Instead of starting with a research question which identifies the meanings of concepts and explores the relationships between these – thereby assuming a unified, subjectively shared world in which key objects are already those which we have a familiar political grammar to explore – a problematisation approach reflects upon why particular problems emerged at particular historical moments. As Shapiro (2013) discusses at some length, this approach does not therefore start with a statement of purpose linked to existing concepts – for example it does not ask what our responsibilities are to citizens in contrast to non-citizen strangers, or to women, or to the third world in the name of modernity or progress. Rather it involves taking a step back to think about these dominant formulations and asking how has something like 'responsibility' come to demand thinking and command representation in terms of citizenship versus non-citizenship, or in terms of the third world and associated ideas of underdevelopment, modernity, gender inequality, etc.? It shifts from a focus on what 'faithful representation involves' (ibid.: xv) – the supposed truth of the matter – to that of asking 'how a particular actualisation [of political life] becomes sedimented … over a period of time'.

It is useful to explore how a problematisation approach is employed in more detail in the work of specific scholars. And for this task I have chosen the work of

R.B.J. Walker and Julia Kristeva, as their work allows us to focus on two very relevant concepts to IR, namely sovereignty and foreignness respectively.

Interrogating sovereignty

It is commonplace for IR theorists to ask questions about democracy, global justice, citizenship and gender, etc. in light of an assumed division between national politics (inside) where order and political authority is presumed to reside, and international politics (outside) where lack of order and authority are presumed given the absence of any overarching international government. To do so is to take this division as a starting point. This issue is summed up in the notion of 'sovereignty' within the discipline of IR; this is the idea that a state's authority over a particular jurisdiction (inside) is (or should be respected as) absolute and territorially limited, and only comes into conflict with the authority of other states beyond its borders (outside) in the international realm.

What Walker (1995, 2010) does is to consider how sovereignty has been posed in terms first, of the problem of universalism to which state particularism is understood as a solution (a compromise), and second, the problem of state particularism to which universalism (humanity) is understood as a necessary solution. He considers how this results in prioritising political possibility in terms always of a trade-off between particularism and universalism which in turn prompts the question time and again – as Wheeler's work demonstrates above – about the rights which states have to citizens within their borders (inside) *or* to strangers beyond their borders (outside); a constant trade-off *between* political community ('thick bonds' [Walzer 1994]) and universal humanity ('cosmopolitan citizenship' [Linklater 2007]).

Instead of taking this as a necessary and inevitable starting point which simply reflects the common sense of the social order, Walker explores the historical basis of this horizontal (inside/outside) ordering of political community and traces this back to the collapse of Christendom and Empire which resulted in a shift from hierarchical to horizontal understandings about what and where political life could be. Politics shifted at this point from being defined in terms of the status of others above and below to being defined in terms of membership of a territorial community: a self-legitimating status. It is by pointing to the contingency of how we have come to understand sovereignty as territorial and horizontal (inside/outside, particular/universal) that Walker is able to achieve distance from the familiar 'problem of sovereignty' and explore its genealogy as a concept (see also Bartelson 1995). By focusing on the division between the national and the international (between inside the state and outside the state) as a particular horizontal way of understanding the world, and showing the historically contingent nature of this, Walker is able to demonstrate and discuss how current understandings of possibility in IR (including the possibility of new forms of politics) are specific rather than infinite. The possibility of new forms of politics are based on a horizontal spatial and temporal understanding of what politics *must* look like: an understanding of space with clear boundaries – between the individual, the sovereign state, the system of sovereign states and the world – and an understanding of time that moves in a progressive manner from past through to present and on to the future always contained within bounded space(s) (see Agnew and Lundborg in this book).

This type of approach to knowledge practice should not be understood as unveiling simple alternatives to current dominant ways of thinking. Rather it helps us understand and engage more directly with the way in which possibility in politics has become linked to certain understandings about the world.

Interrogating foreignness

In her work (1986, 1991), the concept which Kristeva problematises is that of foreignness. Foreignness in IR is seen at worst as that which undermines important institutions such as political community, nationality and citizenship; or at best that which needs to be integrated into these institutions to be dealt with and to avoid conflict. What Kristeva does however is to consider *how* foreignness has been posed in terms of the problem of difference and as that which undermines identity: understood as the unity of personhood which is realised in its purest form in the individual citizen-subject through statehood. She explores specifically how the problem of foreignness is tied into the establishment of the nation-state. She points out that the foreigner is by definition s/he who does not belong to the same state in which we are: 'the one who does not have the same nationality' (Kristeva 1991: 14).

Kristeva's work thus enables wider reflection in this manner on how the nation-state has become both the problem *and* the solution to the question of foreignness. She notes that it is in the search for and emphasis upon the need for greater hospitality that the state produces the foreigner – understood as the immigrant, the exiled, the deported or the stateless person who requires universal hospitality. As such, she does not take the distinction between foreignness (as difference) and that of nationality (as identity) for granted. Instead, Kristeva emphasises the historical basis of how foreignness and nationality have become separated through the nation-state model, given how this model defines the limits of nationality as the limits of belonging. She points to the vicious circle therefore through which any attempts to improve the status of foreigners also reinforces the idea of foreigners. This is because it is the state which defines the boundaries of 'exclusion', which are *then* used to (re)define who needs to be 'included' in the state. The call for universal hospitality by the state, in other words, is based on the initial exclusion of those who do not belong through the idea of nationality itself.

The point of problematising key concepts such as sovereignty and foreigneness in this manner is to attempt to undermine the claims of truth attached to these concepts – the supposed natural separation between universalism and particularism or between foreignness and nationality – while not ignoring the significance of these concepts and the way in which they have very real effects on people's lives. Another step in taking a critical attitude seriously requires the ability and willingness to disorient ourselves and to question the position (foundations) upon which we have come to stand.

Disorienting ourselves

It is important to note that disorienting ourselves in the world (what Judith Butler [2004] refers to as 'making strange' the world) is not about making the world unintelligible. It is however about challenging the accepted frameworks (grammars of inquiry) which we have come to rely upon when thinking and talking about the world. Accepted frameworks explored above include the association of sovereignty with absolute and territorially limited state authority (clear boundaries between inside and outside the state), or the association of foreignness with otherness and exclusion. Butler (ibid.: 328) argues that a 'making strange' approach can be contrasted with the approach taken by 'those who believe that we have a certain responsibility to write not only in an accessible way, but within the terms of already accepted grammar'. She goes on to explain that this approach is not about making things difficult for difficulty's sake but a response to the way in which 'much in ordinary language and in received grammar ... constrains our thinking – indeed, about what a person is, what a subject is, what gender is, what sexuality is, what politics can be'. The move towards making the ordinary world seem strange, she indicates, can therefore be seen as constituting 'a move towards a more capacious understanding of otherness' (ibid.: 326) and thereby opening up what political possibility can be. It helps 'to encourage a hospitality towards ambiguous, protean and unsettled modes of selfhood and community' (Shapiro 2013: xiv) rather than only towards fixed, clearly defined ideas of selfhood and community which is in keeping with the recognised changing nature of the world linked to globalisation.

In an attempt to think about selfhood and community in such indefinite terms – what Shapiro refers to as 'ambiguous, protean and unsettled' – many scholars have turned to arts-based resources, such as novels, music and poetry, as places where the life worlds of subjects are demonstrated to be much richer – because questions of experience such as emotion, sense, unconsciousness as well as historicity (rather than mere causal relationships) are brought to the fore. These sources allow reflection on how subjects are the result of a mixture of accomplishments and historical contingency rather than already informed in light of accomplished meanings.[2] The aim is not to try to emancipate ourselves from existing understandings of who we are and of the world in which we live that these enable but to replay and recite these existing understandings in different ways in order to reveal the instabilities in meanings *within* these terms: that is, the contradictions and inconsistencies in how ideas such as human, citizen, order, authority, mobility, etc. are played out in everyday life.

What is stressed is the manner in which drawing lines – between citizen and stranger, national and international, inside and outside – is constitutive of the world, but that this constitution is contingent as these distinctions constantly slip and slide (Edkins et al., 1999). This brings attention to the *interplay* between these dualisms – their unsettled and ambiguous nature – and away from the idea that they are stabilised in and of themselves. For Butler, thinking about the world as constructed in this manner involves rethinking the meaning of construction itself away from the idea of construction as a singular or deliberate act. '[C]onstruction is neither a subject nor its acts, but a process of reiteration by which both "subjects" and "acts" come to appear at all' (Butler 1993: viii). Rather than focusing on the idea of a singular subject (an agent) or group who construct, the emphasis needs rather to turn towards the collection of narratives, statements, groups of images, actions, modes of representation through which the world is known.

Disorienting sovereignty

In his work, Walker sets about disorienting the position on which our knowledge of sovereignty has come to stand by positing sovereignty as a process of drawing lines – between one state and another state, between citizenship and humanity – rather than as absolute and territorially limited state authority. This is to think about sovereignty as a *process* (as that which is constructed), instead of as a condition 'to be confirmed as either present or absent' (Walker 2010: 14). It is disorienting because it turns attention away from the question about authority of a state over a particular jurisdiction as a starting point – and the question about the responsibility which the state then has within this versus beyond this – towards a focus on the processes through which state authority is *implemented* in a particular socio-political and legal manner. These processes discussed by Walker (ibid.: 14) include points (moments of origin, such as the founding moment of the state and centralised authorities invested in ideas such as Republicanism); lines (borders of secured identity in nationality, ethnicity or language, etc., limits of legal authority, or trajectories of future possibilities); and planes (different levels of scale such as regional, national, sub-national and supra-national).

By thinking about the state and its sovereignty as a process (part of constructing the world), attention turns towards the ways in which different types of lines, points and planes are engaged *in the name of* 'state sovereignty' rather than simply being mere (legal, economic, moral or ethical) reflections of state sovereignty. What this raises is questions about the role of space and time in how we understand the world. Lives can be linked to various times and spaces plural, rather than only to a particular time and space: they can be linked to the question of how borders, mobility, colonial history, economic opportunity, and so on produce different experiences of time (as immobility, irregularity and inconsistency rather than just regularity, mobility and consistency) and space (as fluid rather than just bounded and contained spaces) (see for example, Mezzadra and Rahola 2006; Nyers 2013; Shapiro 2010; Squire 2011).

Disorienting foreignness

In her work, it is through the idea of a subject-in-process rather than a subject defined by its identity (as citizen, or as stranger, or as human) that Kristeva sets about disorienting the way we have come to understand foreignness. She continues to focus on foreignness but not in a way we are familiar with within IR. Rather than locating foreignness somewhere ('to turn the otherness of the foreigner into a thing' [1991: 3]) – for example to locate it in a person who does not have a particular nationality – and thus solidifying it, she considers how foreignness can be understood as 'scattered throughout history' permeating 'even the most familial, the most tightly knit communities' and therefore the self (ibid.: 4). Kristeva removes foreignness from its association with the outside and the unfamiliar by drawing on Sigmund Freud's work on the unconscious as 'the strange in the psyche' (ibid.: 181). Freud is credited with the discovery of the unconscious as that part of the brain which is neither driven by rationality nor clearly accessible. Unlike Cartesian philosophy which posited that the conscious was primary, Freudian philosophy argued that consciousness was a particular aspect of the mind and not its most general feature. Kristeva therefore posits that because the unconscious is part of thought in general, this allows us to consider how 'foreignness' is not something which can only be associated with Others (such as migrants), but is something which is integral to all our lives: an other*ness* which is both biological and symbolic.[3]

In other words, rather than focusing on the question of the lives of citizens (identity) *or* of foreigners (difference), Kristeva focuses on the notion of a subject-in-process *across* identity and difference here. A subject-in-process is a subject which is both citizen and foreigner, rather than one or the other, insofar as being a citizen is associated in her work with biological otherness (the unconscious of the mind) and therefore also symbolic otherness: 'foreignness is within us: we are our own foreigners, we are divided' in our selves (ibid.: 181). It is in this manner that she is able to turn her attention towards encounter itself (and social relations) in their unsettling, ambiguous and protean manner which is so important in a critical attitude, and away from a unified, subjectively shared world with already established meanings of personhood which are clearly fixed and stable.[4]

This understanding of foreignness as integral to the self undermines (rather than eradicates) the need to constantly think about extending hospitality beyond the nation-state. What it undermines is the cycle of reproducing ad nauseam new exclusions – those who are of a different nationality and thus new types of foreigners – who then need further hospitality, and in doing so, raises new questions for us to consider. '[B]eginning with the moment when the citizen-individual ceases to consider himself as unitary and glorious but discovers his incoherencies and abysses … the question [that] arises … [is] no longer that of welcoming the foreigner within a system that obliterates him but of promoting the togetherness of those foreigners that we all recognise ourselves to be' (ibid.: 2).

This type of work, as such, does not seek to only temporarily or momentarily disorient in order to resume existing frameworks in a fresh way. Rather, in disorienting our understanding of the world, it forces us to rethink what 'moving forward' would and should involve because 'already-institutionalized identity spaces within the prevailing power arrangements' are no longer available (Shapiro 2013: 8). It forces us to think about practices in the world which exceed the categories which we *already* have. This brings us to a third aspect of a critical attitude, which is scepticism towards 'some romantically conceived subject of history'

(Shaw and Walker 2006: 158) such as 'the individual' on one hand or 'humanity' on the other. Put simply, a critical attitude rethinks existing understandings of 'what needs to be done', which is such a central question in international politics. For a critical attitude does not only provide a historical basis for how we have come to understand issues such as sovereignty and foreignness as problems in international relations, thus undermining their eternal truth. This work also undermines the solutions which have been offered *to* these problems, such as 'humanity' as that which can act as a counteracting force to sovereignty, and 'individuality' as that which can transcend nationality.

Against emancipation: rethinking the way forward

As with so many problems in international relations (such as poverty, gender inequality, conflict, global justice) the solution to the extremely important question of sovereignty – which is understood as the authorisation and delimitation of state authority – has been defined as the need for a move from prioritising the particularism of statehood and the inter-national system of states to foregrounding the universalism of humanity (see for example, Linklater 2007; Wheeler 2002). This is a move 'from a politics of "the international" to a politics of "the world"' (Walker 2010: 1). 'The world' as a basis for politics rather than mere states or an unequal system of states is seductively appealing. It allows for a different grounding of politics; a grounding in what people share as members of a single humanity and thus what is held in common, rather than a grounding in particular nations which merely focuses (and reinforces) what distinguishes people, places and interests. Yet, to distinguish between a politics grounded in particularism and one grounded in universalism is to reinforce the idea of limits and borders – between the individual, the sovereign state, the system of sovereign states and the world – which is central to the idea of statehood and particularism *in the first place*.

It is with this in mind that Walker challenges any temptation to turn readily to this solution. Instead he considers at length the manner in which this solution has become so entrenched in political imagination, reusing a very familiar conception of space as absolute (defined by limits) and time as progressively extended always within absolute space. He discusses, for example, how such attempts to distinguish a here (particularist politics) from there (universal politics) echo previous distinctions between in here (one nation-state) and out there (another nation-state). He emphasises (echoed now in critical attitude scholarship more widely), the way in which boundaries, borders and limits are also complex sites, moments and practices of political engagement through which politics is articulated and constantly reconstructed: for example, through practices of (im)mobility, (inter)dependency, social struggle, communality and resistance (see also for example, McNevin 2011; Squire 2011; and Shindo in this book). This draws attention to and focuses on borders, boundaries and limits themselves as that which *enable* ideas of particularism and universalism in significant yet contingent ways, rather than focusing on the state or the international system of states and humanity as spaces in which particularism and universalism can be grounded as if they were simply true (Mezzadra and Neilson 2012; Vaughan-Williams and Parker et al. 2009). It opens up, for example, the possibility of discussions about how 'humanity' can be (and has been) invoked to authorise discriminations and practices of judgement between those who are deserving and those who are not – for example, in the name of 'global security', or 'humanitarian intervention' (Butler 2006).

The point is not that there remain no options or ideas which can be taken forward; but rather that the existing particularist options (statehood, the international system of states) and universalist options (ideas of a common humanity) are focused upon in terms of how they are *intertwined*. A critical attitude forces us to consider how any attempt to think about political alternatives must do so through an appreciation of the political nature of the points at which they intersect – and the way in which borders, boundaries and limits are *drawn* between particularism and universalism at the limit of the state, the system of states and the world to include some forms of community and subjecthood and exclude others – rather than manifesting as a simple trade-off between natural borders and boundaries, between the state and the international system.

Coming back to Kristeva's work, we can say that typically, overcoming foreignness is linked – as is the case with many questions in international relations – to becoming a citizen-individual. This is because the citizen-individual has come to represent freedom (autonomy) from the problems of being defined as Other, and is linked to acceptance and inclusion. However, rather than putting faith in individuality again going forward, Kristeva (1991: 3) urges us to consider the individual as a foreigner *to* him/herself. She urges us to begin with 'the moment when the citizen-individual … discovers his incoherencies and abysses'; in short the moment s/he discovers their 'strangeness'. This is explored by Kristeva through what she calls instances of 'permanent marginality' within the structures of society.

In her own work Kristeva explores permanent marginality through her personal experience as someone who lives in France and is a key figure in French intellectual life but was not born there and so speaks a foreign mother tongue; in her role as a mother who carries another within her (an other foreign body); and as a successful woman within a public intellectual life which is dominated by men. This emphasis on intimacy and permanent marginality shifts attention away from the researcher's role as master and authority on a topic towards exposing struggles which researchers and students are as implicated in as the people, ideas and events they explore and thus 'to the complexity of the world and … [our] own frailty in the face of it' (Inayatullah 2010: 8). This can be seen recently reflected in a turn by some towards autobiographical approaches in IR where researchers discuss their own personal journeys and feelings, hopes and fears in the context of IR (see for example, Dauphineé 2012; Inayatullah 2010; Salter and Mutlu 2013; and also Moulin in this book).

This complicates 'the subject' who enquires into international relations as an authoritative voice: as researcher or academic. It emphasises their intimacy and permanent marginality as part of the political process by putting questions of vulnerability to the fore rather than trying to erase them. Indeed increasingly, what has become an important focus in IR is how questions of intimacy and permanent marginality can be understood as part of political agency rather than operating outside it: for example, through explorations of subversive practices in irregularity (Ní Mhurchú 2015; Nyers 2011), in experiences of exile (Jabri 2012; Sajed 2013) or in domesticity and the body (Enloe 2008; Masters 2005).

The point is not that there is no subject of history left, but that these subjects no longer exist as presence in essential form which can be pointed to as, for example, 'non-European migrant' or 'European citizen', as 'woman' or as 'man', as 'researcher' and 'object of research', as 'citizen' or as 'foreigner'. Instead the subject remains as presence in subversive form, defined across such categories rather than grounded in one or two of them. As a result we are left with no easy alternative in which to ground a different politics going forward. Foreignness from this point of view is no longer a source simply of hopelessness and confusion nor something to be unconditionally celebrated. The instability of the relationship between identity and difference, citizenship and foreignness, us and them instead becomes that which enables different articulations of being political *across* individuality communality, plurality and vulnerability.

The possibility of agency as such – thinking differently and moving forward in alternative ways – within a critical attitude is paramount; however this needs to be engaged in such a way that recognises how our ability to challenge institutionalised methods of reproducing and understanding phenomena are 'immanent to power and not a relation of external opposition to power' (Butler 1993: xxii). In other words, a critical attitude involves reflection on the lack of an obvious alternative (a better politics) outside existing power relations.

Indeed, the work of those who espouse a critical attitude can appear frustrating because it provides very few, if any, easy or clear answers as to what needs to be done and what a 'better' approach to/in politics might look like. However it only appears frustrating because we have come to expect answers within received grammar about what is to be done in the world. Easy clear answers merely delay and obscure questions about the complex nature of the world – for example, about the complex ways in which citizenship and strangerhood overlap and certain types of people (such as migrants, women and marginalised populations) get caught between citizenship and strangerhood; or the complex way in which sovereignty is not just an attribute – for example of statehood – but formed through limits manifested as points, lines and planes. Such a critical attitude forces us to rethink the necessity of limits associated with inside and outside, citizen and foreigner, the national and the international as the place where we must begin to think about international politics. It encourages us to challenge this and all other supposedly necessary starting points and instead, to begin by interrogating them.

Conclusion

This chapter has explored the way in which knowledge can be understood as a practice of different interpretations of knowing and of Being which emerge in encounters; rather than as a practice of observation, reflection and measurement about a world and by a subject who is already formed with accomplished meaning. The chapter emphasised three core approaches which characterise what is involved in such a crtitical attitude to knowledge practice: that of reflecting on how key ideas have come to be oriented around particular problems and solutions; that of disorienting the ground upon which we stand; and of rethinking the way forward. In order to think through these three core approaches in some detail I looked at the work of thinkers including Butler, Kristeva and Walker; as well as associated thinkers such as Foucault and Shapiro.

The point is not that the critical approach to knowledge practice explored in this chapter avoids the difficulty of understanding the world. Its critical potential is that it offers analytical perspectives and engaged political actions which consider the limits of what we think we know about the world: and allows us to develop the ability to recognise inherited problematics and reformulate them where appropriate. It allows us to develop new places to start our inquiries – for example, with political identity and belonging as defined through foreignness rather than only though citizenship; with citizenship as defined through otherness rather than only through commonality; or with universalism and particularism as intertwined rather than separate competing perspectives. This provides the opportunity to hear voices and ideas which have been silenced by the well-worn paths we have become so accustomed to taking when trying to understand ourselves, and our place in the world. Its critical potential is embedded in how it opens up what politics can be: 'contributing to a re-articulation of political possibility rather than a re-inscription of political necessity' (Shaw and Walker 2006: 161).

Rather than focusing on producing more progressive and more holistic knowledge about ourselves and about the world, we need to focus on how we engage in the process of knowledge (re)production: to focus on the question of how knowledge is linked *to* practices of knowing and Being which are always incomplete, as opposed to either false or true; and how at their limits, these open up new ways of thinking about the world and about our role in this world. In the words of Foucault (1980: 133): 'The political question, to sum up, is not error, illusion, alienated consciousness or ideology; it is truth itself.'

Notes

1   This is drawn from an idea in Kant's own notes. This is the idea of a constant need to develop oneself beyond immaturity through the Enlightenment (see Foucault 2000) which Kant believed makes 'it difficult to achieve the "subjective necessity" that legislates in favour of common sense' (Shapiro 2013: 2).

2   For a discussion on the merits of using novels to draw out the richness of 'aesthetic subjects' see Shapiro (2013); for an example of how novels can be used when thinking and talking about the political lives of subjects see Closs Stephens (2013).

3   See also Judith Butler's (1993: 46) notion of 'my own foreignness to myself' which she argues is 'the source of my ethical connection to others'. Albeit with a slightly different focus (war and conflict rather than migration), Butler's work builds on Kristeva's to help

us think about how 'we' are constituted and dispossessed by our relations to others. I'd like to thank Laura Brace for prompting me to highlight this.

4 See Lloyd (2005) for a very good discussion of what is involved in this shift towards thinking in terms of a subject-in-process and the question of encounter.

Further reading and useful weblinks

Edkins, J. (1999) *Poststructuralism and International Relations: Bringing the Political Back In*, Boulder, CO: Lynne Rienner. An excellent starting point for thinking about the narrow ways in which 'politics' has been understood as well as the broad ways in which it has been interrogated within and beyond the boundaries of IR through the work of Michel Foucault, Stuart Hall, Jacques Lacan and Slavoj Žižek.

Foucault, M., *Essential Works of Foucault 1954–1984, Vol. 1: Ethics, Subjectivity and Truth*, ed. P. Rabinow, London: Penguin, pp. 303–319. This volume provides a series of short pieces by Foucault where he considers and discusses both what he means by a critical attitude and how he has engaged this in his own work. It thus provides many examples of how this works in practice.

Halberstam, J. (2011) *The Queer Art of Failure*, Durham, NC: Duke University Press. A book about finding alternatives to conventional understandings of success! It challenges the reader to fail and to lose one's way in order to explore counterintuitive questions about the politics of resistance, agency and truth. Drawing in particular on animation, it pushes the reader to think at the limit of what is acceptable, and to dig deep within themselves to imagine how they might pursue creative forms of political engagement.

Ní Mhurchú, A. and Shindo, R. (eds) (forthcoming, 2016) *Critical Imaginations in International Relations*, Abingdon: Routledge. Each of the other chapters in this edited volume is exemplary of the critical approach to knowledge practice explored in this chapter. They seek in various ways and to various degrees to think about their concept – by interrogating, unpacking and exploring the different ways of acting and being in the world which their concept enables.

Shaw, K. and Walker, R.B.J. (2006) 'Situating Academic Practice: Pedagogy, Critique and Responsibility', *Millennium: Journal of International Studies* 35(1): 155–165. This article emphasises the importance, for academics, of asking difficult questions and constantly interrogating how they 'teach' IR in order to resist simplifying (explanatory) dualisms about consciousness, matter or language in world politics.

Acts: The Archive Project – www.enginfisin.eu/cms. This project reflects on the manner in which political subjects and ways of acting politically are produced in complex ways through 'acts'. It attempts to explore the political potential of an act itself in order to reflect on the performative nature of political subjectivity and the manner in which ideas of belonging, foreignness, resistance, etc. are reshaped through acts.

Playing for Change Project – http://playingforchange.com. This project looks at how music connects communities and in doing so reshapes subjects and their life worlds in the process.

'Mansplaining International Relations? What Walt Misses' – http://relationsinternational. com/mansplaining-international-relations-walt. A short blog piece which points to IR as a very complex field and discusses what is lost in ignoring this complexity within IR through attempts to 'explain' it to students.

Bibliography

Aradau, C. and Huysmans, J. (2014) 'Critical Methods in International Relations: The Politics of Techniques, Devices and Acts', *European Journal of International Relations* 20(3): 596–619.

Balibar, É. (2012) 'The "Impossible" Community of the Citizens: Past and Present Problems', *Environment and Planning D: Society and Space* 30(3): 437–449.

Bartelson, J.A. (1995) *Genealogy of Sovereignty*, Cambridge: Cambridge University Press.

Bosniak, L. (2006) *The Citizen and the Alien: Dilemmas of Contemporary Membership*, Princeton, NJ: Princeton University Press.

Butler, J. (1993) *Bodies that Matter*, Abingdon: Routledge.

Butler, J. (2004) 'Changing the Subject: Judith Butler's Politics of Radical Resignification' in S. Salih and J. Butler (eds) , *The Judith Butler Reader*, Malden, MA: Blackwell, pp. 326–328.

Butler, J. (2006) *Precarious Life: The Power of Mourning and Violence*, Abingdon: Routledge.

Campbell, D. (1998) *National Deconstruction: Violence, Identity, and Justice in Bosnia*, Minneapolis: University of Minnesota Press.

Closs Stephens, A. (2013) *The Persistence of Nationalism: From Imagined Communities to Urban Encounters*, Abingdon: Routledge.

Dauphineé, E. (2012) *The Politics of Exile*, Abingdon: Routledge.

Edkins, J. (1999) *Poststructuralism and International Relations: Bringing the Political Back In*, Boulder, CO: Lynne Rienner.

Edkins, J., Persram, N. and Pin-Fat, V. (eds) (1999) *Sovereignty and Subjectivity*, Boulder CO: Lynn Reinner.

Enloe, C. (2014) *Bananas, Beaches and Bases: Making Feminist Sense of International Politics*, 2nd edition, Berkeley and Los Angeles: University of California Press.

Foucault, M. (1980) *Power/Knowledge: Selected Interviews and Other Writings 1972–1977*, ed. C. Gordon, Brighton: Harvester Press.

Foucault, M. (1982) 'Afterword: The Subject and Power' in H.L. Dreyfus and P. Rabinow, *Michel Foucault: Beyond Structuralism and Hermeneutics*, Brighton: Harvester Press, pp. 208–227.

Foucault, M. (1986) *The History of Sexuality, Vol. 2: The Use of Pleasure*, London: Viking.

Foucault, M. (2000) 'What is Enlightenment' in *Essential Works of Foucault 1954–1984, Vol. 1: Ethics, Subjectivity and Truth*, ed. P. Rabinow, London: Penguin, pp. 303–319.

Inayatullah, N. (2010) *Autobiographical International Relations: I, IR*, Abingdon: Routledge.

Isin, E. (2002) *Being Political: Genealogies of Citizenship*, Minneapolis: University of Minnesota Press.

Jabri, V. (2012) *The Postcolonial Subject: Claiming Politics/ Governing Others in Late Modernity*, Abingdon: Routledge.

Kristeva, J. (1986) *The Kristeva Reader*, ed. T. Moi, New York: Columbia University Press.

Kristeva, J. (1991) *Strangers to Ourselves*, New York: Columbia University Press.

Linklater, A. (2007) *Critical Theory and World Politics: Citizenship, Sovereignty and Humanity*, Abingdon: Routledge.

Lloyd, M. (2005) *Beyond Identity Politics: Feminism, Power and Politics*, London: Sage.

Masters, C. (2005) 'Bodies of Technology', *International Feminist Journal of Politics* 7(1): 112–132.

McNevin, A. (2011) *Contesting Citizenship: Irregular Migrants and New Frontiers of the Political*, New York: Columbia University Press.

Mezzadra, S. and Neilson, B. (2012) 'Between Inclusion and Exclusion: On the Topology of Global Space and Borders', *Theory, Culture and Society* 29(4/5): 58–75.

Mezzadra, S. and Rahola, F. (2006) 'The Postcolonial Condition: A Few Notes on the Quality of Historical Time in the Global Present', *Social Text* 2(1).

Ní Mhurchú, A. (2014) *Ambiguous Citizenship in an Age of Global Migration*, Edinburgh: Edinburgh University Press.

Ní Mhurchú, A. (2015) 'Ambiguous Subjectivity, Irregular Citizenship: From Inside/Outside to Being-Caught-Iin-Between', *International Political Sociology* 9(2): 158–175.

Nyers, P. (2011) 'Forms of Irregular Citizenship' in V. Squire (ed.), *The Contested Politics of Mobility: Borderzones and Irregularity*, Abingdon: Routledge, pp. 184–198.

Nyers, P. (2013) 'Liberating Irregularity: No Borders, Temporality, Citizenship' in X. Guillaume and J. Huysmans (eds), *Citizenship and Security: the Constitution of Political Being*, London: Routledge, pp. 37–52.

Nyers, P. and Rygiel, K. (eds) (2012) *Citizenship, Migrant Activism and the Politics of Movement*, Abingdon: Routledge.

Parker, N. and Vaughan-Williams, N. et al. (2009) 'Lines in the Sand: Towards a an Agenda for Critical Border Studies', Special Issue, *Geopolitics* 14(3): 582–587.

Sajed, A. (2013) *Postcolonial Encounters in International Relations: The Politics of Transgression in the Maghreb*, Abingdon: Routledge.

Salter, M. and Mutlu, C. (eds) (2013) *Research Methods in Critical Security Studies: An Introduction*, Abingdon: Routledge.

Shapiro, M. (2010) *The Time of the City*, Abingdon: Routledge.

Shapiro, M. (2013) *Studies in Transdiciplinary Methods*, Routledge: London.

Shaw, K. and Walker, R.B.J. (2006) 'Situating Academic Practice: Pedagogy, Critique and Responsibility', *Millennium: Journal of International Studies* 35(1): 155–165.

Squire, V. (ed.) (2011) *The Contested Politics of Mobility: Borderzones and Irregularity*, Abingdon: Routledge.

Walker, R.B.J. (1995) *Inside/Outside: International Relations as Political Theory*, Cambridge: Cambridge University Press.

Walker, R.B.J. (2010) *After the Globe, Before the World*, Abingdon: Routledge.

Walzer, M. (1994) *Thick and Thin: Moral Argument at Home and Abroad*, Notre Dame, IN: University of Notre Dame Press.

Wheeler, N. (2002) *Saving Strangers: Humanitarian Intervention in International Society*, Oxford: Oxford University Press.

9

LAW

Andreja Zevnik

Introduction

In studies of international politics, especially when we speak about critical or post-structural approaches, the idea of law (or legality) seems to be curiously absent. That is of course not to say that no discussion about law takes place in critical international politics. Quite on the contrary. Since 9/11 many discussions about issues of humanity, security, war on terror and exceptionalism take a note of law (Aradau 2007; Neal 2006); yet they see law as a limitation, a practice of governance, and thus a mechanism of repression rather than as a vista with emancipatory potential.

To fully understand the importance of law and why – for a critical mind – it all too often comes with a negative connotation, we first need to look at the relationship between law and politics. The modern society, which is often portrayed as a society of control (see Dillon and Neal 2008), places politics and law in an ever-changing and reverberating relationship, where boundaries between the two are commonly blurred. It could be argued (see Stone et al. 2012) that modern normative, ethical and legal challenges have transformed law into a new being (a kind of lichen) whereby the one (law) cannot exist without the other (politics), and further, where the two are becoming so intrinsically interlinked that their different bodies, while belonging to separate and distinct traditions, appear as one. The US strategy of the war on terror or the status of combatants in this war (Guantánamo detainees), are illustrations of the complexity of this relationship. In situations when law is 'abused' for political purposes and goals, it is indeed difficult to speak about law's emancipatory or critical potential; but that is not the only way in which law as an idea and a concept intervenes into politics. In fact, I intend to demonstrate how the core critical potential of law is precisely its power to change and institute a different idea of politics, political space, and how one thinks and conducts politics.

With an aim to present the critical potential of law in politics and international politics, this chapter focuses on the sources of legal authority – that is, where legal authority comes from and how law as a legal system relates to it. In doing so, the purpose is to show that legal authority is rather arbitrary, that there are different ways in which it can be thought about, and that a different understanding of authority can lead to a somewhat emancipatory rather than a repressive function of law and from it, emerging legal subjectivity. To illustrate the idea of authority and law that is at stake here I turn to psychoanalytical conceptions of law, which most heavily draw on the work of Jacques Lacan. Lacan provides perhaps the most fundamental engagement with legal and political authority, as he places sources of authority beyond what we commonly consider and associate with 'law': that is legislation, legal rules and norms. Instead, law, as it will be demonstrated and as understood in this critical context, is much more fundamental to the structure of society and to legal and political subjectivity.

This chapter thus opens with a discussion about the relationship between politics and law as two ideas but also two disciplines that – curiously – have not yet been in much discussion. The opening discussion will initiate a reader into the idea of law and provide a broader understanding of the critical legal field and its legacy. Whereas, the rest of the chapter outlines and focuses on the core ideas within law: first, on the mentioned authority of law where mythical authority and authority in the system of law are discussed; and second, on the emergence of a legal subject and its relation to authority. The so-called mythical origins of legal authority and psychoanalytical interpretations of legal and political subjectivity are further con- textualised in reference to legal discourse surrounding the war on terror and in particular the Guantánamo detention centre. Through the discussion of these core ideas, the significance of law in critical international politics is presented and offered for further exploration, engagement and critical thinking.

Politics and law as two ideas and two disciplines

As a movement, Critical Legal Studies emerged in the late 1980s in the US and was closely followed by the so-called 'Brit-Crits' – a critical legal movement across Schools of Law in the United Kingdom. The main target of the two 'critical strands' was to contest the image of law as objective and an impartial system. By means of different methods such as semiotics, hermeneutics and deconstruction, Critical Legal Studies opened up law and legal discourse and began showing how homophobia, sexism and racism persist in legal texts. In doing so, they exposed the perceived yet unquestionable neutrality of legal texts. Their intervention was thus political and methodological. It was political for it challenged the neutrality and objectivity of legal assumptions, and methodological for its introduction of different 'non-legal' methods to the discipline of law. Moreover, their intervention was also trans-disciplinary, for it drew on aesthetics, literature and politics to expose the aforementioned biases. Literary texts such as Franz Kafka's *Penal Colony*, Shake- speare's *Hamlet* or Sophocles' *Antigone* (see Hirvonen 1998, forthcoming 2016), or

Francisco Goya's drawings of torture, war and violence were mobilised as tools to analyse and expose the existing contradictions, biases and obscenities of law. Such an intervention inevitably opened legal discourse to other disciplines, expanded its relevance but also provoked a stark critique of traditional legal studies. Critical Legal Studies departed from a common understanding of law as a system of norms, provisions, or court practices and as a result, similarly to the critical engagement in international politics, faced questions of the relevance of their critical endeavour. An engagement with arts and humanities also called for a different theoretical and philosophical framework; which were unsurprisingly found in philosophy, especially French continental philosophy, and in thinkers such as Jacques Derrida, Michel Foucault, Jacques Lacan, Judith Butler or more recently, Giorgio Agamben, to mention only a few.

The opening up of legal texts and the exposure of their injustices or institutionalised discriminations came with one end goal in sight, namely, the emancipation that is to take place in the law itself: either through the transformation or transgression of law. The emancipatory ideal remains one of the critical investigative stands of Critical Legal Studies until today. As Emilios Christoloulidis (2009: 17) one of 'Brit-Crits' writes, it was 'the promise of the "exploitation" of the institutional imagination to disturb or reverse what appear as legal determinations and legal givens' that drove critical investigations. But Critical Legal Studies did not remain at the level of deconstruction. They did not solely aim at disturbing or reversing the exposed legal biases but strategically aspired to a different legal framework. By strategic mobilisation, consideration and response, as Christoloulidis continues (ibid.), 'there is a shared assumption in much post-structural critical legal theory that what the law has silenced or systematically excluded will return in the modalities of responsiveness and questionability'. In other words, with the popularity and a growing size of the movement, its modes of engagement with law, legal text, strategic goals of critical scholarship as well as the fields of study radically stratified. What became increasingly obvious was that law is not a neutral mechanism of governing society towards its 'more just' or 'more ethical' end but rather a mean of ironing out differences and mediating or solving rather than eradicating disputes. Critical Legal Studies painted an image of law as ideologically and thus a heavily political societal phenomena; law does not only govern society, but creates and re-produces conflicts, injustices and grievances that in turn it is also asked to solve.

The emancipatory and deconstructing task of law is similar to critical international politics' engagement with legal discourse. In the aforementioned example of the war on terror and detention practices, scholars of international politics mainly following the work of Agamben and Foucault, have highlighted the political and ideological side of law and exposed its role in the abuse of the detainees (Aradau 2007; Johns 2005; Neal 2006). However, the discussion absent in critical international politics is one about where law can act as a force of emancipation. In contrast, earlier engagement with law in critical international politics is somewhat different and falls within a normative angle (Campbell and Shapiro 1999). Works inspired by these earlier engagements following the legacy of deconstruction and the work of Derrida or Emmanuel Levinas, speak about the impossibility of ethics and absolute justice, and in such a context challenge the status of law in the modern international (Bulley 2011; Fagan 2013). Their engagement aims to show how ethical claims distinguishing between that which is right or good and that which is wrong or bad cannot be universalised. While we can speak about right and wrong in a particular moment in time, those qualifications are not universal or absolute. Human rights in its various forms of humanitarianism, mechanisms of aid, laws of war, as well as theoretical investigations into universalism, have been at the centre of these discussions (Pin-Fat 2010). However, similar to the more recent discussions of exceptionalism (noted above) this discourse of 'ethical impossibility' leaves the account of law as an emancipatory function untouched. Thus to mobilise the idea of law as a force of change, critical scholarship in international politics might indeed need to refer to Critical Legal Studies. It is by understanding how law operates, how it carves out, closes and opens a particular political space, that practices of resistance (either through or outside the law) can be thought about.

By looking at how the two disciplines of law and politics see and discuss law, the above discussion has suggested that the concept of law with which critical international politics operates could be enriched with the discussions taking place in Critical Legal Studies. As the two disciplines share a concern for a better life in a community, such an exchange of ideas would come quite naturally. What is more, following the arguments of critical legal scholars, law is always already political, and legal issues cannot be analysed independently of political struggles and ideological biases. Thus law, to take it to the extreme, is a form of politics and part of society's not only legal or political, but also ideological struggle. Indeed, legal texts, court decisions, judgements and legislation all come as a result of political and ideological struggles and legal decisions cannot be devoid of their socio-political and historical context. In fact US-based academics already in the late 80s pointed out the influence of politics on the law and the politicality of those in *charge of law*. In other words, law-makers are political animals by virtue of living in a society and their citizenship. But to take a step further, law is not only made political by its subjects, it is political already in itself, for it regulates, governs, determines what is right and what is wrong, and splits the population into subjects: those who break the law and constitute danger on one hand, and on the other hand, law-obeying citizens.

Such a governing and regulating function of law is often described as biopolitical. If law is seen through this biopolitical lens it inevitably appears as one of the governing technologies of society. In such a view, law is not *made* political it *is* always political. It is, in other words, a tool in the hands of politics. In such a biopolitical society, what we witness is a tendency, as Stone, rua Wall and Douzinas (2012: 2) argue: 'to render law at the heart of things, subjecting ever-growing demands of life to a knowledge structured by legal concepts, practices and methods'. A biopolitical society is obsessed with law and legality; it strives to regulate every aspect of social and individual life and subjugate it to legal regulation. If a common aim of politics is a good life for the people living in a community (the common good), the aim of biopolitics is a regulation of life where common good becomes overshadowed by the very need for regulation and control. Such biopolitical space almost 'naturally' brings together politics and law. Law is called in to legitimise political action. Examples of law doing the 'dirty' job of politics are antiterror laws, laws and policies concerning surveillance, control and the abrogation of human rights, and civil and political freedoms. On the back of political necessity, survival and security, politics justifies the institutions of law that abrogate fundamental individual civil and political freedoms. Politics employs law in way that breaches the fundamental principles that constitute good life in a community. A direct example of such 'reductionism' are antiterrorism laws whereby 'people can be excluded, detained and stripped of their rights in the name of security', as Stone, rua Wall and Douzinas highlight (2012: 3).

This opening section of the chapter outlined the existing discussions about law from a perspective of critical studies of law. The aim was to show that in international politics, critical engagement with law exists; yet it is focused on its negative conception. The discussion in critical international politics could be enriched if they took into account the emancipatory readings at the heart of which is a reconceptualisation of legal authority, to which this chapter now turns. In doing so, the chapter aims to outline ways in which law can be understood as an emancipatory force or an institution which offers different ways of conceptualising legality and understanding legal subjectivity.

The mythical origins of legal authority

Where the authority of law comes from is a question politics often asks. It is important for legal authority to determine how the subject relates to law (how it becomes a legal subject), and how the society distinguishes between valid and invalid laws and norms. In the tradition of positive law, the authority of law comes from a law-giver (see Hart 1961). However, for a critical eye, such an explanation does not stand for long, and hence a question as to why the law-giver is endowed with authority should be asked next. Speaking of authority in ontological terms, it is then often said that authority comes from a divine source. Alexandre Kojève (2014), for example, would see the master, the judge, the father and the sovereign as four different positions of absolute, even divine, authority. It is not that these four figures literally occupy the place of authority; rather, as Kojève explicitly states, the four places are functions of authority. That is, any person occupying either of these four will be endowed with authority. Because they transcend the actual person occupying them at a particular space and a moment in time, these positions of authority rely heavily on a myth. For example, in his books *Totem and Taboo* (2001a) and *Civilisation and Its Discontents* (2001b), Freud addresses the problem of law in modern society by focusing on law's inscription on the body and the prohibition of incest and murder. He argues that it is only by means of prohibitions, such as the prohibitions against incest and murder, as the two 'primordial' and in turn mythical prohibitions, that the structure of society and modern form of coexistence of individuals is imaginable (Freud 2001a). For Freud these two laws lie at the very foundations of the evolution of society and form a precondition of civilisation.

Despite shortcomings, what was particularly groundbreaking about Freud's ideas, as Lacan (2008: 216) emphasises, was a discovery of a common logic of ordering social life. The two most significant elements of this logic are the structuring principle of subjectivity, which explains how a person becomes a member of a community and with it a subject of law, and social bond, which outlines why every attempt to create successful universal moral codes or acceptable ethical practices fails. The value of Freud's explanation stands precisely at the point of the myth, which substitutes the authority of the actual person with the authority emanating from a particular position in the social structure. The mythical foundation of law, as Lacan (1993: 176–177) explains, transfers law's authority from a 'living person' onto something that is fundamental to, yet absent or somewhat removed from, the society. In modern political regimes, the constitution could resemble the mythical empty place of authority. It is set up to uphold legal foundations of authority and protected by a range of rigid legal and political mechanisms, which reaffirm but also testify to a special – if not mythical – nature of its authority.

If the myth of authority (prohibition of murder) explains how the law makes society possible, the prohibition of incest, in contrast, enables the internalisation of law and the emergence of what is today known as the idea of modern political community.[1] One can argue that the relations between the subjects and the community are ordered by the prohibition of murder, whereas the prohibition of incest organises the way in which a person becomes a subject of law. At the point of introduction into law, a legal subject becomes aware of laws and norms, but also of penalties for breaking them. As a normalising force, the internalisation of law forms a particular type of a subject, which relates and understands law in a particular way. Thus the incest institutes logic of obedience: that is, it does not determine what the subject should be afraid of, but rather, how it should understand and follow the law.

The logic of incest is, in psychoanalytical language, congruent with the logic of the Name-of-the-Father (the murdered father whose position of authority remained empty). In a traditional psychoanalytical discourse, the Name-of-the-Father is associated with the intervention of the father in the union between mother and child (see Lacan 2006: 671–702). The father, by intervening into the bond between mother and child, prohibits the child to enjoy or see the mother as a sexual object or an object of his desire. Such a prohibition of sexual intercourse between a child and a mother manifests itself in a child's unconsciousness, in the realm Lacan named the Real. Yet the prohibition it imposes is not only a prohibition of incest, but also a prohibition from enjoying the body of the mother (committing incest) (Lacan 2007: 123). As the child before the father's intervention knows no limits to its enjoyment or to its body, the father's intervention institutes the first prohibition, which is a sexual prohibition, and makes some objects unacceptable as the objects of desire. The key here is not the mother–father–child relation (which has been heavily caricatured and criticised as reductionist in philosophy as well as in legal studies and psychoanalysis itself) but rather the logic in which the 'father' as a place of authority intervenes into what is otherwise a pre-social relation. The subject can only enter law once it realises that not everything is allowed, accepts the penalties for breaking the law and begins to relate to the figure of authority in a particular way. Instituted in the image of the Name-of-the-Father logic, legal authority resembles a hierarchical relation where the subject looks up at the authority, and whose subjectivity always depends on the recognition the subject receives from the place of authority. In this way the two mythical laws build the foundations of authority in modern society around the function of the father.

From what has been discussed, it follows that the subject, by becoming the subject of law, internalises the rules of society and the notion of what is right or wrong, acceptable or prohibited (Lacan 2006: 66). In such, psychoanalytical legal realm, the law does not require nor does it seek external legitimacy. To an extent one could comment that the legal constitution is here only to guarantee the symbolic figures such as the Sovereign, the Legislator or the Law with the authority that must be obeyed (Douzinas 2000: 309). Lacan (1988: 201), to further this argument, does not detach sources of law from the symbolic, not even material power, and hence suggests that every legitimate power, even the police, rests on the symbol, and further, that any articulation of the subject or the social cannot occur outside the legislative function (Lacan 2007: 125).

This 'paternal' aspect of law also bears broader legal and political dimensions. The mythical authority is at the same time both a product and a creator of a modern individual and the social order. It is not outside the system but a force creating and shaping it from the inside, while also being created by that very same order. A political example of this paternal authority is Carl Schmitt's (2005: 5) concept of the sovereign as the one who can decide on the exception. Schmitt's idea is an example of how paternal authority is translated into 'positive law'. In the realm of the political, the sovereign is the one who can abrogate the existing laws and set new ones or persist in the exception.

The institution of law and legal authority

As Pierre Legendre (1997: 177), a prominent French psychoanalyst, historian and legal theorist, would argue, the entire structure of legality with principles of authority and legitimacy is built upon the two totemic laws and a paternal ordering logic explained above. If the above section looked at the origins of authority and its intervention into the social realm, this section looks at how authority is translated into legal institutions. Legendre, in his genealogical study of the origins of institutions and authority, emphasises a particular interdependence between the institution of the subject as a subject of law and the institution of law itself. He claims that the 'history' of Western legality and subjectivity is in a particular way continuous. The origins of power and law are inscribed in a set of vital social representations where representation is the only mode of 'knowledge transference' (ibid.: 118). He takes this further by arguing:

> [T]he discourse of legitimacy remains an unavoidable precondition of sociality. [And as in nuclear 'medieval' family], everything to do with law has to do with paternity. There is a paternity of institutions because Law needs a legitimate author. The mythological order of the West is founded on a living Writing which acts as the sign of a place, that of reference to pure power. [In Lacanian language] this place can be occupied by any signifier capable of guaranteeing the Law, whether be it Justinian, science or the class struggle.
>
> *(Ibid.: 118)*

The empty place Legendre refers to in the above text is a place of a murdered father; that place is, at least in an imaginary way, filled by a signifier or an image of authority. It does not matter what exactly the signifier or the image in question is, whatever occupies that space should automatically come into possession of authority pertaining to that place. The question of the subject and its relation to law is then played out in the field of authority. The powers of authority represent a reference point in relation to which the subject is created and introduced into the field of language and legal rules. It is for this reason that the subject does not question the legitimacy of social rules as such. For the subject is being subjectivised – it is given a meaning, a symbolic mandate and a place in the order – by these very same rules, therefore the subject does not know anything else, no other form of organisation, conduct, purpose or anything different to which it can compare the existing rules. In the process of subjectivation an individual is turned into a subject of that particular legal and symbolic order.

Yet, a problem appears when the mythological foundations of authority are questioned. The mythological foundations of legal authority are crucial for the functioning of society and for the process of subjectivation. Legendre (1997: 118) reiterates the importance of mythological foundations by claiming that 'what matters in the political destiny of the societies is not the scientific genealogy of their institutional development, but the mythological narrative which mobilises unconscious beliefs and binds them to a discourse inspired by the mystical truth of the all-powerful signifier.' An obvious question is: how do the institutions mobilise mythological discourse, make it their own and sell it as the story that legitimises them? One such institutional discourse is for example the discourse of human rights, which promotes rights based on universality, shared responsibility, equality and dignity. There is nothing inherent in the idea of rights as such (no material or natural instantiation) that would determine or call for the existence of particular institutions. Instead particular mythical foundations combined with political desires call them into existence.

However, in 'the modern world', mythical authority is questioned by a scientific discourse of law or positive law (Duxbury 1989: 89). An example of how the scientific discourse questions the mythical origins of the existing legal authority (and also fails in doing so) is the way in which the US attempted to institute a new law post 9/11.[2] Particularly interesting is the need to legally back up any actions the US took in the war on terror. Their conduct was either legitimised within the existing law or a new law was drawn for that purpose. After 9/11 the US Congress gave the President almost unlimited means by which to defend the nation (US Congress 2001); the military actions were taken yet almost simultaneously the US pushed forward an international discourse whereby the individuals caught in the so-called war on terror were to be exempted from the legal framework of the laws of armed conflict. While on the level of the international, the former saw no major upheaval, the latter – legal – was met with more resistance. Instead of 'simply' excluding the 'prisoners of the war on terror' from all the existing legal conventions and mechanisms of protection, the US began to re-draw the existing lines of legal protection concerning the conditions of detention in the times of war; amongst others, a category of 'unlawful enemy combatant' was created. However, the 'new' laws and legal frameworks were too arbitrary and lacked authority for them to receive wider international as well as public legitimacy and acceptance. Thus the US, despite its attempts, failed in re-drawing new laws and building solid arguments for exclusions from the existing laws. Nonetheless, in this attempt two very interesting aspects about the nature of legal authority were revealed. First – returning to the discussed 'mythical authority' of the sovereign – the case of the war on terror and the attempt to re-draw new laws pertaining to this situation only reveals the absence of authority of a modern sovereign. In other words, the sovereign's word *per se* is no longer the instance of law. It requires something else for it to become law (something that pertains to the realm of public opinion, international mandate or legal system, and is thus external to the sovereign). And second, continuing from the previous point, for the lack of mythical authority of the modern sovereign and its inability to presents its words as the letter of law, the sovereign always seeks the authority of written law (and thus of legal rules). To illustrate, President Bush could not proclaim the exception or, solely on the basis of his order, institute a new system of detention and conduct concerning the prisoners of the war on terror; instead he sought legal opinions, interpretations of the existing laws, to address the situation or asked for new laws to be drawn to support his 'political will'. But as law cannot be re-drawn on the basis of a sovereign's will, the new laws lacked 'mythical origins'. They were incomplete.

What exposed the incomplete foundation of new law and what questioned the legitimacy of sovereign decision? By understanding the politics of the war on terror and Guantánamo through the perspective of a myth, one could make an observation that what the US has done as a response to 9/11 is to redraw the old colonial lines that determined who is a legitimate opponent with rights that have to be respected, and who is not. A retreat to the politics of drawing lines between barbarian and civilised nations re-invoked a discourse of colonialism and imperialism that has, or so it was thought, long been left behind (at least since World War II). The principles upon which the international community is based today precisely deny any division or asymmetrical power relations based on the colonial past and advocate universal human rights for every living person. After World War II when the discourse of colonialism was still very much alive, the principles of international society were translated into different legal mechanisms and international institutions such as the United Nations, with one purpose, to prevent the same atrocities from happening again. The principles of international law and a process of decolonisation have removed the discourse of colonialism, which can be seen as the major factor in the events that led to World War II, from the political arena. New mechanisms, or so it was thought, no longer divided states along the colonial divide (something that remained present in the period between the World Wars), where some states were privileged and legally allowed to do more than others, even to decide on the fate of another state. International law and the international society that emerged as a result of World War II were perceived as being freed from the old colonial divides.

However, the US with their response to the 9/11 attacks questioned the universality of these principles and cast a shadow of doubt over their validity. In doing so, they did not only question the validity of the principles, but most importantly, they uncovered the hidden truth of the system, which is that the validity of the principles is based on hypocrisy and that the equality between nations and individuals, which was deemed to be essential for the working of the international society after World War II, is in fact only a façade. In this respect the US response to the war on terror has made the system face its inner truth, or as Lacan would describe it, its perverted side. The uncovering of hypocrisy and the mythical origins of law (or legal principles) is what took place in the US legal and political framework of the war on terror.

This section has explored how the law functions on the level of society and where the institutions gain their legitimacy. Throughout the discussion the main problem institutions face in search of their authority was indicated – that is the interplay between the mythical and scientific sources of authority. In what follows, the institution of legal subject – that this section touched upon – is explored. The section problematises the subject–law relationship and indicates different ways in which a subject within law (but also law as such) can be thought about.

Thinking legal subjectivity otherwise

The subject of legal studies is a subject of law as an ideational construct not a 'natural form' in which individuals appear in the realm of the social, legal and the political; and it is the process of subjectivation that turns the individual into a subject. Thus, the subject is first born in nature and only for the second time in the institution of law, or, as Legendre (1997) puts it, the first birth occurs upon the subject's encounter with paternal metaphor, whereas the second in the encounter with the institution of law. The problem with such an understanding of legal subjectivity is twofold. First, it is exclusionary, as only a limited number of subjects are recognised by the institution of law. Historically, for example, full subjects of law were only the adult white man; people of colour, women or children were not considered as full subjects of law. They were only – to different degrees – included in the law or appear in law as objects rather than subjects. Nowadays, a similar example applies to stateless people; they too cannot be protected by law and thus do not feature in the realm of law as its subjects. Second, the Oedipal (or paternal, hierarchical) logic that is still ordering the legal discourse is no longer predominant. The postmodern space of politics inhabited by the de-centred subject no longer relates or is no longer ordered according to a hierarchical authority (that is the master, judge, father and the sovereign are no longer absolute positions of authority). In turn this has an implication on the way the individual becomes a subject of law, for the subject is no longer subjectivised according to paternal logic. Thus it seems that a gap between the legal subjectivity valid in the institution of law and the postmodern subject is formed. Arguably such a gap brings to light the injustices and leaves different groups of individuals at the margins of politics as well as stripping them of any legal and political protection. The most obvious examples are asylum seekers or undocumented migrants, but also Guantánamo detainees who, in their struggle for the recognition of their existence, remain outside the law (despite the fact that courts have heard and made decisions on their habeas corpus petitions). Thus, it emerges as necessary to re-think the parameters according to which an individual appears in the realm of law, and, consequently, address this gap between law (what law does) and its subjects (how it addresses subjects whom it is referring to). The task of such re-thinking is ontological and begins at the level of a life in a society.

That societies consist of human beings who are endowed with reason and subjected to inalienable and sacred human rights should not be taken for granted. The image society has of its subjects is rational and scientific, *and* subjective and mythical. The two images play along various dualisms prominent in modern thinking of the self: body–mind, person–thing, mind–matter, all constructing a way of reasoning that legitimises the existence of 'one' in relation to the existence of the 'other' (Supiot 2007: 11). The modern Western metaphysics relies on such dualisms, which in turn imply that aside from 'internal forces', the subject equally requires an external impetus for its formation. The example of the individual's subjectivation into the subject of law follows this logic. An individual requires external impetus to be recognised (or turned) into a subject. That does not mean that the subject needs an external impetus for it to be able 'to form itself', but rather that the external impetus is essential for it *to be constructed* as a subject in relation to or in a particular context (that is, either in the context of law in general, of a court, political order, but also to be recognised as a specific social form – the father, daughter, etc.). In the discourse of the institution, the state law or legal order is one of such external mechanisms, determining subjects' existence, belongingness to society and existence within and for the law. An example of how law determines the type of legal subject and limits its conduct is legalised security practices and surveillance measures. On the one hand increased security measures and on the other hand growing precarity and insecurity of individuals living in a community, push subjects (of law) to seek security/stability in law. In doing so they subjugate their legal existence to laws, which heavily infringe on their personal freedoms and civil liberties, all allegedly for the benefit of (their personal or national) security. In contrast to the 'enhanced security' for those belonging, is the ever-growing group of those who remain outside and become victims of the perceived 'security for the few'. The legal subjects are thus only those who belong.

As legal personality does not address the changes taking place in the modern social, legal and political realms, how is one to re-think legal subjectivity outside the constraints of the group or exclusions of the type suggested above? And what is at stake in such thinking? The above example of a subject's conduct within and in relation to law (security measures) suggests that legal subjectivity is no longer only determined through legal forms or a subject's spatial belonging (the territory), but also on the basis of subject's conduct. That is, through subject's subordination to rules and laws and through its obedience. It is thus no longer through an external form that the individual internalises and in turn becomes the subject of law, but it is rather the behaviour of the individual (or his characteristics) that determines its belonging to law (or community). Thus we need to understand law no longer as an abstract and universal discourse but rather as an actor; and reconfigure it by looking at the effects it has on the subject. As Véronique Voruz (2002: 28) in her psychoanalytically influenced comment writes: 'not only is there no law without a subject – for law only exists in the moment of its inscription onto the subject – but also the subject is the primary instance of all discourses, that of law included'. The problem facing the critical thinking about law in a biopolitical world is then how to 're-capture' the subject (including those who are on the political margins) so that it begins to count within and as a legal subject. How to counter-balance the modern practice of subject formation where the subject emerges through its own actions and recognises those as actions of 'belonging'. Nevertheless, to be a legal subject means nothing else but to exist for and in the law, to exist not only for the law, and, importantly, to also exist for those who interpret and make law.

'Legal existence', as such, is key in our endeavours as to how one is to break with the deadlock of legal subjectivity emerging on the back of the differences of security and insecurity or inclusion and exclusion. Legal existence in question no longer operates on the aforementioned binaries or duality of the two births of the subject and/or the self–other divide whereby 'the Other' represents the institution of law. Ultimately, what is at stake in a different thinking is a different becoming of the subject of law; one that no longer relies on the intervention of one of the classical figures of authority, or one that operates as a constituting relationship and subjectivises in a less hierarchical structure. In psychoanalysis, the theory which was used as our guidance in this contribution, forms of subjectivation that pre-exist or are found alongside those of paternal nature, exist. Politically such forms are non-existent as there is no language with which one could locate them or determine their stake in the political realm. Yet, these different forms of subjectivation find their own relation to the institution and the law. The subject is left to its own capacities to create and re-create itself in different forms of legal existence. To return to the aforementioned example of asylum seekers or Guantánamo detainees:

a sense of a different legal existence can be spotted in their struggle for legal recognition. Through their behaviour, which counters law, they seek their own place within the law. Guantánamo detainees, for example, brought the language they knew – that is the language enriched with the stories from their childhood and the poetics of the Arab culture – into the rigid legal discourse of Western law and demanded recognition of their tradition. They persisted in claiming the rights of the animals rather than human rights; they referred to the abuses of the Koran rather than their own abuses and mistreatments in their attempts to re-gain some of the basic human rights or humane treatment (Zevnik 2011). With such endeavours they voiced their expectations and asked for legal protection but in a way uncommon to Western legal practice. All these practices of course do not bring to life an entirely different legal subjectivity; but instead demand recognition of something different from or external to the existing legal language (and Western law). Through such a practice they attempted to address the law as a living body, which is there to facilitate the openness rather than to create a closure of legal existence.

Thus rather than rejecting law and legal discourses in political thinking, what is suggested in this contribution is that the law, and its legal categories, are mobilised for political purposes and used creatively to support critical engagement with the existing political practices. In this task the knowledge about the origins (or the sources) of law is crucial, for only by being aware of what is at stake in legal authority can one begin to think, re-think and re-invent subjects' actions within and in relation to law, and in doing so revolutionise the law or use it as a practice of emancipation.

Conclusion

By adopting critical thought and psychoanalysis this chapter aimed at evaluating and exposing the critical potential of law for critical thinking in international politics more broadly. Its key aim was to highlight the centrality of the idea of law for thinking about political and social phenomena. Thus two different yet interrelated discussions took place. The first one (in the opening part of the chapter) put in conversation 'politics' and 'law' as two ideas as well as two disciplines and made an argument for an interdisciplinary engagement. It was discussed how Critical Legal Studies can enrich critical international politics' engagement with law, for CLS understands law as a social phenomenon which is broader than a system of rules. It allows us to see law as a force of emancipation, rather than as a mere repressive force or a mechanism of control. The second part of the chapter then explored the breadth of the humanist idea of law by following the thought of Sigmund Freud and Jacques Lacan. Two cornerstones of law – the authority of law and legal subjectivity – were looked at and discussed in reference to a political situation, namely the legal provisions concerning the war on terror and the detention of Guantánamo detainees. Through this discussion the chapter made an attempt at problematising legal authority, pointing to mythical foundations that uphold it and suggesting the problems that recent security-oriented politics faced in their attempts to change laws. Such problematisation of the idea of law on the one hand and recent political endeavours on the other hand were taken further in a discussion of legal subjectivity, where an argument for a reconceptualisation of who or what is the subject of law and how law should be understood is suggested. That is, the legal subject is no longer only a form applied to individuals who through the process of internalisation (or subjectivation) become subjects of law; rather individuals can also act, react and challenge law, and through such actions demand or fight for their legal recognition. As Guantánamo detainees, such individuals might not be full subjects of law, yet despite not being recognised as such, they deployed law for their benefit. The almost guerrilla actions displayed in the context of Guantánamo posed a challenge to law, and as Christoloulidis (2009) wrote, ruptured and opened law to a change, or perhaps even created an emancipatory moment in law.

Law as a governing practice, it should be remembered, underlies political categories and spatial orientations. Thus the most fundamental question that law poses to politics and the political is precisely the question of exclusion and belonging; it invites politics to re-think its inside/outside distinction not only on the level of space, identity or community, but more inherently on the logic which orders these three aspects into a particular constellation of political landscape. Thus, to think politics anew, as a force of emancipation, self-realisation or a form of freedom rather than repression, what are considered as key ends of critical thinking, politics needs to re-think its engagement with law, and in particular it needs to open up its discussions and understandings of authority and legal subjectivity. An ontological discussion of these phenomena, as suggested here, has enough critical potential and capacity for an institution of a different politics as both an ideational concept and praxis.

Notes

1 Within political theory one could perhaps draw an analogy with the social contract seen as an act in which an individual gives away some of its freedoms in exchange for security and a place in a political community. In a similar sense, incest provides the 'anthropological contract', by which individuals recognise who are 'socially acceptable' sexual partners, and with that, give away part of their personal freedoms.
2 By legal scientific discourse I mean the foundations of positive law that lay, amongst others, also in utilitarian practices and what Jeremy Bentham saw as legal fictions.

Further reading and useful weblinks

Agamben, G. (2005) *The State of Exception*, Chicago, IL and London: The University of Chicago Press.
Aristodemou, M. (2014) *Law, Psychoanalysis, Society: Taking the Unconscious Seriously*, Abingdon: Routledge.
Cage, an independent advocacy organisation campaigning against the war on terror. Available at: http://cageuk.org, accessed 5 October 2015.

Critical Legal Thinking: Law and the Political, blog discussing emerging theoretical and social questions in the intersection of politics and law. Available at: http://criticallegalthinking. com, accessed 5 October 2015.

Dayan, C. (2011) *The Law is a White Dog: How Legal Rituals Make and Unmake Persons*, Princeton, NJ: Princeton University Press.

Derrida, J. (1989/1990) 'Force of Law: The Mythical Foundation of Authority', *Cardozo Law Review* 11: 920–1046.

rua Wall, I. (2012) *Human Rights and Constituent Power: Without Model or Warranty*, Abingdon: Routledge.

The Rendition Project, website dedicated to researching globalisation of rendition and secret detention. Available at: www.therenditionproject.org.uk, accessed 5 October 2015.

Tomsic, S. and Zevnik, A. (eds) (2015) *Jacques Lacan: Between Psychoanalysis and Politics*, London: Routledge.

Zartaloudis, T. (2010) *Giorgio Agamben: Power, Law and the Uses of Criticism*, Routledge: Abingdon.

Bibliography

Aradau, C. (2007) 'Law Transformed: Guantánamo and the Other Exception', *Third World Quarterly* 28(3): 489–501.

Bulley, D. (2011) *Ethics as Foreign Policy: Britain, The EU and the Other Interventions*, London: Routledge.

Campbell, D. and Shapiro, M.J. (eds) (1999) *Moral Spaces: Rethinking Ethics and World Politics*, Minneapolis: University of Minnesota Press.

Christoloulidis, E. (2009) 'Strategies of Rupture', *Law and Critique* 20(3): 3–26.

Dillon, M. and Neal, A. (2008) *Foucault on Politics, Security and War*, London: Palgrave.

Douzinas, C. (2000) *The End of Human Rights: Critical Legal Thought at the Turn of the Century*, Oxford and Portland, OR: Hart Publishing.

Duxbury, N. (1989) 'Exploring Legal Tradition: Psychoanalytical Theory and Roman Law in Modern Continental Jurisprudence', *Legal Studies* 9(1): 84–99.

Fagan, M. (2013) *Ethics and Politics After Poststructuralism: Levinas, Derrida and Nancy*, Edinburgh: Edinburgh University Press.

Freud, S. (2001a) *The Complete Psychological Works of Sigmund Freud: Totem and Taboo and Other Works, Vol. 13*, London: Vintage.

Freud, S. (2001b) *The Complete Psychological Works of Sigmund Freud: 'The Future of an Illusion', 'Civilization and Its Discontents' and Other Works, Vol. 21*, London: Vintage.

Hart, H.L.A. (1961) *The Concept of Law*, Oxford: Oxford University Press.

Hirvonen, A. (1998) *Policentricity: Multiple Scenes of Law*, London: Pluto Press.

Hirvonen, A. (forthcoming 2016) *The Ethics of Tragedy*, London: Counterpress.

Johns, F. (2005) 'Guantánamo Bay and the Annihilation of the Exception', *European Journal of International Law* 16(4): 613–635.

Kojève, A. (2014) *The Notion of Authority (A Brief Presentation)*, London: Verso.

Lacan, J. (1988) *The Seminar of Jacques Lacan, Book II: The Ego in Freud's Theory and in the Technique of Psychoanalysis, 1954-1955*, New York: W.W. Norton & Co.

Lacan, J. (1993) *Seminar of Jacques Lacan, The Ethics of Psychoanalysis, Book VII*, London: Routledge.

Lacan, J. (2006) *Écrits: The First Complete Edition in English*, London and New York: W.W. Norton & Company.

Lacan, J. (2007) *The Seminar of Jacques Lacan: The Other Side of Psychoanalysis, Book XVII*, London and New York: W.W Norton & Company.

Lacan, J. (2008) *The Seminar of Jacques Lacan, Book VII: The Ethics of Psychoanalysis*, London and New York: Routledge Classics.

Legendre, P. (1997) 'The Masters of Law: A Study of Dogmatic Function' in P. Goodrich (Ed.), *A Legendre Reader*, Basingstoke: Macmillan Press Ltd, pp. 98–133.

Neal, A. (2006) 'Foucault in Guantánamo: Towards the Archaeology of Exception', *Security Dialogue* 37(1): 31–46.

Pin-Fat, V. (2010) *Universality, Ethics and International Relations: A Grammatical Reading*, Abingdon: Routledge.

Schmitt, C. (2005) *Political Theology: Four Chapters on the Concept of Sovereignty*, Chicago, IL and London: University of Chicago Press.

Stone, M., rua Wall, I. and Douzinas, C. (eds) (2012) *New Critical Legal Thinking: Law and the Political*, Abingdon: Glass House Publishing/Routledge.

Supiot, A. (2007) *Homo Juridicus: on the Anthropological Function of the Law*, London and New York: Verso.

US Congress (2001) *Congressional Joint Resolution, S.J. Res. 23*, 14 September 2001. Available at: www.law.cornell.edu/background/warpower/sj23.pdf, accessed 8 June 2015.

Voruz, V. (2002) *Psychoanalysis and the Law Beyond Oedipus: A Study in Legal Fictions* (Ph.D. thesis), London: University of London.

Zevnik, A. (2011) 'Becoming-Animal, Becoming-Detainee: Encountering Human Rights Discourse in Guantanamo', *Law & Critique* 22(2): 155–169.

10

NARRATIVE

Carolina Moulin

The name of the bloodsucker superstition is Mumiani [...]. The Mombasa incident took place ... in May or June [1947]. A man ... started a story that the Fire Brigade were Mumiani people and had been seen walking around with buckets filled with blood, and had taken a woman as prisoner at the Fire Station with intent to take her blood. [...] Fire Brigade men took this woman while she was sleeping ... off to the Fire Station.

The story ran round rapidly and aroused a great deal of excitement...about noon on the day the rumours got started ... the Municipal Native Affairs Officer heard the yarn, and ... went to the Fire Station. ... By that time excitement was rapidly rising. ... Very soon after the MNAO's arrival at the Fire Station a larger and angry mob gathered and started to get rough. Responsible Africans told the mob there was nothing in the story and certified they had searched the Station and found all in order. The mob refused to believe them. The MNAO with a few African police tried first to reason with the mob and then to disperse them. They were however heavily stoned and had to beat a rapid retreat ... soon after an adequate force of police came up and after a few baton charges dispersed the crowd and made a few arrests [...] The unfortunate Fire Brigade have I believe from time to time been suspected of Mumiani practices, because they wear black overalls, which are reputed to be similar to the dress of the alleged Mumiani men.

(White 2000: 1)

The Mumiani story is one of a series of rumours and altercations heard in the East African Coast about the role played by firemen, police officials and health workers in colonial times. These stories, passed orally through generations, though fantastic and ridden with superstitions and fears, helped local communities make sense of the violent nature of practices of care and control introduced by colonial power structures. As White argues:

they offer historians a way to see the world the way the storytellers did, as a world of vulnerability and unreasonable relationships. These stories of blood-sucking firemen or game rangers, pits and injections, allow historians a vision of colonial worlds replete with all the messy categories and meandering epistemologies many Africans used to describe the extractions and invasions with which they lived.

(2000: 5)

These narratives do not purport to provide an all-encompassing understanding of what the colonial project entailed, nor do they substitute other, alternative or official, historiographies of life and death under European rule. But they do speak about the 'aggressive nature of colonial extractions', giving them an intimate meaning. After all, what can be more personal and yet so universal than the blood that runs through our veins? The blood may operate here as a metaphorical representation of all resources that sustain life as we know it and as a metonym for the multiple ways in which colonised bodies have been subjugated. What are the consequences of considering such acts of storytelling and their narratives as significant elements for our contemporary understanding of colonial politics? The British rulers might not have believed in vampires, but they had, at a certain point, to resort to force and to dismantle local beliefs in order to operate their systems of domination. Even if these narratives lacked 'authority' or 'credibility' in the eyes of the coloniser, they had nonetheless to negotiate and deal with them on a daily basis.

This chapter is not about colonial politics, nor about vampires – though it could have been. This story serves instead to illustrate the role of narratives as reality constructs and as elements of power relations. International relations is also marked by its own ways of speaking with vampires, even though most of them have remained hidden, in the shadows, for quite a long time. To talk about global politics as an ensemble of narratives about the world, its processes and relations, its operations and circulations, is to consider that what we researchers and students of IR do is much similar to what local Eastern Africans did in our Mumiani tale: we are storytellers, we are both narrators and audiences to competing, conflicting, and, most often, incoherent and incomplete versions of the political processes we take part in.

In this chapter, we explore a discursive understanding of narratives: how the idea of narrative has been incorporated into the grammar of International Relations, what sorts of questions and research projects it has inspired and how a critical stance towards such a powerful concept can assist us to better understand and bring to the fore the multitude and variety of subjects, things and their relations that compose the kaleidoscopic world of contemporary global affairs. In order to do so, we begin by a reading of IR theories as ensembles of contesting narratives about the nature of global relations. We then turn to alternative forms of narrating international relations by focusing on the stories, voices and social dynamics of groups – central to the making of world orders but usually relegated to the sidelines of scholarly analysis. We focus on contributions and examples coming from studies oriented by feminist, de/postcolonial, and postmodern questions and methods. We then conclude with some reflections on the epistemological and ontological underpinnings that the concept of narrative can bring to the study of global affairs, focusing particularly on issues of authority and ethical responsibility.

IR as narration

A narrative is a way of making sense of the world around us. Narratives are '"equipments for living", tools to understand, negotiate and make sense of situations we encounter [... they are] a mode of reasoning and a mode of representation, a way to conceive of and also tell about the world' (Adams 2008: 175–176). Narratives tell us a lot about the limits and possibilities of political life, since they articulate particular worldviews, create and enable certain political subjects, and (re)produce specific understandings about facts, relations and peoples. Narratives can be understood as discursive formations that put in motion a series of political claims about international relations, such as who can act in the international system, in what conditions and under what circumstances. Narratives construct realities. By telling a particular story, one selects events and genres, categorises actions, and organises the unfolding of facts and perceptions about those facts. Narratives are also premised on assumptions about who can be the narrator and thus about who can speak of certain themes/events and about/for someone.

Most contributions that engage with the concept of narrative in IR, or what Dauphinee (2013a) calls 'narrative IR', have derived from strong criticisms of how the discipline understands what knowledge is and the appropriate ways of telling those 'knowledge stories'. In a way, the turn to IR as narration is an effort to enable creative forms of writing and to recognise the relational, expressive nature of our roles as researchers, students, witnesses and active participants in the (un)making of global politics. This is not to say that a turn towards narration necessarily entails a radically different way of performing and understanding our political realities. But, if we engage with our own research from a narrative standpoint, we are prone to take a more reflexive stance about our place in the knowledge production system, about our relations with those that are part of our research designs and about the consequences of what we say and do to those (things and peoples) that surround us. In that sense, a turn to narration provides a potential stepping stone to more diverse and polylogical forms of representation of the politics and ethics of IR. In so doing, narrative-oriented research produces ways of seeing/being/writing the world that 'should be evaluated not by some a priori standard of reference, but by their ability to generate new and valuable insights for particular knowledge communities' (Brigg and Bleiker 2010: 792). These are not new endeavours in our field. Feminist, postmodern and postcolonial approaches have long been at the forefront of employing a discursive approach, expanding and challenging the boundaries of a discipline linked to strongly oppressive, colonial, and state-oriented projects and ideals. They have built on developments in the fields of anthropology, literature, philosophy and cultural studies (to name but a few) to articulate new epistemologies and methodologies suited for complex, changing and contingent political realities.[1] Narratives provide us with one of many ways of contributing to such attempts.

Some authors have argued that International Relations (IR) as a discipline – and as a series of stories that help us understand the world of international affairs – is itself built on a set of narratives about the international system (Bartelson 1995; Onuf 1989; Walker 1993; Weber 1995). Therefore one might suggest that International Relations is itself the product of competing and contesting narratives, some of which have become so dominant that they have, for quite some time, been taken to represent the sole explanation for the realities and nature of international political life. Perhaps the most well-known and quoted narrative at the basis of IR is the Peace of Westphalia, a historical narrative that purports to explain the emergence of the state as the primary actor in modern world politics. According to this longstanding narrative, the modern international system began with a series of principles accorded in 1648, particularly related to the process of centralisation and autonomisation of political authority among European parties. The rise of sovereign political unities was premised on the defence of the principle of territorial integrity and non-interference in domestic affairs. This narrative tells us that the consolidation of territorial states within Europe created an independent actor (the sovereign state), that these actors are legally equal, that they have autonomy, that what states do and 'say' define the content of international affairs and that the domestic sphere is qualitatively distinct from the international realm. The power of the Westphalian understanding stems precisely from its ability to resolve the problem of political affairs by dividing the world into territories of belonging and authority that are both particular (since all states can decide who belongs, what principles and norms apply, and so on) and universal (statehood becomes the norm of political subjectivity in global affairs). This move allows for difference to be erased within (nationalisms operate precisely by homogenising the people) (Rae 2002) and to be domesticated outside (through war, balance of power, imperialism, international norms and institutions, etc.) (Walker 1993; see Blaney and Inayatullah in this book).

Others might claim that the modern international system actually began with the first navigations and the colonial enterprise of European empires in the late fifteenth and early sixteenth centuries (Amin 1992). In this case, the international system is built not on the principles of autonomy and independence, but on profoundly unequal and exploitative relations between the colonies and the metropolis. The story of the modern world is thus the story of the global expansion of Europe and of its mode of production, capitalism. The rise of the international system is consequently the rise of a world economy based on the unequal division of labour between peoples and nations, the destruction of alternative forms of life and the ruin of competing forms of 'local' capitalism in tributary societies in the Americas, Africa and Asia. Wallerstein (1996), for example, contends that the interstate structure and a capitalist world economy are the two significant elements of the modern world system, articulated around core and periphery relations. For him, the state was the historical political construct necessary for capitalism to thrive, since the interstate system creates the condition of possibility for free markets to operate and for capital and labour to compete. Cox (1996), on the other hand, argues that world orders are the product of relations between production and the social forces it engenders as well as the state forms they create. States cannot be seen as rational unitary actors, that have a single undisputed voice, but as state/society complexes. States advance and work for particular interests and social groups who control and mobilise resources. In that sense, states' power does not derive from a set of principles that grant them autonomy, or from their ability to coerce others to do what they want, but from a historical process sustained by articulated productive relations and social forces. Hegemonic relations, on a global scale, are not solely premised on material power, but on a particular configuration of material capabilities, ideas and institutions.

These are two contending narratives about the origins of the modern international system that highlight different and conflicting readings about political processes, the rules of interaction and the relations established among primary international actors. These narratives construct, therefore, different understandings about the logics and dynamic of world politics. If we narrate world politics from the standpoint of the Westphalian world order, we might argue that power politics is the essential nature of interstate relations since autonomy and juridical equality make for an uncertain and unsafe international environment. Therefore, states can only count on themselves to ensure their survival. A so-called self-help system emerges and the tragic tale of international relations becomes one of a permanent search for stability (since change is to be feared for it necessarily involves war) and control. This is the realist view of international politics that makes us hostages to a statist and static understanding of political life. This is international relations as war and peace; this is the IR of the Cold War and of great power politics. If we narrate the world from the standpoint of core–periphery relations, we still argue that power politics is the central feature of interstate relations, but we redefine what power actually means. It is no longer defined solely in terms of military capabilities, but also in relation to productive and ideological capacities. Destructive and productive forces operate hand-in-hand to produce an unequal order of developed/civilised vs. underdeveloped/uncivilised nations, of those who control resources and those who operate them. This narrative contends that such power relations engender institutional settings able to bring together social forces, state structures and international forms that reproduce hierarchical forms of world orders. Although the state remains a central actor, *state power* is no longer taken for granted. This is international relations as capital and labour; this is the IR of transnational corporations, of global financial institutions.

Both narratives are convincing in what they purport to explain, but are purposefully exclusive in what they silently obliterate. They left unhinged a significant part of the world's relations and peoples and, dangerously, lead us into thinking that change is either undesirable or untenable. They mediate our being in the world through the state and its surrogates, while condemning a great part of the globe to the sidelines of history past and present. They are consequently and necessarily partial and incomplete. Neither true nor false, they tell the story of IR from the standpoint of particular actors (states) and from a consideration of certain values (such as order and stability, for example) as intrinsically superior and desirable. Hence, rather than scientific, uncontested explanations about what international relations are, we can say that they are political narratives based on ethical choices about how one perceives, categorises, selects and reorganises the events and processes we call international. As Weber points out, these narratives produce myths:

> If IR theory narrates a particular view of the world from the perspective of various IR traditions, an IR myth is what helps make a particular view of the world appear to be true. The myth function in IR theory is the transformation of what is particular, cultural, and ideological (like a story told by an IR tradition) into what appears to be universal, natural, and purely empirical. It is naturalizing meanings – making them into common sense – that are the products of cultural practices.
>
> *(2001: 7)*

Many scholars have questioned what international relations would look like if seen and narrated from a different vantage point.[2] What if we changed the narrator, allowing not only unspoken, unauthorised voices to speak truth to power, but making these silences the point of departure of our narrative of international relations? What if we redefined the terms of the conversation by including different genres of narration? What if we allowed for a different temporality of narrations of the international, that no longer privileges the coming and going from a point of origin in the past to a point of arrival in the future, according to some sort of teleological route that somehow will lead us to a more 'developed', 'civilised', 'educated', 'normalised' world (see Lundborg in this book)? What if our narratives decentre the way we understand the political world, embracing uncertainty, mobility, ambiguity and incompleteness as our condition of being (and understanding) in the world (instead of the security, stasis and disciplined normality promised by the sovereign resolution of the statist version of IR) (see Brace, Nyers and Sleiman, and Shindo in this book)?

To take these questions seriously requires considering the critical potential of narratives as productive strategies of relating with things, international and otherwise, that surround us. Narratives are, in this sense, modes of acting unto the world and, as such, they are themselves profoundly political. Narratives should never be read in isolation, as stand-alone stories that somehow illuminate aspects of past, present and future realities. They are always partial and incomplete, embedded in values and in personal judgements; they always present us with a perspective, usually connected to other sets of narratives and stories, that can not and should not be seen as singular or unproblematic. Critical reflection upon the role of narratives in the understanding of world politics is fundamental if we want to question and raise awareness about their consequences for all relations *international*.

Listening to narratives

Narratives are imbricated in questions of authority. The mechanisms through which certain narratives come into being, circulate and become accepted among a particular community have much to do with the subjects from which they emerge and the normative context in which they take place. As Adams points out, narrative privilege demands us to question 'who is able to tell a story and who has the ability to listen' (2008: 180).

The narrator is a central figure in these processes for he/she provides the point of reference upon which the whole narrative is constructed. 'The term "narrator" designates the inner-textual highest-level speech position from which the current narrative discourse as a whole originates and from which references to the entities, actions and events that this discourse is about are being made' (Margolin 2012). There is a co-constitutive relation between narrative and narrator that is linked to issues of power and authority. Narratives construct subjects by specifying roles, defining characters, allowing some to alter the course of events and preventing others from entering the scene. One might argue that certain narratives become more acceptable, and therefore more powerful, precisely because their narrators stem from sites of authority. And as they turn into hegemonic statements about the nature of reality, they also reinforce the authorised status of the narrator. In the narration of IR, issues of authority and the role of the sovereign state work in a symbiotic manner. When we take the state, be it 'the United States' or 'Mexico' as the authorised narrators of international tales, as the centres from which our international stories revolve, we necessarily 'underestimate the amount and varieties of power operating in any interstate relationship and mistakenly assume that the narrative's "plot" is far more simple and unidirectional than it may in truth be' (Enloe 1996: 190). In order for 'Mexico' to negotiate with 'the United States', and for certain people to claim to have the right to speak on behalf of these fictional entities we call states, multiple narratives and political disputes have to be sidelined and, often times, strongly repressed. Enloe gives the example of Mayan landless peasants and the Zapatista movement as central actors in the dispute about the economic model of income distribution and land regulation in Mexico, usually sidelined by scholars trying to 'make sense' of regional economic agreements such as NAFTA. But even if these narratives are buried as background noise, they somehow continue to affect the ongoing rituals of interstate affairs.

As such, one of the critical potentials of taking narrative as a central concept in international relations analysis resides precisely in the opening up to the multiplicity of unauthorised narrators and voices – collective, singular, fragmented and unsigned – that continue to creep in the cracks of the interstate relations. As Meuter (2011) argues, 'narrative makes visible something that would otherwise remain unperceived'. Feminist scholars have been frontrunners in fostering research that reorients the question of authority and subjectivity. Take Cynthia Enloe's (2000) *Bananas, Beaches and Bases*, a groundbreaking feminist work in the field of IR, for example. She analyses women voices and strategies of mobilisation across a wide range of international clusters, from the global tourism and agroindustry business to the politics of US military bases around the world. Focusing on feminist questions such as 'where are the women?', Enloe (2000) shows how gender relations work to sustain international power hierarchies among, for example, plantation corporations, female mediatised figures and North American housewives. Rather than focusing on the intricacies of free trade agreements and global market relations, Enloe's provocative essay invites us to navigate the stories of female travellers, workers, wives, prostitutes, all of whom help to sustain a series of power relations that allow transnational corporations to increase their reach and profit, military officers to perform their 'duties' and white tourists to enjoy a relaxing vacation in the Caribbean, while governments increase their revenues and poor working women clean hotel toilets. Her work does not necessarily argue that statist narratives of the international are irrelevant or unimportant, but conveys the idea that they are both profoundly simplistic and incomplete. The relations that make the 'world go round' are complex and involve a series of actors that are at once objects and subjects of power. To incorporate their narratives and stories into the international picture allows the analyst to have a less distorted and less parochial understanding of what is at stake in international affairs, be it in the high circles of security and defence or in the local habits of consumers increasingly affected by global products and producers. It provides an interesting example of narrating international power relations from the feminine margins of politics and of deconstructing the centre place granted to men (and its masculine surrogates such as the state) and male values.

In the context of global circulations and of social processes that challenge the primacy of the state as a locus of political belonging, many scholars have embraced mobility and mobile subjects as alternative standpoints for telling and seeing global affairs (see Brace, and Nyers and Sleiman in this book). Johnson's (2014) research on refugee and migrant communities brings to light the tensions between efforts of states and international organisations to control and discipline human movement and the lived experiences of those on the move. Focusing on sites of profound political tension, such as the enclave of Melilla, a hub for migrants trying to enter into Spain and the EU territories, Johnson articulates a set of multiple stories of migrants and refugees themselves, how they become mobile, the tragedies of personal loss, the tropes of hope and sorrow, and the resilience to face ongoing adversities and to challenge simplistic classifications of their status as either il/legal or victims/criminals. By listening to migrants' stories, her work elucidates a different and often silenced set of relationships central to the making of borders and to the current institutional apparatus of global migration control. More than that, because of the central place granted to migrants and refugees as subjects of their own narratives, she was able to convincingly argue that a global shift in migration politics is in the making. First, the traditional analytical divide between forced and voluntary migration that seemed to structure our understanding of human mobility is being replaced by a dichotomous opposition between authorised and unauthorised movement. Second, the legal categories through which migration is made intelligible have become more important than refugees and migrants themselves. In this sense, much of the work done by actors within the business of governing global migration has been increasingly premised on highly technical and expertise-oriented grammars and has focused more on protecting the legal framework than the people the legal framework refers to.

But not all narratives come from a particular narrator. Sometimes the narrator is hidden, fragmented or turns into an unidentifiable collective. Sometimes narratives lack signature (Das 2007). Rumours provide a good example of social mechanisms of narration particularly suited for subaltern groups. In my own research with urban and rural refugee communities in South America, many instances of rumours and gossip were central to understanding the power relations in which these communities were imbricated (Moulin 2010). Racial tensions, institutional mistrust, confusion over authority systems, and fear were evident traits of the living world of refugee groups and structured in important respects, their relation with governmental officials, local communities and other refugees. Among Colombian migrants in border areas, rumours were a recurrent way of communication because of prevailing norms relating to violent control of peoples among drug warlords and armed groups. As silence became a strategy of survival in dangerous situations, rumours and collective forms of authorship turned into an important way of constructing social meaning. Without taking these utterances as expressions of knowledge and as elements of specific worldviews, much of political life would be either missed or misunderstood. The rumours spoke to and affected the political landscape of life in these sites and therefore provided an alternate narrative central to the making of power relations in these spaces.

It would be impossible to summarise the many contributions that have advanced a curious and detailed look into marginal narratives in international relations. These few examples above illustrate however, I hope, the potential of narrative as both an analytical tool and as a profound epistemological critique of what constitutes knowledge – and under what conditions it can be produced and recognised. The question of who can speak, or the problem of 'narrative privilege' (Adams 2008), is consequently tied to the multiple genres of narration and to the different paths critical research in IR can follow.

Which authors, what/whose stories?

The role narratives (can) play in current IR scholarship is connected to the epistemological critique advanced in the area and relates to a growing awareness for methodological pluralism and openness. Epistemologically, for narratives to be considered a mode of knowing, one has to move away from traditional positivist criteria of knowledge production. Narratives cannot be taken as objective realities, as empirical data, nor are they merely an effort at collecting and grouping a series of events into a storyline framework. Narratives necessarily blur fact and value, authorship and readership, characters and audiences. Narratives escape claims about mere truth, and about reality, for theirs is the realm of performativity. As Sandelowski (1991: 165) argues, 'what preoccupies the storyteller and audience is not how to know the truth, but how experience is endowed with meaning'. A narrative approach to international politics also disrupts a Western conventional reliance on the written word as the primary means of engaging with the world. After all, narratives are stories that circulate and their means of circulation are both varied and dialogical. Some narratives escape any form of 'plot' control, like rumours and gossip; while others seek precisely to restore some order to things that got either too messy or unintelligible.

Narrative as a concept is intrinsically connected to critical epistemological claims within IR that aim at reclaiming the importance of everyday life to understanding global processes, usually based on more ethnographically inspired research. These contributions have been fundamental in presenting alternative voices (and consequentially unheard stories and narratives) of peoples, places and events that are central to the unfolding of international affairs. It should not come as a surprise then that scholars sympathetic to a narrative-oriented reading of the field have resorted to forms of ethnological research.[3] If narratives are modes of knowledge and expressions of particular ways of understanding the world, one is pressed to think about how to participate, or to use an anthropological shorthand, to 'be initiated' in this dialogical enterprise. After all, narratives are not self-evident: they resort to specific rhythms, they adopt particular languages and grammars, and they speak from different vantage points (some of which are quite hard to grasp and even relate to). Narratives bring to the fore the problem of translation, a problem that is particularly acute for IR scholarship since difference is at the heart of its subjects.

Carol Cohn's 'Sex and Death in the Rational World of Defence Intellectuals' (1987) is one of the first works to bring ethnography's resourceful toolkit to narrate the world of defence intellectuals (and through such narratives, understand the more general dimensions of nuclear politics and international security). In her paper, Cohn shows how the everyday politics of a nuclear research centre, through its daily rituals and ordinary characters, is central to producing and sustaining a particular nuclear strategy by the US government. Rather than analysing presidential speeches, defence ministers' addresses, or international accords, protocols and regulations, Cohn reconstructs the multiple daily narratives that permitted the adoption of nuclear deterrence as a central strategy. Of particular relevance are the mechanisms of mobilisation and socialisation of nuclear experts and the ways in which a sense of community is built around certain grammars, rules of interaction and system of meaning. She reorients the analysis to the reconstruction of a language system that enabled a particular collective view of nuclear power and that sustained strong narratives about US power relations, the relationship between men and arms and the ordinary ties among nuclear lab workers, their families and their communities. Cohn convincingly shows how weaponry became the hegemonic narrative of international security through the daily use of domestic and abstract references to bombs and their victims (clean bombs, collateral damage, 'patting the bomb') and the highly technical and hyper-masculine nature of the nuclear business (widespread use of jargon and acronyms, religious references to godlike nature of creative/destructive power). Nuclear bombs were embedded in sexual imagery, making the option for disarmament, for instance, an act of emasculation (Cohn 1987: 693). The power of a gendered and domesticated language was fundamental in defining the narrative terms. And the reliance on a highly technical grammar, as a means of structuring conversation, proved hard for an uninitiated researcher. It took her several months to be able to make sense of physicists' altercations and eventually to be able to take part in their conversation. Only when she was sufficiently proficient to cope with these linguistic structures, was she precariously capable of reconstructing and retelling these narratives in the larger context of US nuclear politics.

An ethnological stance is not the only means through which one can approach politics in narrative terms. Efforts to narrate IR in multiple media are also worth noting. Many scholars have engaged visual culture as narrative modes of seeing/ being/representing the world of global politics. From critiques of popular culture to serious engagements with cultural artefacts, monuments and photography,[4] these contributions aim at enlarging the sources from which we hear/tell stories about global politics. They take these media as critical sites from which to question our disciplinary mythologies and to bring to light insights and perspectives into how IR is made and unmade. Debbie Lisle's work on travelogues (2006), for example, articulates the ways in which contemporary travel writing (or 'trip lit') and their narratives are embedded into visions about cultural difference and circulation that are central to modern global politics. Tourism and travelling are perhaps the most basic activities related to the international and therefore travelogues provide an accessible and widespread tool for understanding, experimenting with and 'narrating' the world. By interpreting these texts, in the light of globalisation pressures and dreams, and colonial histories and legacies, Lisle shows how these particular narratives can be used as resources to make sense of the world and to reproduce specific visions of how this world should be. Following an ethnography on the travelling trope, Vrasti's analysis of volunteering tourism (2013) provides a critical reading of the relationship between subjectivity production and compassionate travel. After taking part in volunteer programmes in Guatemala and Ghana, Vrasti builds on her own experience to show how narratives of help and assistance, intrinsic to volunteering experiences, are less about others and more about creating individuals who are entrepreneurial, creative and autonomous. As such, global volunteering narratives, she argues, are part of a larger logics of neoliberal capitalism aimed at designing selves capable of economic rationality combined with affective traits, flexible belonging and competitive drive.

Also worth noting are explorations on how different media have the power to help us better tell stories and engage audiences in the field of IR (rather than being taken as sources for these stories). Cynthia Weber's project 'I am an American'[5] is a good example of combining visual and written forms of narration into the framework of research. Her analysis of what it means to be an American citizen today revisits the lives of several people/characters in the form of fourteen short video documentaries that somehow help the audience to: 1) capture the ambiguities, tensions and contingencies of the lived lives of ordinary Americans in relation to the grand narrative of national American identity (and national security); and 2) provide a powerful aesthetic critique of foundational concepts of modern political life, notably the idea of citizenship and national unity, by embracing the mess of everyday forms of belonging and affection. IR scholars have also been taking a more active role in the critical film scene, by participating in festivals, acting as jurors, and working along photographers, producers and artists themselves.[6]

Narratives involve a choice about what stories to tell and how to tell them. But they also put into question the relationship between authorial and narrator voices. After all, the privileged position from which we tell IR stories, as authors/researchers, requires a certain mode of critical reflection over how to locate oneself within the research narrative and what sorts of mediation are required to transform our/others' stories into knowledge that is relevant for a particular community. By taking seriously the role of the knower subject (or the privileged author/narrator), Brigg and Bleiker suggest to 'bring the self back in' through autoethnography 'as a methodological resource [... that problematizes] the strict object-subject separation that characterizes quests for scientific legitimacy' (2010: 788). The turn to autoethnographic accounts is perhaps the most innovative and challenging appropriation of narratives in current international politics. This is in part due to the fact that autoethnography involves a clear, transparent (and often troubling) position about authorship that attempts to produce an ethically responsible stance to how authors relate to and negotiate with peoples and world events. As the introduction to a forum on critical methodological and narrative developments in IR notes:

> Autoethnography and narrative writing [...] involve storytelling, explicit use of the 'I' as a narrating subject, and deep exploration of the interface between writers and their subject matter. [...] They are showing that researchers are always personally present in their writing, that narratives – both written and oral – are knowledge-producing activities, and that the claim to scientific objectivity is not only impossible but also, critically, undesirable.
>
> *(Dauphinee 2013a)*

Making narratives 'personal' forces scholars to consider their own complicities, partialities and problematic placements in the unfolding of the plots that constitute their argument/understanding of particular international problems. Elizabeth Dauphinee's *The Politics of Exile* (2013b) is a remarkable example of an autoethnographic account in IR. Written in the interstitial form of a novel/academic book, she traces her own encounter with the Bosnian War and its aftermath and affectively narrates the difficult and impossible choices of one's research position amidst the relationships inevitably woven in the 'field'. In her contribution to a forum on autoethnography, Dauphinee summarises some of the questions her own experiences have brought about:

> Autoethnography in contemporary IR [...] asks us to explore the manner in which we evacuate ourselves from our writing, and to consider the implications of this. It has the potential to open us to a certain kind of scholarly exchange that does not seek unproblematic truth, but which propels fruitful exploration of a range of concerns in IR: the place of the self in writing, and the ethical risks of ignoring this; our relationship to those whose lives we research; the ways in which scholarly writing forces us to dismiss elements of our research findings into footnotes or acknowledgements (or to dismiss them entirely); to accept clear and present responsibility for what we write by stripping us of the armour of unproblematic 'data' and 'theories' that we use to protect ourselves; and to rethink the structured and silencing model of 'debate' that stultifies our scholarship and frightens our students and ourselves into making only the most minute, defensible claims.
>
> *(2010: 818)*

What's in the way of narration?

A binding element of all these narrative efforts in IR scholarship resides in their ethical horizon. When we intervene in international problems through narrative rhythms, we are forcefully presented with the limits of our reasoning, of our ability to communicate and relate to others, and of our own place in the world. Narrative thinking opens up authors, readers and narrators (often blurring these roles) to alternative forms of writing/reading/telling the world of international affairs and turns IR analysis into a site of dialogical knowledge production. They require a degree of ethical responsibility that is usually evaded when we sanitise our scholarly practices. But narrative approaches are also wrought with dilemmas and flaws.

A recurrent critique points to the fact that the act of narration is necessarily violent to those that are narrated. After all, the story of the refugee interviewed in Melilla is told, not by the refugee herself, but by the writer/academic who once talked to her. As Dauphinee eloquently states:

> ours is a discipline built on the deaths and losses of others, and these are deaths and losses that we never personally experience. [...] We don't invite them to our homes. [...] We don't love them. If we do, we do it secretly and we never, ever admit it.
>
> *(2010: 802)*

The fact that the subjectivity of our narrative characters is always and necessarily mediated by the writer/author/researcher produces an intractable problem for narrative approaches. Forms of collective writing and of narrative self-awareness are proposed as methodological ways of minimising the risks associated with turning academic narrative into a master narrative. Alternative forms of writing through fiction, prose and more expressive/creative modals are now being experimented with and provide a respite from criticisms of self-indulgence and logocentrism.

Narratives as tools for imagining IR are not a fashionable solution to the discipline's dogmatic and parochial underpinnings. They are not a shorthand for making IR problems and analysis more empathetic or intelligible, even though some narratives might just do that. Narrative approaches do not promise to take us on a less violent, more humane global journey. In fact, narrative approaches can actually be instrumentalised by disciplinarity efforts – as Vrasti's critique on ethnography aptly reminds us (2010) – and/or 'the narrative turn [can] result in a renewed cycle of seemingly new stories about the diversity and humanity of Europe and single and simple stories about its Others' (Muppidi 2013). These are actual dangers and we have to be constantly reminded of them.[7] But there is a seduction about the way in which engaging narratives invite us into an uncertain picture, a certain intangible promise that gets actualised in the means through which our reading of IR changes as we delve with these authors' contributions. There is an untouchable complexity to narrative approaches that makes IR both more difficult and more interesting, that makes it more 'real' when the factual and the fictional are no longer antonyms. Narrative approaches put a lot of responsibility on our shoulders. Taking narratives seriously demands way more from us, as players in the multiple plots of IR, than our conventional myths. And I think it is this responsibility that makes it so relevant yet so scary, as the colonial vampires that haunt IR mythologies.

Acknowledgements

My sincere gratitude to the editors for their careful reading and constructive feedback on earlier versions of this chapter.

Notes

1 For a good overview of the role of narration stemming from different areas of study, see Meuter (2011). In IR, among the many theoretical works that critically engage with a discursive approach, see: Campbell (1992); Der Derian and Shapiro (1989); Elshtain (1987); Enloe (2004); Milliken (1998); Weber (2006).
2 For interesting examples, see Wibben (2011) – the first study, to my knowledge, to actually engage with narrative theory as a way of thinking about IR puzzles from a feminist perspective; Dauphinee (2013b), Ling (2014) and Lowenheim (2014).
3 For a good overview and debate on ethnography's place in IR, see Lie (2013) and Vrasti (2008).
4 Examples abound of analysis of film, TV series and popular culture icons as relevant sites for telling international relations. For examples of a political critique of the role of culture, media and the aesthetics of representation in IR, see: Davies (2010); Doty (2006); Edkins (2013); Neumann (2001); Shapiro (2004, 2009).
5 The project's website can be accessed at www.iamanamericanproject.com. A book companion was published (2011) under *I am an American: Filming the Fear of Difference*, Chicago, IL: Intellect, The University of Chicago Press.

6 See Michael Shapiro's (2009) recounting of his own experience in such settings.
7 For an interesting and more radical critique of the limits of narrative approaches in IR, see Park-Kang (2015).

Further reading and useful weblinks

For a general, introductory reading about the multiple concepts on narrative theory and the epistemological aspects of narration, see Peter Hühn et al.'s web-based collection of articles, *The Living Handbook of Narratology* (available at www.lhn.uni-hamburg.de) and Abbott, H. Porter (2008) *The Cambridge Introduction to Narrative*, Cambridge: Cambridge University Press. For a discussion on the role of narrative history in the study of international relations, check the lecture given by Geoffrey Roberts at the British International Studies Association in December 2005. A revised transcript has been published under Roberts, G. (2006) 'History, Theory and the Narrative Turn in IR', *Review of International Studies* 32(4): 703–714.

A good analysis (with many interesting examples) of the potential of autobiography in IR is Innayatullah, N. (2011) *Autobiographical International Relations: I, IR*, London: Routledge.

For a powerful example of ethnographic research (in line with Carol Cohn's critique of the nuclear complex), see Gusterson, H. (2004) *People of the Bomb: Portraits of America's Nuclear Complex*, Minneapolis: University of Minnesota Press. See also for a powerful reading of ethnographic IR from indigenous cosmologies, Beier, M. (2005) *International Relations in Uncommon Places: Indigeneity, Cosmology, and The Limits of International Theory*, Basingstoke: Palgrave Macmillan.

A very interesting example of how cultural narratives produce particular legal representations (thus enabling mechanisms of discipline and regulation in the international realm) is Ann Sagan's (2010) award winning essay 'African Criminals/African Victims: The Institutionalised Production of Cultural Narratives in International Criminal Law', *Millennium: Journal of International Studies* 39(1): 3–21.

Aside from her own project 'I am an American' (see note 6), readers might also be interested in Cindy Weber's analysis of movies and popular culture icons and their relation to particular narratives about power in international relations. See, for example, her 'Popular Visual Language as Global Communication: The Remediation of United Airlines Flight 93', *Review of International Studies* 34(S1): 37–153. Her 2014 textbook *International Relations Theory: A Critical Introduction*, London: Routledge, in its 4th edition, also relies on cultural representation and cinematic narration to present and critique the main theoretical streams in IR.

For a discussion on visual politics (and their role in narrating international politics), check David Campbell's website at www.david-campbell.org.

An excellent venue for those willing to know more about the multiple readings on the current status of narratives in IR is the forum published by the IR blog *The Disorder of Things* (available at: http://thedisorderofthings.com/2013/03/12/critical-methodological-and-narrative-developments-in-ir-a-forum). For a reflection on the role of storytelling and the 'personal' in academic fora, see particularly this post: http://thedisorderofthings.com/2015/02/16/why-tell-stories.

Finally, recent debates on narrative developments in the field of IR have resulted in the innovative publication *Journal of Narrative Politics*, available online at http://journalofnarrativepolitics.com. Published since 2014, the journal provides a collection of essays, reviews and academic/activist analysis that resorts to creative modes of writing in the spirit of a more open, accessible and diverse understanding of knowledge-producing practices.

Bibliography

Adams, T.E. (2008) 'A Review of Narrative Ethics', *Qualitative Inquiry* 14(2): 175–184.

Amin, S. (1992) '1492', *Monthly Review* 44(3): s.p.

Bartelson, J. (1995) *A Genealogy of Sovereignty*, Cambridge: Cambridge University Press.

Brigg, M. and Bleiker, R. (2010) 'Autoethnographic International Relations: Exploring the Self as a Source of Knowledge', *Review of International Studies* 36(3): 779–798.

Campbell, D. (1992) *Writing Security: United States Foreign Policy and the Politics of Identity*, Minneapolis: University of Minnesota Press.

Cohn, C. (1987) 'Sex and Death in the Rational World of Defence Intellectuals', *Signs: Journal of Women in Culture and Society* 12(4): 687–718.

Cox, R. (1996) 'Social Forces, States and World Orders: Beyond International Relations Theory', in R. Cox and T. Sinclair (eds), *Approaches to World Order*, Cambridge: Cambridge University Press, pp. 85–123.

Das, V. (2007) *Life and Words. Violence and the Descent Into the Ordinary*, Berkeley: University of California Press.

Dauphinee, E. (2010) 'The Ethics of Autoethnography', *Review of International Studies* 36(3): 799–818.

Dauphinee, E. (2013a) *Critical Methodological and Narrative Developments in IR: A Forum*. Online. Available: http://thedisorderofthings.com/2013/03/12/critical-methodological-and-narrative-developments-in-ir-a-forum, accessed 24 October 2014.

Dauphinee, E. (2013b) *The Politics of Exile*, London: Routledge.

Davies, M. (2010) '"You Can't Charge Innocent People for Saving Their Lives!" Work in Buffy the Vampire Slayer', *International Political Sociology* 4(2): 178–195.

Der Derian, J., and Shapiro, M.J. (1989) *International/Intertextual Relations: Postmodern Readings of World Politics*, Lexington: Lexington Books.

Doty, R. (2006) 'Fronteras Compasivas and the Ethics of Unconditional Hospitality', *Millennium: Journal of International Studies* 35(1): 53–74.

Edkins, J. (2013) 'Politics and Personhood Reflections on the Portrait Photograph', *Alternatives: Global, Local, Political* 38(2): 139–154.

Elshtain, J.B. (1987) *Women and War*, New York: Basic Books.

Enloe, C. (1996) 'Margins, Silences and Bottom Rungs: How to Overcome the Under-estimation of Power in the Study of International Relations', in S. Smith, K. Booth and M. Zalewski (eds), *International Theory: Positivism and Beyond*, Cambridge: Cambridge University Press, pp. 186–202.

Enloe, C. (2000) *Bananas, Beaches and Bases: Making Feminist Sense of International Politics*, Berkeley: University of California Press.

Enloe, C.H. (2004) *The Curious Feminist Searching for Women in a New Age of Empire*, Berkeley: University of California Press.

Johnson, H.L. (2014) *Borders, Asylum and Global Non-Citizenship: The Other Side of the Fence*, Cambridge: Cambridge University Press.

Lie, J.H.S. (2013) 'Challenging Anthropology: Anthropological Reflections on the Ethno-graphic Turn in International Relations', *Millennium: Journal of International Studies* 41(2): 201–220.

Ling, L.H.M. (2014) *Imagining World Politics: Sihar and Shenya, A Fable for Our Times*, London: Routledge.

Lisle, D. (2006) *The Global Politics of Contemporary Travel Writing*, Cambridge: Cambridge University Press.

Lowenheim, O. (2014) *The Politics of the Trail: Reflexive Mountain Biking Along the Frontier of Jerusalem*, Ann Arbor: University of Michigan Press.

Margolin, U. (2012) 'Narrator', in P. Hühn et al. (eds), *The Living Handbook of Narratology*, Hamburg: Hamburg University. Online. Available: www.lhn.uni-hamburg.de/article/narrator, accessed 17 November 2014.

Meuter, N. (2011) 'Narration in Various Disciplines', in P. Hühn et al. (eds), *The Living Handbook of Narratology*, Hamburg: Hamburg University. Online. Available at: www.lhn.uni-hamburg.de/article/narration-various-disciplines, accessed 8 June 2015.

Milliken, J. (1998) *The Study of Discourse in International Relations: Reflections on Research and Methodology*, Budapest: Central European University. Online. International Relations and European Studies.

Moulin, C. (2010) 'Border Languages: Rumors and (Dis)placements of (Inter)national Politics', *Alternatives: Local, Global, Political* 35(4): 347–371.

Muppidi, H. (2013) *Reflections on Narrative Voice*. Online. Available: http://thedisorderof things.com/2013/03/23/reflections-on-narrative-voice, accessed 24 October 2014.

Neumann, I. (2001) '"Grab a Phaser, Ambassador": Diplomacy in Star Trek', *Millennium: Journal of International Studies* 30(3): 603–624.

Onuf, N.G. (1989) *World of our Making: Rules and Rule in Social Theory and International Relations*, Columbia: University of South Carolina Press.

Park-Kang, S. (2015) 'Fictional IR and Imagination: Advancing Narrative Approaches', *Review of International Studies* 41(2): 361–381.

Rae, H. (2002) *State Identities and the Homogenisation of Peoples*, New York: Cambridge University Press.

Sandelowski, M. (1991) 'Telling Stories: Narrative Approaches in Qualitative Research', *Image: the Journal of Nursing Scholarship* 23(3): 161–166.

Shapiro, M. (2004) *Methods and Nations: Cultural Governance and the Indigenous Subject*, London: Routledge.

Shapiro, M. (2009) *Cinematic Geopolitics*, London: Routledge.

Vrasti, W. (2008) 'The Strange Case of Ethnography and International Relations', *Millennium: Journal of International Studies* 37(2): 279–301.

Vrasti, W. (2010) 'Dr Strangelove, or How I Learned to Stop Worrying about Methodology and Love Writing', *Millennium: Journal of International Studies* 39(1): 79–88.

Vrasti, W. (2013) *Volunteer Tourism in the Global South: Giving Back in Neoliberal Times*, London: Routledge.

Walker, R.B.J. (1993) *Inside/Outside: International Relations as Political Theory*, Cambridge: Cambridge University Press.

Wallerstein, I. (1996) 'The Inter-State Structure of the Modern World-System', in S. Smith, K. Booth and M. Zalewski (eds), *International Theory: Positivism and Beyond*, Cambridge: Cambridge University Press, pp. 87–107.

Weber, C. (1995) *Simulating Sovereignty: Intervention, the State, and Symbolic Exchange*, Cambridge: Cambridge University Press.

Weber, C. (2001) *International Relations Theory: A Critical Introduction*, London: Routledge.

Weber, C. (2006) *Imagining America at War: Morality, Politics and Film*, London: Routledge.

Weber, C. (2011) *I am an American: Filming the Fear of Difference*, Chicago, IL: Intellect, The University of Chicago Press.

White, L. (2000) *Speaking with Vampires: Rumor and History in Colonial Africa*, Berkeley: University of California Press.

Wibben, A.T.R. (2011) *Feminist Security Studies: A Narrative Approach*, New York: Routledge.

11

POWER

Rita Abrahamsen

The concept of power is at the heart of International Relations. Since its inception as an academic discipline, power and the varying capacities and abilities of states to wield it have defined and animated debates, as evidenced by terms like the balance of power, super powers and hegemony. Rethinking the concept of power was equally central to the critical turn in IR, and a more complex, dispersed and relational understanding of power now informs diverse approaches within the discipline. This chapter begins by explaining how the concept of power has traditionally been understood and employed in IR, before contrasting this with less state-centric, non-sovereign conceptualisations. It shows how Foucault's insistence that we need to move away from the obsession with sovereignty, or in his words, to 'cut off the King's head' (1980: 121), has spurred more multifaceted understandings of the technologies and effects of power and also helped challenge the Western-centric character of much mainstream IR. By focusing on the North–South relationship – an issue area where the rethinking of power has been particular influential – the chapter shows how the discipline of IR is not merely describing the world, but also helps produce and maintain it. It argues that an understanding of power as productive and as governmentality is crucial to an appreciation of contemporary global politics, but also underlines the continued relevance of coercive power.

Power as domination and persuasion

In everyday parlance, as well as in much political science and IR, power is understood primarily as the ability of actors to influence and determine the actions of others, or as a form of domination and compulsion. A classic formulation of this view comes from Max Weber, who defined power as 'the probability that one actor within a social relationship will be in a position to carry out his own will despite resistance, regardless of the basis on which this probability exists' (1947: 52).

The most influential definition, however, is undoubtedly Robert Dahl's statement that power is the ability of A to get B to do what B would not otherwise do (Dahl 1957). Power, in other words, is coercive and intentional, and B is compelled or forced to act in a particular way; if someone mistakenly changes behaviour because they believe this to be what A wants, it does not in Dahl's definition count as an exercise of power. This requirement of intentionality has been challenged in later engagements with Dahl's claims. Bachrach and Baratz (1962), for example, drew attention to non-decision as a form of power and suggested that intentionality is not a definitional requirement of power. Instead, power is also present in the ability to shape and control political agendas, thus preventing issues from entering public debate. In this way power can be exercised even when A is unaware of its effects on B, an aspect that is also stressed in Barnett and Duval's important contribution to debates about power in IR. As they highlight, victims of 'collateral damage' certainly experience the power of the state behind bombing campaigns, even if that state did not intend to cause such damage (Barnett and Duval 2005: 50).

In a well-known contribution, Steven Lukes (1974) summarised the above views as the two faces of power; first, the deliberate exercise of power by A over B; and second, the ability of prevailing political values and institutional arrangements both to limit opportunities and bias the directions of political choices. To these, Lukes famously added a third dimension of power, focusing on the ability to form the very interests and values that determine action in the first place. In his words, 'A may exercise power over B by getting him to do what he does not want to do, but he also exercises power over him by influencing, shaping or determining his very wants' (1974: 23). For Lukes this is the 'most insidious exercise of power', as it works to shape people's 'perceptions, cognitions and preferences' in ways that may be contrary to their own interests, making people accept the existing order of things, including their own domination (ibid.: 24).

The understanding of power as domination and coercion maps readily onto many approaches and debates in IR, and has given us a vocabulary of super powers, regional powers, middle powers, great power politics, the balance of power, etc. More concretely, the ability of A to get B to act in particular ways usually translates into the capability of states to use their material resources, be they military or economic, to get other states to do what they would not otherwise do (see e.g. Mearsheimer 2001; Waltz 1979). Thus, the military might of Western states figures prominently in analyses of the Cold War, as well as in discussions of various military interventions ranging from the allied invasion of Iraq in the aftermath of 9/11 to more recent operations in Libya and Mali in 2011 and 2013 respectively. Economic superiority often informs discussions of globalisation, showing how despite the dispersal of power to a multiplicity of actors, poorer states remain subservient in the international system. Similarly, multinational corporations are frequently seen to have been empowered by globalisation and by virtue of their immense monetary resources to be able not only to disrupt and destroy local economies, but also dictate favourable terms of operation to weaker states.

While military and economic power occupy pride of place in IR, it is increasingly recognised that the ability to make states do what they would not otherwise do stems not only from heavy arsenals and deep pockets, but also from the power of ideas, values and norms. Such ideational or normative power can be exercised not only by states, but also by international organisations and non-governmental organisations (NGOs) that have acquired increasingly important positions in global governance (Barnett and Finnemore 2004; Katzenstein 1996). Sometimes also referred to as 'soft power' (Nye 1990, 2004), such analyses highlight how military or economic might alone cannot explain the course of international politics and correspond in many ways to Lukes' third dimension of power. As Nye observes, 'Seduction is always more effective than coercion, and many values like democracy, human rights, and individual opportunities are deeply seductive' (2004: x). The global spread of democracy, human rights and neoliberal economic policies are in part a function of such ideational power, and can be traced in part to the growing influence of various international organisations and NGOs. Soft power thus co-opts rather than coerces, persuades rather than dominates, and includes rather than destroys.

In practice, these various forms of power interact, sometimes reinforcing each other and occasionally pulling in different directions. This can be seen clearly in the North–South relationship, and more particularly in development aid. The aid relationship has predominantly been understood in terms of the superior economic and coercive power of the rich countries, which has enabled them to dictate the conditions of development assistance. The structural adjustment programmes of the 1980s and 1990s are a case in point; through these programmes the International Monetary Fund (IMF) and the World Bank were able to make poor countries adopt neoliberal economic policies, including privatisation and various austerity measures, due to their control of financial resources and their ability to deny future loans and development assistance to countries that did not liberalise according to the dictates of structural adjustment. It was this form of conditionality that prompted President Julius Nyerere of Tanzania to condemn the IMF and the World Bank as Africa's new colonial masters, arguing that there was little difference between his country's colonial past and its independent present (Nyerere 1980). In Nyerere's view, structural adjustment was a clear expression of domination or coercive power; economic might trumped sovereignty and the right of poor countries to determine their own economic policies. The demand for democratisation has been seen in similar terms, with donor countries being able to impose a particular vision and model of democracy by making financial assistance conditional on political reforms (Abrahamsen 2000). But ideational power and persuasion is also at work in this relationship, with the values of democracy, freedom and rights spreading through various forms of teaching, training, normative pressures and global standard setting. The three dimensions of power, as identified by Lukes, are thus all at work within the aid relationship and North–South relations more generally. Economic and military might interact with the power to persuade and also with the power to determine the political agenda, each playing a role in shaping global politics.

Productive power in global politics

Insightful as these interpretations are, important aspects of power in global politics cannot be adequately captured by approaching power as domination and persuasion alone. Instead, we require an expanded understanding, drawing on perspectives that regard power as relational and productive of identities and subjectivities. In what follows, I focus on the work of Michel Foucault (1970, 1977, 1980, 1991, 2004), whose analysis of power has been particularly influential in developing new 'critical imaginaries' in IR and new perspectives on the position of the South within global politics. Emerging from Foucault's thinking is a 'new conceptual architecture of power' that seeks to displace the conventional identification of power with domination and with the state (Dean 1999: 46). Foucault conceives of power as a 'structure of actions' (1980: 220) bearing on the actions of those who are free, that is to say, power is no longer perceived only as repressive, nor is it understood in purely material or institutional terms. Instead, it is relational and simultaneously productive and creative of subjects.

A useful starting point is the manner in which Foucault links power and knowledge, not in the purely instrumental sense that knowledge is always in the service of the powerful, but in terms of the production of truth and rationality. For Foucault, the possibility of a positivist, objective science is a myth, and the problematisation of a particular aspect of human life is not natural or inevitable, but historically contingent and dependent upon power relations already having rendered a particular topic a legitimate object of investigation. For example, in one of his early books, *Madness and Civilisation* (1965), Foucault shows how madness is understood differently throughout history and how with modern society it becomes synonymous with mental illness and a natural object worthy of scientific investigation and medical cure. In this way, Foucault draws attention to the way in which the sciences do not merely describe the world as they find it, but instead construct it and create the manner in which it is perceived and understood. Accordingly, any object of scientific investigation is simultaneously its effect and there can be no object of knowledge in the absence of a method for its production. Truth, in short, cannot be found objectively, but is the effect of discourse.

This expanded understanding of power as productive of truths has helped produce powerful critiques of the conventional telling of international relations, drawing attention to the power embedded within the discipline's own terminology and conceptualisations (see Chen and Cho, Moulin, and Ní Mhurchú in this book). In the Foucauldian sense, discourses are 'practices that systematically form the objects of which they speak', practices that have material effects (Foucault 1972: 49). It follows that the discipline of IR does not merely describe the world, but also helps produce and maintain it. This perspective thus encourages us not to accept at face value any particular categorisation of the world, but instead seeks to establish how certain ways of understanding and representing the world became dominant and acquired the position to shape the manner in which a particular aspect of social reality is imagined and acted upon.

The rethinking power and the power/knowledge nexus have found particular resonance in analyses of the North–South relationship and the manner in which this has been discussed in IR. The locus classicus in this regard is undoubtedly Edward Said's *Orientalism* (1979). Said argues that the Orient (or the East) does not exist objectively as a geographical, cultural or political space but was produced in Western scientific, literary and administrative discourses about the Orient. Orientalism is thus defined as a 'systematic discipline by which European culture was able to manage – and even produce – the Orient politically, sociologically, militarily, ideologically, scientifically, and imaginatively during the post-Enlightenment period' (ibid.: 3). In the case of the Orient, knowledge and power went hand-in-hand, and there was no such thing as an innocent, objective academic standpoint because there is 'no such thing as a delivered presence; there is only a re-presence, or a representation' (ibid.: 21). This is not to say that knowledge was produced in advance as an instrument to justify colonialism, but rather that it is in discourse that power and knowledge are joined together. Said provided a compelling demonstration of how the West had managed to establish an authoritative and dominant knowledge about the Orient and its peoples, and argued that the study of the Orient was ultimately a political vision whose structure promoted a binary opposition between the familiar (the West/us) and the strange (the Orient/them). The Orient, in other words, is revealed as central to European self-understanding and identity; it advanced a self-image of the West which in turn underpinned and legitimated its policies towards the Orient. By drawing attention to the intimacy of power and knowledge, Said made a first step towards challenging the hegemonic narratives of the West, a process which has been referred to as 'the Empire writing back' and destabilising the discourses that construct the 'other' (Ashcroft et al. 1989; Said 1993).

In IR, the recognition of productive power has helped to illustrate the discursive production of subjects and identities and the manner in which this in turn influences action (see el-Malik in this book). As Barnett and Duval observe, basic categories of classification such as 'civilised', 'rogue' and 'democratic', represent productive power, generate asymmetries of social capacities and enable action (Barnett and Duval 2005: 56). In the case of the North–South relationship, this can be seen in the terms development and its opposite, underdevelopment. By recognising power as productive, these are no longer self-evident or preordained categories, but discursive constructs; particular ways of seeing and acting upon the world that reflect not only the conditions they describe, but also the constellations of social, economic and political forces at the time of their emergence. The term 'underdevelopment' came to prominence with US President Truman's inaugural speech in 1949, and social reality subsequently became ordered into new categories such as underdeveloped, malnourished, illiterate, etc. (see Escobar 1995). Pointing to this new classificatory scheme does not entail a denial of the material condition of poverty or the disparities between rich and poor, but rather serves to challenge their conceptualisation and the political practices that they make possible. Through these categories, developing countries became established as objects of intervention, and this in turn normalised the right of the North to intervene and control, adapt and reshape the structures, practices and ways of life of the South. Development discourse thus helps legitimise interventions in the South and thereby remodel it according to Western norms of progress, growth and efficiency, and whenever a new problem of underdevelopment is identified, new practices of intervention are devised to rectify the deficiency. In this way, development can be regarded as analogous to what Foucault termed the realm of 'the social' in domestic politics, instigating practices through which the underdeveloped subject becomes known, categorised, and incorporated into statistics, models and graphs, which in turn legitimate practices and facilitate the emergence of the developed, disciplined subject. Development itself is accordingly revealed as a complex form of power in global politics; not simply a benign act of altruism, but neither a straightforward pursuit of self-interest or the exercise of raw domination.

An important aspect of this understanding of power is that systems of knowledge and discursive practices provide the meanings, norms, values and identities that not only constrain actors, but also constitute them. In Foucault's inimitable formulation, humans are not only power's intended target, but also its effect (Foucault 1970: 170). It follows that every identity or subjectivity is contingent and shaped by power, and there is no essence or intrinsic properties to human nature or the self. Instead, all identities are produced through diffuse and contingent social relations that cannot be captured through a focus on domination and coercion alone. As Foucault writes: 'What makes power hold good, what makes it accepted, is simply the fact that it doesn't only weigh on us as a force that says no, but that it traverses and produces things, it induces pleasure, forms of knowledge, produces discourses' (1980: 119). Foucault often spoke about this as discipline, a form of power that does not simply threaten punishment but promises health, happiness and fulfillment. Disciplinary power is ubiquitous in modern society, and through its techniques of continuous categorisation, supervision and normalisation, the self comes to act on itself. Power thus offers ways of being and forms of pleasure, and in this sense the analysis differs from that of Lukes, where the shaping of identities is seen only as an insidious form of power that presumably should be eradicated or overcome.

Within IR, such concerns with the individual subject have played an important role in redirecting attention away from states towards the people who inhabit them, and facilitated important work on identities in global politics. In this way, the understanding of power as productive has been central to opening up new lines of inquiry in IR, and drawn attention not only to the 'contingent social processes that produce particular kinds of subjects, fix meanings and categories, and create what is taken for granted and the ordinary of world politics' (Barnett and Duval 2005: 57), but also laid bare the discipline's own involvement in these processes.

Governmentality in global politics

More recently Foucault's idea of governmentality has become influential in analyses of global politics, often challenging entrenched understanding of how power works and produces its effects (Larner and Walters 2004; Neumann and Sending 2010). Governmentality, or the 'conduct of conduct', refers to the way in which government works 'at a distance' from the state (Foucault 1991). In Foucault's words, governmentality expresses itself through an ensemble of 'institutions, procedures, analyses and reflections' (2007: 108), which in turn means that power is best analysed at the micro-level, at the point where it inserts itself into daily practices and routines. Again, this is an encouragement to avoid state centrism and to focus less on sovereign power; 'rather than asking ourselves what the sovereign looks like from on high, we should be trying to discover how multiple bodies, forces, energies, matters, desires, thoughts and so on are gradually, progressively, actually and materially constituted as subjects' (Foucault 2004: 28).

Importantly, power in this conceptualisation is again not the antithesis of freedom; instead, governmentality is based around and works through the exercise of freedom. These insights have found fruitful adoption in contemporary social theory, and have been particularly instructive in unpacking the functioning of the neoliberal state. As Dean notes, with the turn to neoliberal modes of governance, the 'notion of freedom and the free conduct of individuals … becomes the principle by which government is to be rationalised and reformed' (1999: 155). The policies of decentralisation and the pluralisation of centres of decision-making away from the state towards various quasi-autonomous, non-governmental organisations and institutions, or 'partners', show how the 'conduct of conduct' increasingly obtains in sites 'at a distance' from the state itself (Rose 1996). At the same time, decentralisation is accompanied by a vast array of new mechanisms and techniques of auditing, accounting, monitoring and evaluation which link these various and disparate entities to political strategies at the state level (Rose and Miller 1992). While such networks and techniques are the condition of existence for rule at a distance, they simultaneously accord actors a degree of autonomy and responsibility for decisions and actions.

In domestic social policy, this often entails engaging target populations as active and free subjects, as informed and responsible actors capable of taking control of their own lives and futures. The 'unemployed', 'drug users' and 'single mothers' are thus no longer simply victims or passive recipients of policies, but subjects to be empowered. Frequently this involves the deployment of contracts through which subjects are committed to a range of 'normalizing, therapeutic and training mechanisms' designed to empower them, optimise their skills, their entrepreneurship, and so on (Dean 1999: 168). Top-down directives and impositions give way to, or exist side by side with, forms of self-rule, or what Rose terms 'the instrumentalization of a regulated autonomy' (1996: 57). Modern liberal rule in this sense governs through the management of freedom, and the retreat from direct state intervention is simultaneously a technology of government through various strategies of 'responsibilisation' and empowerment (Cruikshank 1999; Donzelot 1979).

Transferred to global politics and the North–South relationship we can trace similar moves towards rule at a distance and efforts to shape and influence state behaviour (and the behaviour of populations) through a multiplicity of different techniques of observation, calculation and administration. An instructive example is the abandonment of overt aid conditionality in favour of a focus on development partnerships (Abrahamsen 2004). Reminiscent of Dahl's definition of coercive power, development assistance in the 1980s and 1990s was only granted on condition that recipient countries implemented economic and political reforms specified by donors. At the close of the century, however, the World Bank and the IMF abandoned aid conditionality. Responding to persistent critiques of these policies as excessively intrusive, the World Bank President launched a new focus on partnership and ownership, declaring that henceforth 'the recipient country must be in the driver seat', exercising choice and setting its own priorities (Wolfensohn 1999). Developing countries were now renamed 'partner' countries and asked to produce their own development strategies, known as Poverty Reduction Strategy Papers (PRSPs). These development plans should be produced in consultation with civil society and donors, and should be 'owned' by government and citizens as opposed to imposed from the outside.

Development partnerships are formalised through a series of contracts, memoranda of understanding and best practice guidelines, and through such agreements, recipient countries are enlisted as the active agents of their own reform. Instead of overt conditionality and criteria that must be met prior to the release of funds, compliance is now achieved through a series of inbuilt audits, benchmarks and triggers. An instructive example is the World Bank's Poverty Reduction Matrix: presented by the Bank as a 'critical management tool', the matrix includes fourteen different prerequisites for sustainable growth and poverty reduction – ranging from good governance, justice and education to health, water and culture. Countries are advised to have programmes under each heading in the matrix, plus a detailed annex containing the specifics of short- and long-term goals, their present status, timing, costs and progress. From the point of view of the World Bank, 'the matrix allows us to see quickly what is going on in a country and what is not going on' (Wolfensohn 1999: 27–27). Supported by the PRSP Sourcebook of twenty-five chapters and 600-plus pages, the mechanisms of oversight multiply at every turn. In this way, conditionality has become routinised and institutionalised in the bureaucratic policy process, and as a result, arguably also depoliticised in the sense that it is removed from the arena of political discussion and influence and instead appears as a series of measureable, technocratic procedures.

Partnerships are forms of power that serve to make governments and their citizens more responsible for their own development, while simultaneously legitimising new forms of interventions and practices. The matrix is only one of many mechanisms that contribute towards making partnerships a self-disciplining device embedded in the structure of the aid relationship, and partnerships do to a significant extent decentre power, which now works through the regulated freedom of recipient governments and state bureaucrats. In this sense, partnerships function as a technology of agency and responsibilisation that engage their target countries as active and free subjects, as responsible actors capable of taking control of their own development strategies and populations, as opposed to objects of external benevolence or sanctions. This is not to say that governmentality has replaced sovereign or coercive power – importantly, the World Bank and the IMF retain veto power over all PRSPs, and there is little doubt that donors continue to influence policy directions in poor countries, especially due to their superior economic resources. Instead, partnerships govern recipient countries through a combination of inclusion, consent and coercion. While voluntary, this new aid regime provides the conditions for a more detailed micro-management of countries by donors and creditors, only now the medicine is largely self-administered. This is the contradiction at the heart of the partnership discourse; it is at one and the same time less coercive and more intrusive than the good governance agenda of the 1990s.

Conclusion

The rethinking of power has been central to the critical turn in IR and a reconceptualisation of power along the lines sketched above informs and underpins many of the other concepts discussed in this volume. For the purpose of illustration, let's mention two – difference and resistance. The issue of difference and identity (Chapter 6) is intimately linked to an expanded definition of power as productive of subjectivities through various micro-technologies and relations. In the North–South relationship, this has often been analysed by postcolonial perspectives of hybridity and the way in which identities – such as the coloniser and the colonised – are forged in relationship with each other. Nowhere are these mutually constitutive identities better illustrated than in Frantz Fanon's haunting statement that 'the Negro is not. Any more than the white man' (1986: 231). The white man's self-perception as moral, rational and civilised required the image of the Negro as barbaric and uncivilised. In contemporary global politics this finds clear echoes, for example in discussions of the 'Islamic other' and responses to what is sometimes called the 'war on terror', and the understanding of power as productive of subjectivities has helped challenge such essentialised, binary oppositions (see e.g. Cloud 2004; Jackson 2007).

Discussions of resistance (see Shindo in this book) too have been facilitated by the reconceptualisation of power. For Foucault, where there is power there is always resistance. Power operates in and through micro-practices, and this has facilitated analyses of everyday struggles as resistance, as in James Scott's explorations of how the subaltern, despite oppression, frequently avoids and mocks power through 'hidden transcripts' and veiled forms of practical resistance (Scott 1985, 1990). Similarly, the recognition of the intimate relationship between power and knowledge has led to a focus on epistemic violence, and resistance can also be seen to encompass efforts to give voice and make visible those who are not normally heard or seen in dominant discourses (Prakash 1992; Spivak 1988). Put differently, resistance extends beyond challenging the economic and political structures of domination to include its epistemological underpinnings. The rethinking of power is thus a contribution towards reconfiguring the conceptual space in which we understand and act upon the world, and thereby create the space for alternative ways of being and acting.

Perhaps more than at any other time we need analyses of power that take account of its multiple modalities and technologies. While the approaches described here have been successful in analysing the productive dimensions of power, we need simultaneously to ensure that this is not at the expense of the material and coercive dimensions of power. As Dean has observed, focusing too exclusively on productive power and governmentality can lead to the conclusion that 'sovereign power is being undermined, decentred, flattened, deterritorialised, pluralised, and conceptually displaced', and as a result it appears as a 'second order phenomenon, even as an archaism or survival of absolutist or monarchical power' (2007: 133). Yet, coercive power remains central in the global order, not merely in the sense of superior military and economic might, but also in their interaction with productive and disciplinary power. This is perhaps especially the case in the North–South relationship.

A key question for future critical IR is thus how these forms of power interact, and how some forms of productive power help make some forms of coercive power legitimate and acceptable. To continue the focus on North–South relations, we can see this imbrication of multiple forms of power in the case of so-called failed states. In recent years, these have been constructed and classified as a particular category of states that are not simply a risk to their own neglected and poor populations, but also to global security and the security and welfare of rich states in the North (see Abrahamsen 2005). This in turn has facilitated and legitimised particular types of interventions in these countries, where military and security responses go hand-in-hand with interventions designed to win hearts and minds. Any attempt to understand the emergence of failed states, as well as global policies towards them, accordingly requires a multifaceted approach that takes account of the manner in which various forms of power interact and combine.

Writing a short, yet comprehensive chapter on the complex concept of power is inevitably fraught with difficulties and dangers, not least the temptation to simplify in order to facilitate comprehension and illustrate differences. In the above discussion, numerous nuances and complexities are overlooked and omitted, and important contributions to our understanding of power (such as those of Antonio Gramsci and Pierre Bourdieu) are not included due to space restrictions.[1] The very framing of this volume with its focus on 'critical imaginations' also carries an inherent risk of constructing an artificial dichotomy between critical and traditional approaches, where the 'other' is by its very nature unable to be critical. Little is gained by such dichotomies and there is a need to be alert to the dangers of caricaturing other approaches as somehow stuck in outmoded understandings of power. IR has come a long way from a preoccupation with 'raw' power, and while sharp contrasts and delineations can be useful in illustrating difference, they rarely capture the nuances of what lies between. In discussing so-called critical approaches, we need therefore to be sufficiently reflexive and attuned to the forms of productive power at work in designating some approaches as 'critical' and others as 'traditional' or 'conventional'. My hope is that my account has navigated these challenges with sufficient subtlety and openness to inspire readers to explore the concept of power in more depth, both through the key theoretical texts and through more empirical explorations of contemporary global politics. Our understanding of global politics has been challenged and expanded by the rethinking of power, and this rethinking must remain an ongoing project.

Note

1 Gramsci's key contribution to the study of power in IR stems from the concept of hegemony, whereas Bourdieu analyses power in terms of different forms of capital. The classic statement of Gramsci's relevance to IR is Cox (1983). For an application of Bourdieu in IR, see Williams (2007).

Further reading

Bourdieu, P. (2011) 'The Forms of Capital (1986)', in I. Szeman and T. Kaposy (eds), *Cultural Theory: An Anthology*, Oxford: Blackwell, pp. 81–93.
Crush, J. (ed.) (1995) *The Power of Development*, London: Routledge.
Hindess, B. (1996) *Discourses of Power: From Hobbes to Foucault*, Oxford: Blackwell.
Scott, J. (2001) *Power*, Cambridge: Polity Press.

Useful websites

Edward Said on Orientalism, www.youtube.com/watch?v=fVC8EYd_Z_g. Interview with Said, where he talks about how the book was conceived, its main themes and how it relates to contemporary world politics.
'Africa for Norway', www.youtube.com/watch?v=oJLqyuxm96k. Funny parody or spoof of charity videos, illustrating the power of development to shape perceptions and identities.

Bibliography

Abrahamsen, R. (2000) *Disciplining Democracy*, London: Zed Books.
Abrahamsen, R. (2004) 'The Power of Partnerships in Global Governance', *Third World Quarterly* 25(8): 1453–1467.
Abrahamsen, R. (2005) 'Blair's Africa: The Politics of Securitization and Fear', *Alternatives: Global, Local, Political* 30(1): 55–80.
Ashcroft, B., Griffiths, G. and Tiffin, H. (1989) *The Empire Writes Back: Theory and Practice in Post-Colonial Literatures*, London: Routledge.
Bachrach, P. and Baratz, M. (1962) 'Two Faces of Power', *American Political Science Review* 56(4): 947–952.

Barnett, M. and Duval, R. (2005) 'Power in International Politics', *International Organization* 59(1): 39–75.

Barnett, M. and Finnemore, M. (2004) *Rules for the World: International Organizations in Global Politics*, Ithaca, N.Y.: Cornell University Press.

Cloud, D.L. (2004) '"To veil the threat of terror": Afghan Women and The "Clash of Civilizations" in the Imagery of the U.S. War on Terrorism', *Quarterly Journal of Speech* 90(3): 285–306.

Cox, R. 1983 'Gramsci, Hegemony and International Relations: An Essay in Method', *Millennium: Journal of International Studies* 12(2): 162–175.

Cruikshank, B. (1999) *The Will to Empower: Democratic Citizens and Other Subjects*, Ithaca, NY: Cornell University Press.

Dahl, R. (1957) 'The Concept of Power', *Behavioral Science* 2(3): 201–215.

Dean. M. (1999) *Governmentality: Power and Rule in Modern Society*, London: Sage.

Dean, M. (2007) *Governing Societies*, Maidenhead: Open University Press.

Donzelot, J. (1979) *The Policing of Families*, London: Hutchinson.

Escobar, A. (1995) *Encountering Development: The Making and Unmaking of the Third World*, Princeton, NJ: Princeton University Press.

Fanon, F. (1986) *Black Skin, White Masks*, London: Pluto Press.

Foucault, M. (1965) *Madness and Civilization*, London: Vintage Books.

Foucault, M. (1970) *The Order of Things: An Archaeology of the Human Sciences*, London: Tavistock.

Foucault, M. (1972) *The Archeology of Knowledge*, London: Tavistock.

Foucault, M. (1977) *Discipline and Punish: The Birth of the Prison*, London: Allen Lane.

Foucault, M. (1980) *Power/Knowledge: Selected Interviews and Other Writings*, London: Harvester.

Foucault, M. (1991) 'Governmentality', in G. Burchell, C. Gordon and P. Miller (eds), *The Foucault Effect: Studies in Governmentality*, London: Harvester Wheatsheaf, pp. 87–104.

Foucault, M. (2004) *Society Must be Defended*, Harmondsworth: Penguin.

Foucault, M. (2007) *Security, Territory, Population*, Basingstoke: Palgrave Macmillan.

Jackson, R. (2007) 'Constructing Enemies: "Islamic Terrorism" in Political and Academic Discourse', *Government and Opposition* 42(3): 394–426.

Katzenstein, P. (ed.) (1996) *The Culture of National Security: Norms and Identity in World Politics*, New York: Columbia University Press.

Larner, W. and Walters, W. (eds) (2004) *Global Governmentality: Governing International Spaces*, London: Routledge.

Lukes, S. (1974) *Power: A Radical View*, London: Macmillan.

Mearsheimer, J.M. (2001) *The Tragedy of Great Power Politics*, New York: W.W Norton and Company.

Neuman, I.B. and Sending, O.J. (2010) *Governing the Global Polity: Practice, Mentality, Rationality*, Ann Arbor: University of Michigan Press.

Nye, J. (1990) *Bound to Lead: The Changing Nature of American Power*, New York: Basic Books.

Nye, J. (2004) *Soft Power: The Means to Success in World Politics*, New York: Public Affairs.

Nyerere, J. (1980) 'No to IMF Meddling', *Development Dialogue* 2: 7–9.

Prakash, G. (1992) 'Postcolonial Criticism and Indian Historiography', *Social Text* 31/32: 84–98.

Rose, N. (1996) 'Governing "Advanced" Liberal Democracies', in A. Barry, T. Osborn and N. Rose (eds), *Focuault and Political Reason*, London: UCL Press.

Rose, N. and Miller, P. (1992) 'Political Power Beyond the State: Problematics of Government', *British Journal of Sociology* 43(2): 172–205.

Said, E. (1979) *Orientalism*, London: Penguin.

Said, E. (1993) *Culture and Imperialism*, London: Vintage.

Scott, J. (1985) *Weapons of the Weak: Everyday Forms of Resistance*, New Haven, CT: Yale University Press.

Scott, J. (1990) *Domination and the Art of Resistance: Hidden Transcripts*, New Haven, CT: Yale University Press.

Spivak, G. (1988) 'Can the Subaltern Speak?', in C. Nelson and L. Grossberg (eds), *Marxism and Interpretation of Culture*, Basingstoke: Macmillan, pp. 271–313.

Waltz, K. (1979) *Theory of International Politics*, New York: McGraw Hill.

Weber, M. (1947) *The Theory of Social and Economic Organization*, New York: Free Press.

Williams, M.C. (2007) *Culture and Security: Symbolic Power in International Security*, Abingdon: Routledge.

Wolfensohn, J.D. (1999) 'A Proposal for a Comprehensive Development Framework (A Discussion Draft)', Washington DC: World Bank, http://web.worldbank.org/archive/website01013/WEB/IMAGES/CDF.PDF, accessed 5 October 2015.

12

RESISTANCE

Reiko Shindo

Introduction

Any inquiry into resistance should start with the recognition that resistance is not something that can be named in an absolute sense (see Walker 1994). While the term, resistance, has been frequently used in various strands of IR scholarship, the precise definition of the term remains unclear. For instance, James Scott describes the forms of protests hidden in everyday practices as resistance, in contrast to actions that are 'organised' and 'principled' with 'revolutionary implications' (Scott 1993: 22). His definition is, however, no more than '[a] kind of individualistic resentment' for someone like Sydney Tarrow (1998: 7), who perceives the nature of resistance to be collective and structured. Tarrow calls actions of this kind social movements; they manifest *'collective challenges, based on common purposes and social solidarities, in sustained interaction with elites, opponents, and authorities'* (ibid.: 4, emphasis original). Some theorise resistance in relation to power relations (Agamben 1998, 2005) while others link it to the idea of hegemony (Laclau and Mouffe 1985). In some cases, resistance is used to describe struggles against colonisers and oppressive regimes (see Suhl 1968).

Louise Amoore points out the futility, and even danger, of defining the phrase 'global resistance': 'Understandings of the meanings of global resistance, together with perceptions of the scope and possibility for concrete resistances, are shaped by competing views of the world' (Amoore 2005: 2). I concur with Amoore and view her point as going beyond the debate on global resistance. I consider that a particular world view we hold is necessarily reflective of the way we talk about a particular concept, in this case, resistance (see Moulin in this book). This view informs the starting point of this chapter. To put it differently, given a variety of contexts and intentions invested in the concept of resistance, a productive framing would be neither to look for the definition of resistance nor to specify the essence of resistance. Instead, this chapter examines resistance in the specific context of analysis. Given the purpose of this book, the chapter is primarily driven by the following questions: how is the concept of resistance associated with a world view that challenges the centricity of the state in IR scholarship? How does resistance function as a catalyst in which state-centrism is called into question?

The chapter shows that the concept of resistance contributes, in two ways, to an understanding of world politics which challenges state centricity. First, resistance can be used to develop the view that practices and movements can no longer be solely understood from the perspective of the state. These practices have been discussed in the context of globalisation and recognised as concrete examples which question the claim that politics primarily takes place within and through the domain of the state. Second, resistance is connected to practices that challenge sovereign authority to produce certain types of subjects as 'political'. These practices refuse to accept the state prerogative to define the ontological status as a subject and monopolise the question of who is regarded as an authentic political being. This approach to resistance is reflective of an increasing interest in seeing the state not just as a political organisation but as 'a principle, institution, and practice that always works both as abstraction and as a material social form' (Walker 2004: 245). Sovereignty is not merely understood as an institutional manifestation of state organs but as a form of governance which controls behaviour and conduct. In this line of thinking, resistance is not simply associated with practices that liberate oneself from the state and the system of the state. Instead, it is linked to practices that manoeuvre, shift, and unsettle the existing form of governance that determines one's subject status.

The subsequent two sections will discuss these two different ways to link resistance to political activism. Given that they reflect a different view of the state, one may interpret the difference of these two approaches as 'traditional' and 'critical'. Such interpretation is helpful in some respects, especially because it enunciates 'traditional' and 'critical' understandings of power. As Catherine Eschle (2005) argues, the studies on global resistance tend to situate dissident voices and actions in opposition to those with power, such as the state and international organisations. Taking up on this point, Maurice Stierl points out that such inclination is 'tied to a static understanding of power' which 'naturalises conceptions of "powerless social movements" and "powerful state politics" as opposing forces' (2012: 427). While studies on global resistance perceive power between the 'haves' and 'have-nots', studies on resistance and political subjects perceive power relationally (see Abrahamsen in this book). Given that these different approaches to resistance show two distinctively contrasting ways of thinking about the state in relation to power, the present chapter benefits from the traditional–critical distinction in understanding resistance.

However, such a distinction can be misleading in other respects. In the third section of the chapter, I will argue that both types of studies on resistance share a similar inclination which focuses on practices driven by the desire to change the status quo. Reflecting on this tendency critically, I will argue that there is a need to incorporate unintentional and hidden practices into studies on resistance and world politics.

Resistance in the age of globalisation

In the 2003 special issue of the journal *Review of International Studies* (*RIS*), titled 'Governance and Resistance in World Politics', resistance was examined in relation to the changing conditions of politics. The editors argued that globalisation had given rise to 'two implicit, but under-theorised conceptions of politics' in IR, resistance and governance. The former is called 'politics from below' and consists of 'social movements, global civil society actors such as NGOs and potentially, coalitions of Third World states' (Maiguashca 2003: 5). The latter is dubbed 'politics from above' which indicates globally developed structures and entities such as 'formal institutions like the WTO or the proposed International Criminal Court to informal market mechanisms, all developing alongside and to some extent in harness with an increasingly directive role played by the major Western powers, especially the United States' (ibid.). The editors presented the view that it was the changing condition of world politics called globalisation that characterised the tension between 'politics from below' and 'politics from above'.

The *RIS*'s special issue exemplifies one dominant way in which resistance is discussed in IR scholarship: it is associated with practices and movements which have emerged in the context of globalisation. Globalisation is generally understood as 'a number of interacting socio-cultural, economic, political and technological developments that appeared to erode and/or transcend state/nation boundaries [...]' (Peterson in this book: 87). In this regard, it is argued that changes associated with globalisation 'are qualitatively "different"' because they 'unsettle ideas and practices that seemed familiar' to state-centred world politics (ibid.). As Amoore points out, whereas the discourse of globalisation has been circulating both in media and academia since the 1980s, it was only in the mid-1990s that resistance started gaining attention in association with globalisation (Amoore 2005: 4).

The connection between resistance and globalisation should not be understood as suggesting that there were no practices of resistance organised outside the narrow confines of national boundaries prior to the late 1990s. People such as Frantz Fanon and Ernesto 'Che' Guevara advocated internationalist revolutionary ideologies; movements such as the Non-Aligned Movement and the Organization of Front-Line States suggest that there were practices to be described in the language of resistance before the term 'globalisation' was invented (see also Gilroy 1993). Thus, it is not that globalisation is a necessary condition which initiates practices of resistance but that 'the politics of these [global] resistances has come to be floodlit by a broader set of connections to globalization and the oft-cited neoliberal restructuring strategies of states, multinational corporations and international organizations' (Amoore 2005: 4).

In the context of globalisation, resistance is associated with practices that unsettle the idea that the state is the main player in politics. The state centrality in politics can be manifested in various ways. For instance, as Thomas J. Biersteker and Cynthia Weber point out, the state relies on the drawing of a boundary around itself for 'having a territorial basis' and 'the construction of domestic communities'

(1996: 13). In other words, the state 'requires enclosure' (Magnusson 1990: 49) to uphold its unity. As Warren Magnusson (1990: 51) argues, this enclosed space of the state is instrumental to 'proper' politics: 'politics proper is impossible without a protected space where ideals can be realised and interests ideally adjudicated'.

Together with phrases such as 'global resistance' and 'transversal dissent', there has been growing attention to political activism which 'claim[s] maturity and legitimacy at the centres of political life' (Walker 1994: 669). Resistance gives a language to examine such activities that are led by individuals and groups of people other than the state, take place within, across and beyond states, and are formulated around issues that are no longer confined to state boundaries. For instance, information about demonstrations spreads instantly to various parts of the world and is shared simultaneously on the global scale. As Keck and Sikkink's idea of 'boomerang pattern' (1998) exemplifies, political activism in the age of globalisation is considered to be 'transnational' because individuals and groups mobilise resources available beyond national boundaries and use new tactics to communicate their messages.

Implicitly or explicitly, studies on global resistance envisage the emergence of a separate spatial entity from the national one (Guillaume 2011: 460). This space is given names such as 'global civil society' and 'international political sphere'. Dissident voices are understood to be formulated and mobilised in this kind of global arena. For instance, Richard Falk argues that, in response to global market forces, there has been an emergence of 'the field of action and thought occupied by individual and collective citizen initiatives of a voluntary, non-profit character both within states and transnationally' (1998: 100). Calling this field global civil society, Falk argues that the role of global civil society is to mitigate the negative effects of global market forces in areas such as environment and poverty. Thus, voices of global civil society are expected to address 'the moral emptiness of neo-liberalism, consumerism and most forms of secularism' (ibid.: 106).

Importantly, globalisation is linked not only to conditions where practices of resistance are mobilised but also to sources of dissension. Among the various facets of globalisation, the economic aspect is often regarded as a major source of anger which engenders different practices of resistance. As Barry Gills argues: 'The key political tension in the coming era will be between the forces of neoliberal economic globalisation, seeking to expand the freedom of capital, and the forces of social resistance, seeking to preserve and to redefine community and solidarity' (2000: 3). Brassett and Higgott point out that the free-market ideology of the 1990s Washington Consensus led to 'a number of significant points of resistance to globalisation' (Brassett and Higgot 2003: 35). For Rupert (2003), the globally developed system of capitalism brought about the movements to resist that system. The Zapatistas movement in Chiapas, Mexico, anti-World Trade Organization (WTO) movements in places like Seattle (Gill 2000), and the Occupy Wall Street movement are some concrete instances where activism is organised around problems related to global financial markets, global expansion of production networks, and domination of a market-oriented ideology. The encroachment of economics into our lives is thus seen as a source of increasing anger and frustration with globalisation.

The works of two thinkers, Antonio Gramsci and Karl Polanyi, are often used to explain such dissident voices in the language of resistance. Drawing on Gramsci's writings, some perceive globalisation as an embodiment of world hegemony, an overarching world economic order (see Arrighi 1990). This order dominates a mode of production across states, shapes the social, economic and political structures of our lives, and produces norms, institutions and mechanisms applied on the global scale (Cox 1983: 171–172). World hegemony can be met by counter-hegemonic forces built on alliances of people who are marginalised and oppressed by the world economic order, such as 'the new working classes generated by international production' and 'peasants and urban marginals' (ibid.: 174). A series of movements that have been organised to resist and redress the effects of economic globalisation are considered to represent counter-hegemonic movements.

Polanyi's idea of 'double movement' refers to two opposing forces that characterise the development of a market economy: one leaves the expansion of a market economy to its own self-regulating mechanisms and the other intervenes in the market to regulate and control its development and expansion (Polanyi 1957). In analysing the development of the market economy in the nineteenth century, Polanyi points out two opposing movements: 'While on the one hand, markets spread all over the face of the globe and the amount of goods involved grew to unbelievable proportions, on the other hand, a network of measures and policies was integrated into powerful institutions designed to check the action of the market relative to labor, land and money' (ibid.: 76). Using the idea of double movement, some interpret anti-globalisation movements as a counter-movement which curtail and control the influence of the global expansion of the market economy (see Mendell and Salée 1991).

This section demonstrated that resistance is used to explain practices and movements that are associated with different aspects of globalisation. These practices mobilise resources and technologies which become accessible and available at their disposal in the age of globalisation. The target audience of this activism is in the global arena. Furthermore, people constitute forces to intervene in the expansion of the global market economy and address issues which are perceived as negative consequences of economic globalisation. Such political activism is regarded as a concrete manifestation that politics can no longer be contained within the state's domain.

Resisting the state monopoly of political subjectivity

Resistance is not only linked to political activism in relation to globalisation but also practices which challenge sovereign authority to produce certain types of subjects. This approach to resistance echoes Michel Foucault's argument that the sovereign's control over subjectivities should be at the forefront of studies on resistance. He argues:

[…] the political, ethical, social, and philosophical problem of our days is *not to try to liberate the individual from the state, and from the state's institutions, but to liberate us both from the state and from the type of individualization linked to the state.* We have to promote new forms of subjectivity through the refusal of this kind of individuality that has been imposed on us for several centuries.

(Foucault 1994: 134, emphasis added)

What underlines Foucault's argument is that power and resistance do not work separately but always in tandem: 'there are no relations of power without resistance […] It [resistance] exists all the more by being in the same place as power […]' (Foucault 1980: 142). From this perspective, resistance is no longer situated in battles between powerholders and those who have no power. Instead, resistance is constitutive of power relations. Foucault's understanding of resistance draws attention to 'forms of resistance not only at macro-levels, such as the state and the capitalist system, but also at micro-levels' (Rygiel 2010: 38) where certain types of political subjects are configured through power relations. Thinking from this perspective, it is not sufficient to focus on practices that are aimed at liberating individuals or groups from organisations, such as the state and WTO, or the system which these institutions create and sustain, because policy changes and institutional reforms 'leave certain forms and technologies of power firmly in place' (ibid.: 37).

By asking the question, 'Is today a life of power available?', Giorgio Agamben (2000: 8) argues that Foucault's theorem on resistance and power needs to be modified in the contemporary context of what he calls 'the state of exception' (Agamben 1998, 2005). The general idea behind the state of exception is that law can be suspended in exceptional circumstances where the preservation of the state is in grave danger. Since the state has the sole power to declare what such exceptional circumstances are, the line between exception and rule becomes indistinct. It is this indistinctiveness that prepares the very ground where sovereign power is materialised. The suspension of law indicates that, in the state of exception, a life is placed outside law but solely under the power of sovereignty. Agamben calls a life under such status as 'bare life'. For someone whose life is rendered 'bare life', the political relevance of his/her life is exclusively decided by sovereign authority (ibid.: 142). To illustrate how one's life is at the mercy of sovereignty, Agamben uses an example of the Nazi concentration camp (ibid.: 166–174). The value of the detainees' lives in the camp were exclusively at the hands of the sovereign. In other words, their lives were politicised and it was the sovereign who decided whose lives 'cease to be politically relevant' (ibid.: 142). For Agamben, the state of exception is the fundamental aspect of the society we are living in (ibid.: 115). Sovereign power to suspend the value of life is not an exceptional event, limited to the case of the concentration camp. Exception can be declared at any time, and hence the state of exception is now becoming the normal condition of our society.

Some interpret Agamben's argument as offering little possibility of resistance to sovereign authority.[1] For instance, William Connolly argues that, in the world described by Agamben, there is no way out from the logic of sovereignty

(Connolly 2004). Drawing on the example of migrant activism, William Walters also criticises Agamben as follows:

> For all its critical thrust, Agamben's line of thinking seems to lead us away from a dynamic agonistic account of power relations and instead fosters a rather one sided and flattened conception of migrant subjects. Things are always done to them, not by them. Only occasionally are they granted the capacity to act, and then in desperate ways. For the most part it is a narrative in which authority is just that and sovereign power has the last laugh.
>
> *(Walters 2008: 188)*

Jacques Rancière offers one way of locating a site of resistance in the contemporary world where the mechanism of sovereignty seems to allow little space for resistance. Rancière argues that Agamben misses the process in which people who are rendered nameless enact the rights denied to them. Rancière calls this process politics: politics is an interruption to the sovereign social order which determines who has the right to speak and who does not. Rancière is critical of Agamben's thesis because it merely traps us in 'a sort of ontological destiny' where 'any kind of claim to rights or any struggle enacting rights is thus trapped from the very outset in the mere polarity of bare life and state of exception' (Rancière 2004: 301). Rancière's concern can be explained as, in Agamben's terminology, how bare life gets out from the excluded status of invisibility and how it claims a part in the realm of visibility.

In other words, for Rancière, the moment of politics is that of introducing egalitarian logic into police logic. He explains that, while police logic determines who is visible and who is not, whose voice is heard and whose voice is made sheer noise, egalitarian logic assumes that all human beings are equal as speaking beings (Rancière 1999: 30). Since the essence of police logic 'lies in a certain way of dividing up the sensible' (Rancière 2010: 36), egalitarian logic interrupts the allocation of senses, of visibility and invisibility, legitimised by police logic. In this way, Rancière's idea of politics is able to highlight instances where people who are assumed to be invisible challenge their own silenced position.

Rancière's, and Rancière-inspired, works have led to an important area of research where resistance is understood as challenging the power of sovereignty (see Nyers and Rygiel 2012). They focus on practices that bring a disruptive moment into sovereign control over subjectivities. The 'autonomy of migration' scholarship exemplifies this type of research.[2] It looks at various forms of irregular migrant protests to argue that migrants question the sovereign's monopoly on subject formation and determine what they are on their own terms (see Papadopoulos et al. 2008). In other words, irregular migrant protesters are what Nyers (2008: 132) calls 'emerging political subjects', because they are not a priori subjects defined by the sovereign's claim on who can act and speak. Instead, protesters 'emerge … as beings acting and reacting with others' (Isin 2008: 39). In this regard, resistance is associated with practices that enact a nameless subject. As Rygiel puts it, 'Whereas an Agambian approach downplays the active role migrants play as political subjects, the autonomous migration perspective emphasizes their capacity for action' (Rygiel 2011: 4). Irregular migrant activism reifies the moment when sovereign authority is called into question. Migrants claim their own power to name themselves and enact themselves as political subjects.

While Rancière offers one way to theorise resistance, Judith Butler's intervention in Agamben's argument can be read as doing so in a different way. By proposing the idea of petty sovereigns, Butler argues that Agamben's analysis is too general to understand different treatments of people subjected to sovereign power (2004: 67–68). She argues that some groups of people, such as racialised minorities, are more susceptible to such power and more likely to be rendered to the status of bare life. For her, important questions are: 'how this [sovereign] power functions differentially, to target and manage certain populations, to derealize the humanity of subjects who might potentially belong to a community bond by commonly recognized laws' and 'how sovereignty [...] works by differentiating populations on the basis of ethnicity and race' (ibid.: 68).

Butler introduces the idea of petty sovereigns to offer a more nuanced reading of the mechanism of sovereignty than Agamben. Petty sovereigns refer to people who are 'reigning in the midst of bureaucratic army institutions mobilized by aims and tactics of power' (ibid.: 56). Although petty sovereigns 'do not inaugurate or fully control', they 'are delegated with the power to render unilateral decision, accountable to no law and without any legitimate authority' (ibid.). For Butler, petty sovereigns play a central role in the sovereign's function to suspend the rule of law because they are the ones who actually make decisions about the exception. Government officials with 'managerial power' exercise 'a set of administrative power' (ibid.: 55) in their daily activities and, in this way, perform sovereign power on the ground. In other words, performing the suspension of law is constitutional to the configuration of sovereign power (ibid.: 61–62). And it is petty sovereigns, or 'the newly invigorated subjects of managerial power' (ibid.: 62), that carry out this performance.

> they [the newly invigorated subjects of managerial power] are not fully self-grounding; they do not offer either representative or legitimating functions to the policy. Nevertheless, they are constituted, within the constrains of governmentality, as those who will and do decide on who will be detained, and who will not, who may see life outside the prison again and who may not, and *this constitutes an enormously consequential delegation and seizure of power. They are acted on, but they also act,* and their actions are not subject to review by any higher judicial authority.
>
> *(ibid.: 62, emphasis added)*

Butler's idea of petty sovereigns not only shows concrete instances where sovereign power works (see Amoore and de Geode 2005) but also poses formidable questions regarding resistance. Namely, what kinds of practices can be regarded as resistance in relation to the petty sovereign's ability to make the exception? If the task of performing the suspension of law is ultimately left in the hands of government officials, what sorts of possibilities for resistance emerge?

Here is an example which nicely illuminates the importance of thinking about resistance together with the idea of petty sovereigns. There was recently a case in Japan where a government official from the Ministry of Economy, Trade and Industry (METI), which is in charge of nuclear energy policies, exposed the bureaucrats' exclusive power to interpret law related to nuclear power plants to serve the benefits of some politicians, METI officials, and the energy industry. By using a pseudonym, Retsu Wakasugi, this official published a two-part novel called *Genpatsu Howaito Auto* [Nuclear Plants White Out] (2013) and *Tokyo Burakku Auto* [Tokyo Black Out] (2014). The novels extensively use classified information, only available to some senior METI bureaucrats, to describe the government's decision-making process in detail. If we were to think of this instance in relation to the idea of petty sovereigns and resistance, a series of questions will arise. Can the moment of resistance be initiated by petty sovereigns? If yes, what kinds of political subjects are enacted by petty sovereigns? If not, how could we understand this official's decision to reveal his own 'sovereign power' as other than resistance?

To sum up, this section introduced a different way of understanding resistance from the previous section. While the previous section discussed resistance in connection with globalisation, the present section did so in relation to the power of sovereignty. In the latter case, resistance is regarded as a way to produce new political subjects. In particular, I have introduced three key ideas in this line of studies: the state of exception, Rancière's idea of politics, and Butler's concept of petty sovereigns. Agamben's idea of the state of exception illustrates the ways in which state sovereignty monopolises the process of subject formation. Both Rancière's and Butler's works identify practices that can be understood as challenging this monopoly.

Everyday forms of resistance and the role of researchers

I have so far focused on two approaches to resistance which reflect different ways of understanding the state in relation to resistance: one looks at the state as a political organisation and the other as a source of power that monopolises the process of subject formation. This does not mean that there is no overlap between the two. For instance, there are studies that implicitly or explicitly use the Foucauldian understanding of power to investigate practices of resistance in the global resistance literature (see Drainville 2002). In this section, I will focus on one commonality between the two approaches: the tendency to associate political activism with the intention to change the status quo.

In examining global resistance literature, Xavier Guillaume is critical of its tendency to assume that participants in social movements seek to express defiance. Guillaume argues that resistance should not be merely associated with 'practices of collective mobilization publicly striving for changes' (2011: 461). Instead, it should also include 'the almost daily mediation individuals have to face in their relations to diverse and diffuse forms of domination and hegemony *without necessarily possessing the ability and/or will to actually fight against or transform the power relations they are enmeshed in*' (ibid., emphasis added). Underlying Guillaume's argument is James Scott's contention that there are two types of resistance: volitional and unintentional. The former refers to practices that are organised and self-sacrificial, bring about revolutionary consequences, and communicate 'ideas or intentions that negate the basis of domination itself' (Scott 1985: 292). The latter refers to unplanned and individualistic practices that bring no revolutionary consequences because people do not wish to change the status quo (ibid.). Scott argues that not only the former but also the latter constitutes resistance (ibid.). Following Scott, Guillaume suggests the need to rethink resistance in global resistance literature by taking full account of practices that 'offer no gain, and do not transform, but only provide a fleeting moment of re-appropriation' of everyday life (Guillaume 2011: 461).

I argue that Guillaume's observation can be extended to the Rancière-inspired studies on resistance. In this line of research, too, there is a marked focus on practices that are articulated through volition to change the status quo. As Rancière argues, to disrupt the sovereign social order and bring in the political moment, there needs to be a declaration of assumption in terms of visibility, an assertion that everyone is an equal speaking being. A demonstration of this kind requires a clear desire to change the present power relations on the part of those who declare such equality. For Rancière, the agency of protesters plays the central role in thinking of resistance. Hence the Rancière-inspired scholarship predominantly focuses on the intentional type of resistance. By focusing on practices organised by people who are rendered speechless, such as irregular migrants, the existing research regards voices and actions exhibited by them as the crux of the refusal to accept the sovereign's control over subjectivity.

Not surprisingly, therefore, the existing literature mainly investigates observable and visible practices of resistance related to both globalisation and sovereign power. These practices include street demonstrations, occupying public spaces, strikes, sit-in demonstrations, hunger-strikes, and demonstrations which use various innovative methods to draw public attention. The anti-WTO protests, the Occupy movement which started from the Occupy Wall Street protest in 2011, and the Sans-Papiers movement in France exemplify these visible practices. They are designed to declare and disseminate anger and frustrations about the status quo as widely as possible. In each instance, a display of dissenting voices is vital for protesters to openly communicate their demands with others. Visible practices do not necessarily require words: they sometimes rely on means of communication other than words. For instance, some irregular migrants sew their lips to send a symbolical message that they are rendered silent because of illegality attached to them. Lip-sewing can be seen as a silent protest without words. And yet, its symbolic meaning cannot be communicated if protesters hide the actual exhibition of their sewed lips from others.

Even if overt forms of protest, discussed above, receive most of the scholarly attention, to gain a full picture of resistance we must also consider unintentional and hidden protests. These consist of practices where the people engaged in resistance have no intention of risking retaliation to change the status quo. Scott calls this 'everyday forms of resistance' (1985) or 'infrapolitics' (1990). These practices employ the tactics available in everyday situations. They are 'the ordinary weapons of relatively powerless groups' such as 'foot dragging, dissimulation, desertion, false compliance, pilfering, feigned ignorance, slander, arson, sabotage' (Scott 1985: xvi). What is distinctive about this quotidian type of resistance is that it is undetectable as 'resistance'. There is no open declaration of dissent and expression of antagonism from the side of subordinate groups. Instead, they use tactics that evade open confrontation. As Scott argues, this is 'a tactical choice born of a prudent awareness of the balance of power' (Scott 1990: 183) because people engaging in these types of activities have no desire to challenge the oppressors, at least not immediately (ibid.: 196–197, 201). Fearing retaliation, the oppressed are not willing to exhibit their opposition in an open manner (Scott 1985: xvi–xvii). In this respect, everyday forms of resistance are in the 'unobtrusive realm of political struggle' (Scott 1990: 183). They are hidden from the eyes of the dominant.

Incorporating everyday forms of resistance into studies on resistance and world politics gives rise to a number of questions. To begin with, what is the political significance of everyday forms of resistance to our understanding of world politics? How to conceptualise such politics through practices which carry no intention to problematise state centricity and rather, in some ways, prefer to maintain the status quo? What examples of everyday forms of resistance can contribute to critical examinations of a state-centred approach to world politics? In relation to the global resistance literature in particular, a relevant question will be: how to conceptualise the international through everyday forms of resistance? With regards to Rancière's idea of politics and Butler's petty sovereigns, I also wonder: how does one consider agency in relation to quotidian forms of resistance? Especially together with questions raised earlier in relation to Butler's work, it is also important to ask: what kinds of everyday forms of resistance are available to petty sovereigns? What sort of politics is enacted by petty sovereigns' participation in quotidian forms of resistance?

The perspective of unintentional resistance also requires a rethinking of the role of researchers. Given that some practices do not articulate clear defiance, it may be unavoidable to wonder: how do we, as researchers, know which practices are worth examining through the concept of resistance? What is at stake in identifying some practices as resistance when they are specifically developed to hide defiance from the sovereign? I am not alone in wondering about researchers' involvement in naming some practices as resistance (see Ortner 1995). For example, Michael Brown (1996) argues that researchers project their own values in calling some practices resistance. He engages in critical self-reflection on his own research on the struggles in eastern Peru that involved Marxist guerrilla fighters, called the Movimiento de la Izquierda Revolucionaria (Movement of the Revolutionary Left,

MIR), the Peruvian armed forces, and the Asháninka Indians. When Brown conducted the research, he regarded the alliance between MIR and the Asháninka Indians as representing 'a classic case of active resistance to the oppressive conditions of eastern Peru' because 'a score of Asháninkas participated in an MIR-led attack on the hacienda of an abusive landowner' (ibid.: 730). However, in hindsight, he regrets using the concept of 'resistance' to analyse the Asháninka Indian's cooperation with the MIR and reading the struggle through the framework of the oppressed Indians versus the oppressive government. Doing so, he argues, distracted him from examining the internal politics and specific circumstances that necessitated the alliance between MIR and the Asháninka Indians. Later his remorse grew deeper as the Asháninkas eventually fought on both sides of the conflict, with the government and the revolutionaries (ibid.: 731).

For Brown, it was moralism invested in the concept of resistance that made it difficult to even question using it. In some cases, he argues, researchers benefit from more careful reading of practices if they do not rely on the concept of resistance to begin with:

> Because the concept of resistance is informed by an explicitly moral sensibility, […] there is an inexorable tendency for it [the concept of resistance] to spill over into contexts of questionable relevance, since no analysis wishes to be seen as politically naïve or morally insensitive.
>
> *(ibid.: 733)*

Our own perceptions and beliefs shape what we as researchers take up as research topics and how we examine these topics. That is, there is always an intellectual bias in the process of doing research. Brown describes this intellectual bias as moralism attached to the concept of resistance. When the concept of resistance is used as an analytical tool, I think there are other kinds of intellectual biases as well. For instance, at the beginning of this chapter, I narrowed my focus to approaches to world politics that reflect critically on state-centrism. By doing so, I create a sort of legitimate excuse to ignore some other practices, such as movements for national liberation developed through anti-colonial struggles. I assume that these movements can be safely excluded from the present chapter because their main purpose was to gain independence for their countries, which sustains the system of the state. This understanding, however, is biased by what I know and what I understand. There might be other studies, archival documents, analytical frameworks, and stories of people's lives that I am not aware of but which would justify focusing on national liberation movements as a challenge to state centricity.

Researchers are always in precarious positions because of their embeddedness in their own research topics. This precariousness is even more relevant when we investigate practices that operate in the hidden realm of political struggles. These practices carry no actual declaration of confrontation or expression of resistance. In this regard, there are questions that need to be asked to put the involvement of researchers at the foreground of the analysis of resistance. To name but a few: how do researchers know, at the time of analysis, which practices and movements can be called 'resistance' and have the potential of challenging state centricity? What political costs do researchers risk in identifying some practices as resistance when these practices do not necessarily use the language of resistance? In what way does researchers' involvement in naming some practices as resistance contribute to, or limit, a non-statist world view?

In relation to the purpose of this present book, researchers' embeddedness in their research topics also raises a different set of questions. The political project that we are participating in through this book, either as writers or readers, or both, is to resist the state-centred understanding of world politics. To look for a way to widen the scope of imaginations in thinking about international relations, the book encourages us to resist assuming state centricity. I wonder then: to what extent such a 'resistance' approach to world politics aids us to have meaningful conversations with someone who refuses to challenge state-centred approaches to IR? Are there more productive approaches, other than resisting state centricity, that might generate conversations with someone who prefers understanding world politics through the lens of the state?

Conclusion

In this chapter, I have shown that the concept of resistance is linked to two different types of political activism. The first refers to practices that have been developed in relation to globalisation. In terms of agendas, locations, target audiences, strategies, and resources, these practices are analysed through the language of resistance. Thinking about this activism as resistance provides a way of understanding its political significance: politics is no longer confined within national boundaries. The second type of activism refers to practices that challenge sovereign authority over subject formation, such as irregular migrant activism. By using the language of resistance, these practices refuse to accept the sovereign's control over the subject status and attempt to disrupt the control. Rancière's idea of politics highlights such moments of disruption. The concept of resistance is also linked to the idea of petty sovereigns, which locates possibilities of resistance within the functioning of sovereign authority. Despite these two different ways of speaking of resistance in IR, resistance tends to be associated with practices that exhibit a clear intention of defiance. While taking this tendency seriously, I argued that there is also a need to focus on less obvious and more subtle forms of resistance. Lastly, we must be aware of the role of researchers in identifying some practices as resistance. My hope is that this chapter helps readers to create their own intellectual map of resistance. By putting forward a series of questions in the final section of this chapter, I hope to provoke readers to explore a new intellectual terrain of resistance.

Notes

1 This interpretation of Agamben's work is contested: some read his work as not necessarily foreclosing possibilities of resistance. See, for instance, Edkins and Pin-Fat (2005).

2 The precise definition of 'autonomy of migration' differs.

Further reading and useful weblinks

Readers are encouraged to discuss the following books and activities through the questions listed in the third section of this chapter.

Bring-Back-Our-Girls campaign (www.bringbackourgirls.ng). This campaign was started by a group of parents in Nigeria whose daughters were abducted by the insurgent group Boko Haram. This quickly spread to other countries to form a global outcry on the issue.

Hašek, Jaroslav (1973) *The Good Soldier, Švejk*, trans. Cecil Parrott, London: Heinemann. This entertaining novel describes the life of a soldier, Švejk, who gets what he wants without appearing to openly resist the state's order.

Klein, Naomi (2000) *No Logo*, London: Flamingo. This accessible book illustrates what kinds of resistance can be possible against the global capitalist market system.

Mahmood, Saba (2005) *Politics of Piety: The Islamic Revival and the Feminist Subject*, Princeton, NJ and Oxford: Princeton University Press. This brilliant book on the Muslim women's piety movement in Egypt tackles the question of agency and offers an alternative way of thinking about resistance by looking at how the women inhabit norms and practices.

Said, Edward W. (1983) *The World, the Text, and the Critic*, Cambridge, MA: Harvard University Press. This book explores what resistance means to researchers and what it means to be critical for them.

Wedeen, Lisa (1999) *Ambiguities of Domination: Politics, Rhetoric, and Symbols in Contemporary Syria*, Chicago, IL and London: The University of Chicago Press. This remarkable book focuses on the regime of President Hafiz al-Asad in Syria, mainly between the 1970s and early 1990s. Wedeen situates resistance in the tension between cohesion and consent and challenges us to rethink the meaning of resistance under an autocratic political system.

WikiLeaks (https://wikileaks.org/index.en.html). Launched in 2007, WikiLeaks serves as a platform for whistle-blowers to leak classified information about governments and corporations. Can be read in conjunction with Butler's idea of 'petty sovereigns'. A thought-provoking article by Wong and Brown (2013) illustrates the connection between WikiLeaks and resistance.

Bibliography

Agamben, G. (1998) *Homo Sacer: Sovereign Power and Bare Life*, trans. Daniel Heller-Roazen, Stanford, CA: Stanford University Press.

Agamben, G. (2000) *Means Without End: Notes on Politics*, trans. Vincenzo Binetti and Cesare Casarino, Minnesota: University of Minneapolis Press.

Agamben, G. (2005) *States of Exception*, trans. Kevin Attell, Chicago, IL: University of Chicago Press.

Amoore, L. (ed.) (2005) *The Global Resistance Reader*, London and New York: Routledge.

Amoore, L. and de Goede, M. (2005) 'Governance, Risk and Dataveillance in the War on Terror', *Crime, Law and Social Change* 43(2): 149–173.

Arrighi, G. (1990) 'The Three Hegemonies of Historical Capitalism', *Review* 13(3): 365–408.

Biersteker, T.J. and Weber, C. (1996) *State Sovereignty as Social Construct*, Cambridge: Cambridge University Press.

Brassett, J. and Higgott, R. (2003) 'Building the Normative Dimension(s) of a Global Policy', *Review of International Studies* 29(S1): 29–55.

Brown, M. (1996) 'On Resisting Resistance', *American Anthropologist* 98(4): 729–749.

Butler, J. (2004) *Precarious Life: The Powers of Mourning and Violence*, London: Verso Press.

Connolly, W.E. (2004) 'The Complexity of Sovereignty', in J. Edkins, V. Pin-Fat, and M.J. Shapiro (eds), *Sovereign Lives: Power in Global Politics*, New York: Routledge, pp. 23–40.

Cox, R. (1983) 'Gramsci, Hegemony and International Relations: An Essay in Method', *Millennium: Journal of International Studies* 12(2): 162–175.

Drainville, A.C. (2002) 'Québec City 2001 and the Making of Transnational Subjects', *Social Register* 2002: 15–42.

Eschle, C. (2005) 'Constructing "the Anti-Globalisation Movement"', in C. Eschele and B. Maiguashca (eds), *Critical Theories, International Relations and the Anti-Globalisation Movement*, London: Routledge, pp. 17–35.

Edkins, J. and Pin-Fat, V. (2005) 'Through the Wire: Relations of Power and Relations of Violence', *Millennium: Journal of International Studies* 34(1): 1–25.

Falk, R. (1998) 'Global Civil Society: Perspectives, Initiatives, Movements', *Oxford Development Studies* 26(1): 99–110.

Foucault, M. (1980) *Power/Knowledge: Selected Interviews and Other Writings, 1972–1977*, ed. C. Gordon, Brighton: Harvester Press.

Foucault, M. (1994) *The Essential Foucault: Selections from Essential Works of Foucault, 1954–1984*, ed. P. Rabinow and N. Rose, New York and London: The New Press.

Gill, S. (2000) 'Toward a Postmodern Prince? The Battle in Seattle as a Movement in the New Politics of Globalisation', *Millennium: Journal of International Studies* 29(1): 131–141.

Gills, B. (2002) *Globalization and the Politics of Resistance*, New York: Palgrave.

Gilroy, P. (1993) *The Black Atlantic: Modernity and Double Consciousness*, London and New York: Verso.

Guillaume, X. (2011) 'Resistance and the International: The Challenge of the Everyday', *International Political Sociology* 5(4): 450–462.

Isin, E.F. (2008) 'Theorizing Acts of Citizenship', in E.F. Isin and G.M. Nielson (eds), *Acts of Citizenship*, London: Zed Books, pp. 15–43.

Keck, M.E. and Sikkink, K. (1998) *Activists Beyond Borders: Advocacy Networks in International Politics*, Ithaca, NY and London: Cornell University Press.

Laclau, E. and Mouffe, C. (1985) *Hegemony and Socialist Strategy: Towards a Radical Democratic Politics*, trans. Winston Moore and Paul Cammack, London: Verso.

Magnusson, W. (1990) 'The Reification of Political Community', in R.B.J. Walker and S.H. Mendlovitz (eds), *Contending Sovereignties: Redefining Political Community*, Boulder, CO and London: Lynne Rienner Publishers, pp. 45–60.

Maiguashca, Bice (2003) 'Governance and Resistance in World Politics Introduction', *Review of International Studies* 29(S1): 3–28.

Mendell, M. and Salée, D. (1991) 'Introduction', in M. Mendell and D. Salée (eds), *The Legacy of Karl Polanyi: Market, State and Society at the End of the Twentieth Century*, Basingstoke: Macmillan, pp. xiii–xxx.

Nyers, P. (2008) 'Community without Status: Non-Status Migrants and Cities of Refuge', in D. Brydon and W.D. Coleman (eds), *Renegotiating Community: Interdisciplinary Perspectives, Global Contexts*, Vancouver, BC: The University of British Columbia Press, pp. 123–140.

Nyers, P. and Rygiel, K. (eds) (2012) *Citizenship, Migrant Activism and the Politics of Movement*, London and New York: Routledge.

Ortner, S. (1995) 'Resistance and the Problem of Ethnographic Refusal', *Comparative Studies in Society and History* 37(1): 173–193.

Papadopoulos, D., Stephenson, N. and Tsianos, V. (2008) *Escape Routes: Control and Subversion in the 21st Century*, Ann Arbor, MI: Pluto Press.

Polanyi, K. (1957) *The Great Transformation: The Political and Economic Origins of Our Time*, Boston, MA: Beacon Press.

Rancière, J. (1999) *Disagreement. Politics and Philosophy*, Minnesota: University of Minneapolis Press.

Rancière, J. (2004) 'Who Is the Subject of the Rights of Man?', *South Atlantic Quarterly* 103(2/3): 297–310.

Rancière, J. (2010) *Dissensus: On Politics and Aesthetics*, London: Continnum.

Rupert, M. (2003) 'Globalising Common Sense: A Marxian-Gramscian (Re-)vision of the Politics of Governance/Resistance', *Review of International Studies* 29 (S1): 181–198.

Rygiel, K. (2010) *Globalizing Citizenship*, Vancouver: The University of British Columbia Press.

Rygiel, K. (2011) 'Bordering Solidarities: Migrant Activism and the Politics of Movement and Camps at Calais', *Citizenship Studies* 15(1): 1–19.

Scott, J. (1985) *Weapons of the Weak: Everyday Forms of Peasant Resistance*, New Haven, CT and London: Yale University Press.

Scott, J. (1990) *Domination and the Arts of Resistance: Hidden Transcripts*, New Haven, CT and London: Yale University Press.

Scott, J. (1993) *Everyday Forms of Resistance*, Yokohama: PRIME, International Peace Research Institute Meigaku.

Stierl, M. (2012) '"No One Is Illegal!" Resistance and the Politics of Discomfort', *Globalization* 9(3): 425–438.

Suhl, Y. (1968) *They Fought Back: The Story of the Jewish Resistance in Nazi Europe*, London: MacGibbon & Kee.

Tarrow, S. (1998) *Power in Movement: Social Movements and Contentious Politics*, Cambridge: Cambridge University Press.

Wakasugi, R. (2013) *Genpatsu Howaito Auto* [Nuclear Plants White Out], Tokyo: Kodan-sha.

Wakasugi, R. (2014) *Tokyo Burakku Auto* [Tokyo Black Out], Tokyo: Kodan-sha.

Walker, R.B.J. (1994) 'Social Movements/World Politics', *Millennium: Journal of International Studies* 23(3): 669–700.

Walker, R.B.J. (2004) 'Conclusion: Sovereignties, Exceptions, Worlds', in J. Edkins, V. Pin-Fat and M.J. Shapiro (eds), *Sovereign Lives: Power in Global Politics*, New York: Routledge, pp. 239–251.

Walters, W. (2008) 'Mapping the Territory of (Non-)Citizenship', in E. Isin and G.M. Nielsen (eds), *Acts of Citizenship*, London: Zed Books, pp. 182–206.

Wong W. and Brown P. (2013) 'E-Bandits and Global Activism: WikiLeaks, Anonymous and the Politics of No One', *Perspectives on Politics* 11(4): 1015–1033.

13

SOVEREIGNTY

Jens Bartelson

Introduction

If we take sovereignty to mean supreme authority within a given territory, this notion has been subjected to contestation ever since it was first articulated during the sixteenth and seventeenth centuries. To its first critics, claims to supreme authority were seen as attempts to usurp the fundamental laws and ancient customs of the realm, infringing on traditional liberties and aristocratic privilege (Foucault 2003; Pocock 1987; Thompson 1986). To the Enlightenment, the absolutist doctrine of sovereignty was seen as nothing but a licence for despotism at home and imperialism abroad (Muthu 2003). To many of its nineteenth- and early twentieth-century critics, sovereignty was allegedly so out of tune with the new realities of pluralist democracy that it ought to be abandoned in favour of concepts better suited to make sense of those realities (Bartelson 2001).

Yet for all their differences, the above modes of criticism shared two features in common. Almost invariably they presupposed that the concept of sovereignty had some basic and stable connotations, and almost invariably these criticisms were undertaken on behalf of some group or normative principle that made criticism meaningful and politically consequential. Many of these criticisms were but thinly veiled claims to sovereignty on behalf of those groups or principles, thereby locating the sources of legitimate political authority *elsewhere* than in the person of the king or in the institutions of the state: in ancient law, in republican liberties, in the people or the nation, or in groups and associations existing prior to or independent of the state.

Not so anymore. To many of its contemporary critics, sovereignty is *contingent* in two distinct but related senses. First, since the meaning of sovereignty depends upon the historical and cultural context in which this concept is used, sovereignty is basically what we make of it through our successful manipulation of the linguistic conventions governing this usage. Second, from the above is sometimes concluded that sovereignty – rather than being a necessary condition of political order – is an arbitrary expression of political power. To this is often coupled a *qui bono* argument: the main function of the concept of sovereignty is to legitimise particular claims to political authority. Sovereignty is therefore an ideological concept, and those who are ignorant of this fact will only contribute to its reification and the reproduction of the corresponding institutions and practices.

In this chapter, I shall suggest that while the argument from contingency has helped to defuse some of the most dangerous reifications of sovereignty, this peculiar mode of contestation has been blind to some of its own ideological implications and political consequences. Due to their nominalist understanding of political concepts and their meaning, arguments from sovereignty as contingent find it notoriously difficult to account for in whose name the critique of sovereignty is undertaken, as well as for the alternative sources of legitimate authority on offer. Furthermore, and contrary to its intentions, the argument about contingency lends itself to ideological exploitation by those who would like to see sovereignty restored at home and abroad. This being so, since if we accept that sovereignty has no essence of its own, this implies that everyone is basically free to re-define this concept to suit his or her own ends. Thus the insistence on the historically contingent character of sovereignty has legitimised new practices of interference and intervention that ultimately help to preserve the sovereign state, albeit perhaps in a new and governmentalised form. So although I agree with Levine (2012) that we need a form of critique that admits that our theories have performative consequences that are beyond our control, and that such critique should be geared towards tempering the tendency to reify our analytical concepts, I believe that some of our critical practices are complicit in turning abstract concepts into things, and sometimes with very perverse consequences.

This leaves us with the challenge of devising new forms of critical inquiry that can help us make sense of sovereignty without unwittingly playing into the hands of arbitrary power. As I shall suggest, this should compel us to recognise that for the purposes of critique, it does not really matter whether sovereignty has some timeless meaning or is contingent upon usage, or whether its corresponding institutions and practices are real or constructed: what should be of more concern to us is what is done *to* sovereignty by means of reification, and what subsequently is done *by means* of this concept. The rest of this chapter is organised as follows: In the next section, I shall briefly discuss how the argument to the effect that sovereignty is contingent has played itself out in the context of international relations theory. I shall then describe some of its unintended consequences, before sketching the contours of what I believe may be a more sustainable form of critique that takes the latter into serious consideration.

The contingency of sovereignty

The argument from contingency starts out from the assumption that sovereignty has long been uncontested and taken for granted as an unquestioned foundation of international relations and international law. Those who criticise sovereignty on such grounds normally start out from some conventional definition of this concept – such as supreme authority within a given territory – and then go on to show that such an understanding has long been implicit in theories of international relations, and has thereby helped to create and uphold a line of demarcation between domestic and international politics with profound consequences for political practice and disciplinary identity. As Ashley (1995: 103) noted in an early statement of this view, sovereignty is 'conceived as a transcendental origin of power that is not itself a political power because it is also the timeless and universal source of all that can be meaningful and true in history'. And as Walker and Mendlovitz (1990: 1) continued shortly thereafter, 'its meaning might be marginally contestable by constitutional lawyers and other connoisseurs of the fine lines, but for the most part state sovereignty expresses a commanding silence', a contention later reiterated by other critics of sovereignty (Weber 1996: 2, 11). As Biersteker and Weber (1996: 3) pointed out, the argument made on the contrary was that 'the modern state system is not based on some timeless principle of sovereignty, but on the production of a normative conception that links authority, territory, population … and recognition in a unique way and in a particular place (the state)'.

An important task for these scholars was to re-open the question of sovereignty in order to understand how and why this silence had been maintained within international relations. As Ashley and Walker (1990: 383) argued, 'the word "sovereignty" is often used ideologically, as if it represented some source of meaning, some effective organizational principle, some mode of being already in place, some simply and self-evidently given resolution of paradoxes of space, time, and identity'. Yet they argue that sovereignty is contingent; they do so by pointing out that 'discourses of sovereignty cannot relate to their object, sovereignty, as other than a problem or question. This is so because sovereignty enters discourse not as a matter of describing something that is thought to be real, already present, and perhaps distinguishable from other equally real and present things, but precisely as a reflection on a lack, on a loss, on something that might have been but is no longer' (ibid.: 381). So undeniably the argument made here by contingency theorists is that, 'sovereignty is not a permanent principle of political order; the appearance of permanence is simply an effect of complex practices working to affirm continuities and to shift disruptions and dangers to the margin' (Walker 1993: 163).

To this were added further assumptions by contingency theorists about the causes of the lamentable silence surrounding the question of sovereignty: they argued that sovereignty had remained uncontested as a result of having been *reified*. By reification they meant those practices by means of which abstract concepts had been turned into things, and argued that this had been made possible by a widespread but misguided understanding of political concepts according to which their meaning is given and immutable. According to this understanding, concepts derive their meaning from their referential connections to tangible parts of the socio-political world. Hence to contest sovereignty it was tantamount to show that this meaning always had been subject to change and hence that sovereignty had no essence; and in order to substantiate their case for contingency, critical scholars took the linguistic turn. While there was ample room for disagreement about the nature of concepts and their meaning, those who took the linguistic turn shared the basic conviction that the meaning of political concepts is not conditioned by things, their tangible referents or inter-subjective understandings of these. Instead, those who took the linguistic turn were in broad agreement that the meaning of concepts derives from their usage.

As Skinner (1988: 67) once had argued, '[t]o discover from the history of thought that there are in fact no such timeless concepts, but only various different concepts which have gone with various different societies, is to discover a general truth not merely about the past but about ourselves as well'. Those who accepted this view were therefore inclined to argue that sovereignty has no meaning apart from its actual function. And one of the main functions performed by this concept in international relations has been to legitimise the authority claims made by individual states over their own populations and territories in a context of other competing claims to authority (see for example Werner and de Wilde 2001). To others, the history of concepts initially 'directed itself to criticizing the practice in the history of ideas of treating ideas as constants, articulated in differing historical figures but of themselves fundamentally unchanging' (Koselleck 1985: 80). To those who took this view of the concept of sovereignty, the task was to write a history of the meaningful experience of sovereignty as it has become condensed into this concept across time, thus describing its changing meaning in a variety of different political and ideological contexts (Onuf 1991).

Finally, for Foucault and his followers, not only do our political concepts have a history, but they are in fact nothing but the sum of their histories. In order to analyse the formation of concepts, writes Foucault (1972: 63, emphasis added), 'one must relate them neither to the horizon of *ideality*, nor to the empirical progress of *ideas*'. Concepts are neither words nor things, so rather than exploring their deductive or causal relations, 'one would have to describe the organization of the field of statements where they appeared and circulated' (ibid.: 56). From this it follows that if the concept of sovereignty is a by-product of statements produced within political discourse, then there cannot be any such thing as sovereignty outside the confines of that discourse (Bartelson 1995).

To summarise: quite irrespective of these different understandings of the causes and consequences of conceptual change, those critics of sovereignty who took the linguistic turn were in broad agreement that the meaning of sovereignty is contingent upon the usage of this concept, and that sovereignty also conditions or constitutes the corresponding practices and institutions. Since the meaning of sovereignty did change across time and space, so did these institutions and practices. And if the institutions and practices of sovereignty indeed are contingent and mutable, the concept of sovereignty – however defined – can hardly be understood as a necessary condition of domestic and international political order either, only as a veiled justification of an underlying will to power ever ready to express itself in claims to political authority.

The consequences of contingency

As we have seen above, the argument to the effect that sovereignty is contingent was not only directed against the concept of sovereignty itself. Rather, sovereignty was used as a foil for criticising the disciplinary identity of academic International Relations as well as the practices of power politics. Since these were held to be mutually reinforcing, the critique of sovereignty reflected concerns with patterns of dominance, exclusion and marginalisation in both domains. But what does the argument from contingency imply, and what are the limits of this kind of criticism? I think some of its implications have been counterproductive given its critical intent. First, and repeating myself, although the argument from contingency has provided a welcome antidote against the most dangerous reifications of sovereignty, it cannot itself avoid a reification of sovereignty altogether. This being so since those who have sought to contextualise and historicise sovereignty have been compelled to conform to prevailing academic norms of consistent and intelligible usage. Established definitions of sovereignty are hard to shake off, and however much these critics have disavowed such definitions in favour of inquiries into the changing meanings and functions of this concept, they have nevertheless imputed some basic meanings to this concept in order for their inquiries to get off the ground and for the results to be intelligible. Consequently, even the most critical inquiries tend to presuppose that sovereignty, at a very minimum, denotes the presence of supreme authority within a given territory, and however much labour then has been devoted to demonstrating that the underlying concepts of authority and territory themselves are but contingent constructs, such presuppositions amount to de-contesting the lexical meaning of sovereignty, and de-contesting this meaning implies pushing it further beyond the purview of critique. Thus the argument from contingency, while debunking essentialist renderings of sovereignty, cannot but reaffirm the existence of that of which it speaks, albeit with smaller and perhaps less problematic ontological commitments being made in the process (Bartelson 2008). Thus, as Ashley pointed out quite some time ago, as long as criticism is seen as emanating from the sovereign voice of a sovereign subject, it will necessarily become complicit in the reaffirmation of the sovereign state as the privileged locus of domestic political order (ibid.: 265–8).

Second, and perhaps slightly more problematic, the argument from contingency does not tell us on behalf of whom or what normative principle the critique of sovereignty is undertaken, or what any viable alternative conception of political order would look like. None of this will be problematic as long as the argument from contingency is pursued for reasons of historical curiosity, even if the resulting historiography is likely to have profound implications for how we think of sovereignty in the present. Yet a genealogical inquiry into the changing meaning of sovereignty does not have to be guided by any explicitly critical ambition in order to make plain that sovereignty is historically contingent, and that changes in its meaning have had a wide range of institutional and political consequences (see for example Skinner 2010). So it is perfectly possible to make an argument in favour of the view that sovereignty is contingent without thereby automatically debunking sovereignty. But since many of those international theorists who have argued that sovereignty is contingent have done so with the explicit intent of disputing the necessity and desirability of sovereign statehood, this raises questions about the ethical grounding of this critique and the possibility of alternatives. As I think Bickerton et al. (2006) rightly have pointed out, critics of sovereignty such as Ashley, Walker, and myself were in no position to provide coherent answers to the questions as to what agency or politics might look like in the absence of sovereignty, since 'what begins as a theoretical critique of the limits on our understanding ends by dissolving the very possibility of agency' (ibid.: 29). Hence those who want to argue that sovereignty is contingent *while* advocating alternative sources of political authority and community, are prone to restrict the scope of the contingency argument to sovereignty and its cognates, while saving those forms of authority and community one wishes to vindicate from its bite. So pushing the argument from contingency to extremes comes at a considerable price – ontologically as well as ethically – insofar as it not only precludes a coherent defence of any alternative visions of political and legal order, but also serves to reinforce the view according to which sovereignty is an inescapable condition of all politics, and thus also ultimately a necessary requirement of our understanding thereof.

Here again the argument from contingency bites its own tail, and ends up reaffirming what it sets out to contest. It should therefore come as no surprise that some critical theorists recently have invoked essentialist understandings of sovereignty as a bulwark against what they perceive as illegitimate concentrations of power at the global level. As Jennings (2011: 51) has aptly summarised this renewed quest for the essence of sovereignty, 'unaware of the genealogical linkages that connect the specific terms and assumptions of the contemporary critique of sovereignty to the main currents of political modernity, a surprisingly large number of contemporary scholars have unfortunately entangled themselves in theoretical commitments to a series of categories based on retrograde and reactionary modernist accounts of power and of political history'. I think that this has become plain in the recent revival of the works of Carl Schmitt, as well as in the widespread fascination with exceptionalism within contemporary international theory. Here sovereignty is again interpreted as a brute fact deriving from the very nature of political life, rather than from acts of interpretation and contestation (for an overview, see Teschke 2011).

Third, and perhaps most embarrassing for its advocates, a contingency perspective on sovereignty can easily be twisted into justifications of interference and intervention in the domestic affairs of states. If the meaning of sovereignty indeed has varied across different contexts as a consequence of past rhetorical manipulations, there is no reason to expect that it would not be susceptible to similar licentious re-definitions in the present. And if past attempts to re-define sovereignty were undertaken in order to legitimise new political practices and institutions, there is perhaps nothing to stop this from happening in our present as well. I think that there is some evidence that the argument from contingency indeed does perform such a function in the present, especially when coupled with the tendency to unbundle sovereignty and to insist that the institutions and practices of sovereignty are historically mutable. As I shall exemplify below, I believe that the view that sovereignty is contingent has been crucial to the legitimisation of new forms of intervention in failed and fragile states.

Although hardly theorists of contingency themselves, authors like Krasner and Keohane have made a strong case in favour of the view that sovereignty is historically mutable and therefore ought to be understood as highly malleable in the present. Starting with Krasner's (1999) unbundling of sovereignty into different components, such as domestic sovereignty, interdependence sovereignty, international legal sovereignty and Westphalian sovereignty, it has been a short step to argue that if there is no necessary connection between these components, the a priori exclusion of external actors from domestic authority structures can be compromised or even abandoned without adversely affecting any of the other components. As Keohane has argued, 'troubled societies may have more or less of it, but the classic ideal-type of Westphalian sovereignty should be abandoned even as an aspiration' (2003: 276). Perhaps rather conversely: some proposals for state-building tellingly assume that the involvement of external actors in failed states, or, more generally, in areas in which the scope of statehood is limited, is necessary in order to restore domestic sovereignty, or to provide the functional equivalents thereof. As Krasner and Risse have argued recently, non-governmental and private actors may well be better suited to provide public goods in states whose capacity to govern is weak and where the shadow of anarchy looms large (Krasner 2004; Krasner and Risse 2014; Risse 2013). Hence the unbundling of sovereignty ushers in a powerful recipe for interference that would not have been possible to extract from more traditional and essentialist understandings of sovereignty, with their emphasis on sovereignty as a composite and coherent precondition of domestic and international order.

But the more consistently the argument from contingency is pursued, the more generous the resulting licence for interference becomes. Thus Glanville, contesting what he believes to be the conventional story of state sovereignty, has recently argued that the view according to which sovereignty entails a right of non-intervention is a fairly recent one, dating back to the UN Charter and the Cold War. As he goes on to explain, 'proponents of this standard story reify the rights of self-government and freedom from outside interference as the ahistorical and, for some, logically deducible essence of sovereignty' (Glanville 2011: 234). Hence 'when we historicise the sovereign state, we can recognise that it is not only the responsibilities of states to protect their populations that are socially constructed, but also the rights of states to be self-governing and free from outside interference' (ibid.: 249). To Glanville, unlike the right of non-intervention, the right to intervene in the affairs of other states on humanitarian grounds has long been a fundamental prerogative of sovereign statehood (Glanville 2013: 79). So given that there is nothing new about the interference in the domestic affairs of states in order to protect their populations from gross violations of human rights, it follows that 'while peoples have a right to govern themselves free from outside interference, this should be conditional on their protection of human rights' (Glanville 2011: 249). Irrespective of the validity of this historical account, what I want to draw attention to is how it is indicative of the ease with which the argument from contingency can travel to new ideological contexts, and be harnessed in support of contemporary practices of interference and intervention, in this particular case by means of a leap from 'is' to 'ought' that threatens to turn the armchair debunking of sovereignty into a self-fulfilling prophecy of a magnitude neither anticipated nor desired by its critics.

Critique beyond contingency

So if the argument from contingency itself is contingent on an understanding of political concepts that is prone to backfire whenever harnessed for critical and normative purposes, and if it is likely to have perverse consequences insofar as it offers a *carte blanche* to both statists and imperialists to pursue their suffocating stratagems, what are the prospects for a sustainable critique of sovereignty in the present? While I fully agree with Levine (2012: 67) that 'when theorists of world politics forget that political institutions and social realities are constituted … they forget their own obligations as stakeholders and moral agents', I do not think that the mere debunking of reifications will only take us so far. Rather than merely criticising the tendency to talk of sovereignty as if it were a thing, I would like to suggest that we should actually *study* the practices and consequences of reification in more detail. If indeed Ashley (1989) was right in pointing out that criticism necessarily is complicit in the reproduction of that which is singled out for criticism, I think we should focus more on these unintended consequences of criticism. So instead of lamenting the inevitability of reification, or trying to purify the study of international relations from its undesirable effects, I think that we should focus on what reification actually *does* to sovereignty, and what reified conceptions of sovereignty *do* to the world. From this point of view, a sustainable critique of sovereignty would be tantamount to describing the practices of reification, their discursive effects and their political outcomes, and then leave it to the reader to contemplate the desirability of the latter in the light of his or her own moral and political standards (see for example Orford 2012).

Some valuable work of this kind has already been undertaken. Since the myth of Westphalia was busted by authors like Croxton (1999) and Osiander (2001), historians of international law have been keen to understand *why* the notion of such a system of territorially demarcated and mutually recognising states has been so persistently projected backwards onto a largely alien past (Beaulac 2004). Other scholars have shown how the lexical equation of sovereignty with supreme authority over a given territory not only was a relative latecomer, but also how it constitutes a curious anomaly when set against the backdrop of those imperial forms of rule that long used to be the default mode of governance in Europe and elsewhere (Benton 2010; Brett 2011; Elden 2013). Finally, historians of international thought have been struck by the no less persistent habit among international theorists to saddle dead philosophers such as Hobbes or Locke with conceptions of sovereignty that they could not have articulated given the conceptual resources at their disposal, and which would not have made any sense to them (Armitage 2013).

Taken together, these accounts indicate that the very conception of sovereignty that has been subject to constant contestation by international theorists during the past few decades is *itself* the result of recent processes of reification, as is the related practice of superimposing this conception upon times and places in which nothing of the kind was known. As Hobson (2012) has shown, it has been a widespread practice among international theorists to project conceptions of sovereignty onto non-European peoples and their forms of political association. But rather than remaining content to criticise these practices on grounds of their obvious anachronism and Eurocentrism, I think interesting questions could be raised about their implications for our understanding of sovereignty and its history. As Fasolt (2004: 7) has argued, the sovereign state is as much dependent for its existence on temporal limits as it is on spatial demarcations. Thus, if history – or rather the practice of historical writing – has been integral to the constitution of the sovereign state, then the main methodological principle of modern historical scholarship that states anachronism should be avoided, merely serves to uphold the dividing line between past and present so essential to maintaining the temporal limits of sovereignty (ibid.: 13). Conversely, if we accept that sovereignty constitutes an indispensable starting point for the practice of periodisation, it follows that 'the history of periodisation is juridical, and it advances through struggles over the definition and location of sovereignty' (Davis 2008: 8). This symbiotic connection between conceptions of sovereignty and practices of historical writing goes some way to explain why extant attempts to historicise sovereignty often have reinforced rather than mitigated our sense of epochal entrapment. Many historical accounts of sovereignty – my own included – have ended up reaffirming sovereignty rather than pointing beyond it. Perhaps more importantly, it helps us to understand how such reified conceptions of sovereignty have conditioned the possibility of historical writing since the early modern period, and how the resulting historiography has become instrumental in legitimising the sovereign state by making it appear exhaustive of the possibilities of political order, thereby also concealing the rich variety of human associations that antedated the emergence and diffusion of sovereignty on a planetary scale. I take this to be a consequence of the symbiotic relationship between the state and modern historiography that appeared with Ranke and Heeren, and then became foundational to modern international relations. A historical critique of sovereignty would hopefully be able to expose those alternative forms of political order that predominant modes of historical writing have removed from the reach of our political knowledge.

Another and more malign consequence of the reification of sovereignty that has largely escaped contingency theorists has been the concomitant naturalisation and legitimisation of political violence. Even those liberal cosmopolitan theories that are critical of modern state sovereignty have been complicit in this naturalisation to the extent they have assumed that the sovereign state originates in some foundational act of violence, or that war inevitably will ensue among states in the absence of any authority that could prevent its outbreak. Yet as Hidemi Suganami (2007: 529) has reminded us, 'if the practice of sovereignty is a sufficient condition of the possibility of arbitrary violence ... it follows ... that the possibility of arbitrary violence is a necessary condition of the practice of sovereignty'. Thus an important task of a sustainable critique of sovereignty is to unpack and denaturalise the historical and philosophical symbiosis between sovereignty and violence that seems to have escaped earlier critics. As I have tried to show elsewhere, there is a self-reinforcing double bind between sovereignty and the use of force that runs through Western history, insofar as sovereignty has been consistently justified with reference to the violence that would ensue its absence, while the use of force has been consistently justified with reference to the existence of some legitimate authority (Bartelson 2010). But this double bind does not stop with the sovereign state: there are indications that what is essentially a protection racket is in the process of becoming globalised, with far-reaching consequences for our understanding of sovereignty and the sources of its legitimacy. The Responsibility to Protect is a case in point. According to this doctrine, should a state be unable to protect its own citizens from human rights abuses, other states have an obligation to intervene under certain conditions. As Orford (2011) has argued, this doctrine is reminiscent of absolutist conceptions of sovereignty insofar as it serves to reinforce the executive powers of global governance institutions while justifying the obligation to protect with reference to the will of an international community, whose precise scope and mandate is forever in abeyance. Hence, state sovereignty – rather than being the prize of successful claims to independence and self-determination – becomes more akin to a grant contingent upon its responsible exercise in accordance with norms sanctioned by a more bare form of sovereignty embodied in an imagined international community (Bartelson 2014).

Thus, in sum, a sustainable critique of sovereignty would demand that we take the argument from contingency to another level by attending to the unintended consequences of this argument, abandon the vain aspiration to emancipate ourselves from the spell of reification, and instead focus on what the practices of reification do to sovereignty and what those reifications then do to the world. Taking the argument from contingency to another level is not only a precursor to a critical evaluation of the ethical import of sovereignty in the present, but also a necessary step towards the realisation that the sociopolitical world ultimately is composed of nothing but those past reifications that have successfully sedimented into political facts and taken on a life of their own.

Further reading

Biersteker, T.J. and Weber, C. (eds) (1996) *State Sovereignty as Social Construct*, Cambridge: Cambridge University Press.

Hinsley, F.H. (1986) *Sovereignty*, Cambridge: Cambridge University Press.

Kalmo, H. and Q. Skinner (eds) (2011) *Sovereignty in Fragments. The Past, Present, and Future of a Contested Concept*, Cambridge: Cambridge University Press.

Krasner, S.D. (1999) *Sovereignty. Organized Hypocrisy*, Princeton, NJ: Princeton University Press.

Philpott, D. (2001) *Revolutions in Sovereignty: How Ideas Shaped Modern International Relations*, Princeton, NJ: Princeton University Press.

Spruyt, H. (1996) *The Sovereign State and its Competitors: an Analysis of Systems Change*, Princeton, NJ: Princeton University Press.

Bibliography

Armitage, D. (2013) *Foundations of Modern International Thought*, Cambridge: Cambridge University Press.

Ashley, R.K. (1989). 'Living on Border Lines: Man, Poststructuralism, and War', in J. Der Derian and M.J. Shapiro (eds), *International/Intertextual Relations. Postmodern Readings of World Politics*, Lexington, MA: Lexington Books, pp. 25–321.

Ashley, R.K. (1995) 'The Powers of Anarchy: Theory Sovereignty, and the Domestication of Global Life', in J. Der Derian (ed.), *International Theory: Critical Investigations*, London: Macmillan, pp. 94–128.

Ashley, R.K. and Walker, R.B.J. (1990) 'Conclusion: Reading Dissidence/Writing the Discipline: Crisis and the Question of Sovereignty in International Studies', *International Studies Quarterly* 34(3): 367–416.

Bartelson, J. (1995) *A Genealogy of Sovereignty*, Cambridge: Cambridge University Press.

Bartelson, J. (2001) *The Critique of the State*, Cambridge: Cambridge University Press.

Bartelson, J. (2008) 'Sovereignty Before and After the Linguistic Turn', in R. Adler-Nissen and T. Gammeltoft-Hansen (eds), *Sovereignty Games. Instrumentalizing State Sovereignty in Europe and Beyond*, Basingstoke: Palgrave Macmillan, pp. 33–45.

Bartelson, J. (2010) 'Double Binds: Sovereignty and the Just War Tradition', in H. Kalmo and Q. Skinner (eds), *Sovereignty in Fragments: The Past, Present and Future of a Contested Concept*, Cambridge: Cambridge University Press, pp. 81–95.

Bartelson, J. (2014) *Sovereignty as Symbolic Form*, London and New York: Routledge.

Beaulac, S. (2004) *The Power of Language in the Making of International Law: the Word Sovereignty in Bodin and Vattel and The Myth of Westphalia*, Leiden: Martinus Nijhoff Publishers.

Benton, L. (2010) *A Search for Sovereignty: Law and Geography in European Empires, 1400–1900*, Cambridge: Cambridge University Press.

Bickerton, C., Cunliffe, P. and Gourevitch, A. (eds) (2006) *Politics without Sovereignty: A Critique of Contemporary International Relations*, London: Routledge.

Biersteker, T.J., and Weber, C. (eds) (1996) *State Sovereignty as Social Construct*, Cambridge: Cambridge University Press.

Brett, A.S. (2011) *Changes of State: Nature and the Limits of the City in Early Modern Natural Law*, Princeton, NJ: Princeton University Press.

Croxton, D. (1999) 'The Peace of Westphalia of 1648 and the Origins of Sovereignty', *The International History Review* 21(3): 569–591.

Davis, K. (2008) *Periodization and Sovereignty: How Ideas of Feudalism and Secularization Govern the Politics of Time*, Philadelphia: University of Pennsylvania Press.

Elden, S. (2013) *The Birth of Territory*, Chicago, IL: University of Chicago Press.

Fasolt, C. (2004) *The Limits of History*, Chicago, IL: University of Chicago Press.

Foucault, M. (1972) *The Archaeology of Knowledge*, London: Tavistock.

Foucault, M. (2003) *Society Must Be Defended: Lectures at the Collège de France, 1975–1976*, London: Macmillan.

Glanville, L. (2010) 'The Antecedents of "Sovereignty as Responsibility"', *European Journal of International Relations* 17(1): 233–255.

Glanville, L. (2013) 'The Myth of "Traditional" Sovereignty', *International Studies Quarterly* 57(2): 79–90.

Hobson, J. M. (2012) *The Eurocentric Conception of World Politics: Western International Theory, 1760–2010*, Cambridge: Cambridge University Press.

Jennings, R.C. (2011) 'Sovereignty and Political Modernity: A Genealogy of Agamben's Critique of Sovereignty', *Anthropological Theory* 11(1): 23–61.

Keohane, R.O. (2003) 'Political Authority after Interventions: Gradations in Sovereignty', in J.L. Holzgrefe and R.O. Keohane (eds), *Humanitarian Intervention: Ethical, Legal and Political Dilemmas*, Cambridge: Cambridge University Press, pp. 275–298.

Koselleck, R. (1985) 'Begriffsgeschichte and Social History', in Reinhart Koselleck (ed.), *Futures Past: On the Semantics of Historical Time*, Cambridge, MA: MIT Press, pp. 73–91.

Krasner, S.D. (1999) *Sovereignty: Organized Hypocrisy*, Princeton, NJ: Princeton University Press.

Krasner, S.D. (2004) 'Sharing Sovereignty: New Institutions for Collapsed and Failing States', *International Security* 29(4): 85–120.

Krasner, S.D. and Risse, T. (2014). 'External Actors, State-Building, and Service Provision in Areas of Limited Statehood: Introduction', *Governance* 27: 545–567.

Levine, D. (2012) *Recovering International Relations: The Promise of Sustainable Critique*, Oxford: Oxford University Press.

Muthu, S. (2009) *Enlightenment against Empire*, Princeton, NJ: Princeton University Press.

Onuf, N.G. (1991) 'Sovereignty: Outline of a Conceptual History', *Alternatives* 16(4): 425–446.

Orford, A. (2011) *International Authority and the Responsibility to Protect*, Cambridge: Cambridge University Press.

Orford, A. (2012) 'In Praise of Description', *Leiden Journal of International Law* 25(3): 609–625.

Osiander, A. (2001) 'Sovereignty, International Relations, and the Westphalian Myth', *International Organization* 55(2): 251–287.

Pocock, J.G.A. (1987) *The Ancient Constitution and the Feudal Law: A Study of English Historical Thought in the Seventeenth Century*, Cambridge: Cambridge University Press.

Risse, T. (ed.) (2013) *Governance Without a State? Policies and Politics in Areas of Limited Statehood*, New York: Columbia University Press.

Skinner, Q. (1988) 'Meaning and Understanding in the History of Ideas', in J. Tully (ed.), *Meaning and Context: Quentin Skinner and his Critics*, Oxford: Polity Press, pp. 29–67.

Skinner, Q. (2010) 'The Modern State: a Genealogy', in H. Kalmo and Q. Skinner (eds), *Sovereignty in Fragments: The Past, Present and Future of a Contested Concept*, Cambridge: Cambridge University Press, pp. 26–46.

Suganami, H. (2007) 'Understanding Sovereignty Through Kelsen/Schmitt', *Review of International Studies* 33(3): 511–530.

Teschke, B.G. (2011). 'Fatal Attraction: A Critique of Carl Schmitt's International Political and Legal Theory', *International Theory* 3(2): 179–227.

Thompson, M.P. (1986). 'The History of Fundamental Law in Political Thought from the French Wars of Religion to the American Revolution', *The American Historical Review* 91(5): 1103–1128.

Walker, R.B.J. (1993) *Inside/Outside. International Relations as Political Theory*, Cambridge: Cambridge University Press.

Walker, R.B.J., and Mendlovitz, S.H. (eds) (1990) *Contending Sovereignties: Redefining Political Community*, Boulder, CO: Lynne Rienner Publishers.

Weber, C. (1996) *Simulating Sovereignty: Intervention, the State and Symbolic Exchange*, Cambridge: Cambridge University Press.

Werner, W.G. and de Wilde, J.H. (2001) 'The Endurance of Sovereignty', *European Journal of International Relations* 7(3): 283–313.

14

SPACE

John Agnew

Explicit recognition of terrestrial 'space' (to distinguish the term as used here from 'outer space' and similar usage) as a contextual dimension of the substance of what goes for international relations, be it entirely state-related or extended to include other actors, has been largely missing from the orthodox theoretical repertoire of the field. If, on the one hand, 'the Westphalian straitjacket' of a system of self-evident territorial units imposed an 'ahistorical and Eurocentric arrogance', on the other hand, the abandonment of much interest in meta-theoretical issues such as the spatiality underpinning the Westphalian worldview limited the scope for extending the field beyond a narrow state-centredness (Buzan and Little 2001: 25, 30).[1]

Whatever the specific theoretical proclivity, realist, idealist or constructivist, the tendency has been to beg such questions as: how does territory enter into the workings of politics; is sovereignty essentially territorial; how is the international distinctive from the global; how has the structure of the world economy reflected and conditioned the global hierarchy of states and empires; how do political actors other than the governments of states relate spatially to the workings of interstate relations; and how are knowledge practices about world politics constituted in and circulate across different places around the world?

In this chapter I hope to trace some of the ways in which answering these questions has been inspired by an explicit engagement with imagining politics spatially – in terms of networks/flows and places, as well as the territories and geopolitical spaces of conventional wisdom – and has animated recent efforts at revitalising thinking critically about world politics (politics across a range of geographical scales from the local to the global). Before doing so, I briefly review what can be called the 'silent treatment' given to space in mainstream IR in terms of implicit meanings ascribed to it and the history of terminology relating to space in fields such as political geography from which a more analytic vocabulary for understanding world politics can be drawn. I then describe an approach to thinking about the different potential spatialities of world politics and consider three examples of the rethinking of space relative to IR: the historicity of geopolitics, sovereignty regimes, and the geopolitics of knowledge about world politics.

Silence about space

The closed character of much discussion about international relations has become a popular topic. Accepting as 'obvious' and not worthy of explicit examination is the assumption of an essential identity between a quintessential state and a territorial definition of its limits; this has been a particularly important aspect of this closure. With respect to terrestrial space, one of the most important critiques along these lines was made by Richard Ashley (1983: 464) when he wrote about the centrality of statism in IR as involving a self-conscious obscuring of 'taboo terms' that:

> secure disciplinary boundaries which in turn impose and legitimate limits on political and social discourse, constrain the symbolic resources available to contending parties, and circumscribe the social reordering possibilities imaginable within that discourse.

With respect to space, conventional IR has had two closely related understandings of space that have been mostly taboo. In turn, they have crucially restricted thinking about world politics to the focal point of interstate relations.

One understanding is that the territorial basis of modern statehood (which is put into the deep past of human history) eclipses any other conception of space (as, for example, interaction and flow through networks over space or place making). The division of global space into mutually exclusive territorial chunks of space thus totally defines the geography of world politics. Even when spelled out, this often reduces to the banal proposition that adjacent states are more likely than distant ones to have territorial disputes with one another, or that the 'geography' of global conflicts is entirely a function of states as singular actors banging up against one another (Starr 2005). This logic promises relief from external 'anarchy,' by creating a supposedly pacific domestic space and displacing competition – and violence – beyond state borders. In this construction, states are thus natural adversaries of one another. The second dominant understanding of space in IR, therefore, is that territorial states are 'naturally' aggrandising entities that aspire to maximise their territorial bases in an insecure geopolitical space. Their security being in perpetual doubt because of the pervasive anarchy that surrounds them, territorial states constantly prepare to meet threats to their existence by threatening others. The term geopolitics has long been used to convey this sense of interstate relations as a series of zero-sum games, whether in its classical form as invoking the advantages and disadvantages under different technological regimes of global relative location (sea- versus land-powers, and so on), or in terms of generalised global military and economic competition between states and empires. Only if hierarchy/empire restricts competition or if a set of global norms create an 'international society', in some theoretical renditions, can anarchy be kept at bay without the threat of constant anxiety. But geopolitical space remains in place as animating interstate relations even when the word geopolitics itself remains unmentioned. The absence of a word to describe something exactly does not signify the absence of a concept at work in practice.

Both of these notions of space – as state territory and as geopolitical space for contest between states – have recently been subject to critical examination. In the first case, what has been pointed to is that the territorial assumption is underpinned by three related dispositions. One is that state territory is always and everywhere coterminous with state sovereignty. The subjectivity of the state as an autonomous political actor is thereby set prior to any sort of action by or on its behalf. This has the effect of sanctifying the territorial state as a 'sacred unit beyond historical time' (Agnew and Corbridge 1995: 89). Yet, it is through security discourse that any state is actually produced: the distinction this relies on, between 'inside' and 'outside' the territory, functions to demarcate the domestic 'us' from the foreign 'them' (Walker 1993). A second disposition is that territorial states are the only effective units of global economic organisation. Deriving from old mercantilist theories about the subordination of economy to states, this idea essentially sees the world economy as simply the outcome of transactions between territorial states. This has been reinforced by ideas about the developmental state and the rise of the welfare state in some countries. In furthering economic growth and personal welfare, the governments of states are seen as the primary agents of political progress. Finally, the political is limited to the state by the association made between the nation as the singular social group, on the one hand, and the territorial borders of the state, on the other. The recent reassertion of many international borders in the face of various immigration panics and the growth of global terrorist operations has made this assumption seem even more commonsensical than it was in the past. Together these dispositions protect the enterprise of 'international theory' from critical inquiry beyond crucial limits. In turn, they make for difficulty in accounting for past and present capital mobility, population movements, global supply chains and the chronopolitics (time–space compression) of modern militaries (see Muller and Peterson in this book). Much of the real world escapes its intellectual grasp.

The 'modern geopolitical imagination', a phrase I have adopted for this way of thinking, can be thought of as a 'system' for visualising the world with its most significant roots in the European encounter with the rest of the world in the sixteenth and seventeenth centuries (Agnew 2003). It came to the fore at the time when European states/empires were establishing themselves globally and as a substitute for the previously dominant religious-based vertical cosmology. Its horizontality is based on dividing up the world into zones with various presumed capacities for self-government á la European mode, and the necessity, because of the potential anarchy out there to take charge over this world of potential dangers and threats. The imagination works from the global scale down and involves the identification of zones of danger, the most problematic states as potential adversaries and allies, the challenges to the world political map as presently constituted, and the relations between different geographical scales or layers of political action from the local to the global, but with a strong emphasis on the state and interstate tiers as the most vital for the practice of world politics. Contradictory to the territorial understanding of statehood, given that each state is presumed to provide equivalent sovereignty within its territory to all others, in geopolitical space, sovereignty is up for grabs as states compete for global power and influence and weak states succumb to more powerful ones. This hierarchical and sometimes imperialist geopolitical system is one that has come to be the byword of the political elites who occupy seats of power in the most important Great Powers. Membership in this group 'depends on recognition by existing members. Qualification has depended not simply on coercive power, the ability to force others to do what you want, but also on the capacity to write the political-economic agenda of others, defining appropriate standards of conduct and providing the framing for interstate relations with which others must conform if they are to gain recognition and reward from the Great Powers' (Agnew 2003: 9–10; see also Abrahamsen in this book).

The approach to global space as being totally geopolitical is obviously one that has animated much of what have gone for theories of world politics down the years. But practically it has always been far from total. Legions of private actors representing businesses, churches and charities, massive flows of goods, capital and people, and shifting social boundaries between national and other identities (territorial and non-territorial) have long, and increasingly, disrupted the static billiard-ball world that the geopolitical conception of global space tends to reproduce (see Peterson in this book). Contrary to the video-game version of how politics is spaced, this is only one of a number of models of how global political–economic relations have been and are constituted. This is one that relies on a very constrained understanding of 'how the world works'. It is increasingly limiting. One could make the case that at least from 1914 until 1970 or thereabouts, in the European–American world there was a geographical closure within state and imperial borders that, if episodically erupting into Great Power Wars, nevertheless rested on premises that were much closer to the spatiality of politics implicit in the modern geopolitical imagination. Since then we have experienced what Carlo Galli (2010: 109) calls the 'crisis of borders … a trend towards the obsolescence of the distinction between internal and external'. This is a world of multiple spatialities of power in which political space can no longer be adequately reduced to state territories simply banging up against one another (Ruggie 1993; see also Vaughan-Williams in this book).

Consider, for example, the impacts of supranational institutions such as the European Union on established states, both members and potential ones; the overlapping territorialities of social movements and regional devolution within fragmented states such as Colombia, Spain and Lebanon; the transnationalising of corporate law into the hands of jurisdictionally ambiguous private law firms whose expertise allows them to shop for jurisdictions from which their corporate clients can maximise their possibilities of tax avoidance and regulatory arbitrage (recall tax havens such as the Cayman Islands and Bermuda); the persistence of clan and tribal types of polity that defy reorganisation into strict territorial states that often transgress long-established social boundaries and threaten traditional sources of authority (think of Afghanistan); the tragic trajectories of so many undocumented immigrants attempting to cross the Mediterranean from Africa to Italy or the border between Mexico and the US to seek a better life for themselves in a world with dramatic differences in living standards between some countries and others; and the rise of private and non-governmental actors that exercise true authority over a vast range of financial, product and regulatory activities (credit-rating agencies immediately come to mind). Silence about the view of space underpinning conventional IR theory thereby puts much of what is happening in the real world simply off limits.

The language of space

The vocabulary of space is in fact considerably richer and nuanced than that offered by the two understandings that have tended to prevail, even if silently, within the world of IR. The present purpose is not to recite all that could be said about 'spatial thought'. It is more, as suggested by Galli (2010: 7), to identify some of the main alternative interpretations of space to the mainstream ones such that space becomes 'a category for the thinkability of politics'. From this perspective, such concepts as 'state', 'sovereignty', 'empire', 'globalisation' and 'geopolitics' can be rethought using a different language of space than that of the conventional wisdom. In this regard, three terms in particular, territory, space and place, deserve discussing before moving on to consider their meanings in relation to the specific spatial modalities of world politics.

Territory obviously has a strong association with state sovereignty, particularly in the English language. This has its main roots in seventeenth-century Europe when reactions to the religious wars of the time led political leaders and philosophers alike to posit territorial separation (as in the Treaties of Westphalia) as a solution to internecine religious conflict. Many crucial political terms such as democracy and freedom became defined almost exclusively in state-territorial terms as a result of this historical confluence (Connolly 1994). Yet, a territory can be any unit of contiguous space or place managed by a social group, organisation or individual person. The territorial state has been a highly specific historical entity (Ruggie 1993). In many languages, the more general usage implies that territories result from territoriality or the division of space to help organise social life or to fulfil organisational goals. Such strategising may involve states or it may not. There is simply no necessary relationship between states on the one hand and territories on the other. Be that as it may, territorialisation can be associated with both political and social organisation. In this construction, as with Deleuze and Guattari (1972), for example, deterritorialisation refers to the breakdown of territoriality in thought and practice. Epistemologically opposing 'state philosophy' to 'nomad thought', they see territorialisation as a fundamental aspect of the former and deterritorialisation as associated with the latter. But whether territory is invariably absent for nomads in social practice is empirically doubtful. We should be open to the possibility that reterritorialisations can take place under auspices other than those of states. The territorial state remains the implicit ideal in this and other formulations because they all fail to articulate an alternative global space. 'Ultimately, reterritorialization is another example of how global space is conceptualized as a normative extension of territorial space' (Shah 2012: 13). Even proponents of a world state can think of it only in terms of a 'scaling up' of the territorial state rather than as something that might possibly have a more complex and even permanently deterritorialised spatial form.

Space is the more generic term because of its obvious connotation of elemental necessity associated with its usage in physics. Though typically defined in terms of absolute dimensions, such as latitude and longitude, its usage in contemporary political geography implies attending to how different social and political practices are co-implicated in different spatial manifestations. From this relational perspective, space is, so to speak, folded into social and political activities as they take place over time. State territory is simply only one modus operandi of such a folding. Though its association in recent thinking with such ideas as governmentality and biopolitics has reinforced its hold as the premier way in which space manifests its influence, there is no necessity for this to be invariably the case. In political usage, what is critical is the recognition that power is not simply located in 'the State apparatus, making this into the major, privileged, capital and almost unique instrument of the power of one class over another. In reality, power in its exercise goes much further, passes through much finer channels, and is much more ambiguous, since each individual has at his disposal a certain power, and for that very reason can act as the vehicle for transmitting a wider power' (Foucault 2007: 179).

Power is therefore not entirely about domination or coercion as much conventional theorising would have it. Power is both centred and distributed (see Abrahamsen in this book). From this viewpoint, space can be thought of 'as the meeting up (or not) of multiple trajectories' of different people over space as they actively make their interests and identities (Massey 1999: 283). Yet, there are centres of networked power that operate across and around rather than contained by territories. This is the case, for example, with networks of global corporate control. Many lines of power, therefore, are not necessarily territorialised at all. Territorially configured state spaces are themselves riven through with power networks that challenge and reconfigure 'inherited territorial structures of power' (Brenner and Elden 2009: 355). More radically, as Terrell Carver (1997) says, putting space in these spatial–interactional terms (along with attending to the coeval effects of time and speed) reveals that the established territorialised view is in fact an attempt at stabilising the world through creating rather than just representing already existing neatly bordered enmities and anxieties. In failing to adequately distinguish space from territory, territory is sometimes scaled up as a concept to the global and then essentially confused with the continuing ontology of state territory, only now on an extended basis.

The richer conception of space as entailing more than territory leads some writers to see politics as not entirely just contained territorially by states or networked across space but as actively involving the making of places. Space then is not externally related to society but actually intrinsic to its workings. Conventionally, place usually refers to an area or region that displays some distinctiveness as a result of its 'internal' characteristics. This makes it akin to territory when considered beyond its state-based locution. Places are certainly 'sites where people live, work and move, and where they form attachments, practice their relations with each other, and relate to the rest of the world' (Leitner et al. 2008: 161). But they also have a materiality to them (infrastructure, buildings, and so on) and by shaping everyday social interaction, potentially affect the possibilities of various types of political action. The point here is to suggest how much space qua place mediates popular politics in ways that may or may not fit into the conventional state-territorial framework through which politics is typically pictured (Agnew 1987). States themselves are congeries of places more or less integrated into singular territorial spaces with political commitments often overlapping across state borders, as with irredentist political movements, cross-border commuters and immigrant diasporas. Through agency, people are able to exercise the diffuse power that enables them to be active forces in politics rather than simply dupes and dopes pushed around by state apparatuses. Of course, this is only realisable when they activate their agency by challenging the mystification of space entailed in the dual understanding of territory and geopolitical space that plucks politics out of the hands of people and into the grasp of political–economic elites and strategic specialists educated in the ways of the global chessboard.

Spatialities of world politics

In light of this discussion of the various modalities of space relevant to world politics, three conventions about political power and the state can be briefly challenged en route to establishing a typology of historical spatialities of world politics. The first, of course, is the rigid territorial conception of how power operates: a system of territorial states. A richer conception of space sees state territory as only one of a range of historically plausible geographical forms that the distribution of power takes: imperial, global-network, alliance and supranational, for example. Quite which combinations are at work in any specific epoch depends crucially on the spatial ordering of political, cultural and economic activities at that time. A second is the dyadic understanding of power relationships that pervades the conventional wisdom: be they person–person, person–state or state–state. This individualises and abstracts power from historical–geographical settings and views it as a possession of a pre-given set of individual entities. The embedding of relationships in changing material conditions makes this approach extremely dubious for understanding how actual world politics really works. Third, and finally, states are regarded as the moral and ontological equivalent of individual persons. This assumption privileges the state by associating it with the character and moral agency of individual persons in Western political philosophy. Taken together, these three conventions de-historicise the relationship between power and states.

Crucially, therefore, to truly understand world politics requires taking history and space equally seriously. At least four heuristic models of the spatiality of power and their workings over time can be used to offer an alternative general account to that of the conventional wisdom (Agnew 2005). The theoretical logic of the approach is that specific material conditions and ideological understandings correlate with the relative predominance of different spatialities of politics. The first model is an 'ensemble of worlds' in which human groups live in relative isolation and whose spatiality of politics is that of absolute physical distance constraining interaction and dramatically limiting circulation. This fits best the world before the sixteenth century. The second is of a 'field of forces'. This is the geopolitical model par excellence in which rigidly defined territorial units vie for control over territory at the expense of each other. The dominant spatiality is that of state territoriality run by political elites who mimic one another's discourse and practices. In large part this is a facsimile of the Westphalian world. Third is the 'hierarchical network'. This reflects the political economy of a world economy in which transactions across networks link geographical cores and peripheries, imperial centres and colonial hinterlands and global cities and smaller ones in the worldwide urban hierarchy. The spatiality is that of spatial networks joining together a hierarchy of nodes across space. This is the world of global trade, investment and imperialism. Finally is the model of the 'integrated world society'. This represents both a world facing common problems and the possibility of economic and cultural integration in the face of managing them. Networks are viewed as reticular rather than hierarchical and state territories are seen as threatening to the very possibility of creating any sort of world polity.

One can see evidence for the co-presence of each of these models in the contemporary world with the middle two as still particularly significant, the first one as in eclipse and the final one as possibly emergent (at least in relation to some issues such as global warming). Obviously, the models only make sense as heuristic devices but they do help us think beyond the limitations of the conventional wisdom of space as being entirely a question of state territory and geopolitical space.

Historicity of geopolitics

The first example of rethinking space in IR concerns what I have called the 'three ages of geopolitics' (Agnew 2003: Chapter 6). Rather than a trans-historical geopolitical space in which states/empires have operated independently of changing material and ideological circumstances, I identify three epochs from the early nineteenth century until 1990 between which the idioms and practices of world politics changed dramatically. The purpose is to show that spatial contexts have had shifting contours and in so doing exercised different effects on world politics down the years. Clearly, historicising involves periodising in order to gain purchase on a more complex historical–geographical reality. It does not necessarily entail any sort of teleology about the direction of history or even of a singular logic at work in changing the character of space's effects over time, although shifts in communication and transportation technologies, military weapon systems and global commodity chains have conspired to make speed something of a motif in some of the spatial transformations. Engaging with the temporality of geopolitics in the modern era is one way of drawing into question the conventional singular and trans-historical approach to geopolitical space elucidated previously (Klinke 2013; see also Lundborg in this book).

In brief compass, I distinguish three geopolitical epochs: 1815–1875, 'civilisational geopolitics'; 1875–1945, 'naturalised geopolitics'; and 1945–1990, 'ideological geopolitics'. Since the end of the Cold War in 1990 we can perhaps see a new epoch of 'global geopolitics' (Agnew 2003: Chapter 7). But I do not address that in any detail here. In the late eighteenth century a civilisational geopolitics developed based around the Concert of Europe, on one side, and British hegemony in the wider world, on the other. This was widely seen by political elites in the (European) Great Powers as serving collective as well as national interests. Its main elements were: a commitment to the uniqueness of European civilisation; a sense that Europe had eclipsed other civilisations, notwithstanding their past accomplishments; an increasing identification with the so-called nation state as the highest form of political organisation, but only for Europeans; reliance on the British Royal Navy to protect (and extract rents from) trade and investment; and a mixture of liberal political economy in Europe with global imperialism as the modus operandi of networks of trade and investment beyond European shores. This geopolitical order dissolved as the contradiction between its European and global elements became apparent to rising powers (particularly Germany, but later Japan and the United States) as closing out the extra-European compact.

As a result, two antagonistic groups of states emerged to define the new era of naturalised geopolitics based on inter-imperial rivalry and at the heart of the modern understanding of geopolitical space. One, led by Britain and France (with covert US support) stood for the coexistence of open trade and imperialism. The other, headed by Germany, was revisionist, concerned to build new empires and challenge British (and London-based) financial–economic domination. Initially, under German intellectual tutelage but spreading later far and wide, geopolitical space was seen as a natural zone divided into imperial and colonised peoples, states with 'needs' for space and markets, a closed world in which one state's gains (in imperial annexation, in particular) meant another state's loss, and a world of fixed environmental conditions and resource distributions that had determining effects on a state's global status. This combination of ideas and practices reached its zenith with Japanese militarism and German Nazism in the 1930s. National power was seen as having geographical foundations in the sense of requiring explicit control over territories into which people could be settled, investment could be placed and markets developed. It struck a major blow to the centre of the British-based hegemony that had been dominant in the nineteenth century. In so doing it aroused disparate allies against it: the US rallying to the side of liberal capitalism and the Soviet Union, hitherto sidelined in world politics, but now being forced to choose between the invading forces of Nazi Germany and the more benign bourgeois capitalist world represented by Britain and the US.

Neither the United States nor the Soviet Union, however, managed to produce a via media between their two divergent political economies with distinctive 'lingua-cultural' attributes: democratic and capitalist versus statist and socialist. Of course, each side represented the other as the complete antithesis of itself, irrespective of any overlapping traits. On both sides massive military–industrial complexes emerged based on fear of the other, justified in terms of the 'ways of life' each was supposed to guarantee. This ideological geopolitics of the Cold War did involve episodic geographical zones of conflict, including direct and surrogate military commitments (over Greece, Berlin, Cuba, Czechoslovakia and Vietnam, for example). But each side's nuclear arsenals (and air power) tended to put limits on the possibilities of overt warfare between both sides. The spheres of influence each side established in the 1940s lasted well into the late 1980s, with the so-called Third World of former colonised states in Africa, Latin America and Asia being the only world zone in which there was much possibility of picking up new adherents. Even there, little if any movement took place once regimes were orientated one way or the other. The US and Russia/the Soviet Union shared a longstanding history of internal settlement frontiers that arguably led to a drawing of strong spatial lines between the space of Self and the space of Other. National cultural identities thus fed into this global contest. Ironically, it was conditions internal to the two dominant territorial actors that precipitated the collapse of the Cold War geopolitical order. In the Soviet case, the regime failed to deliver both ever-improving military performance and rising living standards. In the US case, internationalisation of the US economy as a by-product of the open economy that the Cold War mandated as an alternative to the autarky of the Soviet Union, produced both a hollowing out of the US economy and increasing 'imperial overstretch' in performing the role of global policeman.

In each case, therefore, different understandings and practices of space were at work. Only in the period of inter-imperial rivalry was space at work in ways closely analogous to the current conventional trans-historical wisdom in IR. Previously and during the Cold War the world was partitioned in very different ways and with different outcomes. Before 1870, the basic global division was Europe versus elsewhere. After the Second World War and down until 1990, a bipolar world with basic worldwide stability in territorial spaces and borders tended to prevail. Today we live in an epoch in which the territorialisation of world politics redolent of the entire period from 1815 to 1990 is challenged by a world-city network and analogous network-power effects involving myriad public and private actors – from credit-rating agencies to international and non-governmental organisations – as well as states, that portends a very different complex global spatiality of politics than that I have drawn for the three previous epochs.

Sovereignty regimes

A second example of using space to rethink IR considers one of the central concepts of the field: sovereignty. Conventional modernist thinking about sovereignty in the academic fields of political theory and IR sees the world as divided into neat blocs of space or territories over which states exercise mutually exclusive control and authority. In practice, we all know that states are not equally sovereign in terms of their control over their borders, effective central bureaucracy to achieve collective ends, recognition by other states, capacity to influence and coerce others, or domestic legitimacy in the eyes of their populations (Agnew 2009; Krasner 1999). The term sovereignty is used in all of these various ways to express the relationship between states, on the one hand, and people, considered as subjects or citizens, on the other. Yet, the world political map and some international orga- nisations, such as the United Nations, are based on the fiction that each territory claimed by a given state is equally sovereign to all others. This is obviously proble- matic if we consider for a moment how many of the world's putative states are in fact completely ineffective, absent, lacking in control over large chunks of the state's ter- ritory and faced with significant legitimacy deficits. Think, for example, of cases such as Somalia, the Democratic Republic of the Congo, Iraq, Pakistan, Mexico and Greece. Of course, these are all distinctive cases with various degrees of depleted sovereignty. The same might be said of so-called strong states; they have also long faced serious if different challenges to their claims to monopolise sovereignty over a given territory.

Most states have never in fact had much effective sovereignty. Many emerged from colonialism and never achieved any real independence. Across the board, state borders match neither any sort of cultural entity (such as a nation) nor meaningful economic unit (such as a settlement network or a resource base). Some states have become dependents of other states, are fractured by organised criminal gangs or secessionist movements, or are reliant on debt servicing and remittances from external sources. Finally, some, including many economically developed states, have become subject to policing by various public and private agencies such as credit-rating agencies, law firms and courts, human rights organisations, and cha- rities that have become sovereigns in their own right as a result of licensing by states because of their superior knowledge, expertise and claims to neutrality. These agencies and more dominant states exercise their sovereignty through geographical networks rather than by territorial control. Thus immigration enforcement now takes place away from state borders both inside and outside states, credit-rating agencies based in world cities such as New York rank the sovereign bonds of even the most powerful states, such as the United States, and London-based law firms and English courts increasingly adjudicate on cases brought by parties resident in or with assets in long-distant jurisdictions (see Peterson and Vaughan-Williams in this book).

What has been missing in understanding the range of practices that constitute sovereignty is a means of identifying the co-variation between the effectiveness of central state authority, on the one hand, and its relative reliance on state territori- ality, on the other. One useful approach comes from writing on the historical sociology of power. In distinguishing despotic from infrastructural power, Michael Mann (1984) identifies two different ways in which a state acquires and uses centralised power. These words refer to two different functions that states perform for populations and that jointly underpin their claim to sovereignty: respectively, the struggle among elites within and between states and the provision of public goods by states as a result of placating various social groups and pursuing and legitimising despotic power. Before the eighteenth century infrastructural power was relatively less important than it is today. This is because elites have been forced by political struggles to be more responsive to their populations through providing more public goods. But economic development has also mandated increased provision of roads, weights and measures, elementary education, and so on, that will always be absent or underprovided with reliance on private provision. This boosted the territorialisation of sovereignty because demand was defined in terms of territorial populations and provision was orientated to satisfying that demand. Technological change, the increased intensity of all kinds of flows across borders, and the vulnerability of state populations to increased global economic competition, threatening public good provision when foreign competitors provide fewer public goods, have conspired to make infrastructural power increasingly networked. City regions and supranational entities (such as the European Union) challenge the state monopoly over public goods. International organisations, both public and private, have the capacity to deliver regulatory, financial and legal services hitherto usually associated with states.

At much the same time, despotic power has come to rely much more on popular legitimacy. At one time, and this is at the root of Western territorialised conceptions of sovereignty, the ruler relied on the claim to stand in apostolic succession to God, as in the Divine Right of Kings. This eventually translated into the idea of the 'body politic' as a territorialised people/nation (Agnew 2009: Chapter 2). Rulers needed to establish at least a modicum of popular authority before they could pursue their goals. Such legitimacy as they have, however, is increasingly fragile. As interests and identities cease to conform to territorial norms, rulers must adjust likewise. This can involve pursuing increased influence elsewhere (as in an imperium) or ceding authority to other parties in order to manage dissent and resistance. There is no necessary correlation, therefore, between despotic power and central state authority. Elites are increasingly globalised with respect both to pursuing their goals through expanded statehood beyond home shores and in terms of alliances with multinational companies, banks and other agents of a more networked world.

The main theoretical conundrum in terms of the 'where' or spatiality of sovereignty is the relative balance between the strength of continued central state authority (despotic power), on the one hand, and the degree to which public goods are provided and regulated on a territorialised basis (infrastructural power), on the other. The former involves judgement as to the extent a state has acquired and maintains an effective and legitimate apparatus of rule. The latter refers to the extent to which the provision and regulation of public goods is heavily state-regulated and bounded territorially. In different terminology, the question becomes one of the relative balance between territory and networks in the operational scope of the sovereignty of states and the agents they license (Agnew 2005: Chapter 3). The two dimensions of sovereignty define the degree of state autonomy and the extent to which it is territorial. From these, four extreme or ideal-type categories, or what I term 'sovereignty regimes', can be identified. These are relational in character. They refer to the character of sovereignty as manifested by differing combinations of central state authority and territorialised provision of public goods in different places. They are not best thought of as characterising particular states in all their aspects; no particular state fits exactly into any of the boxes in question. But they do provide a heuristic basis for identifying the relative complexity of sovereignty around the world today. This is a patchwork of more-and-less sovereign spaces and flows, not a rigidly territorial order, with some states and organisations more sovereign (in terms of their effectiveness) than others. The simplified relational categories are seen as representing stronger and weaker central state authority and consolidated and open territoriality. The purpose of thinking relationally about sovereignty is to move away from trapping thinking in absolute as opposed to relative distinctions. From this viewpoint, there is no simple 'either/or' to sovereignty when it is, on the one hand, either completely territorialised or, on the other, is not manifested territorially and therefore ceases to exist. This has been the trap into which much thinking about sovereignty has fallen.

Of the four ideal types, the first one, the *classic*, comes closest to the conventional story about sovereignty. Both despotic power and infrastructural power are largely territorialised and central state authority remains effective. Contemporary China perhaps best fits this case. The second case, the *imperialist*, represents best the case of hierarchy in world politics but with networked as well as territorialised reach. It is the complete opposite of the classic case. Central state authority is seriously in question, often exercised by outsiders if in collusion with local elites, and infrastructural power is weak or reliant on external support. Much of the Middle East and sub-Saharan Africa falls under this regime. The other two regimes are more complicated. The first, the *integrative*, is a regime where authority has migrated to both higher and lower tiers of government as a result of a sharing of sovereignty among states and infrastructural power takes both territorialised and networked forms. Various sorts of unions or confederations of states take this form, for example the United States before the US Civil War. The fullest contemporary example would be the European Union from the perspective of its Member States. The second of the two more complex sovereignty regimes is the *globalist*. This regime is closely associated today with the globalisation of the world brought about since the 1960s under US auspices. In this construction, the world city system, particularly the cities at the top of it, such as New York and London, provide the geographical nodes for the agents who are central to this regime. They exercise sovereignty wherever states have ceded authority to external agents because of debt dependence or regulatory oversight. This regime has a potentially worldwide reach but its effects are particularly strong in those parts of the world most integrated into the world economy and without the limits set on integration by, for example, managed exchange rates and capital controls, by states with greater effective central state authority (such as China). The historic basis of this regime in US hegemony means that at least until recently US governments were able to use this regime as an alternative to the imperialist one. But as authority has slowly seeped out of US governmental hands, other agencies including many private as well as public organisations have picked up the slack. Even sovereignty, therefore, hitherto perhaps the most territorialised of IR's concepts, can be rethought as exhibiting more complexity both in the past and today by 'thinking through space'.

Geopolitics of knowledge

The third example of using space to rethink IR involves the geography of how ideas about world politics originate in certain places and then circulate and are read worldwide. Since the *Methodenstreit* of the late nineteenth century, knowledge has been viewed overwhelmingly in terms of the opposition between the particulars of local knowledge, on the one hand, and the universals of objective scientific knowledge, on the other. Academic progress is measured in terms of the shift from the former to the latter. Yet, knowledge is always made somewhere by particular people using the experiences of the places in which they live to understand the world at large. So-called universals arise by projecting these experiences onto the world because of your superior capacity to do so, as well as the persuasiveness of your argument and evidence. This does not necessarily entail endorsing a cultural relativism in which all knowledge is essentially local knowledge, Far from it; rather, places in the modern world never exist in isolation and are subject to crosscutting commitments and all manner of external influences. Nevertheless, a case can be made that there are geographies of knowledge production and circulation that reflect geopolitical hierarchies and the flows of influence and ideas that parallel them.

Ideas about world politics, more narrowly IR theory, are a case in point. I have previously identified five ways in which space enters into the production and circulation of ideas about world politics (Agnew 2007). These are complementary more than competitive in that each tends to privilege a somewhat different spatial dimension such as, for instance, places or global networks. The first approach involves identifying particular venues of knowledge, such as is common in so-called science studies. All knowledge is seen as socially conditioned by the rituals, routines and recruitment practices of the laboratories, classrooms and seminars of powerful educational and research institutions. From this viewpoint, for example, the assumption of 'anarchy' beyond state borders in realist IR is not a simple objective fact about the world but a claim made by theorists who reproduce the assumption, often unthinkingly, based on standardised interpretations of selected intellectual giants (Machiavelli and Hobbes come to mind) in premier universities, think tanks and government offices. Its legitimacy, as that of other hegemonic ideas such as 'rational choice' and 'hegemonic succession', arises from the social power of those promoting it who can then influence others to act in the world as if it were empirically true irrespective of its actual veracity. A second approach focuses on the global scale in terms of how flows of knowledge from Europe and its extensions (such as the United States) have tended to overwhelm knowledge produced elsewhere. A product of European colonialism, this structural geopolitics of knowledge led to the diffusion of European and American ideas about international relations as representing the 'best' of global thinking. The development of counter currents of thought, dependency theory's emphasis on how the growth of Europe has depended on the exploitation of colonial territories, for example, suggests that the flow of knowledge need not always be a one-way street.

The next spatial framing of knowledge about world politics is a phenomenological one in which narratives that reflect the historical experiences of some places are projected onto the world at large. Competing geopolitical visions then come to structure how the world is understood. By way of example, as Lisa Anderson (2003: 90) notes, much of the 'liberal tradition' in US social science has had an American 'geographical, territorial association'. Somewhat similar in origins but relating more to the capacity to project influence elsewhere is a fourth spatial framing in which the ideas of a Great Power with substantial hegemonic sway tend to become the global common sense about international politics. Plausibly, the very field of IR is an American invention and has spread worldwide under US auspices even if there are important 'parochialisms' in IR teaching. Finally, the question of *where* also matters in terms of the reading/interpretation of what are presented as universal theories. This is partly because local norms and translations can lead to different interpretations. But it is also because outside theories become weapons in local ideological struggles. The constitutive ideas of IR realism, for example, developed originally in texts by Machiavelli, Hobbes and others were brought to the US by German political refugees whose ideas were then Americanised in terms of the peculiar rendering known as neo-realism for its combination of liberal economic ideas and statist notions about security.

Each of these perspectives on the geopolitics of knowledge in IR offers a distinctive spatial framing of how particular ideas can achieve both wider audiences and larger universal status. They point to how crucial space is in conditioning the very possibility of knowledge about world politics. They also suggest that knowledge is not best thought of as either immediately objective or as completely culturally determined. As theory develops and travels it is always subject to spatial mediation.

Conclusion

Considering 'space', therefore, allows us to rethink a range of topics conventionally taboo in mainstream IR but increasingly important to improve intellectual purchase on the world we live in. The two preeminent ways in which space has entered into IR, but about which the field has been largely silent, are the singular territorial state and a geopolitical space in which the relations between such states play themselves out. I have countered this account by pointing to a much richer spatial vocabulary – of networks/flows and place making – that can help us understand more adequately the paths of contemporary world politics. By historicising the ways in which the spatiality of world politics can be explained I have looked at how we might provide an alternative to the currently dominant structural approach. I then provided three examples of thinking with space: the historicity of geopolitical space, sovereignty regimes and the geopolitics of knowledge about world politics.

Some years ago, Rob Walker (1987: 21), one of the first writers to actively pursue using space as the basis of a perspective for rethinking IR, wrote that 'Legal sovereignty may still justify Cartesian cartography [of territorial blocs of space], but mapping the important patterns of power in the modern world requires a very different account of political spaces, an account of networks and flows, of shifting boundaries and interpretations rather than the continuing reification of Euclidean geometry'. Much theoretical remapping in this vein remains to be done.

Note

1 'Westphalian' refers to the presumed foundation of the modern state system in the Treaties of Westphalia of 1648 that brought an end to the European religious wars by partitioning space into territories whose rulers represented the contending religious confessions.

Further reading

Agnew, J., Mitchell, K. and Toal, G. (eds) (2015) *Wiley-Blackwell Companion to Political Geography*, 2nd Edition, Oxford: Wiley-Blackwell.
Albert, M., Jacobson, D. and Lapid, Y. (eds) (2001) *Identities, Orders, Borders: Rethinking International Relations Theory*, Minneapolis: University of Minnesota Press.
Crampton, J. and Elden, S. (eds) (2007) *Space, Knowledge and Power: Foucault and Geography*, Farnham: Ashgate.
Dodds, K., Kuus, M. and Sharp, J. (eds) (2013) *Ashgate Research Companion to Critical Geopolitics*, Farnham: Ashgate.
Elden, S. (2009) *Terror and Territory*, Minneapolis: University of Minnesota Press.
Lévy, J. (2011) 'Territory', in J. Agnew and J. Duncan (eds), *Wiley-Blackwell Companion to Human Geography*, Oxford: Wiley-Blackwell.

Bibliography

Agnew, J. (1987) *Place and Politics: The Geographical Mediation of State and Society*, London: Allen and Unwin.
Agnew, J. (2003) *Geopolitics: Re-visioning World Politics*, 2nd edition, London: Routledge.
Agnew, J. (2005) *Hegemony: The New Shape of Global Power*, Philadelphia, PA: Temple UniversityPress.
Agnew, J. (2007) 'Know-Where: Geographies of Knowledge of World Politics', *International Political Sociology* 1(1): 138–148.
Agnew, J. (2009) *Globalization and Sovereignty*, Lanham, MD: Rowman and Littlefield.
Agnew, J. and Corbridge, S. (1995) *Mastering Space: Hegemony, Territory and International Political Economy*, London: Routledge.
Anderson, L. (2003) *Pursuing Truth, Exercising Power: Social Science and Public Policy in the Twenty First Century*, New York: Columbia University Press.

Ashley, R.K. (1983) 'Three Modes of Economism', *International Studies Quarterly* 27(3): 463–496.

Brenner, N. and Elden, S. (2009) 'Henri Lefebvre on State, Space, Territory', *International Political Sociology* 3(2): 353–377.

Buzan, B. and Little, R. (2001) 'Why International Relations has Failed as an Intellectual Project and What to Do About It', *Millennium: Journal of International Studies* 30(1): 19–39.

Carver, T. (1997) 'Time, Space and Speed: New Dimensions in Political Analysis', *New Political Science* 19(1): 33–44.

Connolly, W.E. (1994) 'Tocqueville, Territory and Violence', *Theory Culture Society* 11(1): 19–40.

Deleuze, G. and Guattari, F. (1972) *L'anti-Oedipe*, Paris: Minuit.

Foucault, M. (2007) 'Questions on Geography', in S. Elden and J. Crampton (eds), *Space, Knowledge and Power: Foucault and Geography*, Farnham: Ashgate, pp. 173–184.

Galli, C. (2010) *Political Spaces and Global War*, Minneapolis: University of Minnesota Press.

Klinke, I. (2013) 'Chronopolitics: a Conceptual Matrix', *Progress in Human Geography* 37(3): 673–690.

Krasner, S.D. (1999) *Sovereignty: Organized Hypocrisy*, Princeton, NJ: Princeton University Press.

Leitner, H. et al. (2008) 'The Spatialities of Contentious Politics', *Transactions of the Institute of British Geographers* 33(1): 157–172.

Mann, M. (1984) 'The Autonomous Power of the State: its Origins, Powers and Results', *European Journal of Sociology* 25(1): 185–213.

Massey, D. (1999) 'Spaces of Politics', in D. Masse, P. Sarre and J. Allen (eds), *Human Geography Today*, Cambridge: Polity Press, pp. 279–294.

Ruggie, J.G. (1993) 'Territoriality and Beyond: Problematizing Modernity in International Relations', *International Organization* 47(1): 139–174.

Shah, N. (2012) 'The Territorial Trap of the Territorial Trap: Global Transformation and the Problem of the State's Two Territories', *International Political Sociology* 6(1): 1–20.

Starr, H. (2005) 'Territory, Proximity, and Spatiality: The Geography of International Conflict', *International Studies Review* 7(3): 387–406.

Walker, R.B.J. (1987) 'The Concept of Security and International Relations Theory', *Working Paper No. 3*. IGCC, La Jolla CA: University of California, San Diego Institute on Global Conflict and Cooperation.

Walker, R.B.J. (1993) *Inside/Outside: International Relations as Political Theory*, Cambridge: Cambridge University Press.

15

SUBJECTIVITY

Shiera S. el-Malik

A scholar's story

More than a decade ago, political theorist Norma Claire Moruzzi explained how she struggled to understand the representation of women in the Iranian film *Two Women* (Moruzzi 2001). Made by one of the few Iranian women filmmakers who is a self-identified feminist, the film depicts a woman whose stalker by the film's end kills her dominating jealous husband. For Moruzzi, this film reproduced Orientalist stereotypes of Iranian women's subjugation. In her notes from the field, she expressed surprise that a large number of professional, articulate, urban women in Iran – women for whom Moruzzi expected the female lead's lack of agency would have been a problem – expressed an emotional attachment to the film. In responding to the fact that the film was heralded in Iran and internationally as a feminist achievement she asked, '[w]hat kind of feminist message was being conveyed by a film that depicted a woman who could be saved from her own passive victimisation only by the unexpected (violent) actions of a (crazily) devoted man?' (ibid.: 93). But rather than place the perceived disconnect between her response to the film and the response of women in Iran down to their false consciousness, Moruzzi kept trying to understand what was going on. She found her answer in subjectivities that were constituted in the events of a particular historical moment, the Iranian Revolution of 1979.

Women in Iran have become active participants in what can be understood as the public sphere. Their literacy levels, education levels and general rates of public participation mirror men's (ibid.: 93–94). Thus, the traditional explanations of Muslim women's subjugation or feminist emancipation did not fit the situation Moruzzi was trying to understand. She kept asking questions while she was in Iran. After extensive listening to how people discussed the film, she realised that the film spoke to a set of experiences related to the Revolution, the war with Iraq and the development of the Islamic Republic that she could not have understood without having been there or without her continued inquiries. She learned that the film as seen by women in Iran was not an ahistorical drama of gender oppression as it had been read/viewed/experienced by her and other viewers outside the Iranian national context. Instead, it was understood as an 'accurate emotional representation of their own experience under the specific historical, cultural, and political conditions of the early years of the Islamic Republic' (ibid.: 95). The answer, then, turned out to be a uniquely Iranian perception of the political changes that had taken place in that country, during the decades prior to Moruzzi's 2001 query. Without reference to the context that created specific (and contested) Iranian women's subject positions, and from her own specifically constituted subject position, Moruzzi had struggled to understand the representation of women in the film. By continuing to ask questions that helped her to attend to the complexly located subjectivities of the film's Iranian protagonists and viewers, Moruzzi was able to move beyond the initial limits of her own subjective interpretation. In writing about that process, she made clear that the recognition of constituted subjectivities – and the engagement with the details of their constitution – was crucial to the doing of the research itself.

This story represents an example of a scholar trying to make sense of the world and recognising that her own contextual embeddedness inhibited her in that task. In this case, the researcher's own subjectivity rendered an explanation, but one that yielded a misunderstanding. Moruzzi recognised the limitation and used her understanding of subjectivity to critically imagine how this misunderstanding occurred and to try to explain it. Underlying Moruzzi's struggle are ethico-political commitments that made her likely to observe the subject as both *contextually embedded* and *historically contingent*, and simultaneously *remain cognisant of her own subjectivity*. Moruzzi's story exposes the critical potential of the concept of subjectivity. Her recognition of how widely subjectivities can vary led her to continue to ask questions rather than to retreat to easy explanation. The important point is that she refused to apply to her observations, her own, arguably internationally dominant, form of sense-making.

Subjectivity represents a situatedness in power dynamics that yields variable forms, the contours of which are formed by sometimes very localised contextual relations, dynamics and ideologies. Subjectivities, then, are layered over time by experiences, practices and other historical contingencies. As a result, the concept of subjectivity can facilitate analyses of world politics and in particular a retheorising of the notion of 'the political' (Edkins et al. 1999) that is both *unfixed* and *relational*. This makes the notion of subjectivity useful for analysing how people and communities are embedded in specific contexts and how they perform in those contexts (Biehl et al. 2007). Subjectivity is also useful, as Moruzzi illustrates, in thinking about how people's interactions with the world can produce that world through daily instances of micro-power dynamics (de Certeau 1984). The small, interpersonal, and seemingly inconsequential dynamics between Moruzzi and her Iranian interlocutors emerged as quite consequential after all for answering the question Moruzzi was seeking to answer. In the Iranian context, viewers of the film did not 'make sense' of the film as anti-feminist. Instead, the film was read as an allegorical acknowledgement of women's personal and political experiences as women in (post)revolutionary Iran.

The concept of subjectivity has great radical potential, particularly when the power dynamics that constitute the subject are centred in research questions such as that Moruzzi depicts. From this angle, subjectivity points to the broader power dynamics that are the conditions of its specific possibilities. As Persram writes, 'For power to act there has to be a subject, but that does not make the subject into the origin of power' (Persram 1999: 171). The embodied subject, in this case the Iranian woman of a certain age, can act as a site or nodal point in which dynamics of power can be made visible (see Abrahamsen in this book). This approach both highlights the limitations of a state-centric approach to the study of world politics and answers Himadeep Muppidi's provocation for such studies to recognise bodies – their stench, their pain, their utterances – as evidence of ripples of power in the world, as global power dynamics (Muppidi 2012: 3–7). In other words, people matter to explanations of world politics and subjectivity helps to unpack *how* people matter.

This chapter utilises a theory of constituted subjectivities as a lens to analyse macrological and micrological features of power through the discussion of several parallel discursive examples of controversies over Muslim women's (lack of) agency. Leila Ahmed's classic analysis of the historical debate on veiling in colonial Egypt is linked to two more contemporary eruptions of similar arguments on Islamic veiling: the academic 'Galeotti/Moruzzi' conversation that took place in the journal *Political Theory* (1993–1994), and Femen's social media arguments over Topless Jihad. I suggest that the critical potential of subjectivity in (re)thinking IR is that it can account for how *macrological power* – systemic forces, authority and governance – and *micrological power* – everyday negotiations and navigations – simultaneously represent the subject and are represented by subjects. Veiling or not veiling is an especially apposite practice for examining subjectivity because the discussions of the practice reveal the 'colonial signs of international relations' (Muppidi 2012). Discourses and other relational configurations are important, but the degree to which we can ever 'study' them is beholden to the centring of people's everyday practices.

For the purpose of this analysis, I consider the veil a social signifier – which like the brassiere is an item of clothing generally worn by females – that is neither necessarily oppressive nor necessarily a political statement (although available for politicisation in certain contexts). For the sake of simplicity, I use the term 'veil' to cover the gamut of coverings that Muslim women use. Considered together, these examples of arguments over veiling demonstrate how subjectivity can illuminate the functions of power, not only in controversies over gender and Islam, but within the relations between subjects and objects – which are themselves subjects – within the research and analytic process.

Unveiling a discourse on women

An early debate on veiling

Leila Ahmed's historiographical account of the first major debate on women and
veiling in Egypt is illustrative of how an essentially new discourse on women
emerges, 'in which issues of culture and class, and imperialism and nationalism,
became vitally entangled with the issue of women' (Ahmed 1992: 6).[1] Her depic-
tion of this new discourse on women is particularly important for its framing of
every political discussion of the veil since the nineteenth century, including the
two examples that follow.

The Egyptian ruler Mohammed Ali's (r. 1805–1848) desire for modernisation
resulted in substantial policy changes during his tenure (ibid.: 130–135). While
these changes impacted citizens unequally, they were framed as prerequisites for the
development of a strong nation, which was then perceived as the European model
and based on developing industrial technologies and production. One important
policy change related to education. In the early nineteenth century, demands for girls'
education were frequently justified with the argument that 'modern' countries edu-
cate females.[2] Despite this, female education remained fairly exceptional and the
government was less successful with extending it to public primary and secondary
schools. However, many private girls' schools opened during the mid-nineteenth
century: European missionary schools, but also Coptic, Greek and Jewish schools.
Upper- and middle-class Muslim girls were frequently home schooled (ibid.: 135).
By the 1870s, the government opened girls' public primary and secondary schools.

The arrival of the British (in 1882) had a distinctly negative impact on girls'
education as the British either closed girls' schools or raised fees to such an extent
that a family had to choose which child would be educated. Yet, the British
Consul Lord Cromer and the imperial establishment used ideas of gender relations
and roles to legitimise and justify the colonisation of Egypt in the late nineteenth
century. Ahmed summarises Cromer as follows:

> Whereas Christianity teaches respect for women, and European men 'elevated'
> women because of the teachings of their religion, Islam degraded them,
> Cromer wrote, and it was to this degradation, most evident in the practices of
> veiling and segregation, that the inferiority of Muslim men could be traced.
> Nor could it be doubted that the practices of veiling and seclusion exercised 'a
> baneful effect on Eastern society. The arguments in the case are, indeed, so
> commonplace that it is unnecessary to dwell on them'.
>
> (Cromer in Ahmed 1992: 153)

It was essential that Egyptians 'be persuaded or forced into imbibing the true spirit
of western civilisation' (ibid.), Cromer stated, and to achieve this it was essential to
change the position of women in Islam, for it was Islam's degradation of women,
expressed in the practices of veiling and seclusion, that was 'the fatal obstacle' to

the Egyptian's 'attainment of that elevation of thought and character which should accompany the introduction of Western civilisation' (ibid.); only by abandoning those practices might they attain 'the mental and moral development which he [Cromer] desired for them' (Guerville in Ahmed 1992: 153; Ahmed 1992: 152–153).

Whether or not one really *believes* this is Cromer's motivation, colonisation on the pretext of female emancipation is discursively powerful. The idea that one conception of the social subject, distinct from the Victorian Christian moral subject, served to hinder the development of 'civilised' people, places a great burden on the colonisers to work for the salvation of others. Colonisation was essentially an economic mission, but the Orientalist notion of a civilising mission neutralised the ethical problems of restructuring whole economies (so that they became based on the needs of Europe). Colonialism became the white man's burden. This is part of the discursive context within which particular subjectivities are produced (Mitchell 1991).

Ironically, Cromer co-opted the language of imperial feminism in order to legitimise the process of colonisation, while concomitantly implementing policies curtailing women's educational opportunities in Egypt. He raised school fees, which limited general enrolment, and restricted the women's medical school to midwifery, for example (Ahmed 1992: 153). Ahmed notes this irony when she writes, as imperial Britain 'contest[ed] the claims of feminism, and derided and rejected the ideas of feminism and the notion of men's oppressing women with respect to itself, it captured the language of feminism and redirected it, in the service of colonialism' (ibid.: 151). Thus, using feminist rhetoric, Cromer argued that women were oppressed by men in Egypt. He claimed imperial Britain's burden was in part to spread enlightened ideals and emancipate the women. These conflicting articulations of gendered modernity impacted Egyptian nationalism and yielded a bifurcated response represented by two Egyptian men.

Qassim Amin and Muhammed 'Abdu represent the Western-oriented response and the Islamist-oriented response to British colonialism respectively. These positions directly influenced the two strands of Egyptian feminism. Qassim Amin published his book, *Tahrir al Mar'a (The Liberation of Women)* in 1899. He argued for women's primary education and for reforming laws on polygamy and divorce, ideas that were neither new nor extremely controversial. Amin further argued for cultural and social transformation, proposing the abolition of the veil as a way to accomplish such a goal. His discursive foundations are no different than Cromer's. In his reviews regarding veiling, however, Amin courted controversy. He writes:

> [W]hen [the colonisers] encounter savages they eliminate them or drive them from the land, as happened in America … and is happening now in Africa … When they encounter a nation like ours, with a degree of civilisation, with a past, and a religion … and customs and … institutions … they deal with its inhabitants kindly. But they do soon acquire its most valuable resources, because they have greater wealth and intellect and knowledge and force.
>
> *(quoted in Ahmed 1992: 155–156)*

Amin implies that countries can be categorised on a scale from savage to civilised with the argument that unless Egypt attempts to achieve a greater degree of civilisation, the colonisers will take all its resources. For Amin, as for Cromer, this civilising scale is directly correlated with versions of womanhood and femininity. Amin suggests that men are nothing but what their mothers make them and women require liberation so that they can raise capable men. Since he reserved contempt for all save the British, Amin's book was controversial. Yet, according to Ahmed, Amin reserved his greatest contempt for Egyptian women:

> Most Egyptian women are not in the habit of combing their hair everyday … nor do they bathe more than once a week. They do not know how to use a toothbrush and do not attend to what is attractive in clothing, though their attractiveness and cleanliness strongly influence men's inclinations. They do not know how to rouse desire in their husband, nor how to retain his desire or to increase it … This is because the poor ignorant woman does not understand inner feelings and the promptings of attraction and aversion … If she tries to rouse a man, she will usually have the opposite effect.
>
> *(Amin quoted in Ahmed 1992: 157)*

This diatribe on women is noteworthy in that Amin draws from modern ideas of national progress, the discourse of evolution and conceptions of femininity, and locates them in an embodied subject position. Elsewhere, he also draws from modern conceptions of masculinity when he discusses Egyptian laziness and the value of a man who works hard and reads to inform himself (Ahmed 1992: 155–165). Yet, because of his emphasis on unveiling and primary education for women, Amin is positioned as a feminist and a father of Egyptian feminism, or, rather, the Westernised strand of Egyptian feminism.

Concomitantly, Muhammed 'Abdu influenced what would become the Islamist strand of Egyptian feminism. While Amin argued for modernising Islam, 'Abdu argued that the problem was not Islam; it was cultural (ibid.: 138–143). The essence of 'Abdu's argument was that existing regulation of women's behaviour resulted not from the Qur'an, but from corruptions and misinterpretations of the Qur'an. He argued for a rejection of the backwardness that prevailed when women could not choose whom to marry, did not have access to education, were not allowed to hold a job and could be one of a number of wives. This backwardness, he argued, has no basis in Islam, but was based instead in the patriarchal cultural traditions of Egypt. 'Abdu suggests that the best move for Egypt, as an Islamic nation, is based on a progressive interpretation of the essentials of Islam. He was a student of the influential Islamic scholar, al-Sayyid Jamal Al-Din al-Afghani. Al-Afghani stressed the necessity of 'reforming Islam from within and adapting it to the modern world as a way of protecting Muslim societies against western aggression and exploitation' (ibid.: 138). Similarly, 'Abdu 'deplored … the facile, unthinking imitation of Western ways … instead of the pursuit of a genuine transfer of knowledge and real social reform' (ibid.: 140). He argued for the continued veiling of women under the aegis that Westernisation was dangerously eroding cultural norms and values. As we shall see, the debate resulted in politically formalising the connection between the veil and culture in a way that does not occur when women politicised bra-wearing, for example, perhaps because of the way that the veil has been exoticised.

These two sets of arguments are discursively powerful. They represent a form of macrological power that partially contours the context within which women choose to veil or to not veil. Subjectivity places this context at the centre of the analysis. And, attendance to the notion of subjectivity makes it easier to see the spaces within which people conduct themselves. The next section will show how subjectivity and its insistence on context helps to prevent foreclosures of imaginative possibilities that potentially yield misreadings of people's action.

The Headscarf Affair (1989)

In a French example, known as 'the Headscarf Affair', three North African-descended young women decided to cover their heads, which meant that they would be wearing veils at all times outside their homes, including at school. A scholarly analysis of this event can be found in a four-part conversation between Anna Elisabetta Galeotti and Norma Claire Moruzzi in the journal *Political Theory*. Galeotti used the Headscarf Affair as an entry point into a discussion of the need for toleration to be considered a political virtue (Galeotti 1993: 588). To the extent that Galeotti 'reads' the teenagers' action, she did so from a liberal multiculturalist standpoint that evidences an essentialised notion of identity. She suggested that the teenagers declared 'I want to be what I am and I am proud of it' (ibid.: 596). Galeotti further represented this position when she stated that 'when Muslim girls became students, the equal treatment they received *as students* was unequal to them *as Islamic* students' (ibid.: 599; emphasis in original). Here, Islamic was understood as (an essentialist) religious identity rather than a complex and contested, relational component of the context within which the students were constituted.

In utilising the trope of the veil as a manifestation of religious identity, Galeotti homogenised the meaning of the veil in separate events. For example, she refers to the hijab the young women chose to wear in France as a 'chador', which is a specifically Iranian form of covering that women were required to wear after the Revolution. From an analytic perspective, her approach to veiling as a singular practice equates it in as disparate contexts as late 1980s France and late 1970s Iran. However, these practices of veiling are not necessarily equivalent. In the first instance, young women made a decision in a specific context to present themselves with covered heads, the meaning of which would require unpacking within the French context. In the second instance, a government made legal requirements of some of its citizens thereby limiting their own decision-making capacity in a very different context. Placing meaning *in the veil* (in the fabric and in the practice of wearing it) flattens context to meaningless background, thereby impairing conceptual capacities for evaluating agency as decision-making (and political stand-making) with resultant political implications. It makes it hard to examine veiling as a varied and grounded practice undertaken by actual people.

Galeotti argues in favour of the students being allowed to cover their heads in school. While in agreement with Galeotti's conclusion, Moruzzi argued that 'the significance of *l'affaire du foulard* [the Headscarf Affair] was precisely that it exposed the limitations of a metadiscourse based on political rights, and the structural predispositions of liberal ideology that led, as often as not, to a position opposed to toleration' (Moruzzi 1994a: 654). Moruzzi charged Galeotti with inserting a dangerous ideological platform into her liberal multiculturalist analysis, which is evidenced by the latter's ahistorical take on veiling as a cultural practice of identity. For Moruzzi, the Headscarf Affair was unique insofar as 'it provided a remarkably apt constellation of complications through which to trace, if not unravel, some of the more urgent tangles of contemporary political identity' (ibid.: 656). Moruzzi (ibid.) goes on to develop a rich analysis of 'The Affair', the anxieties it raised in the French Left and Right, and the irresolvable tensions it revealed in a particular historical moment. All the while, Galeotti (1993) avoided contextualising the teenagers' decision and so presupposed that the teenagers were communicating an ahistorical identity, rather than any number of communiqués female teenagers might have expressed in a Parisian industrial suburb in 1989. Moreover, in privileging a dominant discourse regarding veiling – that of cultural identity – Galeotti participated in drawing the academic debate, and scholarly explanations of the social, away from other potential explanations of the practice. Moruzzi offers an explanation of how this happens:

> Without a fixed ideological compass, we stumble through political terrain made unfamiliar, relying on theoretical interpretations that may obscure more than they enlighten. Unfortunately, the response to this aporia is often a retreat to a revised form of the old East/West binary opposition in which the Eastern threat is no longer communist but Islamic, and Western values are still democratic but are also emphatically, ostensibly secular.
>
> *(Moruzzi 1994a: 666)*

In other words, a tension exists between people's action on (perhaps unfamiliar to the researcher) political terrain and the available theoretical interpretations of that action. Responses to this tension are not extra-ideological, as Moruzzi displays in her own experience of managing such a tension. Hence, it is precisely the evidence of Galeotti's liberal multiculturalist position that Moruzzi targets. For her part, Galeotti (1994) misunderstands Moruzzi's concerns in her rebuttal and continues to argue for a pluralistic view of toleration, to which Moruzzi suggests a 'fear of a homogeneous Islamic threat is what created the affair of the headscarves as a national issue' (Moruzzi 1994b: 679). A reading of this case through a lens provided by the notion of subjectivity would have kept the students, their utterances, families, local context, etc., front and centre in explanations or analyses of it. 'But [Moruzzi notes, and despite her own efforts to keep them in focus], the different attitudes, backgrounds and nationalities [the subjectivities] of the students and their families, differences which shaped the local incident, disappeared in the national debate' (ibid.).

The topless jihad

In March 2013, nineteen-year-old Tunisian, Amina Tyler, posted online topless photos of herself on Facebook and added to a public debate about Muslim women's veiling (Greenhouse 2013). In one picture, she had written on her torso, 'My body is my own and not the source of anyone's honor'. In another picture, she'd written 'Fuck your morals' across her chest. As a challenge to dominant forms of sexual differentiation that she viewed as regulating women's bodies with notions of honour and morality, Tyler intended to start up a chapter of Femen (a Ukrainian-based international women's movement that uses breast baring as a tactic of resistance) in Tunisia. In what seems like a serious overreaction, she was quickly disowned by her family and institutionalised. She was physical, assaulted and received death threats. Exacerbating the event, an Islamist cleric was reported to have said, that 'Amina's action could cause "epidemics and disasters" and "could be contagious and give ideas to other women"' (Tayler 2013b). And, Femen launched a 'Topless Jihad' in support of Tyler. In response, a Muslim Woman Facebook page has as its cover photo a woman carrying a poster that says 'Nudity DOES NOT liberate me and I DO NOT need saving #muslimpride #Femen' (www.facebook.com/MuslimWomenAgainstFemen).

Placing social meaning in the veil, Femen leader Inna Shevchenko said in conversation with blogger Laila Alawa, 'How can you wear your scarf with so much proudness … like it's the hat of Che Guevara? It symbolises blood and all the crimes that are based on your religion, even if you don't support them … If you're a feminist, if you're for liberation, then be brave [enough] to say that we are against that and take off your scarf until the moment that your scarf will not be a symbol of crime' (Tayler 2013a). Further, she posited that 'the idea of a Muslim feminist is oxymoronic' (ibid.). Journalist Jeffrey Tayler argued that 'Femen has courageously broken rules and enlivened the debate over religion's role in our world' (Tayler 2013b). Others argue that by equating the veil with oppression, Femen's platform universalised and decontextualised *the practice of veiling* in the process of 'imposing their brand of feminism' (Daher and Daher 2013).[3] Arguably, while assertive responses to the violent reactions to Amina Tyler are politically and ethically appropriate, simultaneously reading the veil as essentially oppressive disembeds practices of veiling (as well as practices of baring one's head) from their specific contexts.

An approach that centres subjectivity alternatively insists on specific contexts and on listening to utterances as we saw in earlier sections. Such an approach might start with questions that not only interrogate the Tunisian context in which Tyler posted her photos, but the local context from which Femen and Shevchenko's interpretive positions emerged. Such questions might include: Who is Femen? What are the conditions that make Femen possible? What is the context that gives form to the particular stance on breast-baring, a practice that could vary widely in comparative significance and consequence? Reportage of the 'Topless Jihad' includes some clues that help make sense of the organisation. Preliminary analyses might point to the following: Femen's emergence out of resistance to local sex-trafficking sheds different light on the tactic of breast-baring (Salem 2012); and its emergence in post-Soviet Ukraine, a place where liberal multiculturalism has few roots, seems to explain its disregard for political correctness (Tayler 2013a). Shev-chenko's attitudes to 'religious symbols' like the cross and the veil reveal new contours when one learns that she is facing charges of 'offending religious senti-ment' for destroying a cross and fleeing to France (ibid.). An interesting question might ask how Shevchenko understands Eastern Orthodox religious symbols like the cross and what are the mechanisms by which she reads an 'Islamic' practice of veiling as a symbol through those grounded forms of sense-making.

Shevchenko's attitude toward veiling reflects a direct lineage to the terms of the ideologically driven debate that were established in late nineteenth-century Egypt on the foundations of conversations that came before it. Contemporary theorists still have to negotiate this legacy and its politics in their analyses of everyday deci-sions such as that of veiling or not veiling. The acts of listening and questioning are active and participatory processes that incorporate the subjective positions of the listener. Subjective positions, whether of interpretation or as interpreter, are con-stituted within a particular context, the masking of which is an act of discursive power. Here, the notion of subjectivity facilitates relational analyses that work against discursive closures and de-centre the totalised subject (a fixed subject rather than relational subjective positions). These include the relations of power that led to a young Amina Tyler to present her body in the way that she did, the practices that led to her maltreatment and that give form to the practices that situated Femen as a widely recognised respondent and spokesperson for this case. Shevchenko's sweeping comments about veiling and Galeotti's (mis)conception of the individual (in reference to the French teenagers) as 'extra-ideological', makes it hard to sense how people constitute their own actions, and reveals more about the speakers themselves than the supposed subjects of their analysis.

Subjectivity and epistemic violence

An episteme is a recurring discourse 'characteristic of the way of thinking or the state of knowledge at any one time, appearing across a range of texts, and as forms of conduct, at a number of different institutional sites within society' (Hall 2001: 73). In other words, an episteme is a system of understanding that gives form to the contours of knowledge. Silences, marginality and discursive closures at this systemic level are forms of epistemic violence. Foucault (1988) presents this idea of epis-temic violence using as an example the redefinition of sanity in eighteenth-century Europe. Acknowledging him and his focus on Europe, Spivak later asks 'what if that particular redefinition was only part of a vast two-handed engine?' (Spivak 1988: 17). What if it was a two-handed engine that reconfigured the knowledge landscape of Europe *and* the colonies by creating a new form of social order? Given Aimé Césaire's dismissal of the geographic or cultural divide between the colonisers and the colonised, Spivak's question is on point. Césaire argued that epistemic violence in Europe and its working in the colonies were part and parcel of the same social disease (Césaire 2000). Edward Said developed a similar position in *Orientalism*, which he argued was a discourse of power in a Foucauldian sense. I have argued elsewhere that less attention is paid to his analysis of knowledge practices, which get embodied in ways that can be understood as subjectivity (el-Malik 2015: 508–510). I have shown that far from being an historical text about colonialism, *Orientalism* (1978) is addressed to a contemporary audience in the context of growing American hegemony and expanding networks of capital, media and globally intelligible norms. Thus, the relationship between Orientalism and everyday decision-making is one that connects discourse and representation and hegemonic knowledge practices through social norms, media and other processes of socialisation.

Said made two arguments in *Orientalism* that are particularly helpful for thinking about subjectivity. He argued that Orientalism is a discourse of power that mediates all representations of 'the Orient' regardless of where these representations emanate. Orientalism results in a set of lenses through which every discussion of, or interaction with, the Orient is negotiated. Arguments 'for' the Orient, 'against' the Orient and 'critical' approaches to examinations of the onto-epistemological space of the Middle East and North Africa must all negotiate Orientalism. Certainly, no analysis of the veil (as worn by Muslim women) can avoid Orientalist and counter-Orientalist readings of veiling. Arguably, the discourse of Orientalism mediates the discourse of identity itself. Contemplate, for example, the staying power of Orientalist tropes that a global consumer public easily recognises, from Mickey Rooney's Chinese character in *Breakfast at Tiffany's* (2006), the genie in *I Dream of Jeannie* (1965–1970), to the Arab Terrorist in any number of films and television shows as noted in *Reel Bad Arabs* (2006), or the character of the Arab woman consumer in *Sex and the City 2* (2010) in which the 'girls' go to Abu Dhabi. However, Said also argued that Orientalism is epistemic in that it carries certain properties that scholars have come to associate with hegemonic knowledge practices (for example, binary thinking, flattening context across time and space, and extracting the observer from observable phenomenon) (Said 1978: 116–119 and 149–156). Subjectivities are constituted within and in conjunction with these epistemic practices, as Moruzzi illustrates when she studies her own initial reading of the Iranian film *Two Women*. She shows her readers both how easily such readings can occur and how to interrupt them through practices of querying and listening.

The constitution of subjectivity

To examine the question of how everyday decision-making gets embodied, enacted and re-enacted, one might point to the idea of practice (e.g. dressing, walking, etc.) as subjectivities performed, experienced and resisted (de Certeau

1984). Often, questions of exploitation and dominance are discussed as macro-level questions. Yet, these workings of power are also micro-level in that people engage in action. Starkly juxtaposed answers might say the structure dictates agency or that agency rests in agents, or that the agent acts within a structure. These attempts centre a totalised or determined subject (again, a fixed rather than relational subjectivities). An alternate approach might start from the relationship; it might suggest that relationships reflect historically contingent and contextually embedded subjectivities. From this angle, the agent/structure divide is itself ideologically constituted, and thereby serves specific dynamics of power. In other words, the agency–structure divide comes to appear as just one outcome of sense-making. One might either focus on that specific way of making sense of the world, or on the processes by which sense-making takes place. I am suggesting the latter. By situating subjectivities in a specific context, the notion of subjectivity makes the constitution of structure and agency visible in that context.

Such a critical approach accounts for how macrological power and micrological power simultaneously represent the subject and considers how these power relations re-represent the subject in response to other representations such that the movement between representation and re-representation appears negligible (as in a tug of war between fairly equal sides) (Spivak 1988: 279). This approach would avoid centring a totalised subject and yet still attend to the macrological aspects of power (ibid.: 264). In other words, processes of identity-making involve acts of conferring and claiming positions. When these acts are obscured, the constitutive moment is similarly obscured and 'identity' appears complete. One might think about it like this: in contemporary parlance, identity is a commonsense term. Everyone has one. It might be used to make social or political claims. Or it might designate a community. But subjectivity might be used to examine 'identity' itself as a product of contemporary political debates.

Returning to the discussion in the introduction, Moruzzi's experience illustrates how, in presupposing a subject and variability of subjectivity, in privileging a complete a priori identity, it would be possible to flatten the specificity of experience. Articulations of the sovereign subject, already presuppose *a* subject, thus questions of ideology and representation are necessary in order to destabilise that subject, and to disengage from the apparently fixed positions. This is necessary because the 'subject' here is,

> [C]uriously sewn together into a transparency by denegations, belongs to the exploiters' side of the international labour. It is impossible for French intellectuals to imagine the kind of Power and Desire that would inhabit the unnamed subject of the Other of Europe. It is not only that everything they read, critical or uncritical, is caught within the debate of the production of that Other, supporting or critiquing the constitution of the Subject as Europe. It is also that, in the constitution of that Other of Europe, great care was taken to obliterate the textual ingredients with which such a subject could cathect,

could occupy (invest?) its itinerary – not only by ideological and scientific production, but also by the institution of the law.

(Spivak 1988: 263–264)

The result of epistemic violence, then, is that the 'other' is rendered unknown, erased or delimited to only a very specific existence; the Other only exists as part of the colonised/coloniser relationship. In keeping with the focus on veiling, analyses of the veiled Muslim woman appear divested of the politics that are the very condition of possibility of her existence and her subjectivity.

Conclusion

This chapter explores a theory of subjectivity by theorising actual examples rather than presenting an overview of theorists. I suggest that the critical potential of subjectivity in (re)thinking IR is that it can account for how macrological power – systemic forces, authority and governance – and micrological power – everyday negotiations and navigations – simultaneously represent people as subjects and are represented by the people and their practices. This chapter presents this claim with a reading of three discussions of veiling: nineteenth-century colonial Egypt, the 1989 'Headscarf Affair', and the 2013 Femen breast baring campaign. Together, these three examples expose the practice of veiling as ideologically laden, and heavy with a powerful historical weight. The act of veiling can be considered a sign of gendered practice that is a consequence of a specific historical context. Further, people's decisions to cover their heads as Muslims or as a feminine practice in certain contexts can be shown to produce various and potentially contradictory meanings. This chapter brings to the fore the combination of these understandings of veiling in order to consider the creative potential of the concept of subjectivity.

A critical approach to IR might use 'subjectivity' to account for the ways in which subjectivities are constituted within a complex nexus of conditions of possibility that include questions of race, gender and class, but also, nationality, citizenship, religion, disposition, and so on, in specific moments in time and space. Yet, a critical approach to subjectivity *in* IR would also begin from the position that subjectivity is constituted in very messy ways that impact how people act in ways that are not necessarily predictable and *not only linked to visible categorical framings* of 'race', 'gender', 'nationality', and 'citizenship', etc. Attending to subjectivity in this way makes contestation explicable and reorients the researcher towards substantive and historicised contexts within which subjectivities are constituted. In other words, the notion of subjectivity centres specific practices, including the practice of devising and asking questions, that presents a challenge to the epistemic violence of knowledge practices. Future work might consider approaching events like those discussed here in ways that develop a complex account for how these positions and arguments come to be articulated in the ways that they do.

Acknowledgements

I acknowledge the editors of this volume and the reviewer of my chapter for their thoughtful, engaged, patient (and very organised) assistance in bringing this to publication. Special thanks also go to Andrew McFarland, Jacob Stump, Robbie Shilliam and Maura Conway for their helpful comments on earlier versions of this chapter.

Notes

1 This discussion did not occur outside the colonial experience, and hence the local response was caged within a particularly British Orientalist vision of Egyptian society.
2 One of the most successful results of this was the women's medical school in Cairo, which opened its doors in the early 1830s.
3 The branding point is interesting given that Shevchenko says 'Women's bodies are used for things like selling beer or fast cars all the time … but we are using our own bodies to promote our own idea about our own freedom. There is no boss who is selling our bodies to earn money' (Tiwari 2013). Her comment points to practices related to a specific context, one that commodifies and consumes women's bodies.

Further reading

Cullinan, Patrick (2005) *Imaginative Trespasser: Letters between Bessie Head, Patrick and Wendy Cullinan, 1963–1977*, Johannesburg: Wits University Press. These letters reflect the thoughtful response of people living through (in very different ways) the violence of South African Apartheid. I find it to be illustrative of the variability of subjectivities. In particular, Bessie Head's writing evinces a unique recognition of the relationship between the complexities of the historical moment and people's sense of self in that context.

Davies, C.B. (1994) *Black Women, Writing, and Identity: Migrations of the Subject*, London: Routledge. This volume presents a reading of subjectivity that centres on the position, role and utterances of the 'black female' subject in different locations. I find it useful for its focus on the people's engagement with their locale which is important for thinking about how subjectivities are embodied and variable in their embodiment.

Hassan, S. (2013) *Ibrahim El-Salahi: A Visionary Modernist*, London: Tate Publishing. This volume represents the Tate Modern's first exhibition dedicated to African Modernism. Some threads of my thinking about subjectivity clicked for me as I wandered through the paintings of a Sudanese artist, ex-politician, past detainee of the Sudanese government. This exhibition and this publication are reminders of the different forms that critical theoretical interventions can take.

Mansfield, N. (2000) *Subjectivity: Theories of the Self from Freud to Haraway*, St. Leonards, New South Wales: Allen and Unwin. This volume traces the idea of 'I' and its connection to broader sets of shared ideas. Mansfield curates and presents a wide range of approaches in a format accessible for beginners in critical social theory.

Martino, W. and Rezai-Rashti, G. (2008) 'The Politics of Veiling, Gender, and the Muslim Subject: On the Limits and Possibilities of Anti-racist Education in the Aftermath of September 11', *Discourse: Studies in the Cultural Politics of Education* 29(3): 417–431. This article connects with the analysis presented here in its focus on veiling and subjectivity. It is a creative analysis of how these practices/ideas intersect in post 9/11 discussions of the Muslim subject.

Mengestu, D. (2007) *The Beautiful Things that Heaven Bears*, New York: Riverhead Books. This is one of the most incredible presentations of the meeting of different subjectivities that I have ever read. The novel explores human agency and interactions within frames of immigration, gentrification, race and tenderness.

Said, E. (1983) *The World the Text and the Critic*, Cambridge, MA: Harvard University Press. This book offers much to students of social theory. I find it particularly helpful for contemplating how ideas 'travel' and transform in different contexts. This is also helpful for historicising forms of subjectivity, performances and how people make claims.

Strozier, R. (2002) *Foucault, Subjectivity, and Identity: Historical Constructions of Subject and Self*, Detroit, MI: Wayne State University Press. This book presents a helpful reading of the notion of subjectivity as related to the work of Michel Foucault. Foucault's careful historical analyses of discursive power offer a useful frame for thinking about how one might conceive of subjectivity as embedded within discursive power and yet also performed.

Bibliography

Ahmed, L. (1992) *Women and Gender in Islam: Historical Roots of a Modern Debate*, New Haven, CT: Yale University Press.

Biehl, J., Good, B. and Kleinman, A. (eds) (2007) *Subjectivity: Ethnographic Investigations*, Berkeley: University of California Press.

Césaire, A. (2000) *Discourse on Colonialism*, trans. Joan Pinkham, New York: Monthly Review.

Daher, P. and Daher, J. (2013) 'Femen: You're Doing it Wrong', *Alakhbar English*, 28 April, http://english.al-akhbar.com/content/femen-youre-doing-it-wrong, accessed 15 May 2013.

de Certeau, M. (1984) *The Practice of Everyday Life*, Berkeley, CA: University of California Press.

Earp, J. and Jhally, S. (2006) *Reel Bad Arabs: How Hollywood Vilifies a People*, Northampton, MA: Media Education Foundation.

Edkins, J., Pin-Fat, V. and Persram, N. (eds) (1999) *Sovereignty and Subjectivity*, Boulder, CO: Lynne Rienner.

Edwards, B. (2006) *Breakfast at Tiffany's*, Hollywood CA: Paramount Home Entertainment.

el-Malik, Shiera S. (2015) 'Why Orientalism Still Matters: Reading "Casual Forgetting" and "Active Remembering" as Neoliberal Forms of Contestation in International Politics', *Review of International Studies* 41(3): 503–525.

Foucault, M. (1988) *Madness and Civilization: A History of Insanity in the Age of Reason*, New York: Vintage.

Galeotti, A. (1993) 'Citizenship and Equality: a Place for Toleration', *Political Theory* 21(4): 585–605.

Galeotti, A. (1994) 'A Problem with Theory: A Rejoinder to Moruzzi', *Political Theory* 22(4): 573–677.

Greenhouse, E. (2013) 'How to Provoke National Unrest with a Facebook Picture', *The New Yorker*, 8 April, www.newyorker.com/online/blogs/elements/2013/04/amina-tyler-topless-photos-tunisia-activism.html, accessed 15 May 2013.

Hall, S. (2001) 'Foucault: Power, Knowledge, and Discourse', in M. Weatherall, S. Taylor and S. Yeats (eds), *Discourse Theory and Practice*, London: Sage, pp. 72–81.

Michael, P. (2010) *Sex and the City 2*, New Line Cinema and Home Box Office Films.

Mitchell, T. (1991) *Colonising Egypt*, Berkeley: University of California.

Moruzzi, N. (1994a) 'The Problem with Headscarves: Contemporary Complexities of Political and Social Identity', *Political Theory* 22(4): 653–672.

Moruzzi, N. (1994b) 'A Response to Galeotti', *Political Theory* 22(4): 678–679.

Moruzzi, N. (2001) 'Women in Iran: Notes on Film and From the Field', *Feminist Studies* 27(1): 89–100.

Mupiddi, H. (2012) *Colonial Signs of International Relations*, New York: Columbia University Press.

Persram, N. (1999) 'Coda: Sovereignty, Subjectivity, Strategy', in J. Edkins, V. Pin-Fat and N. Persram (eds), *Sovereignty and Subjectivity*, Boulder, CO: Lynne Rienner, pp. 163–175.

Said, E. (1978) *Orientalism*, London: Vintage.

Salem, S. (2012) 'Femen's Neocolonial Feminism: When Nudity becomes a Uniform', *Al-Akhbar English*, 26 December, http://english.al-akhbar.com/node/14494, accessed 15 May 2013.

Sheldon, S. (1965–1970) *I Dream of Jeannie*, Los Angeles, CA: Sunset Growers Studios.

Spivak, G. (1988) 'Can the Subaltern Speak?', in C. Nelson and L. Grossberg (eds), *Marxism and the Interpretation of Culture*, Chicago, IL: University of Illinois Press, pp. 271–313.

Tayler, J. (2013a) 'Topless Jihad: Why Femen is Right', *The Atlantic*, 1 May.

Tayler, J. (2013b) 'Tunisian Woman sent to a Psychiatric Hospital for Posting Topless Photos on Facebook', *The Atlantic*, 22 March.

Tiwari, N. (2013) 'Bare Breasts and Radical Cheek', *Tehelka.com*, 27 April.

16

TECHNOLOGY

Benjamin J. Muller

The question of technology and/in IR: introduction

The events of 11 September 2001 demonstrated the devastating impact of asymmetric attacks on a global hegemon. The perpetrators' crude weapons, modicum of good fortune and brute force led to a new chapter being added to the history of global politics, in which the vulnerability of the state was made more obvious than perhaps in any prior epoch since the birth of the Westphalian order. However, the events of that fateful day also demonstrated the centrality of media and mediated representations of violence and the intimate connections between the local and the global, particularly through information and communication technologies. In the subsequent decade we might still remain wary of such conventional threats; however, technologically savvy adolescent hackers with few resources in a garage thousands of kilometres away might possess a far greater threat to ever-changing notions of (in)security. Although admittedly an obvious example, this small vignette helps unpack how complex the question and concept of technology and/in IR has become.[1] Traditional notions of space, inside and outside, us and them, (dis)order, security, threat, and so on, are radically reimagined in contemporary global politics, and IR is increasingly challenged, disrupted, motivated and open to a variety of interdisciplinary influences under these conditions. This chapter begins to unpack this complex relationship by looking at the concept of 'technology', and will hopefully inspire further critical reflection and unpacking.

The chapter that lies before you straddles a variety of lines between various approaches to technology and global politics. Not least, while leaning towards an approach inspired by the work of French philosopher Michel Foucault, the analysis nonetheless attempts to draw attention to a range of other approaches from the fields of Science and Technology Studies (STS), for example, which relies on a different set of thinkers and forwards a different articulation of technology and the relationship with the political. In particular, the Foucauldian-inspired approach engages the manner in which technology in the broad sense – in this case, particularly the IR theories themselves – as technologies of rule or of governmentality, set the limits of possibility for how we come to conceive of and interpret 'world politics'. In contrast, the sort of approach taken up in STS, drawing on the work of Bruno Latour and others, considers artefacts of technology, or the material technologies themselves, and unpacks them in genealogical fashion. In one instance, for example, one might take the concept of anarchy and state centric order as a sort of 'technology of rule' from the Foucauldian perspective; whereas the STS perspective focuses on the artefact of technology, the nuclear bomb itself for example, and how this has a particular history, economy and socio-politics that is mutually constituted in global politics – both making a particular world and made by that world. As will become evident, such an analysis must distinguish between 'world politics', that is a field of knowable relations among states constituted through the academic theories of IR, and the functioning and far more complex and *un*knowable politics in the world, or 'global politics'.

This chapter begins with a few reflections on the notion of technology, technologies and artefacts of technology, reflecting a variety of approaches to the question of technology and/in IR. The discussion then moves to consider the distinction between global politics and world politics, the discipline and constitutive role of IR and its theories, and a range of issues regarding concepts and conceptualising politics in the world. After setting this groundwork, I consider an earlier epoch of IR as an academic discipline, and the specific articulation(s) and conceptualisation(s) of world politics made possible through IR. I consider to what extent IR is a technology of power in the Foucauldian sense – which I elaborate on in the next section of this chapter, drawing specifically on the work of Nikolas Rose – shaping and framing the conduct of conduct in IR and subsequently in global politics, producing desired effects and averting undesired ones, and sometimes failing to do either. I explore the emergence of one technology in particular, that of nuclear weapons, which has had a paradigmatic impact on IR and global politics, asserting particular accounts of central dichotomies vis-à-vis sovereignty, such as order/disorder, us/them, subject/object, here/there, inside/outside, visibility/invisibility, and so on. The emergence of this particular technology is a compelling example of the extent to which IR theory operates as a technology of power, which in turn contributes to the reliance on particular *technologies*, or objects or things, or what STS refers to as artefacts of technology, contributing to specific imaginaries of global politics, associated notions of order and disorder, us and them, and the question of violence. In addition to this, the story of technology and the Cold War also introduces a critical concept of failure. With this in mind I explore in this chapter how engagement in technology studies often raises the issue of failure: technological failure, policy failure and security failure, to name just a few.

After considering the nuclear age and the Cold War, and the concept of technology in IR during this epoch together with the concept of 'failure', the chapter changes focus, examining the post–Cold War, in which both the concept of technology and the proliferation of specific technologies, such as information and communication technologies, surveillance and identification technologies, military technologies (such as drones and autonomous weapons), simulations and video gaming (and the relationship to popular culture), and so on, have created a confluence of questions, challenges and productive critiques for scholars grappling with the nature of contemporary global politics. The technical objects are of interest and relevance as they almost miraculously proliferate, fostering asymmetries of power among international actors, societies and hegemons – for which among others, we can consult the work of Bruno Latour (2005). Following Latour's prompts, we ought to be concerned with the manner in which IR remains beholden to the concept of technology in particular ways, which continue to rearticulate IR as a technology of power itself, attempting to shape conduct, produce affects and avert particular outcomes. This later discussion takes drones as the example, but hints at various other issues and artefacts, and fecund interdisciplinary fields of scholarship, in which the limits of world politics vis-à-vis IR's imagination, and contemporary global politics and what is often termed 'late modern warfare', are tested and reimagined.

What becomes immediately obvious as one entertains the concept of technology and technologies and/in IR, is the extent to which popular culture, information technology and media, and mediations of space, violence, identity, otherness, (dis)order and so on, are intimately connected to this analysis. Both in terms of our examination of the operations of global politics, and reflections on the critical scholarship from the diverse fields that engage in the question of technology and/in IR, the centrality of media and mediated representations of power, authority, (dis)order, identity, violence and sovereignty, is almost immediately evident and ubiquitous. As such, this is present throughout the reflections in this chapter, from the analysis of Kubrick's Cold War classic film, *Dr. Strangelove*, to Josh Begley's 'Drone+' smartphone app, and in concepts like Grondin's 'militainment' and Der Derian's 'Military–Industrial–Media–Entertainment Complex'.

Technology

How are we to understand the academic discipline and theories of IR, its account of global politics, together with the concept of technology? While resisting the impulse to focus the analysis solely on emerging technologies or objects, such as drones, surveillance, GPS, mobile devices and smartphones, video games, the internet, air travel, and so on, one cannot ignore the paradigmatic changes nuclear weaponry, for example, has made to global politics, associated notions of order (state power), disorder (anarchy), civilisation, identities and the like. Although there is more to technology than objects or things, those objects have had and continue to have a significant impact on global politics, dramatically challenging, and providing critical possibilities for disrupting, traditional accounts of IR. However, we must be clear – or as clear as we can be – in terms of what we are talking about when referring to 'technology'.

As noted earlier, in straddling these different accounts of technology and/in IR, one can consider both the Foucauldian-inspired approach – what we might refer to as a governmentality approach to technology, as a technique of rule – and that approach focused more on artefacts of technology, vis-à-vis the work of Bruno Latour and STS. Foucault rarely made mention of particular technologies in terms of artefacts but focused instead on techniques and technologies of rule, such as disciplinary regimes or 'technologies', as stated in the interview 'Space, Knowledge, Power':

> What interests me more is to focus on what the Greeks called *techne*, that is to say, a practical rationality governed by a conscious goal … The disadvantage of this word *techne*, I realise, is its relation to the word 'technology', which has a very specific meaning. A very narrow meaning is given to 'technology': one thinks of hard technology, technology of wood, fire, of electricity. Whereas government is also a function of technology: the government of individuals, the government of souls, the government of self by the self, the government of families, the government of children, and so on. I believe that if placed this history of architecture back in this general history of *techne*, in this wide sense of the word, one would have a more interesting guiding concept than by considering opposition between the exact sciences and the inexact ones.
>
> *(Foucault 1984: 255–256)*

Technologies of the self, in particular, led Foucault to engage in both physical artefacts such as the institutional architecture of prisons, schools, hospitals, asylums, and so on, but also the technologies of the self, reliant on behavioural, disciplinary regimes that governed such institutions and went well beyond their physicality. As noted here, Foucault expresses technology, or *techne*, as a wide or broad sense of the word. The analysis in this chapter, in part, takes up a similar tact, while also considering the artefacts of technology, or what Foucault refers to as the narrow, or 'hard' sense of technology, that is to say, the technologies themselves, such as nuclear weapons, drones, and so on, for which I draw more explicitly on STS approaches to the question of technology and/in global politics.

In this Foucauldian sense, to speak of global politics is to invoke technology. In the fiefdoms of the Middle Ages, the cantons and city-states of the Renaissance, and the early epoch of exploration, compelled by capital conquest and spiritual servitude, global politics had little resonance. Elaborate and diverse cosmologies, ontologies and epistemologies made many worlds possible and one world impossible. The technology of IR, in large measure due to the violent valorisation of the sovereign state, has inherited a lineage of colonial expansion and Western dominance (Hobson 2012; Muppidi 2012), and made *a* particular *world* possible, which valorised territoriality and sovereignty. The intellectual and philosophical ancestry of IR invoked specific and often static, if not ahistorical and apolitical accounts of space, place, time and arguably technology, particularly in so far as it was bound up with questions of order and disorder, violence and development, to name just a few. As such, the question of technology and technologies and/in IR, is a deep and complex one. In this chapter, the primary difference lies in the Foucauldian-inspired account of IR as a technology or rule (and its accompanying concepts such as sovereignty, anarchy, balance of power, and so on), and the artefacts of technology – the technologies themselves, such as nuclear weapons, military hardware, information and communication technology (ICT), and so on, for which STS and the work inspired by Bruno Latour and others is necessary and germane to look at.

In the mid-1980s, Stephen Kline noted that 'technology' is used 'to represent things, actions, processes, methods and systems. "Technology" is also used symbolically as an epithet, for important working procedures, and to represent progress' (Kline 1985: 215). Embracing this understanding of technology is necessary for anything close to a somewhat comprehensive reflection on the impact and critical possibilities that the question of technology can bring to IR. To consider the concept of technology in IR opens up traditional theory to a variety of other disciplines and subfields, not least surveillance studies, science and technology studies, critical geography and international political sociology, in often productive and disruptive ways, which prompts us to reconceptualise and reimagine contemporary global politics. Moreover, it begs complicated questions about the limitations of sovereign power in light of telecommunication technologies, social media, algorithmic stock-trading, drone technology, cyber-security and cyber-war, and surveillance and identification technologies, which disrupt classical categories and units of analysis in IR, like the state, anarchy, citizenship, security, even the global marketplace, global civil society and various associated theories about zero-sum power, unitary actors, their utility-maximising behaviour, and so on (see Peterson in this book). In other words, to raise the 'question of technology' in IR is necessary, productive and critically engaging, but terribly difficult to limit.

In order to examine both the concept of technology in a broad sense, and considering the field of IR, as well as specific *technologies* and/in IR, throughout the course of this chapter I am mindful of Nikolas Rose's Foucauldian-inspired account of technologies of power, which are '… imbued with aspirations for the shaping of conduct in the hope of producing certain desired effects and averting certain undesired ones' (Rose 1999: 52). As such, the state system or anarchy, for example, functions as a technology that in this Foucauldian-inspired approach is about directly shaping conduct and producing desired and predictable outcomes in global politics. For example, in the same way that contemporary air superiority is facilitated by mastery of unmanned aerial vehicles (UAVs) or drones, the technological object itself constitutes certain power asymmetries, and is ensconced in a broader technology/conceptualisation of power. This account of power undermines alternatives as purveyors of disorder and privileges state-centric resolutions, and any such power asymmetries that benefit the state. Moreover, while trying to avoid making the analysis more complicated than it has to be, the discussion is as much about the concept of technology as it is about technologies or artefacts themselves; but to engage both conceptualisations of technology, or as noted earlier, *techne* for Foucault and the hard technologies themselves, we must draw on Science and Technology Studies approaches as well as the Foucauldian account.

Drawing on those from STS, such as Latour (2004) and Langdon Winner (1986), among others, we are encouraged to consider the extent to which artefacts themselves have politics. Winner suggests that artefacts always embody forms of authority and power, and as such, analysis cannot be left solely to the technologist, but to the social scientist, and perhaps in this case, the critically minded IR scholar (see Winner 1986). Similarly, Latour encourages us to pursue more critical scholarship to take stock of the multiple characteristics of these technologies and/or artefacts themselves, and avoid simplistic analysis that represents technology as a question of simply inputs and outputs. To this end, the question of technology and/in IR is not simply about the application of particular technologies in the realm of global politics, but the manners in which certain technologies mediate, (re)assemble, gather, and set the limitations and conduct of conduct of global politics (Latour 2004). Herein we can see some closer relationship between the Foucauldian approach of *techne*, that more obviously engages in a broad understanding of technology as 'government as a function of technology', and the artefacts or hard technologies themselves, which for Latour are central, but do not negate the broader notions considered by Foucault. Before engaging in the analysis of technology and/in IR any further, it is worth engaging in some commentary on the relationship between world politics, global politics and IR theories.

Some comments on world politics, global politics and method

If what we refer to as 'world politics' as the object of study for the academic discipline of IR, ever possessed some knowable quality, this is rapidly effaced in light of what we might now more commonly refer to as 'global politics', characterised by prolific travel, mobility, information and communication technologies, advances in science, atomic and nuclear weaponry, ubiquitous and powerful non-state actors of all shapes and sizes, a range of asymmetries and rearticulations of space and time that are simply not captured by the elegant and previously dominant trope of the sovereign state that grounded IR, and the blurred lines between the mediated representations of IR's core imaginaries. What is called contemporary global politics is often amorphous, defying or at least vividly challenging traditional understanding and explanation from IR. In other words, the distinction between world politics and global politics made in this chapter is deliberate: the former, something constituted by theories of IR, or a product of IR as a technology of power; and the latter, a complicated, complex, overlapping jumble of asymmetries, representations, imaginations, state and non-state actors, conflicting interests and powers, more akin to R.B.J. Walker's 'Many Worlds', from his treatise for the World Order Models Project in the late 1980s (Walker 1988). Walker's analysis began to tease out the distinctions between the single 'world politics' that the academic field and body of IR theory constituted, in contrast with the diversity of 'worlds' or what we might call global politics, or perhaps more apropos, politics in the world. In other words, particularly in the Cold War, IR theory constituted a world politics including the actions of great powers, and a notion of peace and security that ignored the destabilising impacts of bipolarity in the developing wars vis-à-vis proxy wars, as well as more profound understandings of security that raised the economic, social, human and environmental *insecurity* that resulted from the bipolar, mutually assured destruction (MAD) logic of Cold War geopolitics. Related to this, the subfields from within STS, which are of particular interest to our analysis here, also draw attention to the process of design, social construction and constitutive socio-economic forces that not only highlight how the use and reliance on particular technologies, in this case, within the field of IR have particular impact, but also the extent to which the artefacts have a politics, drawing in other actors and logics of rule. For example, the use of the drones becomes less of a choice by one particular actor, and more about changing the terrain of security politics towards autonomous killing that takes the 'human out of the loop' of perpetrating violence in as much as is possible, which is developed in response to political concerns, such as a longing for so-called 'zero casualty warfare' and ongoing interventions by hegemons without sacrifice.

Concerns related to comparing, mis-comparing and conceptual stretching expressed by Giovanni Sartori in the aftermath of the revolutions of 1989, appear prescient to current circumstances in global politics (Sartori 1991). Although Sartori was not simply lamenting Comparative Politics' failure to properly grasp the events of 1989, he was also decrying the general loss of purpose of the field in a dramatically different post-Cold War world. The story of IR and technology is not at all dissimilar, in so far as both the tumultuous events of 1989 as well as the asymmetric attacks on 11 September 2001 perpetrated by non-state actors, raised serious questions and critiques to heretofore notions of security, power, stability, sovereignty, even staid dichotomies such as inside and outside, us and them. Such sentiments are prevalent in contemporary IR scholarship, as some have recently asked whether or not IR theory has ended (see Wight et al. 2013). One might also question the resilience of sovereign power, the state system and other IR technology, in light of so-called virtual borders, widespread extra-legal exceptionalism, the internet, drones, algorithmic stock-trading, and so on. The discussion in this chapter will now move to more specific exploration of technology and artefacts of technology and/in IR, drawing on both Foucauldian- and Latourian-inspired accounts of technology to unpack *some* aspects of the relationship between IR and technology.

Technology, technologies and 'failure': the Cold War, nuclear weapons and *Dr. Strangelove*

Military and strategic technologies as well as information and communication technology have taken a central role in global politics. From its genesis in the early part of the twentieth century, the debates and dilemmas motivating the field of IR were developments in strategic and military technology; however, the field of IR stood as a technology itself. Proposing normative frameworks to avoid the alleged inevitable tilt towards a Hobbesian war of each against all, respective theories of IR, be they so-called realist or idealist, were forwarded as a technology of peace. In the absence of a Leviathan, technologies such as atomic weaponry, the panoply that emerged in the nuclear age, and the range of conventional and unconventional weaponry that has now come to dominate IR, acted as part of the arsenal of IR. These techniques and technologies are framed as ordering principles, ways to manage the anarchy that allegedly governs the international, which were particularly obvious in the Cold War. Even outer space and the 'race' to orbit the earth's atmosphere or land on the moon were part of the technology of IR to potentially rearticulate an 'outside' in an international space that is governed by the dichotomy of inside and outside as dictated by the concept of sovereignty (see Walker 1993; Bartelson 1995 contrast Krasner 1999): arguably IR's most powerful and persuasive technology. Interestingly, emerging information and communication technologies, particularly post-1989, challenge particular narratives of sovereignty, particularly territoriality and more comfortable accounts of us and them, inside and outside, inclusion and exclusion, and so on. As Walker already noted in the early 1990s following the collapse of the Cold War that was so beholden to what Agnew referred to as the 'territorial trap' (Agnew 1994), sovereign lines and divisions atrophied, while IR remained beholden to the discourses and 'technologies' of the Cold War, thus reifying what had become an anachronistic world politics.

In the early part of the twentieth century, Martin Wight (1960) famously stated, 'there is no international theory', and yet contemporaries of Wight were already steeped in a vision of world politics, saturated in what we might call the technology of IR, notably John Herz's *International Politics in the Atomic Age* (1959). Herz contends that the emergence of atomic technology and nuclear weapons so alter international politics that almost all that is solid melts into air, as far as the central concepts of IR are concerned. This provides one example of how the concept of technology was central in IR from the earliest period. Military technologies, lines of communication, and the related assumptions of how and why these technologies might be used according to the assumptions of IR have dominated the discipline for nearly the duration of its existence. For some, this provided fertile ground to theorise about the failure of the international community and the resilience of sovereign power and state centricity (e.g. E.H. Carr's *Twenty Years' Crisis*), and for others, it allowed for an almost mechanistic and technological vision of world politics itself, such as functionalism and neorealism.

Almost ubiquitous throughout IR is the technology and technologies, and what we can refer to as moments of technology rather than deployments. One such moment of technology for IR is the instrumental use of the concept of anarchy, which provides both reason and rationale for much of the action of states and the alleged impotence of non-state actors; counter-technology, such as David Mitrany's functionalism expressed in his valorisation of international organisations in *A Working Peace System* (1944) or that of 'mutually assured destruction' and Kenneth Waltz's neorealism, particularly as transmitted in his 1979 *Theory of International Politics*, provide technical solutions in technical discourses to the problem of anarchy and the system of sovereign states. While not altogether focused on technology in terms of things and objects, these IR accounts of world politics that emerged in the post–Second World War period and throughout the Cold War were certainly preoccupied with the role of nuclear weapons. The dominance of this specific technology motivated the majority of IR theory as advancing either international cooperation and subsequent restrictions on the proliferation of this technology, or security through proliferation vis-à-vis the concept of mutually assured destruction (MAD).

Whether one looked at the composition of the UN Security Council, the organisation of first, second and third worlds, even the concept of bipolarity itself, the world was understood in terms of the possession of nuclear weapons or their absence. Other notable aspects of the Cold War were also preoccupied with questions of technology, be that specific nuclear or conventional weapons, the related arms race between the US and USSR, or the infamous 'space race', which drew in both the America and the Soviet Union in an absurd quest to plant flags on the moon and orbit the earth's atmosphere. Perhaps one of the more bizarre confluences of the space race and the dynamics of the Cold War and the arms race was the so-called 'star wars' or strategic defence initiative: a supposed defence system which would allow the US to subvert mutually assured destruction. As will become evident in the latter part of this chapter, the assessment of the question of technology and IR often invokes popular culture, simulation and theatre, as the alleged vision and articulation of the technologies is often as important, or even more important, than any measureable impact of the technology itself. Moreover, an additional and integral theme of technology and/in IR is that of 'failure'.

As already indicated, to speak of world politics, is in fact, to speak of technology. The global marketplace, global civil society, global development, global politics, warfare, even sovereignty, are technologies, simulations of a 'world' we render knowable that is in fact *un*knowable. Complex algorithms together with elaborate information communication technology (ICT) infrastructure form a global financial marketplace, where the wealth is decided in milliseconds, dislocated from the physical marketplace itself and excluding the vast majority of the global population; generally misunderstood social media networks provide illusions of global civil society and global public space; codes, nuclear physics and assumed logics of power provide a confluence of ideas, technologies and assumptions that render the arms race and bipolar world of Cold War possible. Thinking the 'globe' or claiming to know a 'world politics' is to invoke the technology of the field of IR. However, the question of technology in IR is also one that raises the spectre of failure.

Significant parts the appeals of technology are the various claims related to enhanced visibility, solubility, resolvability and a general belief in technology as a panacea. Particularly during the Cold War, much of the arms race was motivated by perceived inadequacies in technology that had far more to do with perceptions than with verifiable data. On more than one occasion, American and Soviet actors made assumptions, often false, about existing military technologies that required a reaction on their part. While there are examples of specific failure, which I discuss here, there are also broader notions of failure related to the politics of the Cold War, IR and the concept of technology, which again we can draw from the field of Science and Technology Studies. In particular, the work of Donald MacKenzie in *Inventing Accuracy* (1993) in which he exposes the technological fictions that constituted the functions of the Intercontinental Ballistic Missile Programs. According to MacKenzie, much of the technology necessary for the launch and targeting of these missiles was faulty, and simply not precise and accurate in the manner in which they were represented. Like much of the story of technology and IR, representations, or what we might also call the 'Battle in the Wires',[2] come to be of greater importance than the material capabilities of the technologies themselves (see MacKenzie 1993). In terms of some specific examples of failure, I consider briefly the *USS Vincennes* incident, as well as the notion of failure more broadly understood, as the concept of technology and IR bound actors to certain inferiority complexes and insatiable quests for ever greater technological advances. As we move past the Cold War in the final section of the chapter, the more intimate relationship between popular culture and particular imaginaries of technology and world politics become almost indistinguishable from the measureable impact of technology and/in world politics. This too, is not altogether absent from the Cold War, as demonstrated by the account in Stanley Kubrick's famous film, *Dr. Strangelove, or: How I Learned to Stop Worrying and Love the Bomb* (1964).

The film *Dr. Strangelove* provides a cogent account of the question of technology and/in IR. The film tells the story of a rogue American military officer who manages to launch a nuclear strike on the USSR without the approval of the US president. This account not only emphasises the fallibility of nuclear weapons and the precariousness of the international system in spite of complex technologies, but the actions also uncover the possible existence of a 'doomsday machine' in the hands of the Soviets. Again, the question of technology and/in IR in Kubrick's film, in spite of being produced at the height of the Cold War, is prescient in its account of how precarious, unpredictable and potentially volatile global politics were in the Cold War. As such, this account of technology and IR vis-à-vis *Dr. Strangelove* highlights the centrality of failure in a broad sense, and the extent to which in spite of the ubiquity of technology, decisions are nonetheless often motivated by assumptions and that which is invisible.

A second example of failure is a more specific one: the so-called *USS Vincennes* incident in 1988. This account not only provides an instructive example of the technology and world politics in the context of the Cold War, but also highlights the work of an important scholar in this field of technology and IR: James Der Derian. On 3 July 1988, the American naval vessel *USS Vincennes* shot down an Iranian civilian passenger airline (an airbus). The vessel was equipped with the most sophisticated radar system of its time, the Aegis, and it was deemed to be in perfect working order at the time the Iranian passenger jet was shot down (ibid.). Der Derian argues that this incident is a prime case of simulation overpowering reality, as the *Vincennes* crew had spent months in training prior to the downing of the passenger jet, in which all simulations involved only hostile targets (Der Derian

2009a). Der Derian is careful not to refer to this incident as a mistake, as he suggests that the simulated battles 'displaced, overrode, absorbed the reality of the Airbus', so that those making the decision to strike believed they were striking down a hostile target and not two hundred and ninety civilians aboard a passenger jet. In the same manner that the map of glowing targets in *Dr. Strangelove* provides the representation upon which all action must be initiated and taken, similarly, the radar screen on the *USS Vincennes* is more real than the real.

Killer skies, virtual borders and battles in the wires: the concept of technology and IR in the twenty-first century

The technology of IR, and technologies or *artefacts* of technology – again, referring to the hard technologies themselves – applied in world politics are related but different. As a technology, IR renders what it constitutes as 'world politics' as knowable in a specific manner, and yet, *technologies* or artefacts of technology have altered the terrain of IR and of actual politics in the world rather radically. In the same way that a disease is understood vis-à-vis particular theories and technologies, which then contribute to pursuing particular treatments for diseases as they are understood, IR provides particular understandings of world politics, pathologies of violence and anarchy, and resolutions of/for order, such as sovereignty, bipolarity, mutually assured destruction, and so on. In the same manner that specific technologies, such as microscopes of various strengths and types provide both clarity and obscurity – for example, under an electron microscope the limits of the body and the world around us can become less obvious, as matter mixes, and yet the matter is observable in much greater detail – technologies in IR can simultaneously enhance precision and precarity.

Technologies of border security, identity, sovereignty, for example, can both render the sovereign state and the 'international' more knowable and less obvious. An aerial view of a national boundary and border from the lens of a camera mounted on a drone, for example, can provide both clarity and obscurity. Differing land use planning and development models are exposed, population and habitation patters are rendered visible, while the synthetic nature of sovereignty and borders between inside and outside in relation to topographical differences, and so on, is also uncovered. It is in this vein that IR and the concept or 'question of technology' is interrogated here. Geographic information systems and global positioning systems provide precision that can in fact obfuscate lines and boundaries, highlighting the extent to which boundaries are often in flux, not certain, and porous not only in terms of mobility, but even in geological and topographical ways (see Vaughan-Williams in this book).

In contemporary global politics, there are myriad examples of technology and/in IR. In fact, to use a Heideggerean parlance, one might even say IR is itself technological. The state, anarchy, civil society, the market, even war, has come to *be* technology, and not simply subject *to* technology. As noted throughout this chapter, a particularly cogent theme within the discussion of IR and the concept of technology is the relationship between information and communication technology, popular culture and entertainment (such as films, television shows, sci-fi, and video games), and the mediations of global politics. In much the same way that the representation and 'story' of missile technology in the course of the Cold War often trumped material and measurable circumstances, the persuasive imagery and imaginations of military prowess, border security, marketplace dominance, and so on, are arguably of paramount importance in twenty-first-century global politics. In order to provide some theoretical context and grounding for a specific artefact of technology and IR, in this case, the drone, it is worth reflecting briefly on the notion of 'War Beyond the Battlefield' and what Der Derian refers to as the 'Military–Industrial–Media–Entertainment Network' (2009b).

In the collection of essays that originally appeared as a special issue of the journal *Geopolitics*, David Grondin's introductory essay noted that the concept of 'War Beyond the Battlefield' was anything but a claim about the evaporation of the battlefield. If anything, it was a complex claim about the manner in which the battlefield proliferated, altered, was displaced and reimagined the traditional accounts of space, place, time, us/them, friend/enemy, so central to notions of warfare and violence that are integral to the cosmology of IR (see Grondin 2012b). To some extent, the fact that this collection of essays, which focused on the role of blogs, video games, and user-generated web content and the military, found its way into the pages of a journal named for one of the more traditional dimensions of IR – geopolitics – is instructive of the transition of the field and global politics itself. Space has not evaporated, but the spaces of conflict and cooperation have mutated, reconfigured and proliferated, in light of technology and technologies (see Agnew in this book). The so-called 'CNN Effect', contending that mediated images and imaginations vis-à-vis the independent media can act as an independent and significant influence in foreign policy decision-making, is well documented, not least in Babak Bahador's text on the news media's role in Western intervention in Kosovo (Bahador 2007). Our imagination of others, and the places and spaces from which they come or inhabit – in other words, what Derek Gregory (2004) refers to as our 'geographical imagination' – is intimately connected to technology and media/mediated representations of the battlefields of late modern war. There are countless more examples and issues one can point to, many of which are not only cogent examples of the challenges derived from complexities of contemporary global politics and late modern warfare, but also the fecund scholarship throughout IR, and interdisciplinary fields such as critical geopolitics, international political sociology, critical security studies, and science and technology studies, to name a few, which raise compelling and engaging questions and reflections to traditional IR (many of which are referenced here). As a final case study, to sum up this reflection on the concept and question of technology and/in IR with specific reference to an artefact of technology, we can take what might be a somewhat obvious but nonetheless compelling example of the drone.

Drones, or what are euphemistically referred to by some actors hoping to conceal the more nefarious connotations of the term 'drone' as Unmanned Aerial

Vehicles or 'UAVs', are stellar examples of technology and technologies and/in contemporary IR and global politics. Exhibiting a typical profile of scholarship when it comes to technology and IR, analysis of drones comes from a range of disciplines, such as critical geography (Gregory 2014), critical security studies (Grayson 2012), and STS (Kroker and Kroker 2014), to name just a few. Examining the drone as an artefact of technology and/in IR from these varying angles – and there are obviously far more cuts into this from a range of other equally diverse and critically engaging scholars – allows us to consider the political economy from which such technologies emerge, deeper questions about the (im)possibility of assassination as a part of official state foreign policy, our own relationship as citizens to foreign policy and the manner in which drones reimagine the battlefield and even the sky itself, potentially blurring the lines between the two. Gregory's (2014) account, for example, of erstwhile New York University student Josh Begley's struggle to design and successfully make available a smartphone app called 'Drone+', which provides a real-time update with casualty figures for each US drone strike, demonstrates the powerful ways in which technology vis-à-vis the drone enhances the destructive capacity of the state and yet can also open up the possibility for more intimate connections between citizens and their state's foreign policy, which critically challenges some fundamental tenets of IR and its imagination of world politics, with distinct inside and outside, us and them, and the sort of moral double standard or 'exceptionalism' that foreign policy has relied upon historically. Moving into the realm of STS can render the categories that ground IR even more unstable, as the definitions of power, otherness, territoriality, and so on are radically disrupted through technology's rearticulation and reimagination of the here and there, spaces and places of battle and peace, order and disorder, and what is included and excluded in IR's purview in relation to world politics.

In their recent intersession on drones, Arthur and Marilouise Kroker provide a particularly adept account of technology and global politics:

> … the meaning of 'real-time' as part of the contemporary language of power – time itself as an otherwise empty, locative coordinate in the spatial networks of communication surrounding us. But if that is the case, if, indeed, power has taken to the air, literally taken flight with the technological capacity provided by drones to turn the sky into a warlike eye, that would also indicate that the grasp of power on the time of duration, the lived time of territorial and bodily inscription, has perhaps been terminally weakened.
>
> *(Kroker and Kroker 2014: 1)*

The Krokers' account of drones and the warlike eye of the sky begs the question to what extent the materiality of the sky is transformed through the technology of the drone. In other words, the sky shifts from the inert space of matter to a weaponised space. Drone technology rearticulates the space of world politics itself, challenging 'air' and 'space', and underscoring their inclusion in world politics. Moreover, this transformation to weaponised space challenges how IR theory conceptualises world politics, but also how global politics functions. The drone, as an artefact of technology in global politics represents a story of the military industrial complex, the exercise of power by a hegemon with impunity and outside international law, but also the relatively inexpensive promise of air power to non-state actors. However, it also demonstrates the role that the evolution of a particular technology, an arte-fact, can contribute to a new technology of rule, as witnessed by the dramatic increase in drone strikes during the successive years of the Obama presidency.[3] It also begs questions about the post-human, drones, like other technologies, assumed to have agency, actors in world politics the same as a statesman at the Concert of Europe in the nineteenth century. Perhaps an obvious example, drone technology and other autonomous or semi-autonomous weaponry alter dramatically the rela-tions of space, time and subjectivity, that are integral to the technology of IR itself, as an ordering principle for world politics.

Although drones might be both an obvious and ostensibly extreme example of technology and IR, cursory reflection quickly suggests otherwise. Can one, for example, imagine the contemporary global marketplace, global civil society, even a contemporary state military, without imagining technology? The US military, for example, is not in a position to consider relying on technology or not, but rather, the US military *is* technology. Personnel often have video-recording devices mounted on helmets, robots are taking on an ever-increasing amount of responsi-bilities and for some years, the number of drone pilots trained per year has out-paced the number of trained pilots for manned aircraft. State security might be compromised by fence jumpers at the White House, but it also might be far more dramatically and even irreparably compromised by adolescent hackers launching cyber-attacks on the New York Stock Exchange or the Pentagon's website. In some sense, we come full circle, where the seeming absurdity of *Dr. Strangelove* is arguably more possible than ever.

Conclusion

The question of technology and/in IR is not easy or straightforward. This chapter reflects on the manner in which more akin to Foucualt's notion of *techne*, IR is a sort of technology in and of itself, forwarding a logic of rule, a conduct of conduct. As such, it sets a series of disciplinary regimes in motion; states, with rational behaviour, avoiding anarchy, in some cases through the mutually assured destruc-tion of a nuclear bipolar world as in the Cold War, or perhaps through cooperative manners and international institutions such as the European Union or United Nations. However, the question of technology and/in IR also, as Foucault himself recognises when confronted with the concept of technology, begs questions about the role of hard technologies or 'artefacts' of technology, such as drones, nuclear weapons, databases, intercontinental ballistic missiles, and so on. On the subject of the technologies themselves, the field of STS and the work of Latour and others is more instructive, although not mutually exclusive to the analysis pursued by Foucault.

The analysis here has made some attempt to amalgamate these approaches in coming to terms with the question of technology in global politics. The logics of rule of IR during the Cold War, for example, had a mutually constitutive relationship with the hard technology, or artefact of nuclear weapons themselves. Particularly, technology of rule that valorised specific conceptions of order, security, and anarchy led to the development of particular hard technologies to serve these ends, leading to mutually assured destruction, and allegedly secure environment for interstate relations during the Cold War. As the technologies of rule evolved vis-à-vis IR theories, hard technologies themselves also evolved, often in disconnected ways but with sharp consequences to global politics. As such, the analysis presented here introduces a multipronged approach that is attune with both STS and Foucauldian approaches, necessary for coming to terms with the complex relations between technology and global politics today. By no means exhaustive, this chapter is intended to begin a conversation and spark deeper more sustained analysis along the lines of some of the key thinkers and analyses discussed.

Acknowledgements

I wish to extend special thanks to Javier Duran and the Confluencenter for Creative Inquiry at the University of Arizona for their support, which afforded me the time and space to complete this chapter. Thanks also to the editors, Reiko Shindo and Aoileann Ní Mhurchú, the reviewer, as well as to Tom Cooke, for their insight, suggestions and helpful comments on earlier drafts of this chapter, all of which proved invaluable in thinking through the question of technology and/in IR.

Notes

1   Throughout this chapter when referring to the academic discipline of International Relations, I will use 'IR'. This is sometimes contrasted with *international relations*, which is a reference to actually existing relations among states.
2   While it will be discussed in the final section of this chapter, it is worth noting that this concept of IR and the Battle in/for the Wires, and war beyond the battlefield vis-à-vis technology, is developed throughout the contributions in David Grondin's edited collection *War Beyond the Battlefield* (2012a).
3   See particularly useful infographic which indicates the rising reliance on drone strikes during the Obama presidency: http://drones.pitchinteractive.com/.

Further reading and useful weblinks

The sources below provide a glimpse of existing trans-disciplinary approaches to technology and IR, and provide both exemplary publications on this topic, as well as dynamic, evolving and reliable websites and blogs that represent some of the best contemporary research in this field.
Derek Gregory, www.geographicalimaginations.com.
International Relations and Digital Technology Project, www.irdtp.org.
Ctheory.net , www.ctheory.net.

Aradau, C., Lobo-Guerrero, L. and Van Munster, R. (eds) (2008) 'Security, Technologies of Risk, and the Political', Special Issue, *Security Dialogue* 39(2–3).
Grondin, D. (ed.) (2012) *War Beyond the Battlefield*, New York: Routledge.
Singer, P.W. (2009) *Wired for War: The Robotics Revolution and Conflicts in the 21st Century*, London: Penguin Books.

Bibliography

Agnew, J. (1994) 'The Territorial Trap: The Geographical Assumptions of International Relations Theory', *Review of International Political Economy* 1(1): 53–80.
Bahador, B. (2007) *The CNN Effect in Action: How the News Media Pushed the West Toward War in Kosovo*, New York: Palgrave Macmillan.
Bartelson, J. (1995) *A Genealogy of Sovereignty*, Cambridge: Cambridge University Press.
Carr, E.H. (1964) *The Twenty Years' Crisis, 1919–1939: An Introduction to the Study of International Relations*, New York: Harper Perennial.
Der Derian, J. (2009a) *Critical Practices of International Theory: Selected Essays*, New York: Routledge.
Der Derian, J. (2009b) *Virtuous War: Mapping the Military-Industrial-Media-Entertainment Network*, New York: Routledge.
Foucault, M. (1984) *The Foucault Reader*, ed. P. Rabinow, New York: Pantheon Books.
Grayson, K. (2012) 'The Ambivalence of Assassination: Biopolitics, Culture, and Political Violence', *Security Dialogue* 43(1): 25–41.
Gregory, D. (2004) *The Colonial Present: Afghanistan, Palestine, Iraq*, Oxford: Blackwell.
Gregory, D. (2014) 'Drone Geographies', *Radical Philosophy* 183(January/February): 7–19.
Grondin, D. (ed.) (2012a) *War Beyond the Battlefield*, New York: Routledge.
Grondin, D. (2012b) 'The Other Spaces of War: War Beyond the Battlefield in the War on Terror', in D. Grondin (ed.), *War Beyond the Battlefield*, New York: Routledge, pp. 1–27.
Herz, J. (1959) *International Politics in an Atomic Age*, New York: Columbia University Press.
Hobson, J. (2012) *The Eurocentric Conception of World Politics: Western International Theory, 1760–2012*, Cambridge: Cambridge University Press.
Kline, S. (1985) 'What is Technology?', *Bulletin of Science, Technology and Society* 5(3): 215–218.
Krasner, S. (1999) *Sovereignty: Organized Hypocrisy*, Princeton, NJ: Princeton University Press.
Kroker, A. and Kroker, M. (2014) 'Night Sky Drones', *Theory Beyond the Codes*. www.ctheory.net/articles.aspx?id=732, accessed 8 June 2015.
Latour, B. (2004) 'Why has Critique Run out of Steam? From Matters of Fact to Matters of Concern', *Critical Inquiry* 30(Winter): 225–248.
Latour, B. (2005) *Reassembling the Social: An Introduction to Actor-Network Theory*, Oxford: Oxford University Press.
Mackenzie, D. (1993) *Inventing Accuracy: A Historical Sociology of Nuclear Missile Guidance*, Cambridge, MA: The MIT Press.
Mitrany, D. (1944) *A Working Peace System: An Argument for the Functional Development of International Organisation*, Oxford: Oxford University Press.
Muppidi, H. (2012) *The Colonial Signs of International Relations*, New York: Columbia University Press.
Rose, N. (1999) *Powers of Freedom: Reframing Political Thought*, Cambridge: Cambridge University Press.
Sartori, G. (1991) 'Comparing and Miscomparing', *Journal of Theoretical Politics* 3(3): 243–257.

Walker, R.B.J. (1988) *One World, Many Worlds: Struggles for a Just World Peace*, Boulder, CO: Lynne Rienner Publishers.

Walker, R.B.J. (1993) *Inside/Outside: International Relations as Political Theory*, Cambridge: Cambridge University Press.

Waltz, K. (1979) *Theory of International Politics*, Long Grove, IL: Waveland Press, Inc.

Wight, M. (1960) 'Why is There No International Theory?', *International Relations* 2(1): 35–48.

Wight, C., Hansen, L., and Dunne, T. (2013) 'The End of International Relations Theory?', *European Journal of International Relations* 19(3): 405–425.

Winner, L. (1986) 'Do Artifacts have Politics?' in L. Winner (ed.), *The Whale and the Reactor: A Search for Limits in an Age of High Technology*, Chicago, IL: University of Chicago Press, pp. 19–39.

17

THEORY

Ching-Chang Chen and Young Chul Cho

Introduction

People cannot engage in systematic thinking entirely independent from existing theories. International Relations (IR) theories enable us to decide what matters for thinking about world politics but at the same time exclude those ideas and issues deemed unimportant or irrelevant. IR theories also decide what IR is and what it is not, both as an academic discipline and the practice of world politics. Concerning its role, then, IR theory does not simply explain international politics to us but helps to constitute our world in a particular way that a given theory preaches to us. For instance, realism not only explains how the world works by making international politics intelligible to IR students, but also leads decision makers and citizens alike to think and act as per realist instructions, hence (re)producing a particular realist world that vindicates realist lessons (see Moulin in this book). Theorising is thus an intellectual *and* political activity; indeed, IR theories wield enormous power over people.

Given that IR theories are human inventions based on a certain spatial and temporal context (see Agnew and Lundborg in this book), it is impossible for them to be purely objective and completely value-free. IR theory offers not just a way of seeing or not seeing, but also a particular viewpoint on how our world functions, or ought to look like. Producing and consuming a certain IR theory is a political act implicated in the power and interests of those who advocate and practise that theory. As far as the power/knowledge nexus in academic IR is concerned, it is widely held that theory should bear some sort of relevance to the world where we live, and the task has often been narrowly understood as describing, explaining and if possible, predicting strategic behaviour of *states*. Such state-centric orientation, in turn, is informed by a particular understanding about territory, statehood and authority originated in the West. As a result, knowledge production about world politics, IR theory in this case, has been very much by the West for the West but internalised by the Rest (Ling 2014). To address this epistemic violence, the aim of this chapter is twofold: first, it seeks to interrogate state-centrism in mainstream Western IR theories from the perspective of critical IR theory. Second, by looking at two IR communities outside the West – China and Japan – it attempts to assess whether and how far alternative IR theorising inspired by local concepts and experiences is possible. To be specific, this chapter illustrates the 'dark side' of theory in (re)producing the present hegemonic IR embodied in Westphalian state-centrism as well as the potential it possesses in transforming that hegemony, making both the study and practice of world politics more representative and responsive.

The main body of this chapter consists of four sections. The first section looks at state-centrism in three major Western IR theories, namely realism, liberalism and constructivism, while summarising each theory's key tenets. The second section takes issue with mainstream, problem-solving theories' state-centrism in light of critical IR theory. Going beyond Western-originated theory, the third section investigates the extent to which recent attempts by scholars in China and Japan to develop a distinctive '*Chinoiserie*' or '*Japonaiserie*' theory are driven by their respective national identity needs (Chang 2011), which may end up with reinforcing the familiar state-centric trope. The fourth section weighs up the possibility of building alternative IR theory by re-examining the aforementioned home-grown concepts in East Asia, with a brief discussion on this chapter's normative stance on IR theorising.

State-centrism in mainstream IR theories

Traditionally, international relations has often been understood as politics among sovereign states in a world of anarchy. Sovereignty is a modern Western invention that accords a given state ultimate internal authority over the issues and people within its soil, and external recognition from other states as an equal. Since there is no supreme authority over sovereignty, the international realm is anarchical. Sovereign states and the ensuing states system, a particular historical institution that emerged in the West, are widely accepted as core ontological elements of making international politics and IR studies possible. Treating the state as a natural unit of analysis cutting across time and space, three mainstream IR theories – realism, liberalism and constructivism – seek to explain and even predict how the world works, with prescriptive guidelines for academics and practitioners of international relations.

Among them, realism has been one of the most dominant theoretical approaches in IR that treats states as the most central and unitary actors. Without states as essential building blocks of IR, it is meaningless for realists to talk about how the world works; IR studies should, therefore, focus on strategic interaction among states and the structural configurations of the states system that influence state behaviour. In realism, states, like men, make their decision after rational cost-and-benefit calculation, and behave in a self-interest manner. States are essentially guided by consideration of the national interest, with state survival as the funda-mental goal, and implement various policies to realise their interests. To maintain national interests, states must struggle for power, which is defined by most realists in terms of tangible material resources such as the military, national wealth, terri-tory, population, and so on. As John Mearsheimer (2013: 75) indicates, 'Realists believe that power is the currency of international politics.' Engaging in zero-sum games, realists maintain that states are more interested in relative gains than absolute gains, and they often seek their national interests at the expense of other states.

The lack of a central authority above states further leads realists to differentiate between domestic and international politics; unlike domestic politics, a high degree of order, justice and trust is deemed almost impossible to materialise in interna-tional politics. The nature of international anarchy is inherently conflictual, as the relentless security competition among states seeking power and influence makes conflict inevitable. A 'security dilemma' situation is thus pervasive. This pessimism is considered a 'timeless wisdom' (Dunne and Schmidt 2014: 102) offered by rea-lism for statecraft. Given the immutable circumstance of international conflicts under anarchy, states cannot but take care of their own survival (the logic of self-help) by any means available to them, including hard power, alliance and loyalty. In short, realism 'depicts international affairs as a struggle for power among self-interested states and is generally pessimistic about the prospects for eliminating conflict and war' (Walt 1998: 31). Ontologically, state-centrism is firmly embedded in realism.

Emphasising cooperative aspects of international relations, liberalism has been a powerful alternative to realism. Scholars subscribing to this theoretical tradition argue that international relations can be a realm of progress and positive change rather than only or predominantly of conflict and warfare; it is neither necessarily nor always a war of every man (state) against every man (state) (Doyle 1997). Because human beings are rational beings in terms of both instrumentalism and morality, cooperating with each other for better lives and moral integrity is gen-erally preferred over throat-cutting conflicts. As a natural corollary, rational state actors are capable of managing international conflicts through the harmony of interests. It is thus possible to make positive changes in world politics, and in most cases, states under international anarchy do not need to fear each other all the time. In the world of liberalism, there are many important non-state actors such as international organisations, non-governmental organisations (NGOs), multinational corporations (MNCs), and so on. Nevertheless, states remain the major (albeit not unitary) actors, and no non-state actors are more influential than states in international relations.

To achieve international cooperation and peace, four variants can be identified in liberalism. First, a sociological variant stresses relations between non-state actors and people as they are more cooperative and peaceful than national governments in world politics (Rosenau 1990). It does not deny the importance of the state and the states system; rather, this variant seeks to reduce the possibility of inter-state conflicts through non-state actors' interactions. Second, a complex interdependence variant (intensified economic interdependence in particular) would discourage states from using violence, for wars damage each other's stability and prosperity. 'Low politics' also plays a key role in improving relations among states (Keohane and Nye 2001). A third variant is that international politics is inseparable from domestic politics. Since the historical record shows that democracies rarely go to war against each other, the spread of democracy is conducive to international peace. Non-democracies should thus adopt liberal democracy as their regime type (Russett 1993). Fourth, international institutions such as the United Nations (UN) and the World Trade Organization (WTO) can play a vital role in promoting international cooperation, for they help to improve trust and flow of information, reduce transaction costs, monitor and punish rule-breakers under international anarchy (Keohane 1989). Liberalism is not utopian idealism; rather, it attempts to go beyond the all-against-all world of Hobbes via the Kantian triangle of liberal democracy, economic interdependence (free-market economy) and international institutions (Russett 2013). Compared with realism, liberalism brings non-state actors and relevant issues and processes into account. However, these are often used to explain state behaviour and offer foreign policy prescriptions, hence revealing state-centrism in its meta-theoretical underpinning. States come first in liberalism's normative and analytical concern.

Since the late 1990s, constructivism has gained greater prominence as a major theoretical approach in IR. Strictly speaking, constructivism is not a single, coherent IR theory; there are plural, even conflicting constructivism(s) in terms of different meta-theoretical positions. Due to space limitations, this section only deals with 'conventional constructivism' (Hopf 1998), the variant developed mainly by Alexander Wendt (1999). Unlike realists who see national interests as a given, constructivists hold that '[s]ecurity interests are defined by actors who respond to cultural factors' (Katzenstein 1996: 2) such as norms and identity. From this perspective, state identity is crucial because the state cannot figure out its interests without knowing who it is in relation to other states. State identity is largely informed by normative structures – for example, norms, institutions and culture – telling the state about what appropriate actions are, which in turn constitutes the state's particular interests. State behaviour is not simply shaped by materialistic calculations (the realist logic of consequence) but by socially accepted rules (the constructivist logic of appropriateness) in international relations.

For constructivists, norms either define (constitute) or prescribe (regulate) states, or they do both, offering states knowledge about their interests and identities. At the same time, norms are constituted by the social interaction of states. Norms and states are mutually constitutive; they are shaping each other. Similarly, culture in a given states system is constituted by states' social interaction, be it friendly or hostile. This implies that anarchy as a culture is not necessarily conflict-prone across time and space: 'anarchy is what states make of it' (Wendt 1992). To achieve international peace and cooperation, therefore, a friendly culture among states should be constructed through the positive social interactions of states, and that culture in turn can contribute to more peaceful international politics. Progress and purposive change are difficult but by no means impossible, as can be seen from the end of the Cold War. Despite their emphasis on the mutual constitution between structures (norms and culture) and agents (states), conventional constructivists place far more weight on structure than agency because they are interested in 'how structures of constructed meaning, embodied in norms and identities, affect what states do' (Jepperson et al. 1996: 66). In this regard, socialisation (i.e. the adoption of rules and modes of behaviour by actors) is reduced to a causal link of top-down relationship between states and the international system. State-centrism is thus still discernible in the meta-theoretical foundation of conventional constructivism.

Thinking outside the state-centric box of mainstream IR theories

In his seminal essay 'Social Forces, States, and World Orders: Beyond International Relations Theory', Robert Cox (1986) distinguishes between problem-solving and critical theory so as to examine the role of theory in maintaining or transforming the existing world order sustained by its hegemonic relations and practices of power. Problem-solving theory seeks to ensure that existing political configurations function smoothly for the benefit of the powerful and privileged by minimising the potential for conflict and war. It is a system-maintaining theory that is conservative in nature. By contrast, critical theory interrogates how the dominant order came into being, how it has evolved over time and may evolve again in ways that empower the vulnerable and excluded, showing its contingency in time and space. Critical theory does not just attempt to explain the world but to change it, by undertaking a critique involving a series of interventions in taken-for-granted modes of thought and action. It constitutes and instantiates an ethics of alterity through political criticism.

Following this distinction, realism, liberalism and constructivism all belong to the category of problem-solving theory, for the purpose is of securing the hegemonic powers-led international system designed for their interests. For instance, the Melian dialogue, which touches on one of the important episodes of the war between Athens and Sparta, is often used by scholars to sum up realist ethics in international politics: 'the strong do what they have the power to do and the weak accept what they have to accept'. This reveals that realism is about power politics for hegemonic states. Liberalism is subtler in the sense that it presents the Western power-led international system primarily ensuring well-off Western powers' interests as self-evidently legitimate and equally good for all. All states, the argument goes, should support and reinforce the existing international system, by proactively embracing the aforementioned Kantian triangle based mostly on Western values and experiences. As a result, great (and typically Western) powers are privileged rule-makers in international politics. In line with 'the liberal claim that international institutions can transform state identities and interests' (Wendt 1992: 394), constructivism likewise makes little of the power differentials between states in the formation of norms. The norm-makers are often the great powers that can use norms as a means to stabilise and perpetuate a particular order that serves their interests. As Cox (1986: 219) explains: '[norms] may become the anchor for such a hegemonic strategy since they lend themselves both to the representations of diverse interests and to the universalization of policy'. International norms are not value-neutral; power and norms, for the most part, are mutually supportive and imply each other. To borrow from Wendt, perhaps anarchy is 'what states make of it' (Wendt 1992), but one should be reminded that some states are 'more equal' than others. Major IR theories claim that they treat the world as something external to theories of it and the world can be tested against neutral or objective procedures to discover the general laws in world politics; nevertheless, they are value-laden and constitutive in the way that they actually help (re)produce a hierarchical state-centric world order for the great powers. Indeed, 'International relations theory is not only about politics, it also is itself political' (Hutchings 1999: 69; see also Griffiths 2007).

This critique of state-centrism in IR does not imply that states are unimportant in current global affairs, or that the reversion of unequal power relations between dominant states and the weak ones would be a cure-all for world problems. Rather, it points to the need to rethink IR outside the state-centric box so as to develop a deeper, more balanced and representative understanding of world politics in an era of globalisation, which is very complex in its nature and processes (see Peterson in this book). In so doing, it becomes possible to image alternative-life worlds, which could be more just, equitable and sustainable than the current states system. Unfortunately, mainstream theories have not recast their focus on different parts of that complexity such as gender, climate change and global inequality. As shown earlier, realism, liberalism and constructivism all subscribe to state-centrism to varied degrees in their ontological foundation. The state is treated as a pre-given, context-free and full-fledged intentional entity in IR. This 'common sense' has been so pervasive that it creates a permissive condition for both academic IR and its subject matter. To some extent, constructivism seeks to problematise the state by indicating that some properties of state (e.g. power-seeking, egoism, etc.) are socially constructed by norms, but the state still exists of its own accord; as Wendt (1999: 198) puts it bluntly, 'states are ontologically prior to the state system, [and the] state is pre-social relative to other states in the same way that the human body is pre-social'.

Critical IR theory takes the view that the state cannot exist of its own accord, for it has no ontological underpinning aside from the many practices of self (inclusion)/other (exclusion) that bring it into being. To be specific, three traditional components of the state – people, territory and government – do not automatically ensure the identity and functioning of state. To be or become a state that can tell its people about who they are, it needs the unceasing operation of various state-making practices such as border control, military draft, taxation, national education, production and consumption of nationalism, and so forth. In this sense, there is no completed state, since the state is (and has to be) always in a process of becoming (Devetak 1995). This includes even the most powerful state of the international system. Using US foreign policy as an illustration, David Campbell (1998) points out that the United States has relied on a series of representations of danger to produce, reproduce and police its state identity. Rather than function as an instrument employed by the pre-existing US state to cope with external dangers and uncertainties that threaten its physical security, foreign policy actually works to (re)inscribe state boundaries that demarcate an 'inside' from an 'outside', a 'self' from an 'other', a 'domestic' from a 'foreign', hence constituting an identity. Rather than treat it as an already given, essential property of the state, state identity should be examined by looking at self/other practices. By uncovering the contingency of the state as the primary actor in world politics, critical IR theory becomes relevant to practical political action for different kinds of actors and processes. It empowers those who challenge structures of dominance and oppression and opens up the possibility of reimaging world politics in novel ways.[1]

The pitfalls of building national schools of IR in East Asia

The state-centric orientation as revealed by critical IR theory in the previous section does not come from a cultural vacuum. Rather, it reflects a particular understanding about territory, statehood and authority derived from Western/European history, philosophy and culture (Hobson 2012). Eurocentric IR theories have been developed based on the premise that the modern international system was a product endogenous to the West, thanks in particular to the Peace of Westphalia (1648); the European-born system then expanded outwards first through the rise of Western imperialism and later through globalisation, a process which has made world politics into what it is (see, *inter alia*, Bull and Watson 1984). This Eurocentric bias in IR knowledge production is not inconsequential for the actuality of world politics. The presence of such a bias means that policy makers as well as ordinary citizens outside the Western core are handicapped in making sense of their own regions, which have contained some of the world's most populous countries, blossoming economies and dynamic civilisations. Moreover, the familiar Westphalian narrative only gives credits to the West for inventing norms and institutions such as 'international society' that help maintain peaceful coexistence among states, while denying agency to the non-West (Kayaoglu 2010). In this Eurocentric account of unequal diffusion, the latter is no more than a victim of, or a free rider on, Western expansion; only the former can act and speak (compare Hobson 2004).

To redress the aforementioned epistemic (and political) violence, a growing body of IR literature has been exploring historical, philosophical and cultural sources in non-Western sites. For instance, Shilliam (2011) illustrates that non-Western thought should not be treated as a mere object of modern inquiry but rather a source through which to construct legitimate knowledge of subjecthood. Tickner and Blaney (2012) go on to examine how Western-originated key concepts (or, more to the point, means of knowledge production) in IR are understood and employed by scholars from around the world. By interrogating patterns of civilisational encounters before the 'rise of the West', Suzuki et al. (2013) challenge the Westphalian narrative and demonstrate the significance of non-European agency in shaping global history.

Among various geocultural sites in Asia, the extent to which IR academics in China and Japan have advanced their 'home-grown' theory merits attention, not least because their rich and self-conscious culture should be able to serve as a potentially valuable source for IR theorising. As the world's second and third biggest national economy, China and Japan also host two of the largest academic IR communities in Asia. To what extent, then, have scholars in these two countries managed to develop alternative accounts of world politics, without committing the Eurocentric fallacy upon which much of the IR theoretical enterprise is based?

To be sure, IR theory-building in China does not attempt to construct a monolithic 'Chinese School of IR', since theorising there has taken both analytical ('what X is') and normative ('what X ought to be') directions and has contained both discrete (i.e. explaining Chinese foreign policy or strategic behaviour) and universal (i.e. carrying some validity across space and time) claims (Schneider 2014: 685–687). Divergent theorising endeavours notwithstanding, they are united by their concern over IR as a not-so-international discipline and the need to redress the Western bias by bringing in China's own contributions. Since it is counter-productive to develop home-grown theory without making reference to existing theoretical approaches, Chinese researchers recognise the importance of learning from established theories beyond copying.

The problem is that this learning process has not been successful in unlearning colonial power relations between the core and the non-cores, whose lingering continues to make Eurocentrism natural to academics and practitioners of international relations. This helps explain why the English School of IR, a theoretical approach that stresses the central role of an 'anarchical society' (Bull 1995) in creating and sustaining order in international politics, is often cast as a role model to emulate by Chinese scholars. Yiwei Wang (2009: 117), for instance, goes so far as to declare that 'China can probably learn more from the English School than from American IR theory' because the former is 'more open to the idea of variations between different international systems that can accommodate non-Westphalian politics'. Attracted by the English School's apparent success as an established alternative to mainstream/American IR theories, Wang unwittingly endorses its Westphalian narrative that the dynamic West/Europe invented 'international society' for maintaining international order and the stagnant non-Western societies were at the receiving end of the 'expansion' of such a society. In a similar vein, Qin Yaqing, a prominent figure in the Chinese IR community, is convinced that the progress of would-be Chinese IR theory must be judged in accord with the American methodology: 'The American IRT [IR theory] tells Chinese scholars that theorising about important thoughts is a sign of disciplinary maturity. If persistent efforts are made, it will be inevitable for Chinese IRT, with local experience and universal validity, to emerge and grow' (Qin 2011: 253). But the following questions remain unanswered: what modes of theorising are preferred or considered valid? Who decides which thoughts are important? And how much theorising is enough to claim 'maturity'?

One of the most serious attempts to go beyond the state-centric mainstream has been made by Zhao Tingyang, a philosopher and public intellectual. Governed by the Westphalian states system, Zhao (2011: 25) indicates that today's world is in fact a 'non-world', for anarchy continues to exist between states, and inter-state institutions cannot solve world problems from the world's vantage point. A 'worldly world order' must be provided, he argues, by genuine world institutions, which are embodied in the traditional Chinese *tianxia* (天下/all-under-heaven) ideas. On that basis, Zhao conceives his ideal-type *tianxia* system that replaces the states system with a three-layer cosmological order consisting of family, state and *tianxia*. The *tianxia* system operates under the benevolent rule of a virtuous leadership ('son-of-heaven'), whose authority comes from their access to *minxin* (people's heart or public sentiment). Considering that family is the most fundamental and universal social institution whose structure can be found at the levels of state and of *tianxia* (the adult/ruler vis-à-vis the underaged/ruled), Zhao argues that the Chinese philosophy-informed *tianxia* system is universal, transposable and internally consistent; its structure is laudable and more superior than its Western counterparts' because the interests of its members are maximised through their mutually reciprocal relations (i.e. the ruler cherishes the ruled with care and benefits, and the former in turn gains deference and legitimacy from the latter).

Unlike the contemporary US-dominated system of globalisation that promotes American values and institutions as if they were universal ones, the 'all-inclusive' (*wuwai*) principle in Zhao's *tianxia* system seems to echo Beijing's 'harmonious world' mantra that calls for the peaceful coexistence of plural civilisations and different political systems. One might be tempted to associate the popularity of the *tianxia* discourse with the Chinese government's soft power manoeuvre (Callahan 2008), but Zhao already proposed his *tianxia* philosophy in 2003, i.e. two years before President Hu Jintao's 'harmonious world' speech in the United Nations General Assembly. It is more pertinent, then, to analyse Chinese scholars' very desire to build *Chinoiserie* theories against Western ones (Chang 2011).

Indeed, Zhao does not rise above what he attempts to transcend, despite his universalist commitment and his own preach to 'think from the world' (Zhao 2011: 3). To the contrary, Zhao's theoretical construct is motivated by how China, now an economic power, can become a 'real great power' through being a 'knowledge production power' in its own right (ibid.: 1–2). If his primary concern is for developing a philosophy of the world, why does it matter so much that the world be conceived in a Chinese way (Chang 2011: 37–38)? By emphasising China's purported cultural uniqueness, Zhao not only contradicts his concern about the world, but also reveals a competitive and nationalistic mood to demonstrate the superiority of traditional Chinese political thought over the Western ones. Instead of proposing an alternative that transcends the limits and deficiencies of the Westphalian world order, his *tianxia* system actually reproduces the same confrontational logic of the states system therefore.

Elsewhere although the Japanese IR community is not engaging in home-grown theory-building with as much fervour as its Chinese counterpart, academics there have similarly sought to gain wider recognition for their local experiences and intellectual traditions in an IR discipline dominated by Western theories and methods. Inoguchi Takashi, a leading scholar of the Japanese IR circle, laments that if IR theories are not narrowly defined in terms of positivist methodology, as is often the case in the United States, it is possible to identify several 'fledging theories' in prewar Japan (Inoguchi 2007). Inoguchi is right to stress that IR theorising should embrace methodological pluralism, but the way he introduces Japanese approaches is no less problematic than that of Zhao.

When presenting Kyoto School philosopher Nishida Kitaro's concept of nothingness (*mu*), Inoguchi chooses to depict Nishida as an 'innate constructivist' with sophisticated understanding about identity (a concept that, even now, can only be expressed in the more angular form of *kana* used in Japanese, *katakana*, implying its 'foreignness' to the Japanese) and Japan's place in the world. He notes that Nishida adopted a creative method of dialectic in which a thesis and an antithesis may coexist without forming a synthesis. A non-Western account of 'identity/difference' thus emerges, which does not resort to conversion or discipline and, so to speak, Japan's identity is produced through a coexistence of opposite: Eastern and Western civilisations. Curiously, Inoguchi does not examine how home-grown IR theorising might benefit from this insightful formulation and its engagement with like-minded philosophies such as Daoism; rather, Nishida's dialectic is reduced to something 'more Hegelian [than Hegelian]' (ibid.: 379). In so doing, Inoguchi ends up reinforcing the West's assumed cultural superiority that he seeks to problematise. It is self-defeating for a non-Western IR project to look for investiture from a questionable Western authority such as Hegel (who had famously equated Asia with the land of Oriental despotism to be absorbed by the law-based, civilised West/Europe), while ignoring other potentially valuable sources.

Such an omission indicates the extent to which culturally sensitive scholarship in Japan has internalised the Westphalian narrative, that non-European political spaces lack a crucial dimension of 'running' international relations (i.e. Westphalia and all of its positive attributes such as order and tolerance) and thus are not appropriate objects of mutual learning. An interesting precedent can be found in Royama Masamichi's essay '*Toa Kyodotai no Riron*' (The Theory of East Asian Community) (1941). According to Royama, an idealist-turned-apologist during the Second World War, East Asia lacks Europe's common regional ethos and fate (thanks to its Greco-Latin tradition and Christianity); as a consequence, the sense of a common East Asian destiny must be consciously constructed through political movements. Royama believed that an East Asian community (i.e. the 'Great East Asia Co-Prosperity Sphere') could only be built by integration, either politically or forcibly accomplished by Imperial Japan, because East Asia lacked Europe's cohesion. Similarly, the contemporary Japanese IR epistemic community believes that it can learn little from the concepts and experiences of other Asian countries (e.g. Shimizu et al. 2008), because Asia lacks Westphalia. Both are embedded in the same colonial trope that treats the West as the only worthy reference point, a familiar fallacy committed by Chinese scholars working on their national approach/school of IR.

The im/possibility of building alternative IR theory beyond the West

The pitfalls in the recent development of non-Western IR theory in East Asia as discussed above indicate the enormous difficulty of alternative theorising. As seen earlier, Zhao's *tianxia* system as a theoretical construct has backfired because his philosophy of the world is ultimately not an end in itself but a means to highlight the contribution China can make for envisioning a feasible world institution. In other words, his *tianxia* system is not so much a wordlist project as a statist one. However, the concept of *tianxia* as a worldview might have greater potentials for home-grown theory development; in Chinese history it had been used to discuss the arrangements for maintaining relations between China (a polity that was normally at the centre of a hierarchical world order because of its supposed civilisational and moral attractiveness) and its neighbours (surrounding polities that were subordinate to China), which can provide the IR scholarship with a valuable site to explore the different nature of state and constitutive structures of international society in a non-Westphalian context. Those arrangements typically involved the presenting of tributes to the Chinese emperor, which led to the Western invention of the oft-misleading term 'tribute system'. In a nutshell, offering tributes to the 'son-of-heaven' was an act of nominal subordination by China's neighbouring polities for acknowledging the former's access to the will of the heavenly bodies and, so to speak, China did not actually administer them or treat neighbouring peoples as its colonial subjects.

As a foundational institution that sustained *tianxia* or what could be called East Asian international society (Suzuki 2009), the tribute system emphasises a formal hierarchy among its members. Within this hierarchical order, China usually sat highest and subordinate states were ranked by their proficiency with Confucian norms, values and practices, not by their relative power. But the Confucian emphasis on relations and mutual responsiveness (namely *li shang wang lai*, or 'propriety values reciprocity') also means that the legitimacy of this hierarchy entailed a credible commitment on the part of the dominant state to cherish, not to exploit, the secondary states. To understand why this was the case, it is helpful to look at three normative dimensions of the constitutive structure of international society (ibid.: 34–35): the 'moral purpose of the state' (the reasons for establishing a political entity to serve the common good), the 'organising principle of sovereignty' (which legitimises the entity's possession of sovereignty) and the 'norm of procedural justice' (the idea that the implementation of the above principles must also follow certain procedures). In the case of European/Westphalian international society, a legitimate state was expected to enable its citizens to pursue their individual happiness and achieve their potential. As a result, the state's internal affairs were to be free from foreign intervention so long as it commanded popular support. The principle of sovereign equality, in turn, was safeguarded through legislation (i.e. legislative justice) and embodied in institutions such as positive international law and diplomacy. By contrast, the 'moral purpose of the state' for *tianxia* was to promote social and cosmic harmony. Such harmony was maintained when members could conform to their 'rightful' positions within this hierarchical society. The principle of sovereign hierarchy meant that states (both suzerains and vassals) had to perform appropriate Confucian rituals to acknowledge their relative positions (i.e. ritual justice) if their legitimacy was to be respected.

To the extent that the arrival of the Western powers added the Westphalian states system onto the tribute system but did not replace the latter altogether, it is of scholarly and policy necessity to examine the conditions under which relations between the People's Republic of China (PRC), now the world's most populous state and the second largest economy, and its neighbours might be shaped by the *tianxia* worldview. The complicated relationship between the PRC and Taiwan represents a case par excellence, for it can hardly be defined as a sovereign state's domestic affairs or interactions between two such states in Westphalian terms. The conclusion of an FTA-like economic pact between them in 2010 is indicative of the island's increasing incorporation into the residual tribute system, wherein hierarchical relations were affirmed when Taiwan ('vassal state') submitted to the PRC ('suzerain') by upholding the so-called '1992 consensus' (i.e. presenting 'tribute');[2] in return, the Taiwanese were granted generous trade privileges as gifts from Beijing ('son-of-heaven'). Since secondary political entities historically enjoyed immense latitude within the tributary order regarding their economic, cultural and even military affairs, this perspective helps to understand why Chinese leaders formulated the 'one country, two systems' proposal in dealing with Taiwan in the way they did (which precludes Beijing from exerting direct control over the island), and why they have been willing to entertain issues pertaining to Taiwan's 'international space' so long as Taipei adheres to the '1992 consensus'.

The aforementioned discussion regarding *tianxia* and its reemergence is not intended to suggest that the world order it entails is 'better' or more sustainable than the Westphalian one; after all, within the tribute system, unequal power relations also existed between China and its neighbours, in the form of normative hierarchy if not direct physical coercion. The point is that contemporary world politics simply cannot be made sense of by the 'Eurocentric big-bang theory of world politics' alone (Hobson 2012) where the West monopolises all positive agency in terms of self-creation and exporting civilisation to the rest of the world. This is so because such a 'big-bang theory' does not take into account the existence of multiple worlds, which, together with 'Westphalia World', constitute our world as we know today (Agathangelou and Ling 2009). A feasible, more diverse theoretical approach to IR worthy of the name should be built upon an ontological parity between them wherein no mode of thinking, doing, being and relating is structurally privileged against, or imposed onto, the other (Ling 2014). On this basis, equitable engagement and mutual complementarities are more likely to take place between differences rather than violent conversion or coercive discipline. In this regard, Nishida's conception of *sekaiteki sekai* (literally, world-of-worlds) envisioned an integrated world consisting of many worlds established *under* a single overarching rubric guided by Japan, hence falling short of promoting a common world made up from the equitable interactions among various worlds (Ling 2014:

14). It is unsurprising, then, that most Kyoto School philosophers were co-opted by the wartime militarist government, supporting the Great East Asia Co-Prosperity Sphere against the West under Imperial Japan's leadership (Shimizu 2011). Nevertheless, Nishida's concept of a place of nothingness (or a non-place) where differing social beings can meet without mutual naming or judgement, points to an inspiring strategy of withdrawing from the Self/Other logic (Nishida 1993). By retreating from their own national and civilisational conditions, his method of strategic self-denial allows nation-states to enter into a truly universal (and non-confrontational) world (Shih 2012: 57–75); it reaffirms that intellectual and political exits from the hegemonic Westphalian narrative in world politics are immanent, emerging and possible, if by no means easy.

Conclusion

Despite their apparent diversity, contemporary major IR theories are united in the sense that they offer a Eurocentric discourse that sustains the Westphalian world order and its foremost agent, the modern state. While proclaiming their universality and objectivity, they in effect institutionalise a hierarchical dichotomy between the West/Self over the Rest/Other, rendering the subaltern (including their knowledge and ways of knowing) either permanently lagging behind or trying to catch up to no avail. Mainstream IR theories have been, and are still, inflicting an epistemic violence on the Others by denying the latter's various contributions to the thinking and doing of world politics. A taken-for-granted 'division of labour' continues to exist in academic IR where scholars in or associated with the Western core produce the theoretical goods, which are then disseminated top-down to scholars in the non-Western margins. The latter are poorly equipped to speak to the former, except perhaps for providing local empirical materials to confirm the validity of those theories and their underlying Westphalian state-centrism. In short, 'problem-solving theory' continues to dominate the theoretical landscape of the IR discipline, which seeks to make the prevailing social and power relationships *within* the Westphalian states system work as smoothly as possible, but the 'stability' brought by such hegemonic domination comes at the expense of subalterns and is ultimately unsustainable. Hegemony does not dissolve following the mere promotion of more national schools/approaches of IR outside the West, which has so far worked to reproduce, not overcome, the exclusive and confrontational logic of the states system. Indeed, a plausible alternative IR theory cannot but be a Coxian 'critical theory', concerning itself with the change *of* the states system and the origins of relevant power relations and institutions that have made the system possible. Rather than provide exotic non-Western insights to those who subscribe to Western IR as something different yet comprehensible through mainstream jargon, the real challenge for alternative IR imaginaries is to recover the contributions subalterns made to world politics and to enable these subalterns to reclaim a position of ontological parity with Westphalia World. This challenge is an extremely difficult one; without facing it, however, IR scholarship will only confront more and more seemingly unsolvable intellectual and political crises arising from Westphalian state-centrism. After all, as this chapter and the whole volume have illustrated, problem-solving theory itself is part of this bigger problem that must be addressed in the first place.

Acknowledgements

The authors thank Aoileann Ní Mhurchú and Reiko Shindo for their engaging comments that helped improve the quality of this chapter. Financial support from the Japan Society for the Promotion of Science, Grant-in-Aid Scientific Research (A) (15H01855), is also acknowledged.

Notes

1 Although Cox's critical IR theory is also a product of the Western IR scholarship, its Western origin should not be conflated with Western-centricity. Western-centricity privileges Western thought over all other modes of thinking, seeing Western tradition as the sole criterion for valid and universal knowledge. As a result, Western-centric IR theories exclude, silence, undervalue or delegitimatise non-Western thoughts, actors and interactions in world politics. Critical IR theory introduced here allows both Western and non-Western actors to lay bare the Westphalian narrative common in mainstream IR theories. It helps empower, not oppress, the underprivileged and disfranchised in the production of IR knowledge, be they in the Western or non-Western worlds.
2 The '1992 consensus' refers to a modus operandi under which Taipei neither openly challenges Beijing's 'One China Principle' (there is only one China and Taiwan is a part of it) nor accepts the latter's definition of China (PRC).

Further reading

Booth, K. (ed.) (2011) *Realism and World Politics*, London: Routledge. This volume is a comprehensive and critical engagement with Waltz's structural realism.

Brincat, S., Lima, L. and Nunes, J. (eds) (2012) *Critical Theory in International Relations and Security Studies*, London: Routledge. This book contains interviews with some of the pioneers of critical IR theory and critical security studies, combined with reflective essays to discuss the legacy and challenges of critical thinking.

Campbell, D. (1998) *Writing Security: United States Foreign Policy and the Politics of Identity*, Manchester: Manchester University Press. Drawing on Foucault and the philosophy of identity, this book illustrates how foreign policy functions as a boundary-drawing practice that constitutes the identity of the state in question.

Keohane, R.O. (ed.) (1986) *Neorealism and Its Critics*, New York: Columbia University Press. This classic text is a must-read for those who want to understand Waltz's realist theory as well as the so-called 'Third Debate' in IR.

Ling, L.H.M. (2014) *The Dao of World Politics: Towards A Post-Westphalian, Worldist International Relations*, London: Routledge. Integrating folk tales and popular culture with policy analysis, this book offers refreshing non-Western alternative visions (not only explanations) of world politics.

Shilliam, R. (ed.) (2011) *International Relations and Non-Western Thought: Imperialism, Colonialism, and Investigations of Global Modernity*, London: Routledge. Exploring non-Western thought on modernity, this volume examines the contested nature of a global modernity shaped deeply by Western colonialism and imperialism.

Suzuki, S., Zhang, Y. and Quirk, J. (eds) (2013) *International Orders in the Early Modern World: Before the Rise of the West*, London: Routledge. This book challenges the Westphalian narrative of modern IR scholarship by examining cross-cultural exchanges before the development of European primacy in many parts of the globe.

Tickner, A.B. and Blaney, D.L. (eds) (2012) *Thinking International Relations Differently*, London: Routledge. This volume investigates how key IR concepts have been understood and appropriated differently by scholars from around the world and analyses the implications of such differences.

Tickner, A. B. and Blaney, D. L. (eds) (2013) *Claiming the International*, London: Routledge. This volume examines the possibilities of alternative 'worldings' beyond those sanctioned by the disciplinary norms and customs, including the possibilities of doing inquiry without IR.

Zehfuss, M. (2002) *Constructivism in International Relations: The Politics of Reality*, Cambridge: Cambridge University Press. Using Germany's post-Cold War shift towards dispatching its military abroad as an illustration, this book offers penetrating critiques of constructivist IR theories by Wendt, Kratochwil and Onuf.

Bibliography

Agathangelou, A.M. and Ling, L.H.M. (eds) (2009) *Transforming World Politics: From Empire to Multiple Worlds*, London: Routledge.

Bull, H. (1995 [1977]) *The Anarchical Society: A Study of Order in World Politics*, Basingstoke: Macmillian.

Bull, H. and Watson, A. (1984) *The Expansion of International Society*, Oxford: Clarendon Press.

Callahan, W.A. (2008) 'Chinese Visions of World Order: Post-Hegemonic or a New Hegemony?', *International Studies Review* 10(4): 749–761.

Campbell, D. (1998) *Writing Security: United States Foreign Policy and the Politics of Identity*, Manchester: Manchester University Press.

Chang, C. (2011) 'Tianxia System on a Snail's Horns', *Inter-Asia Cultural Studies* 12(1): 28–42.

Cox, R.W. (1986) 'Social Forces, States and World Orders: Beyond International Relations Theory' in R.O. Keohane (ed.), *Neorealism and Its Critics*, New York: Columbia University Press, pp. 204–254.

Devetak, R. (1995) 'The Project of Modernity and International Relations Theory', *Millennium* 24(1): 27–51.

Doyle, M. (1997) *Ways of War and Peace*, New York: Norton.

Dunne, T. and Schmidt, B.C. (2014) 'Realism' in J. Baylis, S. Smith and P. Owens (eds), *The Globalization of World Politics: An Introduction to International Relations*, Oxford: Oxford University Press, pp. 99–112.

Griffiths, M. (2007) 'Worldviews and IR Theory: Conquest and Coexistence?', in M. Griffiths (ed.), *International Relations Theory for the Twenty-First Century: An Introduction*, London: Routledge, pp. 1–10.

Hobson, J.M. (2004) *The Eastern Origins of Western Civilisation*, Cambridge: Cambridge University Press.

Hobson, J. M. (2012) *The Eurocentric Conception of World Politics: Western International Theory, 1760–2010*, Cambridge: Cambridge University Press.

Hopf, T. (1998) 'The Promise of Constructivism in International Relations Theory', *International Security* 23(1): 171–200.

Hutchings, K. (1999) *International Political Theory: Rethinking Ethics in a Global Era*, London: Sage.

Inoguchi, T. (2007) 'Are There Any Theories of International Relations in Japan?', *International Relations of the Asia-Pacific* 7(3): 369–390.

Jepperson, R., Nendt, A. and Katzenstein, P. J. (1996) 'Norms, Identity, and Culture in National Security' in P. J. Katzenstein (ed.), *The Culture of National Security: Norms and Identity in World Politics*, New York: Columbia University Press, pp. 33–75.

Katzenstein, P.J. (1996) 'Introduction: Alternative Perspectives on National Security', in P.J. Katzenstein (Ed.), *The Culture of National Security: Norms and Identity in World Politics*, New York: Columbia University Press, pp. 1–32.

Kayaoglu, T. (2010) 'Westphalian Eurocentrism in International Relations Theory', *International Studies Review* 12(2): 193–217.

Keohane, R.O. (1989) *International Institutions and State Power: Essays in International Relations Theory*, Boulder, CO: Westview Press.

Keohane, R.O. and Nye, J.S. (2001) *Power and Interdependence*, New York: Longman.

Ling, L.H.M. (2014) *The Dao of World Politics: Towards A Post-Westphalian, Worldist International Relations*, London: Routledge.

Mearsheimer, J. (2013) 'Structural Realism', in T. Dunne, M. Kurki and S. Smith (eds), *International Relations Theories: Discipline and Diversity*, Oxford: Oxford University Press, pp. 77–93.

Nishida, K. (1993 [1949]) *Last Writings: Nothingness and the Religious Worldview*, trans. David A. Dilworth, Honolulu: University of Hawaii Press.

Qin, Y. (2011) 'Development of International Relations Theory in China: Progress Through Debates', *International Relations of the Asia-Pacific* 11(2): 231–257.

Rosenau, J.N. (1990) *Turbulence in World Politics: A Theory of Change and Continuity*, Princeton, NJ: Princeton University Press.

Royama, M. (1941) *Toa to sekai* [East Asia and the World], Tokyo: Kaizosya.

Russett, B. (1993) *Grasping the Democratic Peace: Principles for a Post-Cold War World*, Princeton, NJ: Princeton University Press.

Russett, B. (2013) 'Liberalism' in T. Dunne, M. Kurki and S. Smith (eds), *International Relations Theories: Discipline and Diversity*, Oxford: Oxford University Press, pp. 94–113.

Schneider, F. (2014) 'Reconceptualising World Order: Chinese Political Thought and Its Challenge to International Relations Theory', *Review of International Studies* 40(4): 683–703.

Shih, C. (2012) *Civilization, Nation and Modernity in East Asia*, London: Routledge.

Shilliam, R. (ed.) (2011) *International Relations and Non-Western Thought: Imperialism, Colonialism, and Investigations of Global Modernity*, London: Routledge.

Shimizu, K. (2011) 'Nishida Kitaro and Japan's Interwar Foreign Policy: War Involvement and Culturalist Political Discourse' *International Relations of the Asia-Pacific* 11(1): 157–183.

Shimizu, K., Ikeda, J., Kamino, T. and Sato, S. (eds) (2008) *Is There a Japanese IR? Seeking an Academic Bridge through Japan's History of International Relations*, Otsu: Ryukoku University: Afrasian Centre for Peace and Development Studies Research Series.

Suzuki, S. (2009) *Civilization and Empire: China and Japan's Encounter with European International Society*, London: Routledge.

Suzuki, S., Zhang, Y. and Quirk, J. (eds) (2013) *International Orders in the Early Modern World: Before the Rise of the West*, London: Routledge.

Tickner, A.B. and Blaney, D.L. (eds) (2012) *Thinking International Relations Differently*, London: Routledge.

Walt, S.M. (1998) 'International Relations: One World, Many Theories', *Foreign Policy* 110(Spring): 29–46.

Wang, Y. (2009) 'China: Between Copying and Constructing' in A.B. Tickner and O. Wæver (eds), *International Relations Scholarship Around the World*, London: Routledge, pp. 103–119.

Wendt, A. (1992) 'Anarchy is What States Make of It: The Social Construction of Power Politics', *International Organization* 46(2): 391–425.

Wendt, A. (1999) *Social Theory of International Politics*, Cambridge: Cambridge University Press.

Zhao, T. (2011) *Tianxia tixi: Shijie zhidu zhexue daolun* [The Tianxia System: An Introduction to the Philosophy of World Institution], Beijing: Zhongguo Renmin Daxue Chubanshe.

18

TIME

Tom Lundborg

Introduction

The discipline of International Relations (IR) is traditionally concerned with the spatial dimension of politics and the territorial borders of states (albeit it has not always been so good at interrogating this (see Agnew in this book)). Hence, it comes as little surprise that questions of 'time' and 'temporality' have received relatively little attention in the IR literature. Recently, however, a growing number of attempts have been made to take time more seriously. While some of these have focused on the particular assumptions of time that underpin theories of IR, others have sought to develop new ways of thinking about time that move beyond as well as disrupt the disciplinary boundaries of IR. In this chapter I claim that both of these kinds of engagements with time must be taken seriously and that, perhaps, it is the relationship between them that raises the most challenging questions.

In the first section of this chapter I turn to a rather obvious but ultimately inevitable starting point for thinking about time and IR: the relationship between time and space. Indeed, it can be argued that the very possibility of IR as a separate discipline, which seeks to explain interstate politics and the relations between sovereign territorial states, rests on the idea of incorporating time within space, or of closing down time in favour of space; that is, in favour of the territorial units of sovereign states operating within an international states-system. Against this back-drop it is suggested that a critical engagement with time can fill two main purposes. On the one hand, it can be used in order to investigate the various assumptions of time that ideas about the modern state and the modern states-system rely upon. In this context, as the second section of this chapter goes on to explore, it is especially interesting to consider the work that history does – as a technique and a practice of inscribing 'borders in time', which are used in order to separate the past from the present and the future. This practice, it is noted, is inseparable from the processes in which the sovereign state seeks to take charge of time and decide on the proper relationship between a past that is declared dead and buried, gone from the world; a present that is simply taken to mean where we are now; and a future that can be shaped as we, as modern political subjects, desire.

On the other hand, a critical engagement with time can be used in order to explore other ways of understanding and experiencing time, which do not fit the disciplinary limits of IR but rather seem to move beyond as well as disrupt those limits. Against this latter backdrop, the third and final section of the chapter considers some recent attempts to explore what these other experiences of time might refer to and how they manifest themselves in contemporary world politics. Concepts such as 'becoming' and the 'untimely' are especially important when thinking of such experiences since they point to something taking place beyond the linear progressive temporality of the state that traditional IR discourse relies upon.

Time, temporality and the limits of IR

In her book *Time and World Politics* (2008), Kimberly Hutchings explores the philosophical assumptions of time underpinning theories of IR and world politics. Her approach is 'post-Kantian' in the sense that she is interested in particular experiences and understandings of time, rather than with the objective nature of time. In contrast to Kant, however, she does not seek to connect these experiences of time to the 'intuition' of individual subjects but is more interested in the 'inter-subjective time of politics' (ibid.: 4). Political time, she suggests, is essentially contested and can always be used for different purposes. In order to analyse the political inter-subjective dimension of time, Hutchings draws on the distinction between *chronos* and *kairos*, which can be traced back to ancient Greek thought. Whereas *chronos* refers to a Newtonian understanding of 'quantitatively measurable duration, associated with the inevitable birth-death life cycle of individuals', *kairos* refers to the 'transformational time of action, in which the certainty of death and decay is challenged' (ibid.: 5). While *chronos* is associated with clocks, calendars and timetables, which humans have invented in order to measure the 'natural' succession of events, *kairos* refers to the possibility of interrupting such 'natural' succession by making exceptions to *chronotic* time.

Both *chronos* and *kairos* are relevant for thinking about particular ways of understanding and experiencing time inter-subjectively. As such, they can also be analysed as forms of temporality rather than time *per se*. As David Couzens Hoy notes, whereas temporality refers to how time 'manifests itself in human existence', time has to do with the objective nature of time, what time really consists of, and how past, present and future objectively and physically relate to one another (Hoy 2009: xiii). Concerned with the social and political dimension of time (i.e. temporality) rather than with the objective nature of time, Hutchings demonstrates how theories of IR and world politics are based on a range of different philosophical assumptions about *chronos* and *kairos*, as well as the relation between them. In other words, she examines how theories of IR rely on different ways of thinking about the measurable time of *chronos*, the transformational time of *kairos* and the relationship between *chronotic* and *kairotic* time.

Assumptions of time play a crucial role in IR not least because they help constitute ideas about the temporality of international politics and the temporal direction in which interstate relations are heading. Thus, for example, it is possible to analyse the Neorealist emphasis on the eternal cycles of war and peace as expression of a form of *chronotic* time based on repetition. Liberalism, on the other hand, most famous in IR for the democratic peace theory and the notion of continuous progress in relations among states, can be linked to a progressive notion of *chronotic* time. Furthermore, in Marxism we find ideas not only about the measurable *chronotic* time studied through the lens of historical materialism, but also a notion of the *kairotic* transformational time of action in the aspiration towards revolution of the existing social and international order.

Competing notions of time can also be found in the distinction made between the inside and the outside of the sovereign state; a distinction that is crucial for understanding the possibility of international politics outside the state and domestic politics inside the state. As R.B.J. Walker (1993) has demonstrated, the inside/outside distinction can be linked to ideas about the possibility of progress inside the state and the impossibility thereof outside the state. Thus, while the inside of the state is characterised by a progressive understanding of time, the outside is tied to a repetitive or cosmological notion of time. Following Walker's analysis, the distinction between the progressive time of the inside and the cosmological time of the outside can be traced back to the Renaissance period and the transition from medieval conceptions of time/space to early modern attempts to grasp time and space in new ways. While the former medieval conceptions of time/space were based on a hierarchical order of the universe in which everything emanates from God, also known as the Great Chain of Being, the Renaissance period saw the birth of the modern individual subject. Instead of passively following the Word of God, the modern individual subject was free to interpret the meaning of the cosmos; free to determine what the meaning of his place in the universe was, how to relate to the heavenly bodies and interpret the movements of the stars (see also Cassirer 2010). The development towards this notion of the modern individual is commonly associated with the so called 'Copernican revolution', referring to Renaissance cosmologist Nicolaus Copernicus (1473–1543) and his astonishing claim that the earth was *not* the centre of the universe, a claim that went straight against the strict theological doctrines of his time.

A crucial outcome of the Renaissance period was that the relationship between the 'particular' and the 'universal' started to change. Rather than trying to think of the universal as such or in itself, directly given by God, the universal had to be interpreted from a particular perspective. Also, as the finite world of the medieval cosmos and the theological Great Chain of Being were called into question, a newly discovered *infinite* universe had to be made sense of. In the absence of a divine authority, the meaning of the cosmos was no longer given by God but had to be interpreted and represented with the help of the reasoning powers of the individual human subject. Hence, rather than emanating from God, the meaning of the universe as well as of earthly things had to originate from the particular perspective of the individual human subject (Harries 2001: 19).

If we fast forward from the Renaissance period to the Enlightenment period, we find philosopher Immanuel Kant (1724–1804) who developed the first attempt to construct a critical philosophy stressing the limits of the particular. Rather than trying to grasp the universal as such or in itself, Kant emphasised the limits of the particular perspective in relation to the universal. The universal, Kant claimed, can never be known as such or in itself since it lies outside the experiences of the individual subject. While experience takes place within the subject, highlighting the immanence of experience, the universal is placed beyond the subject, highlighting that which transcends experience. Thus, in order to reach the universal one must first try to transcend the limits of the particular perspective, that is, to transcend immanence. For Kant, however, there is an unbridgeable gap between immanence and transcendence – a gap that manifests itself not least in the limits of any attempt to *re*-present the universal on the basis of the particular. Since any such attempt is necessarily based on a particular point of view, we can never know what the universal is as such or in itself. Put differently, we can never gain knowledge of the thing itself (noumena), independently of our experiences of that thing (phenomena).

Returning to Walker's reading of IR and the distinction between the inside and the outside of the sovereign state, it can be argued that this distinction reflects a particular way of resolving questions concerning the relation between the universal and the particular. Crucially, the inside/outside distinction makes it possible to grasp the universal in relation to the particular, for example by defining the meaning of the universally good – justice, responsibility, freedom, and so on – within the limits of the particular community of the state. In this way, while the Renaissance period made it possible to experience time in a new way, by freeing the particular perspective of the individual subject from the theological Great Chain of Being, the distinction between the inside and the outside of the state imposes certain limits on this possibility. This is because in a modern world of sovereign states, the individual experience of time is never fully independent of the territorial borders of states, which clearly distinguish the possibility of political life within the state from the impossibility thereof outside the state. The individual experience of time is thus confined to the limits of what may happen inside the borders of a particular state, whereas the outside is characterised by mere repetition of conflict and war.

Of course, not all theories of IR agree with this modern way of resolving the problem of how to aspire towards the universal within the limits of the particular state. In contrast to state-centric theories like Neorealism and Neoliberalism, there are other theories exploring the possibility of progress beyond the state (e.g. Linklater 1998). Rather than emphasising the limits of the particular perspective, they seek new ways of moving beyond the particular and to actually aspire towards the realisation of the universal. The universal, in this framework, often translates into notions of global justice, global ethics or global democracy. However, it can be argued that any attempt to move away from the limits imposed by the particular perspective and to adopt a more open and all-encompassing understanding of the universal must also try to escape that which makes the universal possible in the first place: the borders of the particular. If IR is an expression of how this relationship between the universal and the particular has played out in modernity, it also marks the limits that any attempt to renegotiate this relationship must face, not least when trying to find new ways of organising time beyond the inside/outside distinction of the state.

Temporal borders and the periodisation of 'modernity'

While the spatialisation of time and the inside/outside distinction of the state can be traced back to the Renaissance period, it can also be argued that this spatialisation is nothing but the outcome of a particular narrative or story of how we became 'modern' (see Agnew and Moulin in this book). This is the story that tells us how we became what we supposedly are: modern political subjects naturally occupying our place in the universe within a system of sovereign states. In order to have any continuing relevance and impact, this story must be told and retold, over and over again. A critical perspective on time can, in this context, be used in order to demonstrate how the 'modern' is produced and reproduced as a particular period in history. The point of doing so is not so much to show how 'modernity' is based on a particular way of conceptualising the experience of time – an issue most famously explored by Reinhart Koselleck in his *Futures Past* (2004) – but rather to demonstrate how, in order to have a period of 'modernity', this period must first be produced.

The question of how periods are actively made and produced, rather than historically given, is explored especially well by Kathleen Davis in her book *Periodization and Sovereignty: How Ideas of Feudalism and Secularization Govern the Politics of Time* (2008). Davis looks at how periodisation functions as a powerful tool in constructing our very understanding of the 'modern'. She does so by investigating how the 'modern' is produced in relation to specific notions of its pre-modern 'others', in particular 'medievalism' and 'feudalism'. This production works in two main ways. On one hand, the modern 'self' acquires its meaning by being clearly separated from its pre-modern 'other'.[1] On the other hand, the former is produced by quietly embedding elements of the latter. One example of how the 'pre-modern' is both separated from and embedded within the 'modern' relates to how some of the key political concepts of the latter, while often being presented as modern secular concepts, are deeply influenced by 'pre-modern' theological modes of reasoning. Drawing on Carl Schmitt's famous treatment of 'political theology', including his definition of the sovereign as 'he who decides on the exception' (Schmitt 2005: 5), Davis shows how the notion of a 'secular modernity' can be linked to a sovereign decision that governs the politics of time. This decision, following Schmitt, highlights a pure decision or a pure event, which is unlimited in its scope. As such it can also be linked to the miracle by which the early moderns were suddenly able to cast off the shadows of the Dark Middle Ages.

According to Davis, the sovereign decision on the exception is crucial, not only for understanding the theological influences on the 'modern' concept of sovereign authority, but also for thinking about the very act of historical periodisation that makes the modern 'modern'. Thus, while the sovereign decision on the exception can be seen as integral to a 'modern' political order, it can also be seen as constitutive of that order. More precisely, it can be seen as a key component of 'modernity' as a self-constituting and self-explanatory process, according to which the 'modern' does not simply exist as one period among others but relies on the act of a temporal cut, or the inscription of a temporal border that enables the modern to become 'modern', and which must be continually reproduced in order to naturalise our understanding of what is meant by this period. As Davis (2008: 5, emphasis in original) explains:

> Periodization as I address it, then, does not refer to a mere back-description that divides history into segments, but to a fundamental political technique – a way to moderate, divide, and regulate – always rendering its services *now*. In an important sense, we cannot periodize the past.

Following this critical approach to periodisation, the Schmittean exception is both what enables and is enabled by the periodisation of 'modernity'. It both enables and is enabled by a form of periodisation that successfully conceals its underlying theological elements, especially the 'miracle' of the sovereign decision. 'Modern' is the name given to a period and a political order through an act of sovereign decision-making, which conceals the 'continuity of theological forms' by pushing them into a pre-modern, medieval or feudal past (ibid.: 81). Charles Barbour (2010: 144) notes along similar lines that much of the work on decisionistic legal and political theory, in which he includes Schmitt:

> contends that every political act emerges spontaneously out of the void, but, as part of that very act, invents the appearance of a coherent past and a determinate future. All sovereign decisions, this line of thought proposes, conceal their miraculous coming into existence behind the veil of some unquestionable natural order, some demonstrable rational norm, or some irresistible course of history.

References to an 'irresistible course of history' can often be found in attempts to explain why and how decisions on the exception are necessary – as illustrated by the ways in which '9/11' is commonly invoked as a historical reference point for explaining the necessities of the exceptional politics of the 'global war on terror'. Adopting a critical approach to historical periodisation, however, we can turn this logic on its head by suggesting that it is the decision on the exception that enables the historical context and its necessary temporal reference points, which in turn make it possible to introduce a series of exceptional measures like torture, extraordinary rendition, global surveillance, and so on (see also Lundborg 2012). Hence, what needs to be analysed first of all is a sovereign politics of time, which conditions the birth and continuous reproduction of a particular historical period in which the exception is considered necessary.

The temporal borders of history and periodisation are also important to consider when analysing the 'sovereign state' as a naturalised ground for practices of sovereign authority. In his book *The Limits of History* (2004), Constantin Fasolt argues that the line between the past and the present enables the state to take charge of time, break free from a past that is dead and buried, and on that basis determine the direction of the future that lies ahead. As he puts it:

> [T]he distinction between past and present does not exist apart from our activity. We place that distinction into the uninterrupted flow of time. We assert ourselves and thereby we transform the world. We claim a place for ourselves in the here-and-now and hold it in opposition to the there-and-then. We draw a fence around a part of reality, call that the past, and mine it for the knowledge in which historians specialize. That is the founding act of history.
>
> *(Fasolt 2004: 12)*

This 'modern' idea of history, Fasolt claims, rests on three main assumptions. First, the past is dead and buried, gone from the present world. Second, the meaning of a text can only be understood in the context of 'its' place and time. Third, ideas about where we are going rely on perceptions of where we come from. Instead of merely accepting these assumptions and using them as the basis for providing a fuller description of the past and its relation to the present, Fasolt puts these assumptions to the test (see Ní Mhurchú in this book). He does so through his own attempt to study history, focusing on the life and work of Hermann Conring (1606–1681), an early-modern political thinker who along with other political thinkers of his time sought to break free from the grips of medieval structures of authority that kept Germany tied to Roman law. Using the established tools of history, and relying on the three assumptions mentioned earlier, Fasolt encounters a series of limits in his study of Conring: limits that in different ways prevent him from gaining full knowledge of Conring's life and work. In brief, these limits can all be linked to that founding act of history, according to which the past is declared 'dead' and the present is simply where we are 'now'. Regardless of how hard he tries, Fasolt finds it impossible to transcend these limits, or to study the objects (texts) in the context of 'their' time and thereby discover a clear point where the past leaves off and the present begins. Instead of transcending these limits, Fasolt encounters them precisely as limits of knowledge about time, or limits of our capacity as individual subjects to discover a natural line between the past and the present. This line is never naturally given but must always be produced, which makes it inseparable from a politics based on modern structures of authority.

Following Fasolt's analysis, the modern subject of history cannot offer a trans-cendent point of view, from which it is possible to provide a trans-historical or world-historical perspective. Rather, history is characterised by particular assumptions of time and progress, which emerged as an outcome of the early-modern thinkers and their struggles to leave the medieval structures of authority behind and construct a new political order, based on completely new structures of authority. Because of the radical incommensurability between these two structures of authority, history played a key role in trying to explain the necessity of leaving one of them behind and adopting a new one. By declaring one structure 'dead' and the other 'present', the move from the former to the latter seemed both natural and necessary. However, there is no clear line between past and present that is simply 'there', waiting to be discovered by the historian. Again, this line must be actively drawn or produced. In this sense a modern understanding of history is inseparable from modern claims to authority. To think of this form of knowledge as 'modern' is precisely to think of it as an expression of a particular claim to authority, as well as to 'reason'. As Fasolt (2004: 228) succinctly puts it: '"Modern" is not what is recent. "Modern" is what occurs in time that can be grasped by reason.' History, in this sense, can also be seen as a deeply political form of knowledge, which is designed to meet the needs of those promising to break free from one political order and enter a different one, a move that ultimately depends on the act of separating the past from the present and the future. It is an act that involves taking charge of time, determining how the present should be distinguished from the past, and on that basis deciding on the direction of the future that lies ahead. State sovereignty, in this sense, is not only based on the idea of claiming authority over a bounded territory, which is separated from other territories. It is also based on the idea of claiming authority over the passage of time and deciding on the conditions for leaving the past behind and moving into the future. The inscription of 'borders in time' can be seen as a precondition for doing this because it enables the past to be clearly separated from the present and the future. As Fasolt (2004: 7) puts it:

> Borders in time are moments of foundation or conversion to mark the point where sovereignty and citizenship begin and the past leaves off. They guarantee presence to the state by setting it apart from the past. Without their assistance, the state would constantly have to look over its shoulder in order to fulfill archaic obligations. The state could not protect the freedom of its citizens or their progress into the future.

With the help of temporal borders the state can claim a certain freedom in time; it can decide on how the present should differ from the past, what should belong to the latter and what should belong to the former, and how to best progress into the future. According to this paradigm, time must necessarily move *forward*, like an arrow rather than a circle. As David Gross (1985: 71) puts it, it requires that 'time is linear rather than cyclical, that the direction in which it moves is always forward rather than backwards, and that most if not all aspects of life have manifestly improved as one travels the distance from the past to the present'. In this way, history and the state can also be said to enter a somewhat paradoxical relationship, whereby the latter draws on the former in order to legitimise its own existence, while at the same time deciding on the conditions for *how* this 'source' may be used. As Jens Bartelson (2001: 39, emphasis in original) puts it:

> if concepts of political community are grafted on to a plane of historicity, this implies that such a historicized notion of community can hardly be used to *justify* particular forms of authority, since any such move exposes that authority to the same profound historicity, thereby depriving it of timelessness and thus of any transhistorical legitimacy.

One way of analysing this paradoxical relationship between the state and the historicity of the state is to view the latter as nothing but the outcome of a self-referential and self-explanatory practice seeking to legitimise the state's existence through the active inscription of temporal borders. These borders can thus be seen as crucial for the reproduction of the sovereign state. The latter is reproduced not just along the lines of Max Weber's famous definition of the state as 'the form of human community that (successfully) lays claim to the *monopoly of legitimate physical violence* within a particular territory' (Weber 2004: 33, emphasis in original). It is also reproduced as a political subject of history that has the authority to separate the past from the present and the future through the inscription of temporal borders.

Time and temporality beyond IR

The preceding sections did not seek to move beyond the limits of IR. The main purpose of those sections was rather to highlight the stakes involved in any attempt to find alternatives to those limits. Such alternatives must always necessarily try to renegotiate the dialectical relationship between time understood as continuous progress inside the state and time understood as repetition of conflict and war outside the state. Moreover, they must encounter the politics of historical periodisation and the production of temporal borders separating a past that is declared dead and buried, gone from the world, and a present in which we as 'modern' political subjects can decide on the direction of the future that lies ahead. Against this backdrop, any attempt to realise ideas about the universally good – justice, freedom, responsibility, and so on – beyond the limits of the particular seems destined to fail because it repeats a move that is already distinctively 'modern': the move whereby some are included by the temporal borders of history and others are excluded and made to disappear as the past is left behind and the future is embraced in the name of *progress*.

While attempts to think of progress and the universally good beyond the state cannot simply escape the limits of the particular historical perspective, there is another literature exploring issues of time and temporality that might at least have the potential to push these limits. This literature is concerned with other ways of experiencing and conceptualising time, which go beyond the linear and progressive notions of time on which concepts of history and the state tend to rest. Notable examples include Friedrich Nietzsche's concepts of the 'eternal return' and the 'untimely' (Nietzsche 1997), Henri Bergson's concept of 'duration' (Bergson 2001), Michel Foucault's concept of 'genealogy' (Foucault 1977), Jacques Derrida's concept *différance* (Derrida 1984), Gilles Deleuze's double temporalisation of Aion and Chronos (Deleuze 1990), and Paul Virilio's concept of 'speed' (Virilio 2006). Together, these concepts highlight an effort to problematise the linear understanding of time on which 'modern' assumptions of progress and history are based. In this way, they can also be seen as important sources of inspiration for those trying to analyse politics beyond the assumptions of time and history that underpin theories of IR and the spatial distinction between the inside and the outside of the state.

One prominent example of how to think the political significance of time beyond the limits of IR is James Der Derian's book *Antidiplomacy* (Der Derian 1992). In it, Der Derian seeks to replace the heavy emphasis on the spatial dimension of politics traditionally found in IR and the inside/outside distinction of the state with a focus on the temporal dimension of politics. This latter dimension becomes especially relevant when considering the significance of speed for understanding contemporary globalisation and transnational processes and phenomena (see Peterson in this book). According to Der Derian, 'international relations is shifting from a realm defined by sovereign places, impermeable borders and rigid geopolitics, to a site of accelerating flows, contested borders, and fluid chronopolitics' (ibid.: 129–130). Virilio provides the main philosophical backdrop for Der Derian's analysis, especially the former's claim that we are moving away from an era of *geo*politics, in which the distribution of space matters most, towards a period of *chrono*politics, in which the distribution of space depends on a prior distribution of time. Modern warfare is one of Der Derian's primary examples of the shift from geo- to chronopolitics since it captures the growing significance of speed of information, communication and different methods of simulation. In this specific context, he argues, 'time displaces space as the most strategic "field"' (ibid.: 134).

With the immediacy of real-time information comes a challenge to scholars of IR: to appreciate the role that speed plays in the sudden irruption of new events, and, not least, to grasp the politics of responding to those events (see also Der Derian 2001). In the 'post-9/11' world, practices of counter-terrorism demonstrate how the politics of response is based, not so much on the idea of trying to respond to events as they emerge or become actualised, but rather by *preempting* events. Preemption involves acting directly on a future event *before* it has passed from a mere potentiality to an actuality. As Brian Massumi (2007) has demonstrated, rather than operating on the basis of a past/present axis, whereby the facts of past events are evaluated and used as a necessary background for predicting what might happen next, preemption revolves around the present/future axis. Preemption, in this sense, implies acting on something that might happen in the future but which nevertheless is taken to have *already* happened, thus highlighting the paradoxical temporality of an event that will have been (*futur antérieur*).

The emergence of new temporalities in contemporary global politics does not necessarily imply that the linear and progressive time of the state has been undermined. It might just as well be taken to mean that new tools have been acquired for keeping the latter safe. In order to undermine the temporality of the state other ways of thinking about the possibility of organising time socially and politically might be necessary. Here it is useful to return to Hutchings, who, in addition to investigating assumptions of time in theories of world politics and IR explores other ways of conceptualising time and what their implications for analysing politics might be. What prompts this latter move is her critique of how time is often conceptualised in homogeneous terms, in ways that block 'the possibility of recognising (or investing in the possibility of) temporal plurality in world politics' (Hutchings 2008: 154). In seeking a way out of the parochialism of 'world-political time', expressed especially well by theories of IR, the idea of a pluralism of time is important, as it offers a useful way of questioning the role of the theorist as someone who occupies a privileged position in a unified present, on the basis of which he or she can act as both 'prophet and time-traveller' (ibid.: 155). The notion of a pluralism of time can be used to highlight the significance of other voices and other experiences of time that have been excluded by the dominance of Western- and Eurocentric views masquerading as universal. In this way, it can also be linked to a post-colonial critique of Western/Eurocentrism – a critique that opens up space for other voices and experiences, which have been excluded from the Western/ Eurocentric gaze (see Chakrabarty 2008; Spivak 1999). Crucially, the point of including these other voices and experiences is not to replace the voice of the imperialist subject with yet another centre of discourse pretending to speak of a universal truth. Rather, the primary aim of doing so is to use these voices to disrupt and displace the universalising pretentions of the imperialist Western/Eurocentric gaze (Bhabha 1994: 342).

The idea of a pluralism of time as a way of resisting the homogeneous and unified world-political time of the Western/Eurocentric gaze can also be linked to different notions of the 'untimely', a concept explored not only in Hutchings' book *Time and World Politics*, but also, for example, in Samuel Chambers' *Untimely Politics* (2003), Elizabeth Grosz's *The Nick of Time* (2004), and in Nathan Widder's *Reflections on Time and Politics* (2008). Moreover, the pluralist politics and ethics that a concern with the untimely opens up to are explored by William Connolly in his book *Pluralism* (2005). An important theme that brings together these works is the refusal to articulate an alternative form of time that is supposedly more 'accurate' or 'adequate' for thinking about contemporary world politics. They rather highlight the existence of multiple temporalities, which refuse to be tied to a universal and all-encompassing perspective. In so doing, they also resist the linear model of time as an unquestionable norm. The 'untimely' must be thought of independently of such a 'norm', free of any limitations that the latter imposes on our ability to think of a pluralism of time. It is therefore important, as Chambers (2003: 3) puts it, that untimeliness 'should not connote an arriving too late or too early, since both of these notions only make sense in relation to a linear notion of time'. Moreover, as

Grosz (2004: 11) notes along Nietzschean lines, a concern with the untimely has to imply a concern with the uncertainty of the future and especially with the openness to 'difference', which is opposed to 'the drive of the present to similarity, resemblance, or recognition'. Openness to difference and openness to the future can also be seen as mutually interdependent. Together they point to the kind of pluralist politics and ethics that many of the authors working on the untimely call for. Hutchings (2008: 173) sums this up as follows: 'An untimely approach to global justice is opposed to the kind of normative arguments that assert their own timeliness without regard for the co-existence of a multiplicity of "clocks" by which world-political punctuality may be measured.'

Conclusion

Following the main argument of this chapter, thinking critically about time in the context of IR can be done in two main ways. First, it is possible to question the assumptions of time that underpin theories of IR and the ways in which they try to make sense of the modern state/states-system. In this respect it is particularly important to study assumptions of how time and space interact with one another, and especially how notions of the latter are often assumed to conquer and close down ideas about the former. IR, in this sense, can be analysed as nothing but a particular spatial–temporal imaginary, according to which, time and space are interlinked in order to think about the possibility of political life in relation to the progressive time of the sovereign territorial state, operating within the static limits and repetitive cycles of the international system of states. The spatial–temporal imaginary of IR can also be linked to the narratives of the modern state/states-system: narratives that rely on a clear distinction between a world before and a world after the birth of the 'modern'. This distinction between 'before' and 'after' is enabled by the act of historical periodisation and the inscription of 'borders in time'. Periodisation is important not only for thinking about history as a particular mode of knowledge and technique for making sense of the past, but also for thinking about the sovereign state and its capacity to negotiate the proper relationship between a past that is declared dead and a future that lies ahead and may be shaped as desired.

Second, a critical engagement with time can be used in order to negotiate and push the limits of IR as a particular spatial–temporal imaginary that rests on the idea of spatialising time in a unifying and homogenising way. Different philosophical and conceptual tools are available here, and there is a broad range of critical thinkers that have sought to think of time in ways that could be used to at least try to take us beyond the linear and progressive time of the state, including Nietzsche, Bergson, Virilio, Foucault, Deleuze and Derrida. In political theory and IR, these thinkers have provided vital inspiration for thinking time and temporality in new ways, and also for articulating what the political and ethical implications of doing so might be. Concepts of becoming and the untimely have proven to be particularly popular in this regard, especially in the sense of opening up to a pluralist politics and ethics of time. Crucially, this form of pluralism cannot be reduced to a unifying and homogenising notion of the world-political present, but must always remain open to the multiple temporalities of global politics, expressed by a diversity of experiences and perspectives otherwise excluded from the disciplinary boundaries of IR.

These two critical engagements with time can also be used to open up to a third kind of engagement: namely to study the relationship between the expression of a broad range of temporalities in global politics on one hand, and on the other hand, the disciplinary boundaries of IR and the inside/outside distinction of the state. While this kind of engagement might draw on concepts that highlight the non-linear dimension of time – such as instantaneity, untimeliness and becoming – it would also involve looking at how these concepts interact with the disciplinary boundaries of IR and the limits imposed by the inside/outside distinction of the state. Examining the underlying conditions of this interaction, and how it may be renegotiated in relation to contemporary political practices, is perhaps the most difficult task facing those interested in studying the relationship between time and IR today, but also, potentially, the most rewarding.

Note

1   This analysis of how time is used to separate the modern 'self' from its temporal 'others' was explored most famously by Johannes Fabian (1983) in his groundbreaking work *Time and the Other: How Anthropology Creates Its Object*. There is also an important post-colonial dimension of this critique, examined for example by Dipesh Chakrabarty (2008) in his *Provincializing Europe: Postcolonial Thought and Historical Difference*.

Further reading

Edkins, J. (2003) *Trauma and the Memory of Politics*, Cambridge: Cambridge University Press.

Gunnell, J.G. (1987) *Political Philosophy and Time: Plato and the Origins of Political Vision*, Chicago, IL: University of Chicago Press.

Hägglund, M. (2008) *Radical Atheism: Derrida and the Time of Life*, Stanford, CA: Stanford University Press.

Heidegger, M. (2010) *Being and Time*, trans. Joan Staumbaugh, Albany, NY: SUNY Press.

Hom, A.R. (2010) 'Hegemonic Metronome: The Ascendancy of Western Standard Time', *Review of International Studies* 36(4): 1145–1170.

Ricoeur, P. (1988) *Time and Narrative: Volume 3*, trans. K. Blamey and D. Pellauer, Chicago, IL: University of Chicago Press.

Solomon, T. (2014) 'Time and Subjectivity in World Politics', *International Studies Quarterly* 58: 671–681.

Bibliography

Barbour, C. (2010) 'Sovereign Times: Acts of Creation', *Law, Culture and the Humanities* 6(2): 143–152.

Bartelson, J. (2001) *The Critique of the State*, Cambridge: Cambridge University Press.

Bergson, H. (2001) *Time and Free Will: An Essay on the Immediate Data of Consciousness*, trans. F.L. Pogson, Mineola: Dover Publications.

Bhabha, H.K. (1994) *The Location of Culture*, London: Routledge.

Campbell, D. (2001) 'Time is Broken: The Return of the Past in the Response to September 11', *Theory & Event*, 5(4), e-journal. Available online at: https://muse.jhu.edu/journals/theory_and_event/.

Cassirer, E. (2010) *The Individual and the Cosmos in Renaissance Philosophy*, trans. M. Domandi, Chicago, IL: University of Chicago Press.

Chakrabarty, D. (2008) *Provincializing Europe: Postcolonial Thought and Historical Difference*, 2nd edition, Princeton, NJ: Princeton University Press.

Chambers, S.A. (2003) *Untimely Politics*, Edinburgh: Edinburgh University Press.

Connolly, W.E. (2005) *Pluralism*, Durham, NC: Duke University Press.

Davis, K. (2008) *Periodization and Sovereignty: How Ideas of Feudalism and Secularization Govern the Politics of Time*, Philadelphia: University of Pennsylvania Press.

Deleuze, Gilles (1990) *The Logic of Sense*, C.V. Boundas (ed.), trans. M. Lester and C. Stivale, New York: Columbia University Press

Der Derian, J. (1992) *Antidiplomacy: Spies, Terror, Speed and War*, Cambridge, MA: Blackwell.

Der Derian, James (2001) 'Global Events, National Security, and Virtual Theory', *Millennium: Journal of International Studies* 30(3): 669–690.

Derrida, J. (1984) *Margins of Philosophy*, trans. A. Bass, Chicago, IL: University of Chicago Press.

Fabian, J. (1983) *Time and the Other: How Anthropology Makes Its Object*, New York: Colombia University Press.

Fasolt, C. (2004) *The Limits of History*, Chicago, IL: University of Chicago Press.

Foucault, M. (1977) 'Nietzsche, Genealogy, History' in *Language, Counter-Memory, Practice: Selected Essays and Interviews*, trans. D.F. Bouchard and S. Simon, Ithaca, NY: Cornell University Press, pp. 139–164.

Gross, D. (1985) 'Temporality and the Modern State', *Theory and Society* 14(1): 53–82.

Grosz, E. (2004) *The Nick of Time: Politics, Evolution, and the Untimely*, Durham, NC: Duke University Press.

Harries, K. (2001) *Infinity and Perspective*, Cambridge, MA: MIT Press.

Hoy, D.C. (2009) *The Time of Our Lives: A Critical History of Temporality*, Cambridge, MA: MIT Press.

Hutchings, K. (2008) *Time and World Politics: Thinking the Present*, Manchester: Manchester University Press.

Koselleck, R. (2004) *Futures Past: On the Semantics of Historical Time*, trans. K. Tribe, New York: Colombia University Press.

Linklater, A. (1998) *The Transformation of Political Community: Ethical Foundations of the Post-Westphalian Era*, Oxford: Polity.

Lundborg, Tom (2012) *Politics of the Event: Time, Movement, Becoming*, London: Routledge.

Massumi, B. (2007) 'Potential Politics and the Primacy of Preemption', *Theory & Event* 10(2), e-journal.

Nietzsche, F. (1997) *Untimely Meditations*, Cambridge: Cambridge University Press.

Schmitt, C. (2005) *Political Theology: Four Chapters on the Concept of Sovereignty*, Chicago, IL: Chicago University Press.

Spivak, G.C. (1999) *A Critique of Postcolonial Reason: Toward a History of the Vanishing Present*, Cambridge, MA: Harvard University Press.

Virilio, P. (2006) *Speed and Politics*, trans. M. Polizzotti, New York: Semiotext(e).

Walker, R.B.J. (1993) *Inside/Outside: International Relations as Political Theory*, Cambridge: Cambridge University Press.

Weber, M. (2004) 'Politics as a Vocation' in *The Vocation Lectures*, D. Owen and T.B. Strong (eds), trans. R. Livingstone, Cambridge, MA: Hackett, pp. 32–94.

Widder, N. (2008) *Reflections on Time and Politics*, University Park: The Pennsylvania State University Press.

INDEX

9/11 17, 120, 128, 129, 154, 225, 228, 234, 267; post-9/11 271

Agamben, Giorgio 20, 21, 22, 122, 171, 172, 173
aid 75, 123, 155, 160
alterity 76, 249
Arendt, Hannah 14, 32,
art 59, 66, 117
anti-war 58, 60, 61, 62
activism: political 167, 169, 170, 174, 178; irregular migrant 173, 178
authority: legal 111, 121, 124, 126, 127, 128, 132; political 11, 12, 13, 72, 108, 121, 139, 182, 183, 186, 187

bare life 171, 172, 173
becoming 126, 131, 250, 263, 273, 274
Benjamin, Jessica 78, 83
biopolitical 20–3, 123, 131; biopolitics 21, 22, 124, 200
binary 30, 78, 92, 157, 161, 219, 222; binaries 2, 92, 96, 105, 131
body 115, 124, 125, 130, 132, 206, 220, 221, , 233, 238, 250; bodies 22, 60, 66, 78, 137, 159, 214, 220, 225, 255, 264
borderzone 11, 21
Bull, Hedley 4, 13–14, 71, 73, 75
Butler, Judith 110, 110–11, 116, 122, 173

capital: accumulation 79, 89; capitalism 48, 71, 75, 78, 81, 89, 90, 91, 97, 139–40, 146, 169, 203; and labour 140; global 79

city 32, 90, 206, 207, 222, 231; rights to the 29; world 204, 207
civil society 30, 49, 93, 160, 238; global 29, 93, 168, 169, 232, 235, 236, 241
Cold War 17, 58, 140, 154, 188, 203, 229–230, 234–239, 241, 242, 249, 259; and Geopolitical order 204,
colonialism 15, 38, 42, 47, 48, 75–6, 82, 128–9, 157, 205, 209, 216, 222, decolonial 138; postcolonial 1, 2, 9, 76, 78, 80, 83, 91, 97–8, 138, 161
communal 44, 48, 50, 51, 113
competition 28, 42, 74, 196, 206, 247
confucian 255, 256
constructivism 246, 248, 249, 250
contingency 12, 16, 18, 22, 23, 46, 108, 110, 183, 184–189, 191, 249, 251
cosmopolitan 28, 88, 93, 108, 191; citizenships 28, 108; cosmopolitanism 30
creativity 3, 4, 5, 58, 59, 60, 62, 65, 66, 67, 71; citizenship as a site of 35; and culture 57; and imagination 56, 57; IR as a site of 56
Critical Border Studies 2–3, 19
critical: approach 19, 103, 105, 116, 117, 222, 223, 224, 267; inquiry 183, 197
critical theory 249, 257
Critical Legal Studies 3, 121, 122, 123, 132

decentre 19, 23, 52, 141, 161, 162; decentralisation 159
Deleuze Gilles 22, 106, 199, 271, 273
Der Derian, James 230, 237, 238, 239, 271

desire 1, 9, 31, 125, 167, 175, 176, 215, 217, 223, 253, 263

deterritorialise 90: deterritorialisation 89, 199; deterritorialised 162, 200

development: aid 155; discourse 158, 231; global 70, 90, 96, 236; models 238; and/ as modernisation/progress/improvement 16, 47, 73 78, 79, 80; national 75, 79, 216; partnerships, 160, 161; Polanyi on 170; political and/or economic 62, 71, 74, 75, 76, 90, 96, 206; projects 77; as sustainable 82; technological 215; and underdevelopment 2, 157

dialogical criticism 79, 81, 82

disciplinary: boundaries 196, 262, 274; boundary 5, 6, 23, 24; habits 79

discursive 137, 138, 157, 158, 189, 214, 216, 221, 226

domination 30, 48, 137, 156, 162, 169, 175, 200, 203, 257; and/or coercion 153, 154, 155, 156, 158, 200; colonial 76; geopolitical 91

drones 230, 231, 232, 234, 239, 240, 241

duties 14, 31, 21, 34–6, 44, 50, 51, 143

Egypt 179, 214, 215, 216, 217, 221, 224

East Asia 246, 251, 254, 255, 257; China 207, 208, 246, 252, 253, 255, 256; Japan 79, 174, 203, 246, 252, 254, 256, 257

emancipation 82, 113, 122, 132, 133, 212, 216

ethics 71, 78, 123, 138, 249, 266, 272, 273

Eurocentrism 89, 190, 252, 272: Eurocentric 70, 71, 75, 79, 81, 195, 251–2, 256, 257, 272; Westphalia/en 12, 13, 15, 17, 139–40, 188–89, 195, 199, 202, 210, 228, 246, 251–8

Europe: Christian 72–73; and citizenship 42; civilisation/civilised 203, 254; and epistemic violence 221; EUrope 18; and exploitation 209, 217; and flows of knowledge 208; and global expansion 139; and hierarchy 38, 204; industrial revolution in 80; and international society 252; medieval 12, 15; non-European 73, 74; Renaissance 15; and sovereignty 139, 190, 199, 241; stories about 149; Western 79, 89

exile 58, 115, 147; exiled 109

everyday 4, 5; decision-making 222; forms of belonging 147; life/lives 20, 64, 65, 88, 91, 110, 145, 175; negotiations 224; practices 8, 19, 87 166, 214; resistance 161, 166, 174, 176; social interaction/ encounters 60, 201

experience 110, 145, 148, 213, 219, 223, 246, 249, 252, 253, 254, 263, 265, 266, 272; common 77; and homelessness 45; and imagination 57; of migrants 96; multiplicity of 77; and Kant 105; new patterns of 96; personal 114; and sovereignty 185; and struggle 45; and war 62, 65, 154; and volunteering 146

family 50, 65, 73, 98, 127, 215, 220, 253; family/household: 94, 96, 97, 98

feminism 216, 217, 220; feminist 1, 2, 4, 78, 95, 96, 99, 100, 103, 138, 212, 214, 216, 217, 220; feminist economics 98; feminist IR 57, 63, 65, 97, 143; feminist scholars 80, 142

foreigner 106, 109, 112, 114, 115

Foucault, Michel 22, 103, 105, 107, 116, 122, 159, 160, 258, 271, 273; and critical attitude 106, 117; and epistemic violence 221; and history 18; and power 156, 158, 226; and resistance 161, 171; and surveillance 20; and technology 228, 229, 231, 232, 233, 241

Freud, Sigmund 112, 124, 125, 132

FRONTEX 18–9, 20

genealogy 108, 127, 271

gender 79, 99–100, 108, 110, 113, 143, 213, 224, 250; based violence 63; and belonging 42; and colonialism 215; equality 63; and identities 60; and Islam 214; as a key concept 103, 107; migration 50; and power 41; and race 49; sex/gender 88, 89, 91, 98; and social relations 52; and structural hierarchies/ inequalities 94–8

geopolitics 7, 196, 197, 199, 202–210, 234, 239, 271

Governmentality 153, 159, 161, 162, 173, 200, 229, 231

Guantánamo 121, 128, 130, 131, 132, 133

hegemony 79, 153, 166, 170, 175, 203, 208, 222, 246, 257

hierarchies 15, 34, 89, 91, 94, 95, 143, 208

histories 71, 79, 82, 95, 146, 185

Hobbes, Thomas 30, 43, 49, 72, 73, 190, 208, 209, 235, 248

humanity 76, 80, 102, 103, 104, 106, 111, 113–14, 120, 149, 173 human rights 24, 30, 34, 75, 123, 124, 127, 129, 130, 132, 155, 189, 191; organisations 205

imperialism 70, 128, 139, 182, 202, 203, 215, 251, 259; imperial 73, 74, 78, 82, 189–190, 198, 201–204, 215, 216, 254, 257
informal work 89, 93–95, 99
Information and Communication Technologies (ICT) 88, 90, 229, 232, 234, 239
inequality 44, 81, 99, 103, 107, 113, 250
insecurity 11, 46, 49, 52, 94, 130, 131, 234
intersectional 88, 91
international society 73–75, 82, 129, 196, 251, 252, 255
International Political Economy (IPE) 56, 75, 77–78, 80, 81
Iraq War 58, 60–1, 154, 212
irregular 12, 18–9, 20, 21, 36, 172–3, 175, 178; irregularity 22, 111, 115

joy 58, 60, 62–5, 66

Kant, Immanuel 43, 265; Kantian 4, 105–6, 248, 249, 263
Kristeva, Julia 108, 109, 111, 112, 114, 116

labour 42, 43, 50, 51, 52, 75, 80, 99, 187; capital and 140, 257; domestic 50, 94; domestic-caring 95; independent 44; informal 94; intellectual division of 13; international 223; power/ power of 89, 93; market 52; masculine 47; migration 95, 97; and racialisation 49; reproductive 95; unequal division 139
Lacan, Jacques 117, 121, 122, 125, 126, 129, 132
language 111, 117, 125, 131, 145, 146, 150; of culture 70; of feminism 216; legal 132; ordinary 110; of power 240; psychoanalytical 125, 127; of resistance 168, 169, 170, 178; of space 199; of threat and control 5
Latour, Bruno 229, 230, 231, 232, 233, 241
law: as a limitation 5, 120; of the father 125, 126; legality 120, 123, 124, 126
liberal: liberalism/s 44, 57, 246–250, 264; neo- 169, 265
linear 263, 269, 271, 272, 273
linguistic: conventions 182; structures 146; turn 185
listening 62, 142, 143, 212, 220, 221, 222

Locke, John 41, 43, 49, 72, 73, 190; Lockean 47

market: free 44, 75, 77, 81, 140, 169, 248; global 143, 169, 170, 232, 236, 241
marginal 30, 37, 46, 47, 50, 144; marginality 221; permanent marginality 114, 115
Marxism 264
method 18, 22, 23, 59, 106, 115, 121, 123, 138, 156, 175, 232, 233, 254, 257, 271; methodology/methodologies 22, 62, 139, 252, 254
migrants: 50, 94, 95, 105, 106, 112, 115, 130, 143–4, 199; as agents 172, 173, 175; and change 96; irregular 18, 19, 20, 21, 36, 175; as outsiders 49; and protest 172; undocumented 130
military 19, 31, 80, 93, 94, 140, 154–155, 162, 196, 202, 204, 232, 234, 239, 241, 247, 250, 256, 259; military-industrial 204, 230, 239, 241; and protest 60, 61; and state building 75, 251; technology 230, 235, 236; US 17, 128, 143, 154, 237, 241
modernity 16, 48, 70, 82, 107, 187, 216, 259, 266, 267
myth 47, 49, 124, 125, 128, 141, 156, 189; myths 70, 71, 72, 141, 149

Nandy, Ashis 4, 71, 75–76, 77, 78, 79, 80, 81, 83
narrative: IR as 12, 30, 31, 137, 138, 139, 140, 141, 145–6, 147, 209, 235, 266, 273; narrating 137, 143, 146, 147, 150; thinking 148–149, 150; Westphalian 251, 252, 254, 257, 258, 259
network 32, 170, 195, 196, 200–206, 208–210, 222, 236, 239, 240
norms 30, 32, 42, 44, 48, 56, 92, 139, 144, 170, 179, 209, 248, 249, 250, 255; academic 186; of belonging 49; Confucian 255; cultural 218; disciplinary 259; European 73, 74; gendered 78; heteropatriarchal 97; international/global 74, 75, 191, 196, 222, 250, 251; and law 121, 122, 124, 125; liberal 8, 38; and power 155; shared 88; social 222; as structure 249; territorial 206; universal 15; Western 158
North-South relations 153, 155, 157, 160, 161, 162
nuclear weapons 229, 231, 232, 234–8-8, 241, 242

orientalism 157, 163, 222
origins 38, 72, 80, 126, 132, 140, 209, 257; of civilisation 73, 89; mythical 121, 124, 127, 128, 129
otherness 70, 105, 110, 112, 116, 230, 240

performance 18, 29, 46, 57, 58, 60–2, 173, 204, 226; performative 15, 19, 20, 28, 29, 30–2, 36, 117, 183
personhood 41–6, 49, 109, 112
petty sovereigns 20, 173, 174, 176, 178, 179
Polanyi, Karl 4, 71, 75, 77, 78, 79, 83, 170
political 2, 4, 23, 90, 114, 116, 117, 137, 197, 198, 229, 263, 271; agency 21; economy 202, 203, 204, 240; and ethical 82; of geography/space 90, 195, 200, 210, 254; and law 122, 126, 127, 129, 131, 133; moment 175; and power 156, 183, 184, 201; present 274; and resistance/struggles 32, 141, 144, 158, 171, 175, 176, 178, 206, 213
political concepts 103, 183, 184, 185, 189, 266
political possibility 104, 108, 110, 116; of knowledge (re)production 116
polities 33, 38, 72, 73, 255; polity 30, 31–2, 71, 74, 199, 202, 255
popular culture 146, 150, 230, 236, 237, 239, 249.
postmodernism 4, 130, 138
poststructuralism 1, 2, 4, 12, 22–3, 91, 117
power: coercive 14, 153, 154, 155, 160, 161, 162, 198; disciplinary 158, 162; productive 4, 140, 141, 156–58, 161, 163
problematise 13, 14, 23, 46, 92, 176, 250, 254, 271; problematising 11, 14, 22, 107, 109, 132
process 48, 64, 105, 107, 117, 139, 172, 178, 186, 190, 192, 213, 214, 220, 221–223, 232, 234, 248, 250, 251, 263, 267, 271; of acting politically 103; of becoming 191, 250; of colonisation 216; of decolonisation 129, 157; historical 140; and imagination 56; learning 252; policy 160; politics 172; political 31, 114; of reimagining IR 9; of reiteration 111; subject-in-process 111, 112; sovereignty as 111; of subject formation 174; of subjectivation 127, 129, 133
progress 11, 107, 160, 185, 197, 208, 247, 248, 252, 264; and development 73; and Europe/the West 70, 80, 158; national 217; and technology 232; and time 6, 16, 269, 270, 271

progressive: politics 5, 8; teleology 16, 108; temporality 263–4, 271–2; time 272, 273
property 8, 41–52, 96–7, 251
protest 60, 71, 176; protests 5, 46, 61, 62, 166, 172, 175; protesters 33, 46, 47, 173, 175
psychoanalysis 126, 131, 132

queer 96, 97, 117; queering 89, 96

race 34, 97, 173, 224, 225, 226, 235,; and boundaries 48; and dispossession 49; and gender 49; and inequalities 42, 88, 89, 91, 94, 95, 97; and intersections 95, 98 and social relations 52; structures of 41
Rancière, Jacques 106, 172, 173, 175
Rawls, John 43, 44, 49, 51
realism 209, 245, 246–250, 258; Neo-realist 264; Neo-realism 209, 235, 265
repetition 16, 264, 265, 270
representation 107, 111, 127, 137, 138, 150, 157, 212, 213, 222, 223, 228, 230, 233, 237, 238, 239, 250
researchers 6, 33, 114, 137, 138, 147, 174–178, 179
rumours 136, 144, 145

Said, Edward 78, 83, 157, 163, 179, 222, 226
sanctuary cities 32, 33–7
Science and Technology Studies (STS) 3, 228,229, 231, 232, 233, 234,237, 239, 240, 241, 242
self-ownership 42, 46, 50, 52
senses 66, 105–106, 172
silence 144, 184, 196, 199, 221, 258; silenced 3, 116, 122, 143, 172
social movements: anti-globalisation 169, 175; anti-war 60; international women 220; liberation 82; Muslim women's peity 179; non-aligned movement 168; revolutionary left 177; Sans Papiers 175; Zapatistas 142, 169
social relations 41, 44, 48, 51, 52, 89, 90, 106, 112, 158; pre-social relation 126; social relationship153
sovereignty: authority 12, 32, 33, 167, 172–3, 170, 171, 173, 178, 189, 207, 208, 267, 268, ; domestic 188, 188–89; historicise 188, 190, 191; interrogating 108, 115; territorial 17, 28, 199, 206, 207, 208, 231, 235; Westphalian 188
spatiality 14, 88, 195, 198, 202, 204, 206, 209

state: state-centric 34, 87, 91, 92, 94, 96, 153, 214, 232, 245, 246, 249, 250, 251, 252, 265; state-centric IR 29; state-centric orientation 245, 251; state-centric thinking 1; state-centric view/visions 6, 7, 37; state-centric worlds 2; state-centrism 29, 32, 96, 177, 246, 247, 248, 250, 258; states-system/ states system 14, 16, 23, 246, 247, 248, 250, 253, 256, 257, 262, 273; Westphalian states system 253
status: gendered 5, 65; human 45, 49, 51; legal 29, 34, 143, 150; non 33; ontological 2, 167; quo 5, 23, 65, 167, 175, 176
stories 132, 136, 137, 138, 139, 141, 142, 144, 146–8, 149, 150, 177; IR 147; migrant 143; unheard 145; of war 58, 64; storytelling 137, 147, 150
structural: adjustments 77, 155; approach 211; configurations 247; hierarchies 89, 94, 95; inequalities 91, 97; possibilities for action 31; predispositions 220; realism 13
surveillance 18, 20, 93, 124, 130, 230, 232, 268
subjectivity: legal 124, 129, 130–3; political 29, 30, 32, 35, 37, 38, 117, 121, 139, 170, 197, 213–4

temporality 88, 89, 141, 203, 262–4, 270–274
territorial: borders 90, 92, 197, 262, 265; limits 12, 13
territory: and authority 182; and force 13; as geopolitical space 198, 202; as given 14; and politics 195; and power 20; and security 22; and space 131, 197, 199, 200; to territorialise 15; territorial state 196, 197, 199, 200, 201, 209, 273,
Third World 74, 79, 107, 168, 204
tianxia (all-under-heaven) 天下 253, 255, 256
Todorov, Tzvetan 71, 75, 76, 77, 78, 79, 83

traditional approaches 4–6, 12, 29, 106, 162, 163, 167
tribute system 255, 256
truth 6, 107, 109, 116, 117, 127, 141, 142, 145, 156, 185; eternal/universal 113, 272; hidden 129; unproblematic 148

untimeliness 272, 274; untimely 64, 263, 271–3

veil 214, 215, 216, 218, 220, 221, 222, 267; headscarf 218, 219, 224
violence 74: and borders 12, 14, 23; and citizenship 30, 104; colonial 76; concealing of 23; and empowerment 64; epistemic 161, 221, 222, 224, 246, 251, 257; homophobic 96; internal 73; and 'outside' 71; political 191, 251; representations of 228, 229; structures of 21; structural 94; and technology 229, 230, 231, 234, 238; and territory 15, 271; and war 122, 239, 248
visible 5, 62, 91, 93, 94, 172, 175, 214, 223, 224; especially/most 94, 95, 98; make/render 142, 162, 214, 238

Walker, RBJ 26, 28–9, 107, 113, 116, 184, 187, 210; inside/outside 16, 108, 264; and lines/divisions 15, 108, 111, 235
'war on terror' 20, 120, 121, 122, 128, 129, 132, 161, 267
Weber, Max 141, 153
Westphalian: states system 13, 15, 253; narrative 251, 252, 254, 257, 258; non-252, 255; order 140, 228; statecentrism 246, 257; straightjacket 195; understanding 139 13, 15; world/world order 140, 202, 253, 257, problem-solving 246, 249, 257, 258
World Bank 155, 160, 161
writing 127, 148, 150, 157, 162, 205, 213, 225; creative 59, 138; fiction 58, 149; historical 190; narrative 147; travel 146

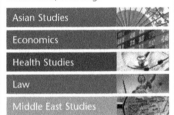